D0327241

The Case FOR Islamophobia:

JIHAD BY THE SWORD;
AMERICA'S FINAL WARNING

BY
Walid Shoebat
AND
Ben Barrack

NEW PROVIDENCE MEMORIAL LIBRARY
377 ELKWOOD AVENUE
NEW PROVIDENCE, NJ 07974

Copyright © 2013 Walid Shoebat Foundation

All rights reserved

No part of this book may be used or reproduced in
any manner whatsoever without written permission
except in the case of brief quotations embodied in
critical articles or reviews.

ISBN: 978-0-9825679-6-8

BJT 25.95 9/13

1st Edition

Printed in the United States

INTRODUCTION

Muslims frequently say that we, the critics of Islam
"know nothing about Islam". They are correct.
The truth is that no one truly understands Islam,
neither Muslim scholars nor Muslims in general.
Even the best of its critics don't understand it. The only
way to fully understand Islam is to be the devil himself.
❖ **Walid Shoebat**

The word "Jihad" has many meanings and takes many forms. Whether it's intended to be overt with a sword or covert with words, the ultimate goal neither changes nor deviates. Islam's agenda is to rule over all of mankind.

Don't believe me? Take a look at the only two definitions provided by a commonly used online dictionary at the time of this writing. One perfectly defines Jihad by the Sword and the other perfectly defines Jihad by the Word:

1. a holy war undertaken as a sacred duty by Muslims.
2. any vigorous, emotional crusade for an idea or principle.[1]

Right there, in black and white English, we find the truth in the most fundamental of places—the Dictionary. The first definition specifically defines Jihad by the Sword, which means that a physical war must take place between Muslims and non-Muslims. Inherent in that definition is that said holy war must take place against non-Muslims because they are not Muslim.

Moderate sounding Muslims who have infiltrated western societies—intent on making Islam the dominant religion—are given the benefit of the doubt by westerners because it's a self-evident truth that they are not waging physical, holy war against non-Muslims. While it can indeed be verified that to this point, leaders of Muslim groups have decried Jihad by the Sword, they have not denounced the religion that has such a mantra as a fundamental tenet.

When Islamic groups like the Council on American Islamic Relations (CAIR) fight for the civil rights of Muslims, it's not because they are a repressed group. It's because groups like it—The Islamic Society of North America (ISNA) and the Muslim Students Association (MSA)—began in the late 1950's and early 1960's. Their founders watched the Civil Rights movement unfold and learned how to leverage political debates in their favor. This brings us to the second definition of "Jihad".

Any "vigorous" or "emotional" effort to push an idea or principle is usually done through communication. That is where Muslim Brotherhood groups in America come in. While they have the weaker hand, they're still quite vigorous and emotional about pushing their principles. Why are westerners not as passionate? Perhaps they have been intimidated with rhetoric.

Welcome to Jihad by the Word.

It's important to remember that the objective of both forms of Jihad is the same. Means is the only difference. If that sounds like ends-justify-the-means type thinking, it's because it is.

When we first set out to write this book, the idea was to include the word "Doublespeak" in the title. We decided against this for a couple of reasons. First, it's a term that has been used with some regularity and we didn't want to give you, the reader, the impression that this has all been done before; it hasn't.

The second reason is that the term "Doublespeak" only describes the tactic, not the strategy. The strategy behind the use of "doublespeak" involves principles used by Jihad—Jihad by the Word (JBTW).

To that end, whenever you see JBTW referenced in this book, know that it once said "doublespeak" but that we decided to take it up a notch.

Some might call that "Islamophobia". We call it a rational concern.

FOOTNOTES

1. http://dictionary.reference.com/browse/jihad?s=t

Table of Contents

ACKNOWLEDGMENTS

Special thanks to Keith Davies and his persistent nature (nagging) urging us to complete this book. To Ben Barrack goes my thanks and acclaim for the outstanding job he's done in writing and editing. Without his contribution, this book wouldn't have happened. I also thank Cheryl Taylor, who labored night and day in designing and preparing the material presented in this book for the printer, and Design by Sarah Lynn, for the superb cover design.

I also want to thank the Muslim world for speaking their mind—in plain Arabic, a language that I understand well. It was their Arabic that revealed what they never say in English, which was the key to reveal to the western non-Arabic speaking world, what are the true intentions and motives of this evil empire.

Finally, I want specially to thank my wife and her support in this dangerous endeavor.

SECTION

1

The Forked Tongues' Attempt To Control

CHAPTER

1

RATIONAL PHOBIA

*A*ttempts by Muslims to place Islamophobia on par with anti-Semitism will never be successful because a diagnosis of Islamophobia includes a prescription that says afflicted individuals must necessarily disagree with the US Constitution, which permits the critique of religion—any religion. Judeo-Christian critics of Islam who believe they are commanded to love Muslims are still identified as being Islamophobic. The anti-Semitism, to which we refer, by its very nature, means hatred for the Jews. See if you can get an anti-Semitic Muslim to admit to loving Jews.

Muslims who complain about Islamophobia ignore the real issues—Judeo-phobia, Christo-phobia and Ameri-phobia. Philosopher Piers Benn suggests that people who fear the rise of Islamophobia foster an environment that is "not intellectually or morally healthy," to the point of what he calls "Islamo-phobia-phobia."[1]

Essentially, this is a fear of being outwardly critical of that which you are critical of internally. People who don't want to be perceived as Islamophobic are succumbing to subtle intimidation. This makes far more sense. After all, a "phobia" is an irrational fear. Fear of Islamic terrorism or creeping Sharia law is not irrational at all. It is actually very rational. An irrational fear is one that says critics of Islam are afraid of being labeled as "Islamophobic." Is this not intimidation of speech by instilling fear and creating a phobia out of thin air?

Benn has a valid point. The notable Islamophobic acts that are recorded hardly constitute any phobia; desecrating a Muslim gravesite or vandalizing mosques are signs of racism, not phobia. Wouldn't a phobia prevent an individual from having any desire to go that far, to go anywhere near a gravesite or mosque? When is the last time you saw someone with acrophobia get on a flight from New York to Los Angeles just so they could trash the inside of the plane? It would appear that we have a problem of mis-diagnosis on our hands.

Despite this, anyone who has diagnosed Islamic fundamentalism as being a jihadist ideology that sanctions financial, political, and murderous terrorism is identified as being Islamophobic. Why would a phobic—of any stripe—call more attention to his fear when doing so only draws that person closer to his fear? Wouldn't people who are stricken with Islamophobia avoid any criticism of Islam entirely, even privately? That's actually what the left does. Left-wing non-Muslims are the true Islamophobes because they attack those who are critical of Islam. Aren't individuals who are afflicted with a phobia supposed to confront the source of their fear? Yet, the Muslim community only attempts to discourage and intimidate those who are unafraid of confronting Islam. This would also make the Muslim community Islamophobic-phobic as well.

Certain Jewish writers critique the New Testament and do not believe in Christian dogma. This would not constitute a phobia but an attempt to defend their flock from going to the other side. Jewish talk show host Toviah Singer runs a program called Jews for Judaism. While Singer encourages adherents to remain true to the Jewish faith, Christians would not identify him as being Christophobic. This would be like identifying a Muslim who does extensive research on Christian Crusaders and reaches negative conclusions as being "Christo-phobic." If he had such a "phobia," he wouldn't have done the research in the first place!

Put simply, writers who address Islamic fundamentalism do not have Islamophobia. If they did, they wouldn't write about it. How could someone who is concerned about the rise of Islamic fundamentalism be a 'phobic' if such a person confronts the subject head on? That would constitute either an anti-phobia or an individual cured of his phobia.

Singer can't be Christo-phobic because he openly welcomes so many Christians on his radio program. Dennis Prager, another radio talk show host who is himself Jewish also welcomes Christian guests. Both Singer and Prager are Bible believers and while they differ on matters of theology with Christians, they find the Old Testament to be a common ground for both faiths. Both realize that neither side can fully please the other so they unite in their efforts to fight tyrannies.

Does this constitute a phobic alliance? Is this the point where oil and water finally mix?

Will the Council on American Islamic Relations (CAIR) ever expose anti-Semitism within its ranks? CAIR takes the lead in exposing me as a racist, bigoted, Islamophobic, divisive, xenophobic and far right-wing Christian fundamentalist. What separates racists from non-racists is that the latter exposes and expels wrongdoers from their own circles. Church-goers will ostracize members of the congregation who spread racism. CAIR must be afraid of doing the same thing by calling out Muslims who persecute Jews—if they disagree with anti-Semitism. Would this not constitute Islamophobia on CAIR's part? It's either that or they agree with the sentiment and are themselves racist, bigoted, Judeo-phobic, divisive, xenophobic and far left-wing Muslim fundamentalists.

Criticism of Islam is no more a sign of Islamophobia than criticism of Nazism is a sign of Nazi-phobia. Both fears are rational, which necessarily means they are not phobias.

FOOTNOTES

1. New Humanist Magazine, [SEARCH] *On Islamophobia-phobia*, by Piers Benn. http://newhumanist.org.uk/

CHAPTER
2

HIDDEN AGENDA

RELIGIOUS DIALOGUE

*M*any westerners believe the Islamic world must pursue the avenue of modernization and secularism in order to advance culturally. The viability of such a strategy is debatable but what avenue should the west take in pursuit of its own advancement?

Problems cannot be solved until they are first accurately diagnosed.

The first inclination of many western thinkers is to engage the Muslim world in *dialogue*. The problem is that all the talk about religious dialogue has nothing to do with religion or dialogue; it has everything to do with a desire to persuade as many people as possible to put blinders on, to avoid real issues and to simply postpone the explosive crescendo until a more opportune time presents itself further into the future.

Sure, dialogue is good and it's better than saber rattling but most of today's dialogue insists on setting aside major differences while focusing on what is labeled "common ground".

So how can we have honest dialogue when Islam fundamentally rejects both Judaism and Christianity? These faiths were abrogated with the advent of Islam. To Muslims, the Bible has been changed and is viewed as corrupt.[1] While the West has a Judeo-Christian heritage, its insistence that secularism is the only answer fails to provide the Muslim masses a different spiritual fountain from which to drink. It also renders the case for Islamic reformation all but impotent by not providing a viable alternative. So dialogue is being restricted in such a way that it lacks arguments for—God forbid—a religious alternative to Islam. Even if we were to accept such a premise, dialogue should be intended to resolve differences, not just search for common ground. The former is sometimes uncomfortable because it involves conflict while the latter often involves the path of least resistance where those most passionate, agenda-driven individuals usually get their way, even if only incrementally.

Such dialogue has already existed in debates between Muslims and Christians from time immemorial. Eventually, the strength of the West prevailed when the Ottoman Empire was dismantled; western concepts were introduced and we had years of peace.[2] Will history repeat itself or will the Muslim and Judeo-Christian worlds find common ground?

This Clash of Civilizations as portrayed in the West by Samuel Huntington will soon transform into the *Dialogue of Religions*.[3] This new dialogue will one day be encouraged as political entities in the West change to face the unmasked threat of Islam. This dialogue must take on a scientific approach, which is lacking from Islamic traditionalists.

The West must stand its ground. Once such dialogue begins, the traditionalist, Islamic teachers will be on the lookout, ready to expose every perceived affront and infraction that either veers away from or impinges upon Sharia (Islamic) Law. This can be used to expose the traditionalists instead of allowing Muslim apologists to hide behind the banner of civil rights while furthering an intolerant agenda. Until this subtle but monumental shift occurs, the traditionalists will continue to gain more ground as the apologists run interference; apologists like CAIR must be exposed before traditionalists can be neutralized.

Less than two years after the Fort Hood massacre in which Jihadist, Major Nidal Malik Hasan murdered 14 and injured 32, Pfc. Naser Abdo attempted to follow in Hasan's footsteps. After going AWOL from Fort Campbell in Kentucky, Abdo planned another attack at Fort Hood. Though he was apprehended before he could carry out his attack, Abdo had published a statement condemning Islamophobia. This is proof positive that at least one Jihadist knows how to hide behind such words.[4]

Muslim traditionalists must *not* be allowed to set the rules or even play the game on our turf. The West needs to fight this battle on Islamic turf; western culture is not in need of moderation; the magnet of Islam is. Arabia, not Rome, is the part of the world in great need of modernity.

It is Islam that lacks a scientific approach to comparative religion—all they really have is whatever was transmitted from their ancestors, a collection of retrograde ideas and laws that the modern logical mind cannot accept. Nearly the entire compilation contradicts western, scientific approaches to religion. Westerners already have a *Biblical Archeological Review*. Why can't the East have a *Qur'anic Archeological Review*?

Whenever comparative religious studies are used in the Muslim world, they are devoid of serious research and are intended solely to provide a one-sided view that confirms the validity of Islam as the only absolute truth. Any serious probe is quickly met with vehemently defensive and narcissistic sensitivity from the Islamists, which simply corrupts the thought process to the point that such people are unable to think freely and openly. As this hypersensitivity escalates, the contentious issues that exposed it are removed from the dialogue by the west, so as not to offend; they are ostensibly tabled to be re-phrased and re-introduced at a later date. This is not dialogue; it is a form of submission Muslims see as an indication that victory will soon be at hand. In essence, appeasing hypersensitivity only reinforces the behavior and breeds more hypersensitivity. An example of this is when CAIR took great offense when then US President George W. Bush referred to his country's enemies as "Islamic fascists".[5] Bush never publicly used that language again.

A desire to set the historic record straight while engaging in dialogue is what the West lacks. The reality faced by Christian minorities in the Muslim world throughout its history is very dark; few westerners focus on it or even acknowledge it. Islam identifies such expeditions (occupations) as *Futuhat* (openings). The objective is to 'liberate' these territories through conquest so that they can accept Islam.

Such occupation is no liberation. What have the Muslims liberated? These Christians were given the choice of Islam or taxation through *Jizzieh*. After this they were given the Omar Declaration. Whether Omar Ibin Al-Khattab or Omar Ibin Abdul Aziz invented this initiative makes little difference; it may as well have been invented through jurisprudence. It is still law and offers no equality to non-Muslims; its objective is to force Christians to accept Islam.

The Muslim world must be confronted on its modern views of subjugation and racism, things that have been purged from Western civilization. It was the West that made null-and-void such treatments in 1885, during the Ottoman rule. Yet, we still have Islamic racism in force throughout the Muslim world. Though appeasement may prevent hypersensitive reactions in the short term, it will also allow the Muslim world's dark past to incubate as it awaits a rebirth through a series of subtly hatched plots. If that happens, helpless Christians will increasingly be forced closer toward the furnace of Islamic persecution. Such a reality might *justify* a little hypersensitivity from the West.

So where are all these moderates?

ISLAMOPHOBIC ASSERTION JUSTIFIED

The Muslim world provides the West with practitioners of *JBTW* while appearing to grace westerners with moderates in order to demonstrate a desire for "common ground". In other words, Islam commands that its proponents hide deceptive hearts behind smiling faces.

This begs a question: How do we recognize *JBTW* artists? The answer is simple; you always find them condemning terrorism while simultaneously condemning free speech and critical thinking. JBTW artists are always ready with an alkaline response, usually written in English, for western consumption. Its purpose is to neutralize the acidic reality of things like terrorism, honor killings and Sharia—things westerners can see—things that cause anxiety, fear, and heartburn. JBTW is meant to be the antacid that extinguishes the already tepid willingness to recognize very painful truths. Though it works, it contains a poison pill.

For example, The "Ten Commandments of Jihad" is used by Muslim apologists who gladly translate into English the words of Caliph Abu Bakr, who commissioned Muslims for Jihad expansions:

> "Listen and obey the following ten commands and instructions: Do not betray anyone (if you give a pledge). Do not ever steal from the war booties. Do not breach your pledge of allegiance. Do not mutilate the body of the killed enemy fighters or deceased. Do not kill a child or a minor. Do not kill an elderly man or woman. Do not kill a woman. Do not pull out a date palm tree (or any other trees) and do not burn it either. Do not cut or destroy a fruit tree. Do not slaughter a female sheep, a cow, or a camel except for your (required) food. You surely will pass by some people who isolate themselves and are secluded for worship of Allah as monks and else, thus leave them alone and do not disturb them ever. You will, surely, stop at some people on the road, who will bring forth for you all types of food dishes. Whenever you eat their food utter the name of Allah each time you eat. You will, surely, pass by a group of people who shaved the hair in the center of their heads, and

left the surrounding hair in long braids. Go ahead; kill these people, as they are the fighters and warriors who carry their swords against you, of the enemies. Go ahead, with the name of Allah." **(Sahih Muslim 1731)**

Isn't there a contradiction between "Jihad expansion" and all this talk of loving captive peoples? Why invade them in the first place? What transgression did the people of Jerusalem commit against Arabia to deserve Omar's invasion? Were the Muslims truly defending themselves when they invaded Spain?

Then you have the acidic reality that is rarely, if ever, translated by JBTW artists. One of the most amazing contradictions comes from Al-Ghazali:

"One must go on jihad (i.e., warlike razzias or raids) at least once a year...one may use a catapult against them when they are in a fortress, even if among them are women and children. One may set fire to them and/or drown them...If a person of the Ahl al-Kitab [People of The Book – Jews and Christians, typically] is enslaved, his marriage is [automatically] revoked...One may cut down their trees...One must destroy their useless books. Jihadists may take as booty whatever they decide...they may steal as much food as they need." **(From the Wagjiz, 1101 A.D., quoted by Andrew Bostom)**.⁶

Muslim apologists love to quote Al Ghazali, the famous theologian, philosopher, and paragon of mystical Sufism as a prime example of moderate Islam. Even Western scholars like the eminent W. M. Watt describe Al-Ghazali as, "acclaimed in both the East and West as the greatest Muslim after Mohammed, and he is by no means unworthy of that dignity."⁷

Had Westerners studied Al-Ghazali regarding Jihad and the treatment of the vanquished non-Muslim dhimmi peoples, perhaps they would not have been deceived by the dialogue of 'peace'. The *Qur'an* even contains an entire chapter entitled Al-Anfal, which translates to mean "the Booty" or "the Spoils of war." The book *Al-Hidayah*—arguably the most widely read book of Islamic jurisprudence in the Muslim world—is used as a primary text in Islamic schools and seminaries. It mentions the motivating factor in the call to jihad:

"After the Battle of Badr, the verse dealing with the booty was first revealed. The verse introduced the rule for the first time that the spoils of war would be the property of the soldiers who actually take part in the battle...That is one of the reasons why the soldiers of Islam fought tooth and nail. They would get Paradise in case of death in a Holy War, and booty in the case of conquest. Jihad is therefore the best source of all acquisitions." **(Al-Hidayah, Mishkat II. p. 406)**

Muhammad attacked numerous tribes, villages and cities in order to raid their wealth, which he gave to his new followers; this is also how the Mahdi (the Islamic Messiah) is expected to imitate Muhammad. The Mahdi, during the seven years of peace proclaimed in Islam, will re-distribute among his followers, the seized property and wealth of the nations that he defeats.

When westerners are encouraged that Sufi Islam is the peace-loving version of Islam and are comforted by the words of the likes of Hisham Qabbani, the Sufi Imam, perhaps they should read the acidic reality of his Arabic words that he would never intentionally have translated into English from Arabic; we did what he would not.

Qabbani is a Mahdist who believes that the Mahdi (Islamic messiah/Christian antichrist) will establish Islam's utopia. One of the most popular traditions regarding the Mahdi that Qabbani writes about is that "He will give away wealth profusely." **(Sahih Hakim Mustadrak, related by Abu Sa'id al_Khudri (4:557 and 558), as quoted by Kabbani p. 233. *Paving The Way For The Coming Mahdi*)** Is this not the redistribution of wealth, a leftist, socialist principle? "In those years (the time of the Mahdi) my community will enjoy a time of happiness such as they have never experienced before. Heaven will send rain upon them in torrents, the earth will not withhold any of its plants, and wealth will be available to all. A man will stand and say, 'Give to me Mahdi!' and he will say, 'Take.'" **(Al-Tabarani, Related by Abu Hurayra, as quoted by Izzat and Arif. p. 9)**

JBTW artists will always say that Jihad is defensive and never point to Islamic invasions as "invasions" but as "liberations". As mentioned earlier, this is known as *futuhat*, which is not intended to liberate *people* but to liberate *land* from *Kufr* (unbelief). No serious historian can deny that Muslims invaded Sicily in 827 AD and then conquered it in 902. In 846, the Muslims entered the city of Rome where they plundered the churches of St. Peter and St. Paul. There were also attacks against Christians in Spain during the 10th and 11th centuries. In the Levant, the Battle of Manzikert occurred in 1071 with the Muslims defeating the Byzantine Christians. In 1091, Muslims drove the Christian priests out of Jerusalem. The Muslims also tried and failed to capture Constantinople, the citadel of Eastern

Christianity, between 668 and 798. *The Great Divide*, By Alvin J. Schmidt, Chapter 6, pgs. 143-144, For further discussion, see Paul Fregosi, Jihad in the West: Muslim Conquests from the 7th to the 21st Centuries (Amherst, NY: Prometheus Books, 1998)

Nearly four hundred years after the Muslim conquests in Palestine, they destroyed the Church of the Holy Sepulcher in Jerusalem in 1009 under Caliph el Hakim. All of these attacks against Christians were perpetrated well before the Crusades were even initiated in 1095.[8] These multiple attacks on Christian sites, which went on for a period of over five-hundred years, provided more than enough justification for the Crusades to begin a defensive attack against the Muslim pagans. Conveniently, support for the Crusades has also been called *Islamophobic*. In reality, if both sides of the debate accept the notion that one side is Islamophobic, the side afflicted with Islamophobia has historical precedent to justify acting on that inaptly named phobia. This is what we've termed *Islamophobic Assertion* and it needs to be exercised in the arena of ideas before it must be exercised in the interest of actual survival.

Emperor Alexius in the East asked Pope Urban II in the West to help him recruit soldiers for the Byzantine army. The objective of the Crusaders was to roll back the Turkish Muslim conquest of Asia Minor, as well as to keep Christianity from being completely destroyed in the East and to also protect Turkish and European Christian pilgrims.[9] The Crusades were not about imperialism, nor a preemptive strike; they were acts of self-defense (Islamophobic assertion). What would leftist historians write had the Christians conquered Mecca and the Ottoman Turks charged there to stop the Crusades from conquering the lands of Islam? The left would be praising the Muslims as great fighters for freedom while referring to the Crusaders as fascists.

The fact remains that it was the Muslims who were the invaders that needed to be met with Islamophobic assertion. Islam conquered Spain and ruled for 800 years; Portugal for 600, Greece, 500; Bulgaria, 500; Romania, 400; Serbia, 400; Sicily, 300; and Hungary for 150 years. If the left is all about fairness and fighting imperialism, where are their writings about how Tariq ibn Ziyad terrorized Spanish Christians when conquering Spain? He ordered Christian prisoners to be "cut to pieces and their flesh boiled in cauldrons." (**Mark Williams, *The Story of Spain* (Malaga, Spain: Santana, 2000)**

Practitioners of JBTW would never debate Muslim fundamentalists or historic revisionists on such issues; they eschew confessions, yet they demand confessions from their victims. While Christendom confesses its wrongs—and we find a litany of such confessions—JBTW artists would justify the torture of Rabbi Kinana by Muhammad while endlessly reminding the West of "atrocities" at Abu-Ghraib. Despite holding all guilty parties accountable for the abuses at Abu-Ghraib, the West never stopped confessing and the JBTW artists never stopped accusing. Islam tortured others for property and has not confessed. The West tortured suspected terrorists and continues to confess despite righting its wrongs.

JBTW artists argue that America is a repressive country while simultaneously enjoying life *in* America. Such hypocrites would even deny Islamic teaching influences them to any real degree. At the end of the twentieth century, a non-Muslim country fought another non-Muslim country to liberate Muslims. During that time, Jewish doctors treated Kosovo Muslims in a way that was diametrically opposed to how those Muslims were treated under Islam.

I've had numerous debates with Muslim callers on radio interviews; I rarely find one that is willing to confess to Islam's bloody history; they never answer the questions or address the evidence. Instead, they attack the Islamophobic questioner.

Until westerners embrace the Islamophobic label as a badge of honor, they will continue to succumb to a bully's tactic of intimidation that is specifically intended to shame them into silence.

THE MODERNITY OF MEANS

When it comes to modernity, westerners have used both debate and discussion to bring the Muslim world into the 21st century. While the western view of Islamic modernity focuses on *modernizing* Sharia, the Islamic east actually welcomes the dialogue for its own selfish reasons; such talk actually simplifies the methods required to implement Sharia in a modern, western world.

JBTW artists use a mix of flowery language that consists of terms that are foreign to westerners, used to hide the true intent; it is devoid of any confession since Islam's version of its own history is devoid of any wrongdoing. Such artists are usually accompanied by western, anti-Salafist professors who are sympathetic to Islam (Salafists are Islamists who don't believe in masking their true intentions); they rarely, if ever, include critics of Sharia. The way to circumvent western suspicions is to condemn violence and terrorism while avoiding condemnation of Sharia.

A google search of "Islam and Modernity" illustrates the point. A forum on Islamic modernity was discussed at the University of Michigan April 23, 2011.[10] The speakers included several prominent Muslim scholars. Al-Habib Umar Bin Hafidh explained in his speech, which was translated into English in such a way so as to soothe American audiences.[11] Al-Habib explained:

> "…many people who dwell on it [modernity] direct themselves to think it's an issue regarding life, whether economic, moral, political or social, and formulate their speech based on this perspective."

Al-Habib then attempts to reveal the intent behind the language of modernity:

> "…the best way to explain it is to modernize or to cause benefit of every aspect of life. If we understand it from this perspective then we can discuss it in this regard. First, no logical mind can erase from humanity its past. Therefore, no logical mind should ignore a past that includes Allah's wisdom and his Sunnah [law]."

Al-Habib gives examples:

> "We do not change how we *eat* food as it was in ancient times…but we modernize how we plant, prepare and cook it…"

> "…we turn to modernity while understanding our inherited Islamic values and we say there are constants and absolutes brought forth by the religion of Allah."

Al-Habib is simply modernizing the means to achieve the same standards established by Islam centuries ago. In much the same way that 'Jihad by the sword' was replaced by Jihad by the gun and espionage found in Jihad by homing pigeon was replaced with Jihad by cell phone (text or call) modernity offers a complete set of opportunities to spread Islam through new forms of Jihad.

The Islamic principles set forth in ancient times are ironclad; they are not subject to change. The Islamic mindset is that ends justify the means. When it comes to economics, neither socialism nor capitalism is acceptable according to Al-Habib:

"...we have no need for modernity that results in a problem found at the root of socialism or capitalism; both endorse usury [interest]. It [usury] is forbidden."[12]

When it comes to Jihad, Al-Habib uses terms the West is not used to, terms like Futuhat, to open the world for the house of Islam via warfare. It is important to note that the term 'occupation' is absent from Muslim terminology when a land is 'occupied' by Islam. Al-Habib begins with what soothes western minds:

"...yes to the Jihad of guidance, not aggression. Jihad of love, not aggression; we have not known in our history a Jihad that is void of benefit for others. We have not seen, especially during the Rashidun Dynasty [rightly guided caliphs] a country opened [occupied] by Islam, without other religions remaining intact and it was under the Islamic rule that they kept their rights."

The first question in the dialogue at Michigan University was, "How do we establish Shariah in a country of unbelievers?" The answer was typical:

"...it was permitted by Muhammad, the prophet of Islam, who ordered the Muslims during his ministry to reside in Ethiopia, the land of the Christians."

Ethiopia was not the only place where Islam 'occupied' a territory that didn't ask for it:

"Muhammad also lived in Mecca and his mission was not to destroy its idols prior to his immigration to Medina...our understanding is that we do not love the rulers we live under...so if Islam was not in control and the Muslim wanted to carry out the commands of Islam under existing rule, it would be contrary to Sharia."

It's all about timing and nothing more.

CREEPING TROJAN HORSE

Through propaganda, the Muslim Brotherhood (Ikhwan) has convinced the power brokers of the West that it has moderated; this is a myth. Today, the Muslim Brotherhood is running Egypt. The AKP Islamist Party in Turkey has become the envy of the Muslim world. It has been decades since Islamists have seen the level of opportunity they see today; Islamists have accomplished more than at any other time in recent history.

The victories are well expressed throughout Middle Eastern news. Yet, the West seems more interested in sex scandals. In the case of former congressman Anthony Weiner, there was an inordinate amount of attention paid to explicit photos he sent out via his twitter account. Virtually no attention was paid to the discovery—made as a result of the heightened attention brought on by the scandal—that Weiner's mother-in-law was a member of the Muslim Brotherhood (more on that later). In the case of former CIA Director David Petraeus, an affair with his biographer garnered more attention than four dead Americans at the consulate in Benghazi, Libya. Two of those four were CIA operatives—former Navy SEALs Tyrone Woods and Glen Doherty—truly courageous American heroes.[13]

In its blind search for Islamic moderation, the West has aided fundamentalist and traditional Muslim scholars in the construction of a Trojan horse. It is a horse cloaked in secularism and moderation but its inhabitants still drink out of the same old dogmatic fountain of mainstream Islam.

The current Muslim reformists prefer to replace the explosive act of terrorist attacks with a time bomb they call political Jihad, which will eventually erupt in chaos. The walls and fortresses of the West were not even breeched or penetrated. Through dialogue, we simply opened the gates for Trojan horses masquerading as moderates, who've entered while raising the shield of hypersensitivity that says: "If you critique my ideological beliefs, then you critique my religion." In this case, the word "religion" is seriously misplaced intentionally by the horse's inhabitants. The real term for it is Sharia, or Islamic law; it's pushed by a political agenda that hides behind a religious facade.

Sharia represents the equivalent of Islam's Constitution, which is what makes arguments from Muslim Americans, that their religion should be afforded first Amendment protections under the US Constitution, invalid. Instead, as the *Team 'B' II Report* rightfully pointed out, westerners should point to Article VI, which asserts that the US Constitution shall be the "Supreme law of the land."[14] If this is what Islam wants for Sharia, it unequivocally proves that these two constitutions *cannot co-exist* in a free society. As long as Americans allow Muslims to set the terms of the debate by insisting that the US Constitution affords them freedom of religion, Sharia will continue to creep.

Here is the relevant portion of Article VI:

*This Constitution, and the laws of the United States which shall be made in pursuance thereof; and all treaties made, or which shall be made, under the authority of the United States, **shall be the supreme law of the land**; and the judges in every state shall be bound thereby, anything in the Constitution or laws of any State to the contrary notwithstanding.*

While there are many insignificant differences between Islamic sects, the honest researcher will quickly discover that none of those differences have anything significant to do with promoting peace.

For example, many Westerners point to Sufist Muslims, focusing on their transcendental meditation and mystical approach to Islam in an attempt to portray Islam as being for personal use. Any endorsement of this approach ignores Sufi Muslims like Qabbani and Sheikh Maulana Nazeem Kibrisi, both of whom have been caught talking from both sides of their mouths.

Another example used by promoters of moderate Islam point to Irshad Manji, a lesbian Muslim who pushed Islamic *Ijtihad* (innovation in Islam) as a tool for reason with Muslim scholars. (**Matthew Kalman, "A Muslim calls for reform – and she's a lesbian," San Francisco Chronicle, January 19, 2004.**[15] But Manji is naïve—*Ijtihad* emanates from the Islamic classical period and cannot contradict the holy writ from the 'absolute' *Holy Qur'an* and *Sunnah*, which restricts the use of these sources from becoming permanent within the Sharia law framework.

Ijtihad is used, but not to conform to Manji's dream world. Tariq Ramadan, the grandson of Hassan al-Banna (founder of the Muslim Brotherhood), is a Muslim apologist in Europe who calls for a "freeze to Islamic capital punishment," while citing *Ijtihad*. (**"Tariq Ramadan Calls for a Freeze on Hudud Punishments," Islamopedia online, March 24, 2010**)[16] Yet, a 'freeze' is not permanent since Islamic laws—according to Ramadan and Muslims in general—are an absolute truth and not malleable to changing times or conditions. These "freezes" Ramadan and others discuss are not in response to changing times or conditions that call for modernizing Islam. On the contrary, such things are done to garner the interests of those—like Manji—whose advocacy for Islam in the short term will help further the true cause of Islam in the long term. The intention is for these laws, while frozen in time, to eventually thaw and return to their original state when the time is right. In essence, people like Manji are nothing more than useful idiots destined to fall victim to the Trojan horse as well.

The evidence for this is clear—Ramadan only calls for this freeze in the West, never in the Middle East where he supports continued implementation, which includes the amputation of hands as well as stonings and lashings for what westerners consider to be minor infractions. If supposed reformers *did* confront Islamism head on, we would find a litany of arguments between Ramadan the reformist and fundamentalist Muslim scholars. Curiously, such arguments don't take place.

A problem confronting the West is that Muslim reformers who represent any form of organized Islam believe that a founding principle is described by the prophet Muhammad, in one of the clearest definitions of Islam: *"Al-Islamu Deen Wa Dawla"*—"Islam is a religion *and* a state." This "and" is a combination of the two, infusing state with religion. That very basic definition strictly prohibits any Muslim from losing focus of the ultimate goal—to spread Islam from the east to the west, never blending western laws with portions of Sharia law that conflict with them. How is this for "common ground?"

According to a 2006 study, the percentages of Muslims in Europe, who proclaim their allegiance *first* to *Islam* and then to whatever home country has adopted them, are staggering. 46% of all Muslims in France, 81% in Great Britain, 66% in Germany, and 69% in Spain hold this view. (**"Muslims in Europe: Economic Worries Top Concerns About Religious and Cultural Identity," Pew Research Center, July 6, 2006**)[17] This only serves to create an apartheid culture *within* a culture; it only adds fuel to the fire that burns with dissent, racism, and terrorism. Paradoxically, anyone who dares to call attention to this problem may as well have the scarlet letters that spell the word "Islamophobe" tattooed to their foreheads.

Ramadan, like most Muslim apologists, simply exploits minority rights issues for his own advantage, focusing on the status of Muslim ghettos in Europe, knowing full well that he aids in creating such separatism by simultaneously calling for it (promoting Islamophobia). (**Khadija Bradlow, "Out of the 'Muslim ghetto'," September 5, 2007**[18] He does so while blaming 'apartheid' in Europe for the eyesore of Muslim poverty. Ramadan and his ideological colleagues use exactly the same argument to defend Palestinian refugees while pointing their collective finger at Israel's 'apartheid' state. This allows Ramadan to kill two birds with one stone. On one hand, he can manipulate European sympathizers into arguing for Islam's advance. On the other hand, Muslims hail him as an icon fighting for their rights.

FOOTNOTES

1. Middle East Forum, [SEARCH] *Islam and Islamism—Faith and Ideology*, by Daniel Pipes. http://www.danielpipes.org

2. BBC Religion & Ethics: [SEARCH] *Ottoman Empire (1301-1922)*. http://www.bbc.co.uk/religion

3. Foreign Affairs, *The Clash of Civilizations?* by Samuel P. Huntington. http://www.polsci.wvu.edu/faculty/hauser/PS103/Readings/HuntingtonClashOfCivilizations ForAffSummer93.pdf (p. 22)

4. Jihad Watch, *New Fort Hood jihadi on ABC News last year: wants to "put a good positive spin out there that Islam is a good, peaceful religion."* http://www.jihadwatch.org/2011/07/new-fort-hood-jihadi-on-abc-news-last-year-wants-to-put-a-good-positive-spin-out-there-that-islam-is.html

5. BBC News, Washington, *Bush's language angers US Muslims*, by Richard Allen Greene. http://news.bbc.co.uk/2/hi/4785065.stm

6. FrontPageMag.com, *When is Jihad Not Jihad?* by Andrew G. Bostom. http://archive.frontpagemag.com/readArticle.aspx?ARTID=4838

7. D*eliverance From Error and Mystical Union with the Almighty,* English Translation with Introduction by Muhammad Ab–ulaylah, Introduction and Notes by George F. McLean, http://books.google.com/books?id=sC2afF7Q_6MC&pg=PA29&lpg=PA29&dq=acclaimed+in+both+the+East+and+West+as+the+greatest+Muslim+after+Mohammed,+and+he+is+by+no+means+unworthy+of+that+dignity.%E2%80%9D&source=bl&ots=gio-V-ZJAk&sig=W2DonIeQnKORAQPerqWjrXQXbd4&hl=en&ei=1lWCTreqEOiFsgLcsPjiDg&sa=X&oi=book_result&ct=result&resnum=1&ved=0CBoQ6AEwAA#v=onepage&q=acclaimed&f=false (p. 29)

8. *The Great Divide*, by Alvin J. Schmidt, Chapter 6, pg. 143-144, For further discussion see, *Jihad in the West: Muslim Conquests from the 7th to the 21st Centuries* by Paul Fregosi (Amherst, NY: Prometheus Books, 1998). Also see *Mending Bodies, Saving Souls* by Guenter B. Risse, (New York: Oxford University Press, 1999), 139.

9. Ibid

10. Arabic website. http://www.alhabibomar.com/Book.aspx?SectionID=6&RefID=160

11. Arabic website. http://www.alhabibomar.com/Lecture.aspx?SectionID=8&RefID=1342

12. Ibid

13. United Press International, *US: CIA Ran Benghazi consulate*. http://www.upi.com/ Top_News/US/2012/11/02/US-officials-CIA-ran-Benghazi-consulate/UPI- 44771351839600/

14. *Shariah The Threat to America, An Exercise in Competitive Analysis, Report of Team "B" II*. http://ebookbrowse.com/shariah-the-threat-to-america-team-b-ii-report- 9-14-10-pdf-d109943273 [SELECT] Download

15. San Francisco Chronicle, *A Muslim calls for reform—and she's a lesbian,* Special to The Chronicle, by Matthew Kalman. http://www.sfgate.com/entertainment/article /A-Muslim-calls-for-reform-and-she-s-a-lesbian-2809919.php

16. IslamoPedia Online, *Tariq Ramadan Calls for a Freeze on Hudud Punishments*. http://www.islamopediaonline.org/ [SEARCH] Muslims in Europe: Economic Worries Top Concerns About Religious and Cultural Identity

17. Pew Research Global Attitudes Project, *Muslims in Europe: Economic Worries Top Concerns About Relitious and Cultural Identity*. http://pewglobal.org/2006/ 07/06/muslims-in-europe-economic-worries-top-concerns-about-religious-and- cultural-identity/

18. *Tariq Ramadan Out of the Muslim Ghetto*, http://www.tariqramadan.com/spip. php?article1179&lang=fr

SECTION

2

Brotherhood Born
Of Demons

NEW PROVIDENCE MEMORIAL LIBRARY
377 ELKWOOD AVENUE
NEW PROVIDENCE, NJ 07974

CHAPTER

3

BROTHERHOOD ANCESTRY

ISLAM'S DIVERGENT PATHS

*P*erhaps the best way to explain Islam's breakup into its Sunni and Shia sects to westerners is to compare the Shia (Shi'ites) to those who subscribe to a monarchical view in which the Prophet Muhammad's living descendants are the ones who should lead the Muslim world. Sunnis, on the other hand, believe that the title should be granted to those most qualified—in the eyes of Allah— to hold it.

For example, Muhammad's cousin and son-in-law, Ali ibn Abu Talib (Ali), is recognized by the Sunnis as the fourth caliph, with Islam's prophet being the first and Abu Bakr being the second. Conversely, Shi'ites view Ali as Muhammad's immediate successor and don't believe Bakr ever rightfully held the honor.[1]

Ali was assassinated by a man named Abdur Rahman bin Muljam, one of a very few number of survivors from a group that went to war with Ali's forces.[2] For all intents and purposes, this is where the divide between Sunnis and Shi'ites started. The Shi'ites consider Ali as the first Caliph (Khalifa), or spiritual head of Islam, while the Sunnis consider him to be the fourth and last 'rightly guided' Caliph.[3]

SUFISM

An important aspect of Islam—if not a sect—is that of Sufism, referred to as Islamic mysticism.[4] In some western circles, Sufism is considered to be a peaceful brand of Islam. Westerners accept this view at their own peril as Sufis desire the return of an Islamic caliphate, just as the Sunnis and the Shi'ites do. Sufism was an integral part of the Ottoman Empire and many of the individuals and entities within Turkey that seek an Ottoman revival have been instrumental in moving their government away from secularism and toward Islamism. Turkey has made quantum leaps in this regard in recent years; Sufi scholars have played huge roles in Turkey's strong lurch toward Islamism.

Despite sharing the common goal of an Islamic caliphate, Sufis are certainly not universally embraced by Islamists with different perspectives. For example, while Sufis seek more emotional or mystical experiences when practicing Islam, Sunnis are much more orthodox and traditional in their approach.[5] This can certainly lead to strife. In an article penned by Islamic fundamentalist Yusuf Hijazi entitled, "Sufism: The Deviated (Muslim) Path," the author argued that Sufism helped lead directly to the decline of the Ottoman Empire:

> The Sufi influence undoubtedly contributed greatly to the decline of the Ottoman Empire. The pacifist views they spread, the lack of Shari'ah knowledge, and their befriending of the disbelievers, made sure that no one would oppose the vast changes being made to the Ottoman Laws.[6]

It is a duplicitous argument. How can Sufism be responsible for the decline of the Ottoman Empire when its proponents have been working diligently toward the empire's revival?

WAHHABISM AND THE HOUSE OF SAUD

If you've ever wondered why Egypt is the cradle of the most fundamentalist forms of Islam, the migration of the Wahhabists to that region from Saudi Arabia goes a long way in explaining it.

Wahhabism is a fundamentalist brand of Sunni Islam that was founded in the 18th century. One of the principles of Wahhabists is that they reject nationalism; they embrace a singular Islamic caliphate, unlike Saudi nationalists. Wahhabists passionately attempted to move Saudi Arabia toward being more fundamentalist in the early twentieth century but something happened in 1920 that would significantly alter their plans; oil was discovered on the Arabian Peninsula.

The Saud family became wealthy as a result of its dealings with the West. Though it wished to satiate the Wahhabists while enriching itself by doing so, the House of Saud became the object of Wahhabist ire as a result of the former's willingness to deal with the West.[7]

Fundamentalists are hardliners by definition and the Wahhabists grew increasingly furious with the House of Saud for dealing with the West. This led to an uprising that was violently put down. An historic figure named T. E. Lawrence—

better known as *Lawrence of Arabia*—was instrumental in developing successful strategies with Arabs in the latter's efforts to beat back the Ottoman Turks in Saudi Arabia.[8] Wahhabists consequently migrated to Egypt, where the Muslim Brotherhood was eventually born a few years later.[9]

Lawrence, a Brit, grew up in Oxford, England where he attended both High School and College.[10] He also became another object of hatred for Wahhabists. As a figure of western colonialism that helped defeat the Ottomans, the legacy of Lawrence is despised by Islamists who long for an Ottoman resurgence. Ironically, in the decades since, Oxford University has become a hotbed for Islamic radicals.[11] In particular, the Oxford Centre for Islamic Studiers (OCIS) features a board that consists of several members sympathetic to Wahhabists and the Muslim Brotherhood. There will be much more on this in a later chapter.

The level of hatred Wahhabists have for the House of Saud is rivaled only by Iran's hatred for Saudi Arabia, primarily for how Shi'ite clerics are treated in the Arabian Peninsula.[12]

SALAFISM

A brand of Islam birthed during the Ottoman Empire's last century of existence is known as Salafism. It was founded at Egypt's al-Azhar University, led by Muhammad Abduh, and is considered an outgrowth of the Wahhabist movement.[13] Wahhabism and Salifism, while very similar, have used different approaches. The former believed in the rejection of modern influences while the latter advocated adopting them in order to achieve the same end. Years later, the Muslim Brotherhood would take Salafism even further, relative to the adoption of modernity.

In the mid to late nineteenth century, as the Ottoman Empire was in decline, the Salafis took notice of Europe's technological rise and colonialism; they decided to incorporate European advancements into their agenda while remaining loyal *to* that agenda.

To illustrate this difference, consider one of the most well known Salafists of today—Anjem Choudary—with one of the most renowned of al-Qaeda's leaders—Ayman al-Zawahiri. Al-Qaeda is widely considered to be the purest manifestation of Wahhabism. As such, the terrorist entity responsible for attacking the United States on September 11, 2001 is unwelcome in any western society. If someone were to announce he were a member of al-Qaeda while in a western country, he could quickly be identified as a terrorist.

Conversely, Choudary is a known Salafist who is permitted to publicly align with Wahhabists while spouting rhetoric that should identify him as an enemy of Great Britain and the West. He is very careful not to declare himself a member of al-Qaeda but it is obvious he shares the group's goals.

While appearing on a panel that aired on *ABC*'s "This Week," Choudary made this very clear:

> "...we do believe, as Muslims, the East and the West will one day be governed by the Sharia. Indeed, we believe that one day, the flag of Islam will fly over the White House. Indeed, there's even an oration of the Prophet where he said, 'The day of judgment will not come until a group of my ummah (Muslim people) conquer the White House.'"

With the birth of the Muslim Brotherhood after the fall of the Ottoman Empire, Salafism's deceit was trumped by that of the Ikhwan. As you will see in a subsequent chapter, *Muruna* allows Muslims to go as far as blaspheming Islam in order to further Islam's agenda. Salafists like Choudary are unwilling to sink to this level of deception.

During his appearance on "This Week," Choudary had a run-in with Daisy Khan, the wife of Ground Zero mosque imam Feisal Abdul Rauf, a stealthy Sufi Islamist who has marinated for years in the more refined, Muslim Brotherhood interpretation of deceit. Any contribution made by the Salafists to the Islamic agenda relative to embracing western modernity has since been trumped by the Brotherhood's advocacy for increased deception, in addition to accepting that modernity.

At issue in this exchange was Choudary's fundamentalism vs. Khan's adaptability to western culture. After Choudary expressed an extremist point of view Khan disagreed with, he doubled down:

> "It's very easy for people to justify the fact that they're not practicing. I mean, this lady in your studio, she should be covering with the hijab. She's obviously not practicing...You cannot be a non-practicing vegetarian. Therefore, similarly, if you're a Muslim, you submit to the Sharia."[14]

Christian evangelist, Franklin Graham, who was on the panel, expressed agreement with Choudary after that statement.

Choudary's response to anyone who challenges him to denounce attacks on westerners by the likes of al-Qaeda always includes an assertion that American attacks on Muslims motivated the terror attacks. This is a manufactured argument that blatantly ignores the principles of martyrdom.

Consider the statement of Abdul Qadeem Zalloom:

> Resisting a ruler who fails to implement the true Islamic system is also of immense importance. So much so that the rule by a Kufr [non-Islamic] system must be prevented even if this led to several years of fighting and **even if it led to the killing of millions of Muslims and to the martyrdom of millions of believers**...[15]

In essence, this assertion torpedoes the primary argument of Salafists like Choudary. If Muslims are taught to martyr themselves in order to push a larger agenda, each explosion gives Choudary new talking points. Any attempt to justify the murder of westerners by pointing to the murder of Muslims must necessarily fall flat if this is true because it means that living Muslims are turned into dead Muslims in order to push an agenda. This point cannot be overstated because it is at the essence of the sympathy the Islamic world receives from the West. When pawns are willing to sacrifice themselves in the name of repression, they tend to make a good case with those who simply cannot fathom such a mindset.

Perhaps this is a lesson learned by the founders of the Muslim Brotherhood or Ikhwan; westerners are gradually waking up to the deception game and Choudary's agenda is simply too visible. The old adage about it being better to face the enemy you know than the enemy you don't applies to the West in its battle with the Salafists and the Muslim Brotherhood respectively. Salafists and Wahhabists telegraph their intentions while many in the West ignore the messages. Unfortunately, those westerners will one day be forced to open their eyes to a new level of deception.

FOOTNOTES

1. Jewish Virtual Library, *Ali ibn Abi Talib,* from *Saudi Aramco World*. http://www. jewishvirtuallibrary.org/jsource/biography/talib.html

2. *A Brief History of Islam*, by Ghaffar Hussain, Quilliam. http://www.multi faiths.com/pdf/briefhistoryofislamism.pdf

3. *Ali Ibn Abu Talib, the Fourth Caliph*, http://www.iccuk.org/media/khutbas/ Ali%20Ibn%20Abu%20Talib,%20the%20Fourth%20Caliph.pdf

4. BBC Religions, *Sufism: history and theology*. http://www.bbc.co.uk/religion/ religions/islam/subdivisions/sufism_1.shtml#h2

5. *Comparison of Shia, Sunni and Sufi Factions of Islam*. http://staff.jccc.net/jbacon /readings/world_religions/Sunni-Shia.htm

6. Bristolblog.com, *Sufism: The Deviated Muslim Path,* From *Nida'ul Islam* Magzine, by Yusuf Hijazi. http://www.sullivan-county.com/wcva/sufism.htm

7. Tell Children the Truth, *Muslim Brotherhood*. http://tellthechildrenthetruth. com/mbhood_en.html

8. T.E. Lawrence Studies, *Thomas Edward Lawrence, 'Lawrence of Arabia'*. http:// telawrence.info/telawrenceinfo/life/biog_biog.shtml

9. The Christian Science Monitor, *The Tenets of Terror*. http://www.csmonitor.com /2001/1018/p1s2-wogi.html

10. First World War.com, *Who's Who—T.E. Lawrence*. http://www.firstworldwar. com/bio/lawrencete.htm

11. Oxford Centre for Islamic Studies. *A Recognized Independent Centre of the University of Oxford*. http://www.oxcis.ac.uk/fellows.html

12. English Islam Times, *Saudi Shia Muslims at risk of torture and ill-treatment*. http://www.islamtimes.org/vdch66ni.23nzqd10t2.html

13. The Jamestown Foundation, *Global Terrorism Analysis,* by Trevor Stanley. http:// www.jamestown.org/programs/gta/single/?tx_ttnews[tt_news]=528&tx_tt news[backPid]=180&no_cache=1

14. ABC This Week with George Stephanopoulos. *'This Week' Transcript: Holy War: Should Americans Fear Islam?* http://abcnews.go.com/ThisWeek/week-transcript -holy-war-americans-fear-islam/story?id=11786745#.TuAep3pcVdg

15. *A Brief History of Islam*, by Ghaffar Hussain, Quilliam, http://www.multi faiths.com/pdf/briefhistoryofislamism.pdf

CHAPTER

4

BROTHERHOOD DESCENDANTS

HATCHING THE BROTHERHOOD

One of the consequences of World War I was the dismantling of the Ottoman Empire, an Islamic caliphate without national borders. That is what Islam desires—a world ruled by Sharia law. Unbeknownst to westerners, the United States became the object of intense, deep-seated Islamic ire when the Ottoman Empire fell in 1924. In 1928, the Muslim Brotherhood was created in Egypt under the leadership of a man named Hassan al-Banna. The Brotherhood was formed with one purpose in mind—to reestablish the Ottoman Empire by defeating the west in general and the United States in particular, through the implementation of a 100-year plan.[1] Brotherhood anger was stoked even further with the defeat of Hitler in World War II. Hitler's closest and most powerful Arab ally was Haj Amin al-Husseini, the Grand Mufti of Jerusalem who would later become the leader of the Muslim Brotherhood in 1945.[2] My paternal grandfather, as chieftain of his village, was close personal friends with Husseini and welcomed him whenever the Brotherhood leader paid a visit to the village. Husseini was also a close colleague of al-Banna.

Hitler/Nazi comparisons are typically frowned upon because they have become rather tiresome and often signal a devolved argument. However, in the case of the Muslim Brotherhood and one of its later leaders—Husseini—such a comparison is indisputable and must be underscored for reasons that will become apparent shortly.

PALESTINE LIBERATION ORGANIZATION (PLO)

Brotherhood anger rose to a new level with the embarrassing Arab defeat in the 1967 six-day war; it gave birth to enough Islamic rage to last for several lifetimes.

I lived in Bethlehem at the time of that war; it was a source of enormous shame for the Brotherhood. It was Israel vs. Egypt, Jordan, Syria, Lebanon and practically the entire Arab world. Israel was victorious in six days. As a child, I remember listening to Arabic broadcasts on the radio. They were filled with lies that Israel was being defeated. It was very similar to the 'Baghdad Bob' moment in Iraq in 2003, when Saddam Hussein's information minister was on television, broadcasting live from Baghdad. 'Bob' was denying that US troops had made it to the Iraqi capital. There was an inconvenient problem for 'Baghdad Bob' though; American troops were visible in the background.[3] This was certainly a different kind of JBTW.

The six-day war was definitely a flashpoint in the Muslim Brotherhood's 100-year plan to overthrow western civilization. The Arab world didn't get much sympathy from the international community after that war. Israel successfully defeated a much larger foe. David and Goliath comparisons were invoked; Israel was portrayed as the successful underdog and the Arab world as the humiliated favorite. To demonstrate how different perceptions were at that time, consider an article written by *TIME* Magazine one week after Israel's victory:

> Historians may argue for years over who actually fired the first shot or dropped the first bomb. But the Realpolitik of Israel's overwhelming triumph has rendered the question largely academic. Ever since Israel was created 19 years ago, the Arabs have been lusting for the day when they could destroy it. And in the past month, Nasser succeeded for the first time in putting together an alliance of Arab armies ringing Israel; he moved some 80,000 Egyptian troops and their armor into Sinai and elbowed out the U.N. buffer force that had separated the antagonists for a decade. With a hostile Arab population of 110,000,000 menacing their own of 2,700,000, the Israelis could be forgiven for feeling a fearful itch in the trigger finger.[4]

Just forty-three years later, that same *TIME* Magazine placed a Star of David on its cover with the words, "Why Israel Doesn't Care About Peace," at the center of the star.[5] There have been, no doubt, countless forces at work which are responsible for this demonization of Israel and support for the Palestinians. Some have suggested Arab oil has westerners over a barrel and that the latter must cater to Arab sympathies as a result. Others assert that there has been a slow, consistent indoctrination of western students and that a left-wing school of thought has infiltrated the media. Both of these arguments have merit but the art of JBTW has been extremely effective and one man masterfully employed it to help portray a Palestinian David and an Israeli Goliath. His name was Yasser Arafat, the man who would head the organization to which I belonged—the Palestine Liberation Organization (PLO). The propaganda campaign was—and continues to remain—fierce.

Moreover, the *Jewish Virtual Library* charges that Arafat became a member of the Muslim Brotherhood.[6] Arafat himself claims to have fought for al-Husseini in 1948 according to a 2002 interview he gave.[7] Some reports place Arafat under the direct tutelage of al-Husseini in 1946, when the former was seventeen years-old.[8]

It has been widely accepted that Arafat was likely the nephew of al-Husseini. This could have contributed to his early success and rise within the Muslim Brotherhood. He reportedly referred to al-Husseini as his 'hero'.[9, 10]

The PLO was founded by Gamal Abd el-Nasser, the leader of Egypt. After the Arab defeat at the hands of Israel in 1967, a change in leadership within the PLO was virtually inevitable. That change came in 1969 when Arafat was handed the reins. Arafat was a master of propaganda who knew how to exploit situations to his advantage.

For example, consider the Oslo Peace Accords. Arafat joined Israeli Prime Minister Yitzhak Rabin on the White House lawn with US President Bill Clinton, just days after the PLO leader had given Rabin a hand-written letter in which Arafat expressed his heartfelt rejection of terror and violence. Rabin, who should have known better, gladly shook hands with Arafat. As this was transpiring, a recorded interview with Arafat—in Arabic—was ironically airing on Jordanian television. During that interview, Arafat said the following:

> "Since we cannot defeat Israel in war, we do it in stages. We take any and every territory that we can of Palestine, and establish sovereignty there, and we use it as a springboard to take more. When the time comes, we can get the Arab nations to join us for the final blow against Israel." [Translation][11]

It was quintessential JBTW. The real shame is that it should be so easy for westerners to spot that one is left to conclude that there is an unhealthy degree of willful ignorance coupled with plausible deniability at play. A consequence of the west's inability or unwillingness to confront leaders like Arafat has been its own defeat in the propaganda war. Shockingly, Yasser Arafat—a member of the virulently anti-

Semitic Muslim Brotherhood—was awarded the Nobel Peace Prize in 1994 on the presumption that he was going to go through with the anticipated agreement reached with respect to the Oslo Accords.[12] Arafat accepted the Nobel Prize but ultimately reneged on the treaty; it was yet another example of JBTW. That Peace Prize wasn't given to him on contingency and history still records his receipt of it; the stain is forever on those who gave it to him. Arafat said what was necessary to get himself notoriety for being interested in peace while eschewing the foundation for it being awarded.[13] Inexplicably, western leaders continued to fall for what as an obvious duping to those who weren't allied with outright evil.

HAMAS AND AL-QAEDA

Despite the mountains of evidence that implicate the Muslim Brotherhood, it is a group that has inexplicably escaped a justifiable level of scrutiny in western lands. During my terrorist days in Chicago, I was an activist for the Brotherhood; I understand their long term objectives as well as the short term tactics they employ in order to achieve those objectives.

My trainer in Chicago was Imam Jamal Said, who is identified as a spiritual leader at the Bridgeview mosque; I know it well. Said is a spokesman for the Muslim Brotherhood; he was one of the unindicted co-conspirators in the Holy Land Foundation trial. To put the extent of his complicity with terrorists in the proper context, consider that a man named Abdullah Azzam was a close friend of Said. Azzam was the mentor to none other than Osama bin Laden.[14] Azzam is also considered one of the founders of Hamas. Terrorism expert Steven Emerson once wrote about visiting the Bridgeview mosque and meeting a "defensive" Jamal Said. During that visit, Emerson said he noticed that the walls were covered with Hamas posters and literature.[15] I knew Said very well and this fits perfectly. I lived on a daily basis what Emerson was exposed to during that visit. I know what the goal of the Brotherhood is. Said supports Hamas and as a Brotherhood activist, I witnessed it.

This reality ties two terrorist organizations—Hamas and al-Qaeda—to the Muslim Brotherhood. So, how does the Brotherhood escape blame? The premise is easy to understand but the answer is complicated.

Yes, it involves JBTW but it also involves multiple front groups that operate under the guise of being motivated by civil rights; this façade puts westerners on their heels. Consider the example of CAIR; it is a group that claims to fight for the civil rights of Muslims. CAIR's leaders have studied American culture; they know that the issue of civil rights is a sensitive one. To their credit, they understand that. To their discredit, one of CAIR's strategies has been to exploit western civilization's bleeding heart and politically correct tendencies relative to civil rights. No one in western culture wants to be accused of being racist or insensitive when it comes to civil rights. CAIR, which has ties to Hamas, understands this and it has worked to their advantage. In this regard, CAIR has been far more effective than al-Qaeda or Hamas, both of whom share the goals of CAIR. The issue of tactics is where they differ.

Hamas and al-Qaeda operate from a premise which says explosive acts of terrorism represent the best way to defeat the West. Muslim civil rights groups like CAIR believe that the best way to achieve victory is to incrementally co-opt western governments and institutions. Think about the Muslim Students Association (MSA). It teaches Muslim students how to navigate through political systems. Both al-Qaeda and CAIR use Jihad but the former uses the sword while the latter uses a pen, not the kind that's filled with ink but a cage that is slowly constructed, one wall at a time, without the captive's knowledge, until it's too late and the captive is penned in.

Consider the examples of CAIR's National and Chicago Executive Directors—Nihad Awad and Ahmed Rehab. Awad expressed solidarity with Hamas in 1994 and Rehab expressed solidarity with Jamal Said in 2008. During an appearance with Bill O'Reilly on *Fox News*, Rehab defended Said as a "great American faith leader."[16]

The common denominator in all of this is the Muslim Brotherhood. Yet, this umbrella organization, under which Hamas, al-Qaeda, CAIR, and many others reside, continues to operate surreptitiously behind the scenes while westerners engage in discussions about whether CAIR is a legitimate civil rights group. The truth is that all of these groups desire the same outcome—Sharia law in America. Until Americans confront this reality, the Muslim Brotherhood—along with its many front groups—will continue to make gains.

An analogy might be the radical 1960's group known as Students for a Democratic Society (SDS), which believed in steady, incremental, and "progressive" change. The Weather Underground was formed when William Ayers and others broke away from the SDS so they could affect change through terrorism and bombings.[17] Eventually, Ayers and company decided that bombings were less effective than education and indoctrination.[18]

A FAMILIAL BROTHERHOOD

Arafat seemed to go to great lengths to keep the origins of any familial connections to the Muslim Brotherhood shrouded in secrecy. His birthplace and original name have been the source of much debate. One person whose lineage is not in question is that of Tariq Ramadan; he is the grandson of Muslim Brotherhood founder, Hasan al-Banna, as mentioned earlier. Al-Banna cooperated with the Nazis in undermining the British and the Soviet Union. (**For further documentation from German archives, see Klaus Gensicke,** *Der Mufti von Jerusalem und die Nationalsocialisten: Eine politische Biographie Amin el-Husseinis* **(Darmstadt: Wissenschaftliche Buchgesellschaft, 2007)**

According to the *Sri Lanka Daily News*, which posted a bio of al-Banna, the Ikhwan founder rejected the sheer notion of separation of church and state:

> To help consecrate the Islamic order, al-Banna called for banning all Western influences from education and ordered that all primary schools should be part of the mosques. He also wanted a ban on political parties and democratic institutions other than a Shura (Islamic-council), and wanted all government officials to have a religious study as main education.[19]

No group in the US is more hypersensitive than ACLU types and left-wing activists whenever there is even a hint of Christianity creeping toward the public square. Yet, those same people don't seem interested in sounding alarm bells when it comes to Muslim Brotherhood groups who operate in the US. The founder of the Muslim Brotherhood, a group thoroughly entrenched in America, rejected the foundational principles of the US Constitution.

It is widely documented that al-Banna was a staunch admirer of Adolf Hitler; he was also a close personal friend of Haj Amin al-Husseini, who had both the ear and admiration of Hitler as well.[20]

It wasn't just al-Banna who pledged allegiance to the Ikhwan. His son-in-law, Said Ramadan, did as well. In fact, Gamal Abdel Nasser, the leader of Egypt who initially welcomed the Brotherhood, ultimately outlawed the group after an assassination attempt was made against him. Brotherhood members were either jailed or exiled. As a member of the Ikhwan, Said was exiled to Switzerland; this is where Tariq was eventually born.[21]

Like his father-in-law, Said was a Brotherhood loyalist and leader. After moving to Switzerland, he co-founded the Al Taqwa Bank in 1988, which quickly began funding radical Islamic groups. Al-Qaeda was reportedly among them.[22] *Newsweek* reported that US authorities raided Al Taqwa Bank in Switzerland about one month after the September 11th attacks. In the article, the bank was identified as having been set up by Muslim Brotherhood members. *Newsweek* proceeded to refer to the Ikhwan as "…radical but ostensibly peaceful…"[23]

How could a group with deep-seated ties to Hitler's Nazis be considered "peaceful" in any way, shape, matter or form? One way is through JBTW, which is where Said Ramadan's son, Tariq, comes in.

By not fully and forcefully denouncing the Muslim Brotherhood, Tariq Ramadan remains tied to the group through his heritage as well as through his refusal to denounce it. It would be like the grandson of the founder of the KKK also being the son of one of its Kleagles, becoming a public figure without rejecting his heritage. If such a person were to have a conversion away from the racist ideology that fuels the KKK, his primary objective would be to denounce his ancestors if he were to be afforded any credibility as an advocate for the end of racism. Tariq Ramadan does not do that; he also doesn't fully embrace the Ikhwan publicly. Instead, he uses JBTW to nurture an environment that allows him to remain a public figure without denouncing the anti-Semitic, Islamo-fascist, Nazism espoused by both his father and grandfather. This is not a gray area; it is black and white. By not denouncing the Brotherhood, Tariq Ramadan—in particular— necessarily and tacitly, embraces it.

Consider a glowing article that featured Tariq Ramadan; it appeared on the official Muslim Brotherhood website and demonstrates clearly how Ramadan attempts to thread the needle between the Ikhwan and western sensitivities about racism. He does so with a public admission that he is Muslim, coupled with a call for secularism in non-Muslim lands. Penned by Mehru Jaffer Vienna, the subtitle of the article is as follows:

> He (Ramadan) is one of the most outspoken intellectuals today in Europe who is dismissed as too modern by the orthodox and too traditional by secularists. Meet Tariq Ramadan, 47, a cult figure with his good looks and gift of the gab.[24]

That part about the "gift of the gab" is important because it segues nicely into a discussion about JBTW. Why would the Muslim Brotherhood portray Ramadan so positively if his goals didn't align with theirs? The answer is that it wouldn't and when one comes to grips with that very obvious reality, the deceit inherent in JBTW screams out from in between the lines of the article.

Consider the following excerpt:

> Ramadan's Swiss wife has converted to Islam and their children attend government schools. He is often accused of trying to impose Islam on the West. He, however, begs to differ. To be engaged in a reasoned but traditional approach to life is no crime, he says.

> This student of French literature, German philosophy and lover of Fyodor Dostoevsky has discovered that Islam offers values as universal as the European Enlightenment. For him, his religious practice and **Islamic identity is very precious**. It keeps him grounded in morals and ethics so **familiar to him from childhood**.[25] (emphasis mine)

Ramadan's love for Islam, coupled with his refusal to renounce the anti-Semitism of his father and grandfather, actually exposes him more than most. He clearly embraces his family heritage, which involves an alliance with Adolf Hitler and virulent anti-Semitism. Yet, he is so adept at JBTW that he has inexplicably been able to fly under the radar of scrutiny. After all, he *does* have the 'gift of the gab' while the west appears to be afflicted with willful ignorance.

In 2004, Tariq Ramadan had applied for a visa and was days away from starting a job with the University of Notre Dame when he was informed by the Department of Homeland Security (DHS) under the George W. Bush administration that his visa would be suspended and that he would be banned from entering the United States. At the time, Daniel Pipes chronicled multiple instances of Ramadan's alleged interactions with al-Qaeda operatives—including a coordinated meeting with al-Qaeda's number two, Ayman al-Zawahiri.[26] In short, if Ramadan's objective was to distance himself from Islamist influences because of his familial ties—which would have necessitated much more distancing than most—he failed to do so. In fact, he did the opposite. Tariq Ramadan was the quintessential example of a public figure that needed to unequivocally distance himself from Islamist influences. Instead, his affiliations seemed to indicate that he *embraced* those influences. He was subsequently banned from entry into the US...for a while.

Pipes predicted in 2004 that Ramadan's fate would be determined by a battle between the State Department, which endorsed granting him entry, and DHS, which rejected it under the Bush administration.

Any conflict that existed between State and DHS essentially dissipated under the Obama administration as the former was headed by ex-first lady and runner-up for the Democratic presidential nominee, Hillary Clinton, and the latter led by former Arizona governor, Janet Napolitano. Assuming Napolitano had any interest in keeping Ramadan out of the US—which would require a heaping helping of grace—she most assuredly would have lost any political battle with Clinton. In any case, Napolitano never put up a fight.

In January of 2010, Secretary of State Hillary Clinton signed Tariq Ramadan's release papers. The grandson of Hasan al-Banna suddenly had the ban on his entry into the United States lifted at the stroke of Clinton's pen.[27]

The *Global Muslim Brotherhood Daily Report* had this to say about Ramadan after learning that his ban had been lifted:

> Tariq Ramadan is perhaps best described as an independent power center within the global Brotherhood with sufficient stature as the son of Said Ramadan, and the grandson of the founder of the Muslim Brotherhood to challenge positions taken by important Brotherhood leaders. His statements and writings have been extensively analyzed and he has been accused by critics of promoting anti-Semitism and fundamentalism, **albeit by subtle means.**[28] (emphasis mine)

Aside from the part about Ramadan's potential interest in furthering the Muslim Brotherhood's agenda surreptitiously, Secretary Clinton had a conflict of interest exposed when she signed on to seeing the grandson of the group's founder go free. That conflict involved Hillary's Deputy Chief of Staff, Huma Abedin, a Muslim woman who had been working for her since 1996. It would later be learned that Abedin's familial allegiances were far more in line with those of Ramadan's than one might suspect. Ramadan is a professor at Oxford University in the UK;[29] He also was appointed to a chair with the Oxford Centre for Islamic Studies (OCIS) according to the *National Observer*.[30] Abedin's brother is on the board of the OCIS. There will be much more on this later. For now, it's important to come to grips with the fact that both families (Abedin and Ramadan) share a common cause when it comes to the Ikhwan. Hillary's most trusted adviser had substantial influence over her decision-making. One of those decisions did indeed involve lifting Ramadan's travel ban.

Regardless of what Ramadan may have stated with respect to his intentions, his actions—as well as the *reactions* of groups sympathetic to the Ikhwan—spoke volumes. For example, shortly after his ban was lifted, CAIR endorsed the act.[31] In addition to receiving the endorsement of Ikhwan-affiliated groups, Tariq, on several occasions, spoke at Islamist-sponsored events whose organizers clearly revered Tariq's heritage as well as the organization his grandfather founded. In his first public speaking engagement after having his travel ban lifted, Ramadan spoke in New York alongside a woman named Dalia Mogahed.[32] Former Muslim Nonie Darwish describes Mogahed as a fierce defender of both CAIR and the Islamic Society of North America (ISNA), both Muslim Brotherhood-affiliated groups. She also served as a faith adviser in the Obama administration.[33] Soon thereafter, Ramadan spoke at a CAIR Chicago event.[34] This is the same CAIR branch headed by Ahmed Rehab, mentioned earlier.

Not long after his speaking engagement with CAIR, Ramadan spoke at the Ronald Reagan Building Amphitheater, just a few blocks from the White House. Joining him was none other than Obama's envoy to the Organization of the Islamic Conference (OIC), Rashad Hussain.[35]

A few short months later, Ramadan spoke at a United for Change event in Canada, where he shared the stage with Jamal Badawi and Abdallah Idris Ali (both members of the ISNA), Zainab Al-Alwani of the Fiqh Council of North America (FCNA), and Yasir Qadhi, a holocaust denier according to an article in the *London Telegraph*.[36]

Speaking of denial, in an op-ed written by Ramadan that appeared in the *New York Times*, the grandson of the founder of the Muslim Brotherhood made a feeble attempt to paint a reality in which Hasan al-Banna and Hilter were opposed to one another and that the Brotherhood's founder opposed Nazism.[37] In reality, they were the closest of allies and shared a common hatred for the Jews. As mentioned earlier, the Grand Mufti of Jerusalem—Haj Amin al-Husseini was not only a close personal friend of al-Banna but he was also Hitler's closest and most powerful Arab ally. If Hitler was a guy who was so ostracized by the Ikhwan, how did Husseini become the group's leader *after* WWII? The answer is that Ramadan is attempting to manipulate language in order to rewrite paradigms, as well as history.

There are countless examples of Tariq Ramadan aligning with Muslim Brotherhood sympathizers, members, and groups. In fact, the evidence is beyond damning; it would assuredly convict him if the power centers of western civilization had any interest in identifying the actual enemy. Instead, those power centers seem more concerned with either looking the other way or aligning with the likes of Ramadan. The case can be made that Ramadan has a tremendous "gift of the gab" but the reality is western leaders have either become corrupt, wicked, or are simply too unwilling to dissect his JBTW for fear of a truth they cannot handle.

As for why the left in America buys what Ramadan is selling, one can only guess, but make no mistake; most of them are buying it. In fact, Paul Donnelly at *Salon* thinks so much of Ramadan's reformation efforts that he once pushed the idea that the grandson of al-Banna could be Islam's Martin Luther.[38]

In an article penned by Shammai Fishman, readers were warned of Ramadan's tendency toward JBTW as well as an ostensibly close relationship he held with none other than Taha Jaber Al-Alwani, whose nefarious, anti-Semitic views are covered in another chapter of this book. To put this relationship into context relative to the leading, rhetorical question posed by Donnelly would necessitate a reality in which Martin Luther collaborated with the Pope in order to christen the Protestant religion.[39] Again, what is it about Ramadan that would so successfully and totally dupe the left's useful idiots? Fishman cites an interesting assertion made by Prof. Emmanuel Sivan of the Hebrew University of Jerusalem:

> Sivan recommends reading Ramadan in Arabic before reading him in any other language, due to the possibility of double messages.[40]

Assuming Ramadan is aware that people are out there dissecting his words (any other assumption would be rooted in a blatant, dangerous and childish form of naiveté), we are left only to conclude that his polished JBTW is being subjected to constant refinement. The problem for him, however, lies in his affiliations; they are damning. Al-Alwani is just another in a long line of them. According to Fishman, both men were registered as guest scholars at the American Learning Institute for Muslims (ALIM) in Maryland as recently as 2005.[41] Al-Alwani was also a founding member of the International Institute for Islamic Thought (IIIT). This is another officially designated Muslim Brotherhood group; Ramadan has already been tied to several others. With his relationship to Al-Alwani, we can add IIIT to the list.

Reformation may be on the mind of Ramadan but his interpretation of it isn't about reforming Islam; it's about reforming Muslims so that they can become more puritan and fundamentalist in how they practice it while giving the perception of reformation. Ramadan is a chip off the old block; he is a branch from the tree with roots that go back to his anti-Semitic, religiously intolerant ancestors.

At Islam Online, Majdi Said quotes from Tariq Ramadan's own testimony:

> "My father was chosen to represent the Muslim Brotherhood in absentia, so from my birth I was surrounded by Islamic thought and talk by Muslims living in Europe and they were fully submerged in the reality of the Muslim world...All my youth I am accompanied with the image of my martyred grandfather Imam Hasan Al-Bana...Everyone in Egypt gave my father the title Hasan Al-Bana, Jr. since my grandfather sent him to speak in the farthest climates in Egypt even though he did not exceed the 16th year of age. From then he was my Imam, a human being in which I can say that the strength of his knowledge was especially overwhelming."[42]

Ramadan then quite specifically asserts that he does not deny his birthright to the Muslim Brotherhood lineage:

> "I studied in depth the thought process of Hasan Al-Bana and **I do not deny my membership**. His spiritual connection to Allah, his **Sufist aspiration**, and his persona, as well as his critical thinking regarding law, politics, society and pluralism, all these are references for me to turn to, via my heart and my mind. His commitment to continue stimulates my respect and admiration...I feel that I am close to his thought and this commitment: to be with Allah, to seek fidelity to his teachings, to stimulate in establishing madrassas, and commit to solidarity with the people for the struggle for social justice...This is my heritage and the meaning of my spiritual and intellectual membership."[43] (emphasis mine)

There you have it, proof that Tariq Ramadan revered his father and grandfather; he didn't renounce them. Consider that Ramadan calls for European style Islam. This is very similar to what Feisal Abdul Rauf has been calling for in the United States.

Liberal Muslim and Egyptian writer Ghada Abdel-Moneim describes Ramadan as a person who:

> ...uses doublespeak: to Muslims and Arabs he is loaded with ideas and views of the Muslim Brotherhood describing Western civilization as morally bankrupt, ideas he derived from his father and grandfather used as a formula for Muslim consumption within the Muslim community. But when speaking to the West uses another version filled with innovative ideas in Islamic law, where he addresses that the goal is to 'purify Islam' and update it, making it in-line with the pattern of contemporary Western civilization. This is why Tariq Ramadan is always accused by anyone that knows both Arab and Western cultures as 'sneaky' and 'elusive' with views that tickle the ears of whatever party line willing to receive him. He Addresses the West with words that totally contradict what he says to Arabs and Muslims. Perhaps the greatest proof of this is an article published by Israeli newspaper *Haaretz*, where he defended the charge of anti-Semitism against him; he also showed entirely different views of his grandfather, which was promoted and advocated to the Muslim youth in his speeches and seminars. What is ironic is that when he was prevented from entering the United States, his strongest defenders were the Jewish students at the University of Notre Dame, where he was scheduled to teach, had it not been for the [Bush] ban. (Ghada Abdel-Moneim in Modern Dialogue, #1319, September 16, 2005)[44]

Let us further consider the Muslim view of Ramadan's doublespeak. Despite Ramadan being banned by Egypt, Syria, and Saudi Arabia, Hillary Clinton signed a document that allowed al-Banna's grandson to enter the United States. Muslim writer Hamid Fadlallah unwittingly exposed Ramadan's attempt to cover-up his intentions while rationalizing his deceptive tactics:

> Ramadan acknowledges that European rejection directs us on how to navigate, evolving ourselves to new direction while remaining loyal to the rules of his faith. Ramadan's position on dealing with issues of faith does not contradict the *Shurah Fiqh Council*, but with his fate living in Europe, he finds listening ears of the new generation of Muslims.[45, 46]

The term "reformist" usually implies something positive, a reference to someone who is eager to right wrongs. In the case of Ramadan and his like-minded minions, the word carries a different meaning entirely: wrongs are covered up by individuals who seek to continue them while doing so behind the façade of making amends for having committed unnamed evils. Those who attempt to identify those evils are themselves identified as *Islamophobic* for having the gall to do so. In essence, deception is used to continue committing evil no one will take responsibility for having committed. It would seem that we are getting ever closer to the very essence of evil itself.

Fadlallah even supports the duality and JBTW as a sign of loyalty. He wants Ramadan to emulate the Muslim Brotherhood's spiritual leader, Sheikh Yusuf al-Qaradawi in his JBTW and even refers to this phenomenon as "clarity":

> "[Ramadan] is also met with much criticism for his swinging views. Sheikh Qaradawi for example, is also met with lots of criticism, but now he is well known to support the heritage of the Muslim Brotherhood and as an Islamist he is securing and defining the Islamic existence in the West, but opposite from Ramadan who lacks this clarity [and ask]—is he an Islamist or is he a reformist?"[47]

In this case "reformist" is nothing more than an Islamist still in the closet, an Islamist who is not yet willing to publicly pledge his allegiance to the cause while having it emblazoned on his heart. That is a rather bizarre definition of "reformist," is it not? A more apt word would be "deceiver." In that respect, Ramadan is more dangerous than Qaradawi.

Fadlallah's summary of German scholar Ralph Ghadban, who is Maronite by origin, provides Ghadban's eight points in the conclusion of Ramadan's book. It is crucial to note that Fadlallah's review was not meant to portray Ramadan in a negative light but to acquit him from Islamic modernity with a wink to those who had doubts. In other words, Ghadban is not pointing to Ramadan as a bad apple; he is telling the general Muslim public not to worry because Tariq follows proper tactics:

> Ramadan's desire to freeze Muslim penalty codes of stoning, flogging and death is simply his way to advertise himself in front of the Western world so as to appear as a Muslim reformist.[48]

The conclusion by Ghadban of Ramadan's thoughts includes 8 "positive" points:

1. Tariq Ramadan rejects freedom of thought or rationality. He comes from an Islamic Unitarian ideology.

2. Ijtihad (innovation in Islam) emanates from the classical period—the tenth to twelfth centuries. This doctrine, which Ramadan adopts, explains the holy writ from the Holy *Quran* and *Sunnah* and restricts the use of these sources. He depends on *Qiyas* [analogical reasoning as applied to the deduction of juridical principles], (the measurement of the absent witness) rather than calling for the diligence of the traditional interpretation of the law to address present problems.

3. The classical approach is not only the expulsion of scientific theology, but also philosophy—Islamic philosophy represents an attempt to reconcile faith with reason.

4. The science of speech has no place in Ramadan's thought process. Philosophy is used as a compromise and he cites those who want to abolish it and fight free thought as wanting to serve the [Islamic] faith as the only source of knowledge. An example of this is Imam al-Ghazali.

5. His speech follows ethical and typical methods limited to classical jurisprudence with no room for maneuver. Islam is eternal and cannot change. Modernity only results in blasphemy.

   The modernization of [Islamic] laws is based on interest in order to correspond with Western societies. [Ramadan] does not recognize any value of the trends of secularization in Islamic history. This includes the reformation of the Ottoman period from the mid-nineteenth century including the work of reformers in the era of the Renaissance, such as Muhammad Abduh, and Tahtawi, Kawakibi and Ali Abd al-Raziq, who Ramadan accuses of loyalty towards the West, which must be combated.

6. Ramadan is against the Enlightenment and does not recognize human rights or the separation of church and state.

7. In order to reach his goal to create an Islamic identity he uses brilliant methods:

A. Taking advantage of western guilt and remorse, referring to the European colonial period as hideous.

B. Failure of western policy in dealing with foreigners and the growing Islamophobia.

C. Use multiculturalism.

8. In Ramadan's view, Muslims are not to integrate into western environment. Instead, he advocates for the integration of the environment into the eternal cosmic Islamic society. Those who believe that [Ramadan's] Islam is a step into European integration are greatly mistaken. Ramadan's Islam is not a way to integration but represents Islamization. European Islam is simply a new façade for an ancient subject that has already been dealt with.[49]

As if it were necessary at this point, Ramadan again revealed his true colors in 2006. During a *Prayer for Palestine* event, Ramadan loudly proclaimed the following in a prayerful chant:

"O Allah, strengthen the faith of our brothers and sisters of Palestine, give them victory over their enemies, your enemies, the enemies of the faith...strengthen the faith of the believers in Palestine, in Chechnya, in Afghanistan, in Morroco, in Algeria, in Tunisia, in Egypt and Sudan, in Kashmir, in every land and in every battleground O Merciful One, accept it from them and strengthen their bond and enter them into paradise alongside the virtuous and righteous and the martyrs the prophets O merciful most magnificent one. O Allah, strengthen the tortured prisoners. Take care of our enemies, the enemies of our faith and give victory to Islam and to Muslims and elevate the truth, the truth of our religion."[50]

Why wouldn't such a prayer, offered to Allah in full public view, with hundreds of Muslims in attendance, and made available for sale on DVD not garner a single peep from the Muslim community about a contradiction between Ramadan's public stance of reformation coupled with his public display of prayerful advocacy for fundamentalism?

Egyptian researcher Husam Tamam refers to Ramadan as:

...an "Islamist" who can open up new frontiers that were not even a subject of discussion amongst Islamists. By approaching his supporters on the left, by using social justice and aligning with the anti-globalization and the third other—the pro-One-World-Government to even re-formulate their ideas into Islamic expressions...He is also the "Islamist" that can confront Jewish intellectuals in France and managed on his own to confront the French influential elite. All of this is achieved without involving the traditional Islamic methods of attacking Jews, which always end up in accusations of anti-Semitism. Instead, he succeeds through humanistic talk that puts them on the defensive in place of self-retreat; it forces them to focus on universal values and the values of justice, freedom and equality instead of allowing the other side to extract their community interests. (Al-Ghad Newspaper, December 22, 2006)[51]

Now that we have established that Ramadan has chosen to align with the Muslim Brotherhood on multiple fronts, what can be deduced about his beliefs? We have proven that Ramadan engages in JBTW based on his actions. In the digital age, any deception once practiced by al-Banna must be made more difficult to decode for the likes of Ramadan if the latter is to maintain his stealth. This is what the grandson of the Brotherhood's founder has proven adept at doing and his relationships necessarily eliminate this from being a matter of conjecture. The case on this is closed. The only things open at this point are the minds of his pawns—both suspecting and unsuspecting—to his JBTW.

With a premise established that says Ramadan agrees with his grandfather's goals but sees the need for implementing different means to achieve them, perhaps it would be a useful exercise to explore al-Banna's beliefs while understanding that Ramadan is unwilling to be as forthright as his grandfather was.

Consider what al-Banna thought about Jihad:

Agree unanimously that jihad is a communal defensive obligation imposed upon the Islamic ummah in order to broadcast the summons (to embrace Islam), and that it is an individual obligation to repulse the attack of unbelievers upon it. (*Five Tracts of Hasan al-Banna* (1906-1949): A Selection from the Majmu'at Rasa'il al-Imam al-Shahid, translated by *Charles Wendell* (Berkeley, University of California Press, 1978), page 150-151).

There is so much overwhelming evidence that Ramadan believes as his grand-father did that anyone willing to give him the benefit of the doubt would deny their own eyes and ears when confronted with the face and screams of a tortured human being. Not only do we assert this without reservation but we now know that Ramadan is hiding his true feelings in order to continue the art of deception.

It is a reality that should have westerners enraged. Yet, so many still remain disengaged.

FOOTNOTES

1. FrontPageMag.com, *The Muslim Brotherhood "Project"*, by Patrick Poole. http://archive.frontpagemag.com/readArticle.aspx?ARTID=4476

2. Tell Children the Truth, *Muslim Brotherhood*. http://tellthechildrenthetruth.com/mbhood_en.html

3. M.S.S. *Updates*. http://www.welovetheiraqiinformationminister.com/

4. Time (Magazine).com, *Middle East: The QuIckest War*. http://www.time.com/time/printout/0,8816,843937,00.html

5. Time (Magazine).com, *Why Israel Doesn't Care About Peace*. http://www.time.com/time/covers/0,16641,20100913,00.html

6. Jewish Virtual Library, *Yasser Arafat*. http://www.jewishvirtuallibrary.org/jsource/biography/arafat.html

7. Discover The Networks.org, *Yasser Arafat*. http://www.discoverthenetworks.org/individualProfile.asp?indid=650

8. CNN report, *Arab use of Nazi propaganda techniques*. http://tellthechildrenthetruth.com/arafat_en.html#_edn25

9. Palestine Facts, *Grand Mufti Haj Amin al-Husseini*. http://www.palestinefacts.org/pf_mandate_grand_mufti.php

10. Masada 2000.org, *The Blood Connection: Grand Mufti Haj Amin al-Husseini*. http://www.masada2000.org/Arafat-Husseini.html

11. Discover The Networks.org, *Yasser Arafat*. http://www.discoverthenetworks.org/individualProfile.asp?indid=650

12. Nobelprize.org, *The Nobel Peace Prize 1994, Yasser Arafat, Shimon Peres, Yitzhak Rabin*. http://www.nobelprize.org/nobel_prizes/peace/laureates/1994/#

13. Palestine Facts, *Arafat and the Nobel Peace Prize: Why did Yasser Arafat get the Nobel Peace Prize?* http://www.palestinefacts.org/pf_1991to_now_arafat_nobel.php

14. History Commons, *Profile: Abdullah Azzam*. http://www.historycommons.org/entity.jsp?entity=abdullah_azzam

15. WND, *Terrorists Among Us, 'Jihad in America'*, by Steve Emerson. http://www.wnd.com/?pageId=13197

16. Doug Ross@Journal, *Obama's Muslim-Outeach Adviser Resigns*. http://directorblue.blogspot.com/2008/08/spin-zone-barack-obama-mazin-asbahi.html

17. http://www.terroristplanet.com/underground.htm

18. Blog at Wordpress, *Bill Ayers Biography/history*. http://billayers.wordpress.com/biographyhistory/

19. Daily News, *ISLAM, Popular Uprising in Egypt*, compiled by Latheef Farook. http://www.dailynews.lk/2011/04/04/fea16.asp

20. The Simon Wiesenthal Center, "Hitler Put Them in Their Place" *Egypt's Muslim Brotherhood's Jihad Against Jews, Judaism, and Israel*, by Dr. Harold Brackman. http://www.wiesenthal.com/atf/cf/%7B54d385e6-f1b9-4e9f-8e94-890c3e6dd277%7D/HITLER-PUT-THEM-IN-THEIR-PLACE_BRACKMAN_FINAL.PDF

21. Discover The Networks.org, *Tariq Ramadan*. http://www.discoverthenetworks.org/individualProfile.asp?indid=1884

22. History Commons, *Profile: Said Ramadan*. http://www.historycommons.org/entity.jsp?entity=said_ramadan_1

23. NBC News.com, *Attacking the Money Machine*, by Mark Hosenball. http://www.msnbc.msn.com/id/3067473/t/attacking-money-machine/

24. The Muslim Brotherhood's Official English web site, *A Man with Qualities*. http://ikhwanmisr.net/article.php?id=22456

25. Ibid

26. Daniel Pipes, Middle East Forum, *Why Revoke Tariq Ramandan's U.S. Visa?*, by Daniel Pipes. http://www.danielpipes.org/2043/why-revoke-tariq-ramadans-us-visa

27. http://www.tariqramadan.com/US-Government-Lifts-Ban-on-Tariq.html

28. The Global Muslim Brotherhood Daily Report, *Breaking News: U.S. State Department Lifts Ban on Tariq Ramadan*. http://globalmbreport.com/?p=1956

29. University of Oxford, Faculty of Theology and Religion, *Prof. Tariq Ramadan.* http://www.theology.ox.ac.uk/people/staff-list/dr-tariq-ramadan.html

30. National Observer, *Security*, by Anthony Glees. http://www.nationalobserver. net/2009_81_glees.htm

31. CAIR, Council on American-Islamic Relations, *CAIR Welcomes Lifting of Ban on Muslim Scholar.* http://www.cair.com/ArticleDetails.aspx?ArticleID=26229&&name =n&&crrPage=1

32. The New York Times, *Muslim Scholar, Formerly Barred, Is to Speak in New York,* by Andy Newman. http://www.nytimes.com/2010/03/18/nyregion/18prof.html

33. FrontPageMag.com, *Appeasing the Muslim Brotherhood*, by Nonie Darwish. http:// frontpagemag.com/2010/04/20/appeasing-the-muslim-brotherhood/

34. CAIR Chicago, *First U.S. Appearance – Tariq Ramadan to Speak at 6th Annual CAIR-Chicago Banquet.* http://www.cairchicago.org/2010/02/22/tariq-ramadan-to-be-keynote-at-cair-chicagos-6th-annual-banquet/

35. Center for the Study of Islam and Democracy – 11th Annual Conference, *U.S.-Relations with the Muslim World: One Year After.* https://www.csidonline.org/ pdf/11th_CSID_Conference_Tentative_Program.pdf

36. The Global Muslim Brotherhood Daily Report, *New Canadian Muslim Brotherhood Organization To Hold "Biggest Islamic Conference in Montreal History".* http:// globalmbreport.com/?p=3342

37. The New York Times, The Opinion Pages, *Whither the Muslim Brotherhood?,* by Tariq Ramadan. http://www.nytimes.com/2011/02/09/opinion/09iht-edramadan 09.html?_r=1&pagewanted=all

38. Salon, *Tariq Ramadan: The Muslim Martin Luther?* by Paul Donnelly. http://www. salon.com/2002/02/15/ramadan_2/

39. Global-Report, *Some Notes on Arabic Terminology as a Link Between Tariq Ramadan and Sheikh Dr. Taha Jabir al-Alwani, Founder of the Doctrine of "Muslim Minority Jurisprudence",* by Shammai Fishman. http://www.globalreport.com/prism/a5009 -some-notes-on-arabic-terminology-as-a-link-between-tariq-ramadan-and-sheikh-dr-taha-jabir-al-alwani-founder-of-the-doctrine-of-muslim-minority-juris prudence

40. Ibid

41. Ibid

42. Arabic website. http://www.islamonline.net/i3/ContentServer?pagename=Islam
Online/i3LayoutA&c=OldArticle&cid=1182774755089

43. Ibid

44. Arabic website. http://www.ahewar.org/debat/show.art.asp?aid=45656#

45. Arabic website. http://www.saudiinfocus.com/ar/forum/showthread.php?t=21099

46. Arabic website. http://www.ibn-rushd.org/forum/TRamadan.html

47. Ibid

48. Ibid

49. Ibid

50. Video in Arabic. http://www.youtube.com/watch?v=onuEStqTk20

51. Arabic website. http://www.alghad.com/index.php/article/125891.html

CHAPTER

5

WELCOME TO
MURUNA

NEW LEVEL OF DECEPTION

*T*here are generally three terms used to describe various types of deception intended to further the cause of Islam. *Taqiyya* refers to the tactic of saying something that is not true in order to guard the faith; *Kitman* is similar but is performed by leaving out elements that would expose the true faith. The third—*Muruna*—is the subject of much controversy within Islam itself and may be the main bone of contention between the Ikhwan and the Salafists. It means "stealth" or "flexibility".

At the root of this controversy exists the meaning of two other terms. They are *abrogation*, which means that a more recent verse on a specific matter always trumps any previous verse, and *Ijtihad*, which refers to realities that are not addressed by existent Islamic rulings. A changing world can often complicate this problem but Islamists have learned to use it to their advantage by citing *Ijtihad* in their attempts to portray Islam's openness to modernity and reform. In both cases, Islam is known to use *Taqiyya* and *Kitman* to deceive non-believers.

According to Yusuf al-Qaradawi, *Muruna* requires Muslims to actually *believe* the lies they are putting forth, at least temporarily. Leaders of other powerful sects, like the Salafis, vehemently disagree with this approach because it can, in part, actually backfire and thereby deceive Muslims themselves. In short, there is a concern on the part of some Islamic scholars that such an interpretation of *Muruna* can cause Islam to out-smart itself.

Sheikh Qaradawi, perhaps the leading authority on Islamic jurisprudence in the Sunni Muslim world, under the instruction of the High Committee to Institute Sharia, began a book series entitled, *Preparing the Atmosphere (to reinforce Sharia)*. The title Qaradawi gives to his first book in the series is: *The Workings of Al-Si'a (Inclusion) and Muruna (Flexibility) in Sharia.* It is about how Islam can be malleable, adaptable in today's world, almost chameleon-like. In the beginning of his book, Qaradawi addresses the purpose of his writing:

> It was imagined by Orientalists and their ilk, writing about Islam in a spirit of bigotry and a mindset of hostility saying that Sharia is stiff and belligerent, that it cannot open its chest to accommodate development in facing modern times with the spirit of modernity...etc. They argue that because [Sharia] and its sources are based on religious inspiration, the Muslim has no choice but to "hear and obey," that this is his destiny, his faith and his Islam. Believers are to reply with "We hear and obey" when they are summoned to Allah and His Messenger so that he can judge between them. They are ones who are successful. (Quran, Nur: 51)".[1]

Qaradawi continues…

> While this [Quranic] instruction is correct, the conclusion they made is in error.

The flexibility that Qaradawi argues is inherent in Sharia has nothing to do with burdensome mandates or rulings that do not jibe with our modern era. Instead, it involves the abolition of rulings that stand in the way of "goals," "necessities," "needs," and "interests" that call on Muslims to shun the most crucial elements of the law. In other words, Qaradawi's claim would allow blasphemy as a form of *taqiyya* or *kitman*; this is difficult for many Muslims to accept.

Qaradawi explains…

> The fourth aspect of Sharia's ability to be flexible and inclusive is that it cares for the necessities, needs and excuses that so **burden the Muslims.** For the sake of their destiny, it was made lawful for them to have exceptions from the law that are appropriate for them since these exceptions match their general goals to **make it easy for humanity by removing the chains of these [Sharia] rules** they were made to follow in previous Sharia rulings. [emphasis mine]

Was that an admission that Sharia law comes with chains? Under certain circumstances, Qaradawi allows Muslims to break the rules of Islam. His assessment of how Sharia can be implemented today is tantamount to self-deception, not just deception of the unbelievers. He unequivocally states—without apology—that "necessities justify" denying the tenets of a Muslim's sacrosanct Sharia law[2] and that when "coercion" is present in "times of weakness and disability," Muslims have legitimate reasons to break Sharia laws. Qaradawi provides such examples:

> One of the conditions for exceptions granted by the general rules is that of weakness and disability, which inflicts Muslim individuals and Islamic entities, which makes Muslims take non-Muslim friends, showing them love and alliance. This does *not* mean that he admires their religion or that he betrays his *own* religion and thereby, his [Muslim] nation. Rather, it is his fear of their dominance that motivates him to protect himself from their evil in accordance with [Allah's] command: "Let not the believers take for friends or helpers unbelievers rather than believers; if any do that, in nothing will there be help from Allah, except by way of precaution, that ye may Guard yourselves from them. But Allah cautions you (To remember) Himself; for the final goal is to Allah.'" (Quran, Al-Imran: 28)

Note that Qaradawi is not attempting to nullify verses which mandate hatred of unbelievers; he actually affirms them. Even in times of need, a Muslim must hate the unbelievers. Qaradawi affirms the ruling thusly:

> Despite this harsh condemnation [in the Quran]: "and as for whomever does this he has nothing to do with Allah" that with another condemnation "whomsoever befriends them [Unbelievers] is one of them" (Quran, the Table: 51), and "You shall find no nation believing in Allah and the Last Day loving anyone who opposes Allah and His Messenger, including their fathers, their sons, their brothers, or their tribe." (Quran, The Reasoning: 22) **Weakness was the only justification for this exception** [to love] that the Muslim protects himself from the evils of his enemies by showing friendship. [emphasis mine]

Note that Qaradawi is making an exception for Muslims by allowing them to **love** unbelievers—people a Muslim is mandated to hate—even if they are members of his immediate family. A follower of Qaradawi is therefore directed to both "love his enemy" and "hate his enemy" at the same time. Qaradawi is careful not to use words like "lie," "deceive," or "connive". Such words are antithetical to love, which he wants Muslims to show to unbelievers, almost unconditionally but with a deceitful core.

Under the section titled, "the necessities of the group," Qaradawi explains that "as Sharia considers the individual's needs, it permitted many exemptions and considers the necessities of the Umma [Muslim Nation] first." It is an ends-justifies-the-means mentality if there ever was one. Consider that it was forbidden in Islam to burn trees before reading this example:

> When the prophet ordered the burning of palm trees belonging to the Jews of Banu Qurayza to force their surrender, he said: "Whatever you have cut down of [their] palm trees or left standing on their trunks—it was by permission of Allah and so He would disgrace the defiantly disobedient." (Quran Al-Hishr, 5)

Here is Qaradawi's justification for the killing of Muslims…

> …killing Muslims whom the unbelievers use as shields…leaving these unbelievers is a danger to the Muslims, so it is permissible to kill these unbelievers even if Muslims are killed with them in the process."[4]

In the modern day, this example may be best illustrated by the killing of al-Qaeda terrorists. While Qaradawi's Muslim Brotherhood spawned al-Qaeda, the latter is despised by the former not because of divergent goals but because the means al-Qaeda chooses to use—terrorism—can have the effect of drawing attention and critique to groups like CAIR, which prefers a more stealthy approach. Applying Qaradawi's logic, such groups may be excused for an outward show of support for the killing of the likes of bin Laden or Anwar al-Awlaqi. If showing support for the death of fellow Muslims reduces suspicion, it might be acceptable.

According to Qaradawi, there are some rulings that are set in Sharia stone and there are other rulings which are more open to interpretation:

> Sharia rulings have two types; the first is firm; that does not change in accordance to place, time or even by Ijtihad, such as duties, prohibitions and criminal law. Ijtihad cannot be used to change what was made firm. The other types of Sharia rulings are those that *can* be changed while keeping Islam's interests in mind."[5]

Qaradawi sees tribal laws as being subject to Ijtihad, not Sharia. This is why we find Feisal Abdul Rauf of the Cordoba Initiative, in Arabic, stating that: "If Sharia is not carried out then we are left with tribal laws."

If Qaradawi is to justify changing laws and Sharia rulings, he must do so by the authority of the Qur'an itself. For that, he brings forth the issue of *Al-Nasekh wal-Mansookh* or the Abrogation in Islam. In this case, Nasekh (rulings that abrogate other rulings) and Mansookh (abrogated rules) involve matters that have been misunderstood in Qaradawi's view. In the Qur'an, one finds verses that permit the drinking of wine and in other verses, it is forbidden. The verse that permits drinking has always been understood to be made null and void (Mansookh) and replaced by a prohibition (Nasekh).

Qaradawi takes an approach different from what has been understood:

> There are no abrogated verses, or verses that abrogate other verses, but to each verse is a condition and a time to use it...one is used in a time of weakness and the other in a time of strength, so on and so forth.

He gives examples...

> Verses that call for peace, forgiveness, sparing the unbelievers and things of that sort which the interpreters say were abrogated by the Verse of the Sword...the truth I say is that such verses have their time and place and the Verse of the Sword has its time and its place".[6]

Qaradawi mentions another definition called "Al-Munsa" (forgotten verses):

> None of Our revelations do We abrogate or cause to be forgotten, but We substitute something better or similar: Knowest thou not that Allah Hath power over all things? (Quran Surah 2: 106)

The term "forgotten" is not meant in a literal sense; it does not mean abrogated or discarded, either; such verses are to be wiped from memory "temporarily," until the right time approaches. It sounds a bit like hypnosis, doesn't it? Qaradawi strengthens his view by quoting Al-Syuti, one of Islam's great sources of jurisprudence:

> ...abrogation has different levels. We have the first, the second and the third. A verse [commandment] has a purpose; when the purpose is finished, such as in being weak and few in number to have peace and forgiveness with the enemy, it is abrogated by the commands of war. This is not about abrogation. Look under the section of forgotten verses, as Allah said "we made forgotten." What is forgotten here is the order to fight until the Muslims are strong, while they are weak the ruling is to be patient.[7]

If you find yourself confused after reading that, it does not mean you have problems with comprehension; it means you are sane.

One of the concerns about Islam expressed by westerners is that it is both a religion and a political system. This is usually an attempt at politically correct word parsing. It is often intended to soften the blow of criticism directed at Islam itself. In other words, instead of criticizing Islam as an all-encompassing ideology, many westerners make attempts at objecting to it due to its incompatibility with western-style governments because it combines politics and religion.

Ironically, and perhaps unbeknownst to those who make such arguments, Islamists like Qaradawi use these attempts at political correctness to fan the flames of anger toward the West. While intending to politely reject Islam with a rhetorical wet blanket so as to avoid an inflammatory situation, secularists who attempt to compartmentalize Islam by placing it into two separate boxes may be pouring gasoline on the fire.

According to Qaradawi:

> One of the most reviled expressions used by secularists and modernists is "political Islam," which is alien to our Islamic society, without a doubt. Here, they are referring to an Islam that manages the affairs of the Muslim Nation and its relationships at home and abroad...The reason for this application is a master plan by the enemies of Islam to fragment it into different divisions.

Whether Qaradawi believes that or not is immaterial; he is obviously highlighting an attempt by Westerners *not* to offend the Muslim world and intentionally interpreting it in such a way so as to *enflame* the Muslim world. The case can be made that westerners should cease trying to appease the Muslim world since any attempts at doing so will only be twisted by Islamic leaders in order to impugn western motivations. Maybe if westerners cast aside political correctness, they might at least garner a modicum of respect.

Qaradawi continues…

> They speak not of the one Islam as revealed by Allah but of manufactured "Islams," plural, several different Islams, which they desire to create. Sometimes they even divide Islam by regions. There is the Asian variety of Islam; then we have the African Islam. Sometimes, according to the ages, there is the Prophet's era of Islam, Rashidi Islam, Umayyad Islam, Abbasid Islam, Ottoman Islam and modern Islam. Sometimes, according to race, there is

Arab Islam, Indian Islam, Turkish Islam, and the Islam of the Malaysian... And so on and so forth. Sometimes, according to the doctrine, there is Sunni Islam and Shiite Islam. They even divide the Sunni and the Shia into divisions. New divisions have also been created; there is revolutionary Islam, reactionary Islam, radical Islam, classical Islam, right-wing Islam, leftist Islam, orthodox Islam, modern Islam and, finally, political Islam, spiritual Islam and theological Islam. Why do they invent such divisions that are rejected in Islam? The truth is that these divisions are all unacceptable in the eyes of a Muslim; there is only one Islam, which has no partners, which recognizes no other; it is the first Islam, the Islam of the Quran and Sunnah. (Accusing Islam with Politics by Dr. Yusuf Qaradawi, 10/28/2011)[8]

Who is the "they" to which he refers? This is quintessential victimology on the part of Qaradawi. The branches, sects and divisions within Islam he speaks about were not created by westerners; they were created and sustained by Muslim leaders who disagreed with one another. Self-accountability and critical thinking are foreign concepts in the Muslim world. This is clearly demonstrated by the fact that Qaradawi appears unable to admit a very basic truth; people are different and unity of thought will never be achieved. Even in Islam—a religion that seeks such unity—multiple differences exist, which Qaradawi himself enumerates. However, he blames the west for those differences. His mind is a forebodingly fascinating study.

So, is the orientalist whom Qaradawi admonished in his 'flexibility' book wrong? Based on Qaradawi's own words, it would appear—to quote the hypothetical orientalist—that Sharia "...and its sources are based on religious inspiration, the Muslim has no choice but to 'hear and obey', that this is his destiny, his faith and his Islam." As Qaradawi denounces the West in his 'flexibility' book, he simultaneously proves the hypothetical orientalist right. Can you say 'schizophrenia'?

Yet, Qaradawi unequivocally concludes in his article:

We must declare explicitly that Islam is the truth—as it was laid down by Allah—it can only be political and if Islam is stripped from politics, it might become just another religion like Buddhism, Christianity or otherwise. It is impossible for these religions to be like Islam for two reasons:

1. Islam directs every aspect of life: The position of Islam is clear and explicit; its very core is political. Islam is not exclusively a theological doctrine, nor is it exclusively about devotional rites. It is not just a relationship between man and God; it is not only about how to run the community and the state. Nay, the doctrine, worship, creation and the law are all integrated. It includes the principles and foundational rules for the enactment of legislation and what was revealed as the direction for the individual, family, society, national foundation and global relations. This is obvious to those who read the Quran and pure Sunna; jurisprudence can clearly see this as well. Even the section of personal devotions is not far from politics. Muslims unanimously agree that anyone leaving his prayers, abandoning alms (Zakat), openly eating during Ramadan and not performing the Pilgrimage to Mecca (Haj) is deserving of punishment. Even fighting is mandated if a group came against it with a gripe.

2. The core of a Muslim is a political one as it was birthed by his ideology, Sharia itself, worship, and upbringing; it can never be anything but political. Islam lays on every Muslim neck the duty titled The Promotion of Virtue and Prevention of Vice." (Accusing Islam with Politics by Dr. Yusuf Qaradawi, 10/28/2011)[9]

Qaradawi was critical of westerners who insisted Islam is a system that is both political and religious. Yet, he makes the point far better than any westerner could, while astonishingly avoiding self-criticism. Qaradawi smeared critics who made the same argument. They were labeled as provocateurs who were seeking to sow division while arguing that political Islam and religious Islam cannot be separated, which is exactly what Qaradawi has argued. Logically, it can be concluded that either Qaradawi was lying in his critique of critics or he himself is attempting to sow division within the Muslim world. Perhaps it is both, which is right in line with our double-the-message theme.

EVOLUTION OF JIHAD BY THE WORD

Muruna's revival was initiated as far back as December 1989 in the US, during the annual conference of the Association of Muslim Youth Forums by one of Qaradawi's allies—Muhammad Al-Hashimi Al-Hamidi. Hamidi was one of the leading rebels in Libya who participated heavily in the Arab Spring more than twenty years later; he is also the head of the Muslim Brotherhood in Mauritania. In what they termed, *The Priorities of The Islamic Movement in the Next Three Decades,* which commenced in 1990 and is to run its course by 2020, "the goals of the Islamic Movement" were laid out. The group has set its sights on lofty aspirations indeed, to include:

> ...organized popular work to return to Islam in order to **lead society, all of society**...to **bring back the caliphate**...to announce Jihad either by arms or by pen or by heart...[emphasis mine]

To outline the grandiose plan, Qaradawi introduces five doctrines, two of which are worthy of a brief discussion. The first is the *Doctrine of Balance* and the second is the *Doctrine of Priorities.*

Qaradawi explains that these doctrines start with the "...balance between good and evil; if the two conflict with one another, **evil takes priority** when it is for the sake of an interest; these doctrines also determine when an evil deed is forgiven for the sake of an interest". [emphasis mine][10]

Even with evils, Qaradawi has a doctrine:

> Though evil and harm are from the same side of the coin, a determination must be made with regard to the least of the two when necessities demand. This is what the experts in jurisprudence decided: we try to remove the evil as much as possible. When the evil is either not removed nor replaced by an equal or greater evil, it is best to tolerate the lesser harm in place of the greater evil that would certainly rear its head when the lesser evil or harm is rejected; we must put up with harms that inflict the private individual so that the harm to the general public is not made more severe.

> Evil and harm can be accepted when it yields a long-term benefit. When interests or benefits are in direct opposition to evil or harms, the consequences of those evils or harms can be forgiven for long-term benefit, even if the evil endured is great.[11]

Qaradawi has created a doctrine that permits the justification of evil. Besides the reversalist, double-minded ideas that Qaradawi promotes, he is also apparently a collectivist:

> When conflicts arise we must take a pass on worldly interests for the sake of higher interests; we must sacrifice individual, private interests for the greater

public interest. The owner of the private interest can be compensated for what is lost but short-term interests are nullified when the alternative is the sacrificing of long-term interests.[12]

Try to follow the ensuing, twisted logic of Qardawi…

Is it permissible then to have alliances with powers that are non-Muslim? Can Muslims work in banks that practice usury (charging interest)? The decision based on these principles is easy but the actual application is difficult since the *Doctrine of Balance* is difficult for the lay Muslim…in the light of this balancing act…for the young Muslims, they should not leave their jobs in banks and insurance agencies. While their work is evil in the short-term, the experience they gain can benefit Muslim commerce in the long-term…entrance into these areas is a preference and a duty. The *Doctrine of Balance* instructs Muslims to endure evil personally in order to overcome it collectively.[13]

In English, we call that masochism. It reminds me of the scene in the movie *Animal House*, when Kevin Bacon was being aggressively paddled as part of an initiation. After each whack, he was instructed to say, "Thank you sir, may I have another?" This appears to be exactly what Qaradawi expects Muslims to do when they experience individual harm that is beneficial to Islam.

Qaradawi is viewed as a moral authority in Islam and his edicts require treating both Muslims and non-Muslims as a means to an end. Muslims are instructed to commit lesser evils for perceived greater goods and non-Muslims are to be deceived in the process. It would seem to be the quintessential playbook for treating people as pawns. On one hand, Qaradawi seems to be saying that Muslims who have a higher calling are permitted to commit acts of evil (according to Islam) against unsuspecting non-Muslims. Even worse, the anger felt by Muslims who do this, is to be directed at the non-Muslims they are deceiving. In short, innocent people are to blame for Muslims having to commit evil against them. Talk about abdicating responsibility!

Contrast these teachings with the work of 18th century German philosopher, Immanuel Kant, a man whose work helped to shape modern western thought. His teachings run exactly counter to those of Qaradawi. Kant, like Qaradawi, believed in a sense of duty but took the view that human beings are ends in themselves and should never be treated as a means to an end. Kant believed in a concept called Absolutivity; doing wrong for some perceived greater good is not permissible. He taught that acting out of morality is not contingent upon outcomes; it is simply the right thing to do and should be done for that reason alone.[14]

Assuming that every human being is equipped with a conscience—an inner gauge that discerns between right and wrong—Kant's teachings attempt to ascertain an understanding of that conscience while Qaradawi seeks to snuff out the consciences of his own followers so that the resultant schizophrenic drones can do his dirty work. The rank and file Muslim in Qaradawi's ideological army is consequently unaware that he is being used as a means to an end that can only be achieved by sacrificing himself to evil or harm.

It would seem that we are getting closer to the motivation behind suicide bombings.

THE ULTIMATE SACRIFICE FOR ALLAH

The extrapolation of Qaradawi's rule—that any Muslim should endure evil or harm if it serves a greater good—to the point of asking a Muslim to strap on a bomb and blow himself up for the purpose of serving that greater good, places a spotlight on the flawed logic for all to see. As if that weren't enough, consider that these suicide bombers are not interested in killing just themselves. They seek to kill as many innocent people as they can with acts that are sanctioned by the likes of Qaradawi because they involve harm to the few for the promised greater good of many more. All the undetonated bombers have to do is look around with open eyes to see that such a promise is—and has long been—empty.

In 2008, Qaradawi was interviewed by both Al-Hiwar and Al-Jazeera. In these interviews—translated by the *Middle Eastern Media Research Institute* (MEMRI)—Qaradawi further demonstrates how lesser harms and evils endured by his subjects are far more desirable than the consequences that would otherwise be suffered by unnamed individuals. In reality, suicide bombers are being used for the purpose of furthering an agenda:

> "I am known in the Islamic world as the preacher of the mainstream but (the British authorities) ignored this and they focused on the issue of martyrdom operations, as if this was something new. I have (supported) this for more than 20 years and I am not the only one to support this. More than 300 Muslim scholars have supported it. I do not automatically support martyrdom

operations. I permit them under specific constraints, when necessary—like in the case of our Palestinian brothers, who are forced to defend themselves by turning themselves into bombs.

It's the ultimate insanity, suicide in the name of self-defense. Are we to deduce that more than 300 Muslim scholars share Qaradawi's view that people should blow themselves—and others—up in order to further a holy agenda? Wouldn't it be nice to know how many followers each of those scholars has? How many of those scholars are standing in line to volunteer to lead by example when it comes to martyrdom operations? Why don't suicide bombers stop and ask themselves these questions? Is it because they have Qaradawi-inspired schizophrenia?

Qaradawi continues…

I said to a British TV broadcaster in the summer of 1983: "Brother, you can prevent these martyrdom operations. Give the Palestinians just one percent of the tanks, missiles, and Apache helicopters that their adversaries have, and they will not resort to martyrdom operations." [**sounds a bit like ransom money, doesn't it?**] They are forced to do so. God has given them this means as a kind of just and divine compensation. [**this is how Qaradawi gets his minions to buy his lines—everyone needs a payoff**] Their only way to defend themselves is for one of them to turn himself into a human bomb. This is divine justice…I sanctioned these operations to anybody who is forced to carry them out in defense of his homeland. In my opinion, our brothers in Palestine are forced to do so. In Iraq, they have a wide variety of weapons. They are able to use weapons against their enemies. But the weapons of the Palestinian brothers are no match for their enemies' weapons—they do not have even one percent or one per mile of their weapons. [**why does he *demand* more instead of build more?**] That's why I sanctioned these operations for (the Palestinians), but nor for (the Iraqis). In addition, I did not approve using these kinds of operations in New York and Washington on September 11, 2001. I did not approve of these operations in the London and Madrid bombings. I sanctioned bombings and sacrifice operations for the Palestinians only—not because their enemies are Jews but because they are occupiers and the Palestinians cannot fight them. They kill Palestinians on a daily basis, destroy their homes, burn their fields, uproot their trees, and so on.

In the early 1800s, the United States was engaged in what is known as the Barbary Wars. Islamic states in North Africa, to include present-day Libya and Tunisia, demanded that American merchant ships pay tribute (ransom) to have the right to do business on the Mediterranean Sea. When tribute wasn't paid, hostages were taken. It had been a long-standing practice of the American colonies and then the new American nation to pay ransom instead of confronting the pirates. That all changed when Thomas Jefferson became president in 1801.[15] The good news for the US was that these Barbary pirates were the reason for the creation of the US Navy and ultimately, the Marines.

Hundreds of years later, US Navy SEAL sharpshooters amazingly delivered head shots to three Somali pirates who had hijacked an American freighter and were holding its captain, Richard Phillips, hostage. Captain Phillips was saved by the descendents of American armed forces pushed for by President Thomas Jefferson. The heroic precision exercised by the sharpshooters was second to none. Phillips was rescued as all three of his captors were simultaneously taken out by three SEALs from 40 yards away, on the high seas.[16]

The hostage taking process was put aside for martyrdom in the case of the September 11th attacks. There have also been countless other suicide / homicide missions perpetrated by Islamic barbarians. Rather than hone their entrepreneurial skills to compete in the market, Islamic leaders during the Barbary Wars did what Qaradawi is doing now; they demanded money in exchange for the withholding of terrorism, intimidation, and bullying all while claiming to be victims.

The Barbary pirates were indeed an extension of the Ottoman Empire itself. The practices those pirates engaged in at the dawn of the United States are still being used hundreds of years later; they are espoused by a man, in Qaradawi, who seeks a return to that same Ottoman Empire.

In another 2008 speech, aired by Al-Jazeera from Qatar, Qaradawi attempted to convince those who were watching that he harbored no ill will toward Jews or Christians.

> "I denounced some contemporary religious preachers, who curse the Jews and the Christians, saying: 'Allah, annihilate the Jews and the Christians.' Where did this come from? There are Jews and Christians in our Muslim countries. There are Copts in Egypt and Christians in Syria. So how can you curse them? Not only that but they curse: 'Allah, turn their children into orphans.

Allah, destroy their homes.' Who sanctioned such prayers? The Qur'an does not call to turn children into orphans or to destroy homes. There are no such things in the prayers of the Prophet Muhammad. I denounced some people who said that Jews are the offspring of apes and pigs. That's not true. When God transformed some people into apes and pigs, they did not have any offspring, as is written in the Al-Muslim compilation. When God transforms people into something else, they do not have offspring. They die and are annihilated straight away. Besides, this is a curse, and Islam forbids cursing.[17]

Based on what we now know, using Qaradawi's own words, that is *Muruna*. Perhaps this is Qaradawi's way of leading by example. After all, he *did* say that accepting a lesser evil or harm in order to prevent a greater evil or harm is the more desirous course. Therefore, in a moment of honesty, devoid of schizophrenic subject-changing, Qaradawi might admit to his followers that it pains him greatly to utter such blasphemous lies but that he does it for the greater good of Islam. A fringe benefit is that it can also take the heat of western leaders off of him for a while as well. That's what we call the removal of a minor harm.

In essence, Qaradawi can blaspheme his own religion while telling his followers to follow his cxamplc. Hc's such a leader!

Now that we've seen what goes through the mind of Muslim Brotherhood leaders like Qaradawi, how should westerners react when they listen to Muslim apologists—many of whom are quite familiar with Qaradawi's teachings—say that "Islam is the religion of the middle"—*Al-Islam Deen Al-Wasat* in Arabic— or that it's "balanced", not extremist?

Doesn't Qaradawi teach that "balance" is to be used to hide Islam's true intentions? It's a word that conveys level-headedness, tolerance, and understanding to westerners but its true meaning to Qaradawi's followers involves making judgments about the level of deception that is needed in order to further the cause of Islam.

The key word in all of the *Muruna* jurisprudence and doctrines is the word "interest" but as Qaradawi demonstrates once again, any interest deemed worthy of fighting for must be subjected to an ends-justify-the-means litmus test. Once westerners accept the premise that the goal of Islamists is sharia law, this rhetoric is easier to comprehend:

> To Balance between one set of interests versus another, in terms of size and capacity, depth and impact, survival and durability; which should be submitted and considered, which should be repealed and dropped. (Qaradawi, Fiqh Al-Muwazanat, the Doctrine of Balancing)[18]

These are essentially excerpts from an operation manual for an entire management system that dictates what plans will be executed, how tactics are chosen, and under what circumstances they should be implemented:

> The balance between evils—for reasons we have mentioned concerning interests—must be ascertained; it must cause certain evils to be delayed or dropped...if the balance between good and evil is in conflict, we must determine when to give priority to evil in order to bring benefit, and when an unforgivable evil can be committed for the sake of what is good.[19]

In Qaradawi-speak, "balance" has nothing to do with balancing between old and modern or western dress over Hijab. Westerners will do themselves a tremendous service when they accept the premise that the main goal of the Muslim Brotherhood is to establish Sharia. Once that transformation takes place, from ignorance to understanding, western civilization takes an immediate quantum leap toward defeating those who seek its extinction. Qaradawi makes this emphasis clear:

> Why was Sharia given to us? It is to fulfill the people's [Muslims] life interests in their known order; necessities, needs and improvements.

Qaradawi shares this example from Islam's history:

> In Hudaibiya, the Prophet (peace be upon him) saw the real interests for fundamental and future considerations instead of what some preferred. He accepted terms and conditions that one might consider blasphemous. In the agreement, he even agreed to strike out the Bismillah, "In the Name of Allah," writing instead, "in your name O God" and described the indelible message of making peace to suffice with "In the Name of Muhammad bin Abdullah."[20]

Qaradawi concludes that Muslims may: "accept the alliance with non-Muslim forces," seek "reconciliation for having a truce with the governments not committed to Islam," "participate in governments that are not purely Islamic," ally with "an opposition front made up of some parties in order to overthrow evil regimes (think Gadhafi in Libya and Saddam Iraq)," and accept "Muslims working in banks and institutions that practice usury."

For those who think these are Qaradawi's private interpretations, consider that he points to the examples of others in order to bolster his case, which he does quite effectively. In Pakistan, Abu Al-Ala' Mawdudi seemed to advocate for a "balanced" form of jurisprudence when he expressed a preference for the election of Fatima Jinnah, a woman, over the male Ayub, regardless of the Hadith, which says, "…it will not work for a people being ruled by a woman." In the Sudan, Dr. Hassan al-Turabi entered into a partnership with the Soviet Union in the era of Ja'far Nimeiri; he accepted some official positions with the Soviets in his reign prior to announcing the application of Sharia. In Syria, members of the movement to overthrow dictator Bashar al-Assad allied with some non-Islamic forces to resist the system that wants to eradicate the Muslim Brotherhood. Even the Prophet himself allied with the tribe of Khuza'a despite their being unbelievers.

This is what is known as "balance" in Qaradawian parlance but he also cites the Qur'an as a source for the view he holds:

> In the Holy Quran, in both Makiyan and Madanian suras, we find a great deal of evidence for the jurisprudence of balances and penalties. We find the balance between the interests.[21]

And if the forbidden month (Muharram) in which warfare and killing is prohibited,

> …the Quran acknowledges that Jihad warfare in the sacred forbidden month is great.[22]

The term "balance" actually seems to mean "excuse-making" when faced with blatant contradictions and having to choose a course that goes against Islam. It is simply a balancing act that should always tilt in favor of choosing the lesser of two evils:

> If they ask you about intoxicants [Alcohol] and gambling, say: these are two great sins, and are benefits to the people, but the sin is greater than what will benefit them. (Quran Al-Baqarah: 219)

The Qur'an seems to argue that neither alcohol nor gambling is all bad. In fact, they carry with them, some benefits but since those benefits are minimal, they are forbidden.

MURUNA AND THE ARAB SPRING

The term, "Arab Spring" is yet another example of how the Islamic world plays word games with the West. Such a name conveys a refreshing and welcome rebirth after a long, cold winter of suppression. In reality, it's more like opening the door that releases a caged wolf. Although the overthrow of Egyptian dictator Hosni Mubarak was swift, Islamists had been working patiently, behind the scenes for years to get to that point. As *Wikileaks* has demonstrated, western leaders are not ignorant of this fact which means they have chosen not to address it publicly, if at all.

Take the example of former International Atomic Energy Agency (IAEA) Director General, Mohamed ElBaradei. As head of the IAEA, ElBaradei was an agent of the United Nations. He held the position from 1997—2009; both he and his agency were jointly awarded the Nobel Peace Prize in 2005. According to the Nobel Prize website, ElBaradei and the IAEA received the award…

> …for their efforts to prevent nuclear energy from being used for military purposes and to ensure that nuclear energy for peaceful purposes is used in the safest possible way.[23]

Four years after receipt of that award, as his time as head of the IAEA was drawing to a close, ElBaradei identified Israel—not Iran—as the greatest nuclear threat to the Middle East while speaking in Tehran.[24] Perhaps this view held by the IAEA's Director General helps explain why little to nothing was done to prevent Iran's nuclear program.

If one had any doubts that ElBaradei was anti-Semitic then, such doubts should have been dashed as the "Arab Spring" unfolded in Egypt. ElBaradei, who had largely been viewed as a secularist Muslim, joined the side of the Muslim Brotherhood in opposition to Mubarak. The issue of *Muruna* can be looked at from two separate perspectives in that scenario. If the Ikhwan believed that ElBaradei was a secularist, they would have applied the *Doctrine of Balance* and viewed aligning with him as the lesser of two evils.

Conversely, if ElBaradei is as anti-Semitic as he appears to be, perhaps it was he who—wittingly or unwittingly—applied the *Doctrine of Balance* when he decided to portray himself as a secularist to the western world. Nevertheless, an alliance with the Muslim Brotherhood necessitates anti-Semitism on ElBaradei's part. It should be noted that after the Muslim Brotherhood's Mohamed Mursi became president of Egypt and made brash attempts to consolidate power, ElBaradei was among the first to plead for help.[25]

ElBaradei's views aside, the Ikhwan aligned with leftist socialists in general to overthrow Mubarak. There is strong evidence that the Doctrine of Balance was used; it was demonstrated perfectly when the revolution's secular hero—Wael Ghonim—was booted from the stage so Qaradawi could accept all of the Tahrir Square praise. When Qaradawi's followers aligned with the secularists, it was quintessential *Muruna*.

While the Brotherhood was careful not to *spark* the revolution, they took the opportunity to infect it in much the same way that a virus does with a host. If Qaradawi's interpretation is a private one, how then did the masses of Muslim Brotherhood members accept partnering with socialists? If he was an ineffective lone ranger with a private interpretation, how then was he able to oust Ghonim and give the victory speech on Tahrir Square to a mass of two million crying loudly, "Al-Quds rayheen shuhada' bil-malayeen" (to Jerusalem we march, martyrs by the millions)?

The West is in need of—and will one day get—an intervention in order to confront these realities but on whose terms it will be administered remains to be seen.

FOOTNOTES

1. *Al-Si'a wa-Al-Muruna*, by Yousuf Qaradawi
2. Ibid, p. 67
3. Ibid, pgs. 70-71
4. Ibid, p. 71
5. Ibid, p. 76
6. Ibid, pgs. 79-80
7. Ibid, p. 80 – Al-Itqan, p. 21 – Al-Halabi
8. Arabic website. http://qaradawi.net/component/content/article/4285.html
9. Ibid
10. Arabic website. http://www.qaradawi.net/library/66/3269.html
11. Ibid
12. Ibid

13. Ibid

14. tutor2u*, Religious Studies Bloq, *Kantian Ethics*. http://tutor2u.net/blog/index. php/religious-studies/comments/kantian-ethics

15. The Library of Congress, *The Thomas Jefferson Papers, America and Barbery Pirates: An International Battle Against an Unconventional Foe,* by Gerard W. Gawalt. http://memory.loc.gov/ammem/collections/jefferson_papers/mtjprece.html

16. ABC News, *Navy SEALs' Simultaneous Headshots on Somali Pirates Were Procedure,* by Lee Ferran. http://abcnews.go.com/International/story?id=7325633&page=1

17. Video in Arabic with English Subtitles. http://www.youtube.com/watch?v=w 2PSbGLJjV4

18. Arabic website. http://www.qaradawi.net/library/66/3269.html

19. Ibid

20. Ibid

21. Ibid

22. Ibid

23. Nobelprize.org, *The Nobel Prace Prize 2005, Mohamed ElBaradei*. http:// www.nobelprize.org/nobel_prizes/peace/laureates/2005/

24. News China View, *ElBaradei says nuclear Israel number one threat to Mideast: report,* http://news.xinhuanet.com/english/2009-10/04/content_12181647.htm

25. The Daily Caller. *White House silent as Egypt's president grabs power, moves toward Shariah Islamic law,* Posted by Neil Munro. http://dailycaller.com/ 2012/11/26/white-house-silent-as-egypts-president-grabs-power-moves-toward-shariah-law/?print=1

SECTION

3

Islamic Nazism

CHAPTER
6

DOUBLE STANDARD

RACISTS GET A PASS

The mainstream (liberal) media in America is almost obsessed with talking about racism but the irony is that America exercises the least amount of racism when compared to any other country on earth. Making that paradox even starker is the fact that America is one of the most—if not *the* most—diverse nations in the world. As a culture, it sets the standard for a nation that polices itself in matters that involve confronting racism; there is one exception and it has to do with racism that targets Jews.

Liberals rarely address Jew-hatred, especially when it comes from Muslim leaders, communities or institutions but they are seemingly all too eager to point out instances of Islamophobia. Hypersensitivity about alleged Islamophobia is almost completely counteracted by the near disregard for anti-Semitism.

Barack Obama's former pastor, Jeremiah Wright, exhibited anti-Semitism countless times both before and after the 2008 election.[1] Yet, the liberal media had to be dragged—kicking and screaming—into the controversy surrounding his twenty year relationship with President Obama. Another example is Wright's friend and Nation of Islam leader, Louis Farrakhan, who once called Judaism a "gutter religion".[2] Both Wright and Farrakhan have a long history of anti-Semitic comments and associations.

Liberal media outlets not only twisted themselves into pretzels to avoid Obama's connection to a racist pastor but they became quite salty whenever the subject was brought up. Defending Obama as the man who would become America's first black and "post racial" president was of far greater import to the media narrative. They didn't much appreciate anyone raining on their "post racial" parade with such inconvenient truths. A media supposedly hypersensitive about racism made an exception when the target of that racism involved Jews. In essence, the liberal western media was willing to overlook racism in defense of *overcoming* it. To the objective eye, it was a hypocritically racist attitude; the double standard proved it.

NAZI-STYLE RACISM AT GSISS

Speaking of those who are supposed to be men of the cloth but who actually espouse racist religiosity, Taha Jaber Al-Alwani is one such individual.[3] After coming across his work by sheer happenstance, I discovered another dangerous conductor in a major three-ring, JBTW circus act. Before we examine his Nazi-style anti-Semitism, it is important to point out that Alwani runs the Graduate School of Islamic and Social Sciences (GSISS), which is a United States Department of Defense program for training Muslim military chaplains. It was the GSISS that produced the United States Marine Corps' first Muslim chaplain.[4]

GSISS is an affiliate member of the Washington Theological Consortium at Cordoba University in which Alwani is president. The significance of the name "Cordoba" cannot be understated. It is of great symbolic importance because it signifies a tremendous Islamic conquest of a Christian cathedral in Cordoba, Spain. When Islamic groups use the name "Cordoba," they do so, almost exclusively, in reference to that conquest (see Ground Zero mosque).

In English, Alwani is another who writes about the need for *Ijtihad*, which is the tradition of independent thinking. Alwani has compared America to the golden age of al-Andalus in Spain and has told Muslims in the mosques he visited that America is the best country in the world in which to live.

To back up that public display of reverence for America and show how much he loves our freedom, Alwani became a signatory with the *Muslim Statement Against Terror* and even issued a fatwa (after consulting with Sheikh Yusuf al-Qaradawi) urging Muslims to fight in the US military in Afghanistan against terrorism.[5] Confusingly, Qaradawi issued a fatwa that called for the kidnapping and murder of American civilians in Iraq.[6] Though he later denied issuing this Fatwa,[7] the proof of the JBTW on the part of Alwani was irrefutable. It would become even more so after reading his works.

TRANSLATING THE RACIST ALWANI

Aside from his attempt to *portray* patriotism, Alwani was revealed to be an ardent anti-Semite. Why would the US military continue to employ this influential figurehead, especially when his hateful writings are so prolific? Alwani should not object to having his writings translated and published in full. In fact, as an Islamic scholar, he should be very appreciative. As a "man of the cloth," translating his Arabic words into English is helping him to "spread the word" of his religion.

In an article entitled "The Great Haughtiness," published in the Islamic *Umma Magazine*[8] and even on his own website, Alwani commented on the Quranic verses:

> "And We [God] conveyed to the Children of Israel in the Scripture that, You will surely cause corruption on the earth twice, and you will surely reach [a degree of] great haughtiness." (*Sahih International*)[9]

Al-Alwani writes:

> "Allah, Mighty and Exalted is He who is all knowing when it comes to his creation and their willingness to do good or evil, told us that, 'the children of Israel will do corruption in the land twice.' That is, two grand events since they have done mischief twice already in the past and many more after that. It is for this reason Allah said "But if you return [to sin], We [Allah] will return [for punishment]" (Isra:8)

So what is this "Great Haughtiness" that was predicted to befall the Jews? According to Alwani, it is:

> "...an intellectual, psychological and mental ability, which they can employ with great efficiency to take advantage of real and objective situations, whatever these situations may be in accordance with their specific visions and goals, in a meticulous fashion."[10]

In his Arabic writings, Alwani targets Judaism for its reliance on the infamous golden calf. Strangely, Alwani sees Jews as a people who exploited the holocaust to their own advantage while continuing to worship a golden calf that has rendered its followers nothing more than cagey animals that have held Muslims back:

> "...the Zionist leaders made this calf a model for today's world so they can be able to control it. Today's world, with its secularism and its phony democracy

alongside its free, controlled trade and national legitimacy and all these other subjects that bellows [*bloviates*] and never dialogues [*engages in real debate*]. This is not a far-fetched notion, an image of a calf that moos with an outward appearance that is beautiful, breathtaking and shiny – one that almost takes your breath away [*the Jews worship an animal god that is deceptive*].

So the giant media assumes the role of a mooing and bellowing entity that never stops. This gives it *an ability to transform humans into animals*; the media consumes (the calf's) energy. It (the media) empties him and fills him with whatever it wants. The nations were transformed under the shade of this calf-like image, into herds composed of individuals that are unable to build relationships or identities [*those who worship the animal god are sub-human*].

They (the Jews) were able to convert a negative incident (the Holocaust), which placed them in a collective apostasy; to a model, which enabled them to make strategies, institutions and plans to ensure that the world—the whole world—remains beneath them [*being subjugated by animals has apparently angered Alwani greatly*]...

...So what can we do, and especially those of us who sit in positions of control over our great battle as we live alongside this calf? How can we first study deeply their psyche and minds? And how can we know their inherited education with its influence as they manage the conflict with the rest of the nations on the earth?

When will the Muslims get out of being a useless reeling multitude to gain the position of imposing ourselves to be respected by the whole world and to employ (our) great abilities for benefiting this struggle with others? Only then will we be able to have dialogue on an equal footing and not through all the bellowing."[11]

Western media is hypersensitive about racism, which is the belief that one class of human beings is superior to another. Alwani takes this a step further by branding Jews as animals who need to be subjugated by humans (Muslims). This isn't racism; it's a script tailor-made for a *Planet of the Apes* film.

Yet, Muslim leaders and pundits like Alwani continue to get a pass from the western media, a western media Alwani perceives as consisting of animals not worthy of his respect. Those who attempt to alert western media outlets to these realities are smeared as Islamophobes. The evidence unequivocally supports the notion that racists are labeling those who expose them as racists. In psychology, this is a defense mechanism known as projection, which is the act of projecting or attributing one's own shortcomings onto others.

MEDIA COMPLICITY

The blatant double standard almost necessarily makes western media derelict at best, wicked at worst. If they're derelict, they could be operating from a position of fear on par with that shared by those afflicted with "Stockholm Syndrome," a survival technique and psychological condition that causes hostages—in this case, weak media executives, producers and pundits—to sympathize with and even actively assist their (political) captors. This syndrome causes its victims to employ a technique designed to avoid the wrath of a superior and threatening force that has the power to exert its influence. It was named after a 1973 bank robbery in Stockholm, Sweden; hostages actually bonded with their captors. They did so to such a degree that they viewed the authorities who were on-hand to rescue them, as the threat.[12] This might at least partially explain why the liberal mainstream media goes to such great lengths to attack those who attempt to warn them about the true intentions of Islamists by exposing their JBTW.

If western media is suffering from a brand of "Stockholm Syndrome," it likely views the forceful side of Islamists as being too much to stand against. This level of cowardice would have to be rationalized; few publicly admit to being afflicted with such a shameful condition. Cowardice is dishonorable; when reality is twisted in such a way so as to vilify those who would otherwise help, it allows for the suppression of the real emotion—fear. One way to do this is to take up the cause of the Islamists. In doing so, admissions of cowardice are not necessary; western media outlets have chosen a side through either vocal support or silence in opposition. In the case of Alwani, for example, media outlets that defend him by ignoring his JBTW don't seem interested in fighting *all* racism, just the brands of racism they deem worthy enough to fight. That qualifier necessarily makes such people and institutions racist themselves; it is quintessential projection. Whether it's a sin of commission or omission, the mainstream media is guilty of that which it claims to decry.

The only other explanation for why the mainstream media carries the water for Islamists like Alwani is *corruption*. By not revealing Alwani's true intentions, the media is actively supporting him. This would involve a shared belief with those Islamists and if this is true, it can only mean that non-Muslims in the mainstream media are comfortable aligning with those who view Jews as sub-human. How is this not racism?

Alwani's incendiary rhetoric reveals racism on steroids but the liberal western media seems more interested in tacitly supporting positions held by the likes of Alwani while simultaneously claiming to reject all forms of racism. The real victims in this scenario are the Jews whose persecution the media ignores.

The comments made by Alwani's readership are even more telling. They are overwhelmingly about how the Jews are treacherous, devious, cunning and plotting.

VICTIMS MORPH INTO JEWS

If members of the media establishment think they are protected by not coming to the defense of Jews who are discriminated against by Islamists like al-Alwani, they are mistaken. Even when non-Jews say or do something Islamists disapprove of, they can find themselves morphing into Jews in the minds of those Islamists. The following three examples demonstrate this very phenomenon. *CBS* news reporter Lara Logan; late night television host David Letterman; and author Paris Dipersico all experienced this firsthand.

As the regime of Hosni Mubarak was falling in Egypt, ground zero for the celebrations was Tahrir Square in Cairo. Logan was covering the story at night with her news team when the battery of her colleagues' camera died. The light went out; Logan was separated from her team. A mob of 200 men or more surrounded her and she suffered a sustained and brutal sexual assault, barely escaping with her life. Her attackers repeatedly shouted, "Jew! Jew!" during the attack; Logan is not Jewish.[13]

When late night television comedian David Letterman told a joke about the death of Osama bin Laden and the ultimate fate of his successor, a Jihadist posted that American Muslims should, "cut the tongue of this lowly Jew and shut it forever." Like Logan, Letterman is not Jewish.[14]

After writing his first book, Paris Dipersico, who was raised Muslim, reported that he had been dragged off of his bike by two Muslims, tied up, and beaten unconscious for writing an anti-Muslim book. The attackers hurled homophobic slurs toward Dipersico and called him a "Jew." Dipersico is not a Jew; he was raised Muslim.[15]

In each one of these cases, the object of Islamic hatred only became Jewish in the *minds* of those who wished to do them harm. This must mean that any non-Muslim can become a Jew, which is the most despised creature among Islamic fundamentalists. Does that not take the racist mindset of Islamists to an entirely new low? This means that at any time, pundits in the liberal media who seem to go out of their way to defend Islam could instantly become Jewish if they say or do something that warrants it.

Logan works for *CBS*, a mainstream media outlet considered *liberal*; Letterman is known as a *liberal* personality, and Dipersico penned a sexually graphic, *liberal* book. In each case, all three people became Jews because they became the object of Islamic hatred.

Take the example of pop icon, Katy Perry, who is a creature of the far left celebrity culture. When she tweeted that she would be praying for Israel in response to a request, she was skewered with vile comments by angry anti-Semites, who posted things like:

> "You heartless lesbian. Israel has killed
> THOUSANDS of PALESTINIANS, yet you're
> gonna pray for Israel? You shiz.

> "I hope you private jet crash lands in Palestine
> so they can stamp on you like the whore you
> are see if Israel come help you."

In a case of proving the point that intimidation works, Perry later attempted to rescind her tweet but to no avail. The damage had been done. By praying for Israel, one must necessarily become a Jew that is to be hated.[16]

Even pop culture icon Kim Kardashian has had a run-in with anti-Semitism. As Israel and Hamas were preparing for yet another confrontation in the fall of 2012, Kardashian sent out a tweet informing her seventeen million followers that she was "praying for Israel". Within five minutes, the hateful reaction to those three words was so bad that she attempted to make amends by sending out a similar tweet for Palestine. That apparently wasn't enough and Kardashian eventually deleted both tweets before posting a rather conciliatory message on her blog with the intention of sending the entire episode down the memory hole and letting bygones be bygones.[17] Isn't it amazing what five minutes of intimidation can do?

ALWANI'S MUSLIM BROTHERHOOD TIES

Alwani also has a connection to al-Qaeda. He was a founding member of the Muslim World League (MWL), which is an al-Qaeda financier. Process that level of insanity for a moment. The US military has entrusted a man who co-founded an organization that funds al-Qaeda with the keys to classrooms so he can train Muslim chaplains for integration into our military.

In addition to the MWL being an organization that funds al-Qaeda, it has extremely close ties with the Muslim Brotherhood.[18] This is the same Muslim Brotherhood that was embraced by the Obama administration as a group with which it could formally deal.[19]

Alwani is also the former President of the International Institute for Islamic Thought (IIIT), whose Virginia offices were raided by the FBI in March of 2002, in connection with the funding of Palestinian Islamic Jihad (PIJ) through Sami al-Arian (this is the same al-Arian whose honor Obama's envoy to the OIC, Rashad Hussain, attempted to defend at a 2004 MSA event). Alwani managed to slip through the cracks of terrorism and is also slipping through the cracks of racism. Remember, his racist rhetoric is only against Jews. IIIT is a Muslim Brotherhood-affiliated group. This put the Obama administration in the camp of embracing very racist individuals and organizations while claiming to be "post racial."

Alwani graduated from Al Azhar University in Cairo in 1959 and was a professor of Usul al-Fiqh at Imam Muhammad Ibn Sa'ud University in Riyadh, a well-known Wahhabi stronghold. His attendance at Al Azhar is very significant because of that institution's connections to Muslim Brotherhood members. Sheikh Dr. Yusuf al-Qaradawi is another example.

In 1988 al-Alwani founded the Fiqh Council of North America, also a Muslim Brotherhood group, and in 1997 he participated in the founding of the European Council for Fatwa and Research, headed by the well-known Yusuf al-Qaradawi from Qatar, one of the Brotherhood's most prominent leaders.

These two councils, along with the Islamic Fiqh Academy in India, are connected to the Organization of Islamic Conference (OIC) through the International Fiqh Academy, based in Jeddah, Saudi Arabia. Alwani is also a colleague of former Islamic Society of North America (ISNA) president, Dr. Muzammil Siddiqi (discussed later). Military enrollment and elections are both major topics on the agenda of al-Alwani. Both Alwani and Siddiqi support the participation of Muslims in all fields of American political life, and thus simultaneously pave the way for Muslim candidates to nominate themselves to various elected posts.

The most effective training grounds for doing this exist on over 600 college campuses across the United States via the Muslim Students Association (MSA). Here is an excerpt from a publication MSA published and sent out nationally to its members:

> "It should be the long-term goal of every MSA to Islamicize the politics of their respective university...the politicization of the MSA means to make the MSA more of a force on internal campus politics. The MSA needs to be a more 'In-your-face' association...For example, the student body must be convinced that there is such a thing as a Muslim-bloc..."[20]

In a 1991 Muslim Brotherhood document that was introduced as evidence in the Holy Land Foundation (HLF) trial, the largest terrorism financing trial in American history, the MSA was listed as a member organization. The document, authored by Mohamed Akram, clearly states that the goal of the Ikhwan (Muslim Brotherhood) in America is to destroy western civilization internally, through deceptive means. Those deceptive means include JBTW. Here is an excerpt from that document:

> The process of settlement is a "Civilization-Jihadist Process" with all the word means. The Ikhwan must understand that their work in America is a kind of grand Jihad in eliminating and destroying the Western civilization from within and "sabotaging" its miserable house by their hands and the hands of the believers so that it is eliminated and God's religion is made victorious over all other religions.[21]

Consider that there are over 600 universities that have MSA chapters and MSA was but one of 29 Muslim Brotherhood groups in that 1991 document. The extent of infiltration in the United States is potentially astronomical at multiple levels and in multiple capacities.

Like the MSA, The Fiqh Council or ISNA Fiqh Committee was also listed in the 1991 document as a Brotherhood group. While the MSA focuses on training Muslim college students how to acquire political power, the Fiqh Committee is a jurisprudence committee that gives religious rulings based on politically established laws within Islam. The problem with these rulings is that they ignore the

US Constitution, which is supposed to be the "supreme law of the land" (Article VI). In typical deceptive practice, groups posing as Muslim civil rights organizations—like CAIR—distract Americans by pointing to the First Amendment, which guarantees freedom of religion, not freedom to usurp the supreme law of the land. Sabotage, indeed.

ALWANI AND AL-QARADAWI

Shortly after the September 11th terrorist attacks, al-Alwani received a question from Capt. Abd al-Rashid Muhammad, a Muslim military chaplain stationed at Walter Reed Army Medical Center in Washington, DC. Alwani was asked if Muslim soldiers in the US military could fight their Muslim brethren in Afghanistan. Alwani forwarded the question to a special committee headed by Sheikh Dr. Yusuf al-Qaradawi (European Council of Fatwa and Research) who is not allowed into the US for his extremist views (at least not at the time of this writing). Qaradawi initially issued his fatwa in the affirmative; he said it was necessary for American Muslims to support the US and fight Muslims in Afghanistan because Islamic law prohibits "terrorizing the innocent, killing noncombatants, and the destruction of property."[22]

Apparently, fatwas can be issued and reversed based on political expediency. Qaradawi issued this particular fatwa in the face of a United States that was in no mood for equivocation. It had been hit by jihadists and ground zero was still smoldering. This may have explained Qaradawi's ruling. Even further validating speculation that the fatwa wasn't made based on righteousness or principle, Qaradawi rescinded it after the angry reaction it garnered from the Arab world. Apparently, though both the American and Arabic wheels were squeaking and in need of grease, the Arabic wheel squeaked the loudest when it was time for the rubber to meet the road. Within days, Qaradawi held a press conference and expressed support for the Afghanis against Americans.

Fatwas are obviously more malleable than absolute truths. This reality not only demonstrates imperfection in such rulings but also their political nature.

RACIST WORLD VISION

Alwani views the Islamic Nation (Ummah) as a global one, without respect for borders. In a chapter from one of his works entitled, "Towards Principles for

Minority Jurisprudence" (*Nahwa Usul Li-Fiqh al-Aqaliyyat*), Alwani presents his definition in a clear way:

"To be committed to the Quranic geographic concept: The earth belongs to Allah, and Islam is His religion. Every place is 'Dar al-Islam,' (Land of Islam) either actively in the current reality, or 'Dar al-Islam' of potential for the future to come. Humanity in its entirety is 'the Nation of Islam,' either being 'a Nation of faith (Millah)' by embracing this religion, or 'a Nation of the religious call (Da'wah)' of which we are committed to approach so that it will arrive."[23, 24]

In essence, al-Alwani argued that the world is made up of Muslims and non-Muslims who must one day become Muslims if the vision of a global Muslim nation is to exist. A better example of racism one is hard pressed to find.

As such, America can be regarded as Land of Islam in the eyes of the Muslims:

"The council (North America Fiqh Council) will work to direct the Muslims to the approach, wherein the identity of the American Muslim is to be loyal to his homeland (Watan), America, due to his obligations towards it as a citizen, because the homeland for the Muslim is considered Dar al-Islam (Land of Islam) for him, as long as he is able to do his religious rituals inside it." (Al-Sharq al-Awsat, 21 July 2002)

Everyone has a mission in Islam. The MSA's is to teach students how to move within the system to gain political power; the Fiqh committee's is to issue religious rulings that place subtle, yet consistent pressure on the US Constitution; Muslim practitioners not affiliated with these organized groups play a role too—perform Islamic rituals. This helps keep pressure on the American system. Everyone serves a purpose in the furtherance of Islam. The twenty nine groups discovered to exist under the Muslim Brotherhood umbrella based on the 1991 document are quite diverse in terms of purpose, if not in terms of beliefs.

JEWS PORTRAYED AS RACISTS

Lecturer-Scholar-in-Residence for the Zaytuna Institute—Hamza Yousuf Hanson—expressed support for none other than Feisal Abdul Rauf on *CBS'* 60 minutes; several meetings with Rauf have been recorded on *YouTube* as well. In English, Hamza seems moderate but he is a rabid racist in Arabic (are you beginning to see a trend?). During his speech at the annual Islamic Society of North

America (ISNA) national convention in 1995, Hamza Yusuf Hanson identified Judaism as "a most racist religion" and said:

> "The Jews would have us believe that God has this bias toward this small tribe in the Middle of the Sinai desert and all the rest of humanity is just rubbish. I mean this is the basic doctrine of the Jewish religion and that's why it is a most racist religion."

On September 9, 2001, two days before 9/11, Hanson hollered in Los Angeles:

> "This country (America), unfortunately has a great, a great tribulation coming to it. And much of it is already here, yet people are too illiterate to read the writing on the wall…Every Muslim who is honest should say, 'I would like to see America become a Muslim country.'"

Daniel Pipes, an established and recognized authority on Radical Islam, calls Hanson "a master of deceit". According to an article that appeared in the *Weekly Standard*, Pipes presented Hanson with a test meant to determine if a Muslim is radical or moderate. The test consisted of a series of questions concerning Islamic radicalization. Hanson refused to take the test but later announced:

> "I took that test and I failed. And I want to say to all of you, I hope you fail that test too."[25]

The *Standard* article went on to describe a speech Hanson allegedly gave to the Islamic Circle of North America (ICNA), which is an arm of the radical organization Jamaat-e-Islami in Pakistan. The name of the speech was "Jihad is the Only Way". ICNA is also one of the 29 member organizations of the Muslim Brotherhood in America according to the 1991 document penned by Mohamed Akram. As such, ICNA inherently wants to destroy western civilization from within, using Jihad. By any rational standard, such facts should make Hanson a domestic enemy of the United States.[26]

FOOTNOTES

1. WND, *Obama Church Published Hamas Terror Manifesto*, by Aaron Klein. http://www.wnd.com/?pageId=59456

2. Docstoc. *Louis Farrakhan*, From Wikipedia. http://www.docstoc.com/docs/640 2032/Louis_Farrakhan

3. http://www.fikercenter.com/fiker/index.php?option=com_k2&view=item&id=153:taha&Itemid=70

4. Cordoba University, *Welcome to Cordoba.* http://www.cordobauniversity.org/welcome.asp

5. Civil Rights Concerns in the Metropolitan Washington, D.C., Area in the Aftermath of the September 11, 2001, Tragedies, *Chapter 3 Understanding Islam in America in the Aftermath of September 11.* http://www.usccr.gov/pubs/sac/dc0603/ch3.htm

6. Discover The Networks.org, *Sheikh Yusus Al-Qaradawi,* http://www.discoverthenetworks.org/individualProfile.asp?indid=822

7. The Middle East Media Research Institute, *Reactions to Sheikh Al-Qaradhawi's Fatwa Calling for the Abduction and Killing of American Civilians in Iraq,* Jihad & Terrorism Studies Project. http://www.memri.org/report/en/0/0/0/0/0/0/1231.htm

8. http://www.fikercenter.com/fiker/index.php?option=com_k2&view=item&id=153:taha&tmpl=component&print=1

9. Arabic website. http://www.alwani.net/articles_view.php?id=80

10. Ibid

11. Ibid

12. MHMatters, *Love and Stockholm Syndrome: The Mystery of Loving and Abuser,* by Joseph M. Carver, Ph.D. http://www.mental-health-matters.com/index.php?option=com_content&view=article&id=167

13. New York Post, *CBS reporter's Cairo nightmare,* by Michael Shain, Kon Kaplan and Kate Sheehy, http://www.nypost.com/p/news/international/cbs_reporter_cairo_nightmare_pXiUVvhwIDdCrbD95ybD5N

14. New York Post, *Internet jihadist calls on Muslims to cut off David Letterman's tongue,* by Michael Blaustein and Chuck Bennett. http://www.nypost.com/p/news/local/manhattan/internet_jihadist_calls_tongue_muslims_yBGLi0l6S70HiJ1cYkOfVI#ixzz1VKKM3z9x

15. Toronto Sun, *Attack on Muslim author may be hate crime,* by Ian Robertson. http://www.torontosun.com/2011/08/25/attack-on-muslim-author-may-be-hate-crime

16. MICHELLE MALKIN, *What happened when Katy Perry tweeted "Pray for Israel,"* by Michelle Malkin. http://michellemalkin.com/2011/08/23/what-happened-when-katy-perry-tweeted-pray-for-israel/

17. Fox News, *Kim Kardashian slammed over pro-Israel tweet, deletes it,* by Hollie McKay. http://www.foxnews.com/entertainment/2012/11/16/kim-kardashian-slammed-over-pro-israel-tweet-deletes-it/

18. The Global Muslim Brotherhood Daily Report. http://globalmbreport.org/?p=482

19. Newsmax, *The Tipping Point: Embracing the Muslim Brotherhood,* by Frank Gaffney. http://www.newsmax.com/FrankGaffney/MuslimBrotherhood-HillaryClinton-Islamist-Israel/2011/07/07/id/402842

20. FrontPageMag.com, *Islamofacism Fraud at Wright State,* by Patrick Poole. http://archive.frontpagemag.com/readArticle.aspx?ARTID=30246

21. IPT – The Investigative Project on Terrorism, *An Explanatory Memorandum on the General Strategic Goal for the Brotherhood in North America,* by Mohamed Akram. http://www.investigativeproject.org/document/id/20

22. *An Activist Guide to Arab and Muslim Campus and Community Organizations in North America,* by Suleyman Ahmad al-Bosnawi. http://www.discoverthenetworks.org/guides/Muslim Booklet.pdf, p. 26

23. http://www.islamonline.net/arabic/contemporary/politic/2001/article1.shtml

24. PRISM, Project for the Research of Islamist Movements, Issues of Present Interest, "Some Notes on Arabic Terminology as a Link Between Tariq Ramadan and Sheikh Dr. Taha Jabir al-Alwani, Founder of the Doctrine of 'Muslim Minority Jurisprudence (Fiqh al-Aqaliyyat al-Muslimah), Shammai Fishman,'" http://www.e-prism.org/

25. The Weekly Standard, *Hamza Yusuf, At It Again,* by Stephen Schwartz. http://www.weeklystandard.com/Content/Public/Articles/000/000/005/174izpiw.asp?pg=1

26. IPT – The Investigative Project on Terrorism, *An Explanatory Memorandum on the General Strategic Goal for the Brotherhood in North America,* by Mohamed Akram. http://www.investigativeproject.org/document/id/20

CHAPTER

7

ARABIC LOVE
FOR HITLER

INVERSE OF GODWIN'S LAW

*T*he insertion of Nazism in general, Hitler in particular, into heated online arguments has become so common that it is actually a point of study. 'Godwin's Law,' named after the man who came up with it, Mike Godwin, states:

> *As an online discussion grows longer, the probability of a comparison involving Nazis or Hitler approaches one.*[1]

When engaging in an argument about matters related to Islam, comparisons to Hitler and Nazis should be laid out at the very beginning; such comparisons are exempt from Godwin's Law, which argues that the party who brings Hitler into an argument signals his own defeat by doing so. Conversely, when arguing that Islam and Nazism share much in common, it is simply a statement of fact, a premise of any sound argument about Islam. Anyone who *denies* it automatically loses the argument; the person who introduces that fact actually wins the argument by doing so.

ARABIC HEROES

The degree to which public or historic figures are loved or hated can perhaps be determined by typing the name of that individual into a *Google* search engine. When typing the names of Arab dictators— in Arabic—into *Google*, one is apt to uncover high levels of dissatisfaction, with comparisons, ironically, to Hitler. Iraq's Saddam Hussein was a dictator who still garners high praise from Sunni Muslims who rarely refer to him as a tyrant. The sentiment reserved for the likes of former Egyptian dictator Hosni Mubarak or exiled Tunisian dictator Zayn Al-Abideen ben Ali is not as kind.

Heroism in the Middle East is not determined by the amount of good that leaders do for others and neither is tyranny determined by how much evil is inflicted on innocent people by dictators. Instead, each distinction is earned by who is identified as friends and enemies. While Mubarak and Al-Abideen hardly measure up to Saddam when it comes to brutality, the latter did something the former two did not; he lobbed scud missiles at Israel and rewarded the families of suicide bombers with thousands of dollars.[20]

GOOGLE EXPERIMENT

In doing research for this book, I entered history's greatest tyrant (Hitler) plainly, in Arabic, into google. What did I find?

In Arabic, "Hitler" has as many hits as the number of Jews he liquidated—over 6 million. While it's impossible to read 6 million blogs and websites to determine what the Arab world thinks of him, a sample population consisting of hundreds of websites in Arabic would shock westerners; comments posted in response to articles were often far more revealing when I attempted to gauge public sentiment. Most of the comments in some way or another either complimented or glorified Hitler. The first Arabic website was a blog that introduces the former Nazi dictator thusly:

> Hitler was not an ordinary individual to be spun by the wheel of history, to sprinkle him behind as dust, to be forgotten across this vast globe. Nor was he the king of the German people alone. He is one of the greatest few. Here is the king of history.[3]

Westerners might think that the first comment in response to such an article would be disgust. They would be grossly mistaken. Muhammad Jasem posted the first comment:

> ...if the greatest leaders gather together they would not equal the magnificence of Hitler.

The remaining comments neither deviated from, nor rebuked that sentiment.

The second hit was a *YouTube* video entitled, "The Cowardly Jews," which featured a Hitler look-alike walking the streets with Jewish passersby supposedly terrified as they moved out of his way. This "proves that Jews are cowards" the narrator interpreted.[4]

The most common and popular quote from Hitler on Arabic websites was him allegedly saying (perhaps posthumously):

> "I could have destroyed all the Jews but I kept some so the world will know someday why I destroyed them."

The next hit was a *YouTube* video entitled, "Hitler's declaration on Jewish Annihilation". The first comment posted was about how Hitler "respected Islam" and enlisted a Muslim SS unit; he even gave them prayer breaks.[5]

A perusal of hundreds of Arabic websites yielded similar comments; when it comes to Hitler, one would rarely find comments that are 'western-typical'. I was elated to find what I thought to be the first positive, western-typical comment among thousands of pro-Hitler comments. It said:

> Hitler was a psychopath. He would also have killed all the Muslims...

I was disappointed very soon thereafter upon reading the rest of the sentence:

> ...but to be frank, I love Hitler for his ability to lead.

Of course, this was quickly met with rebuke by others:

> ...indeed if Hitler hated the Arabs, why would he enlist Muslim soldiers in his ranks? This must be Jewish propaganda.

Accusations of "Jewish Propaganda" and conspiracy theories plague the Internet in Arabic, where factual history is dismissed as a 'Zionist conspiracy'. Yet, there is apparently no equivalent to Godwin's Law in Arabic; such a law would say that anyone who introduces talk of Zionist conspiracies into an argument to bolster his case subsequently loses that argument. This would signify critical thinking but such a thing is in very short supply in the Muslim world.

I concluded from my own anti-Semitic experiences growing up that a culture plagued with conspiracy theories is usually the one producing them.

One very typical comment in response to these videos stated:

> Hitler left the other half (of Jews) alive in order for Muhammad's prophecy to be fulfilled and open the pathway for Islam to destroy the rest.

On *Alsaha.com*, which is a main news source in the Arab Gulf, a report on a newly released film in France depicts for the first time how the Paris Mosque saved Jews and Muslim resistance fighters during World War II.[6] The most common comments stem from Holocaust deniers and long posts on how the Muslim Grand Mufti, Haj Amin Al-Husseini was a hero and how Hitler supposedly quoted the Quran, allegedly saying, "The hour is near, and the moon was rent asunder." This Qur'anic quote was allegedly uttered so often by Hitler that Ayed Al-Qarni, one of the most respected Saudi Muslim theologians, remarked why Hitler had this Quranic quote engraved on the canons and tanks of the SS Army:

> This is a reminder that the end of days has come and the hour is near when the Jews will be totally annihilated in accordance with Muslim Prophecy.

From Muslim scholars to historic references, Hitler is regarded as a hero. Objections to the love of Hitler *do* exist but they rarely escape passionately adamant refutations in great numbers. One comment criticizes such reverence, not because Hitler was evil but because he didn't measure up to others when it came to exterminating Jews:

> *Hitler was a Nazi who believed in the Arian Race...it was obvious that Hitler complimented Islam because he was allied with the Ottoman Muslims. But why do we Arabs have to insist on our love of Hitler, just because he scrubbed away the Jews? Muhammad, then Omar after him, scrubbed them away in Jerusalem, long before Hitler.*[7]

If one imagines westerners in English equating Muhammad, the prophet of Islam, with Hitler, the reaction would be forceful. But it is not unusual to find Arabic websites that compliment Hitler for emulating Muhammad. Hitler was glowingly quoted as saying:

> "The only one in history who was able to win the Jews in order to cripple them was Muhammad."[8]

Al-Riyadh news in Saudi Arabia published an article on Hitler's Conference Center, which was brought down by a controlled explosion.[9] No comments supported it. They were upset that a historic landmark was destroyed and blamed it on Israel.

Such psychopathic comments would undoubtedly find much rebuke in western forums but retorts like that rarely exist on Arabic websites. Arabic critics of Hitler almost seem to paint him as a moderate who doesn't warrant a Muslim's adulation. Here is a typical rebuke of Hitler on Arabic sites:

I am amazed at all the comments that consider Hitler an icon. The only good thing he did was to kill the Jews.

Arab commentators have been known to use Hitler as an example, to compare with Arab tyrants and to combat extremism. *Walfajr.net*, a Middle Eastern news source, in an article by Al-Baqer Ali Al-Shamasi entitled, "Zionists' drum beats of war," he writes the following about extremists:

Hitler, this extremist nationalist, and his friend Mussolini, came and sparked a world war which victimized 60 million. [10]

So far so good, right? The apologist's hopes are dashed just a few lines later:

…when Hitler did what he did with them [the Jews], the Zionists used their tactics to concoct the Holocaust.

Accepting the reality of the Holocaust, while simultaneously denying it, is not unusual to Arabic websites. Those who espouse this view qualify as pathological liars who know they're invested in a lie but choose to believe and promote it anyway. The longer a pathological liar does so, the more the lie is actually believed and the further into the abyss he falls.

Articles remembering Mein Kampf and how Hitler described the Jews as "stench" and "dirty rats" are in abundance on Arabic sites. The first comment after the first article I encountered, said the following:

With all honesty, I admire Hitler but his killing of Jewish women and children was abhorrent, to say the least. [11]

Western readers might ask how a normal human being could admire what he abhors. On its surface, it seems like *doublethink*. The answer is simple; the comment continued and thus, revealed the reason:

Our religion, Islam, forbade the killing of the elderly, women and children. But I thank you for the wonderful insightful memoire about Hitler's struggle with the Jews.

Only men that reach puberty are to be killed according to Islamist scholars.

Hitler's *Mein Kampf* was advertised with multiple complimentary reviews. If one types "I love Hitler" in English, the first things that come up are articles exposing fashion guru John Galliano, who was filmed delivering a vile, racist rant during which he declared, "I love Hitler". Then you have to go through a ton of articles exposing this embarrassment until he was found guilty for his anti-Semitic rants. Typing "I love Hitler" in Arabic will net an entirely different result. In Arabic, the first websites that come up after typing "I love Hitler" consist of romantic messages such as, "I love you as much as Hitler loved Berlin" coupled with instructions to Muslims on why "loving Hitler is a duty" and why you "must not believe what you watch on television; Hitler loved Islam and welcomed Muslims."[12]

The problem in the Arab world is not a lack of sufficient secular education, as westerners think, but a religious conditioning of the Muslim masses. The photos of Haj Amin Al-Husseini that various western websites use to *expose* Islamist-Nazi connections are actually used to argue in *support* of Nazism in the Arab-Muslim world. Even typing, "I hate Hitler" in Arabic yielded the first website on a debate between a hater and a lover of Hitler. The debate concluded by asserting that loving Hitler was an honor.[13]

The second website rebuked all Arabs that love Hitler. Why? Jealously appears to play a role:

> *The Muslims should have been the priority choice to destroy the Jews, not Hitler.*[14]

Perusing through the thirty websites on "I hate Hitler" revealed hatred on every website. Answers varied from "I hate Hitler because his Holocaust hardened the hearts of Jews which made them take over Palestine"[15] to "Hitler was judged because he never got the job done."[16]

Searching "Hitler" in Arabic was a journey akin to entering a tunnel of depressing darkness. "Hitler the artist," says one article. Hitler was the one who even "discovered the Walt Disney cartoons," stated one comment. It was "Hitler who first drew Snow White and the Seven Dwarfs." Commenters from first to last viewed the article as a delight.

The final comment was:

> *Hitler hated Jews because his mother's doctor, who was Jewish, failed and caused her to die. It was a Jew that purchased Hitler's first pieces of art and paid Hitler very little in order to sell them for major sums. Hitler later discovered the theft of his art by the Jews. It is this story that finally awoke Hitler to see that Jews are cheaters.*

It all reminds me of my early days, when I was schooled in Bethlehem; we studied the life and writings of the most notable, respected, and prominent Egyptian writer Anis Mansour, who once wrote:

> People all over the world come to realize that Hitler was right, since Jews are bloodsuckers...interested in destroying the whole world, which has expelled them and despised them for centuries...and burnt them in Hitler's crematoria...one million...six million. Would that he had finished it! (Anis Mansour 1973).

Anis Mansour was nothing more than a sleaze bucket. I know saying this might anger the hundreds of millions in the Arab world who respect him. Perhaps they might say that I was infected by an American conspiracy.

Indeed I was. It's called critical thinking.

FOOTNOTES

1. http://www.wired.com/wired/archive/2.10/godwin.if_pr.html
2. Fox News, *Saddam Pays 25K for Palestinian Bombers.* http://www.foxnews.com/story/0,2933,48822,00.html
3. Arabic website. http://v.3bir.com/77183/
4. http://www.youtube.com/watch?v=c8C_Nq-P7bg
5. http://www.youtube.com/watch?v=FTZrmLZmKo8&feature=related
6. Arabic website. http://www.alsaha.com/
7. Arabic website. http://vb.arabsgate.com/showthread.php?t=522177
8. Arabic website. http://www.law-uni.net/la/showthread.php?t=39037
9. http://www.alsaha.com/users/220153919/entries/295740
10. Arabic website. http://www.walfajr.net/?act=artc&id=16968
11. http://www.inter.ae/forums/showthread.php?t=86419
12. Arabic website. http://www.aljabiya.com/vb/showthread.php?t=2314
13. http://www.facebook.com/topic.php?uid=128261437193375&topic=117
14. Arabic website. http://ejabat.google.com/ejabat/thread?tid=62884513de13f127
15. Arabic website. http://socialwork.yoo7.com/t6802-topic
16. Arabic website. http://yasmin-alsham.com/vb/converse.php?u=3521&u2=1754&page=18

CHAPTER
8

THE MUSLIM SISTERHOOD

BEHIND THE SISTERHOOD HIJAB

*M*any Americans are fascinated with the issue of women in Islam. They believe that most women in Muslim society are awaiting a grand liberation from male supremacy. When it comes to the role of women in the Muslim Brotherhood, most westerners cannot see the error in such thinking since the word, "Brotherhood" is exclusionary. It might conjure up memories of Philadelphia, the "City of Brotherly love" or the film "Band of Brothers".

The truth is that the Muslim Brotherhood is not the Taliban; female activism in the Muslim Brotherhood takes a lead role, as exemplified by an entire division called the Muslim Sisterhood. It is a group that was established in 1933.[1] It was headed by a woman named Lebiba Ahmad.[2]

Contrary to what is said by western media—when it says anything—this elite unit is by no means a tangentially complicit "mule service," consisting of couriers who smuggle secret documents in order to more easily avoid the eyes of surveillance; neither are they made up of innocent women who don benign-looking "hijabs," as portrayed by *Der Spiegel.*[3]

It is time to debunk—once and for all—the myth written by western media about the Sisterhood; any facts it may have presented are rendered infinitesimal after we conduct a more thorough analysis that focuses on what members of the Sisterhood do and say in Arabic.

We should first issue a disclaimer. Be forewarned; entering the minds of the Sisterhood is like entering a horror film, with one exception. This "bogeywoman" is very real and it resembles the reincarnation of another dark side of history—the beginning stages of the growth of Nazism in Germany. This nightmare is alive, well, and very active as it paradoxically lies in wait for its western prey. It would probably take western media, the public in general, and even our intelligence agencies a decade or so to catch up and realize how ill-equipped they are to deal with it.

The Sisterhood is something of an enigma since the role of women in Jihad goes beyond the explosive act. It firmly believes the pen is mightier than the sword, until the pen used by scribes who write about "tolerance" in English, runs out of ink. According to the Sisterhood, political activism is what Islam mandates and it precedes holy war.

Welcome to *Jihad by the Pen*. A foundational Islamist principle is simple, as it is written in the Islamic texts:

> The earth belongs to Allah and His messenger, who allotted the entire earth for His servants—the Muslims who are so willing to take it over—working for the cause of Allah. (Bukhari 63: 2996)

The Sisterhood disregards Judeo-Christian ethics which God Himself used to establish nationalism. In the Islamist's view, ends *do* justify the means and there is no respect for national borders.

Since nationalism is a farce according to Islamic dogma, Islamists pull a secondary principle from the Qur'an, using it as a political ploy:

> Allah created nations and tribes to mingle and reach out to each other (Qur'an 49:13).

While the West is ignoring the first principle, it is drinking up the second as if it were a bridge-building elixir; the bottle they drink from has the word "dialogue" on the label. Through the use of dialogue, the Sisterhood becomes extremely active.

How active? Even the most ardent of skeptics will be stunned to learn that reporting the list of sixty-three Sisterhood agents published in Arab media by moderate Muslims is hardly a case of Islamophobia.[4] That list depicts something very real. It consists of highly educated media icons who speak several languages while traveling the globe. Through dialogue, they wield influence over several international organizations, from the United Nations to women's advocacy groups worldwide. Allegiance and membership usually involves entire families, with male supervisors, along with their activist wives and daughters; additional memberships in Islamic organizations; spies who've proudly disclosed their past "heroic" acts; Nazi affiliates from the time of the Brotherhood's inception; Hijab advocacy groups in Europe; prominent doctors that became public figures; and even media moguls who double as conspiracy theorists while serving as cogs in the propaganda war machine.

The Muslim Brotherhood means what it says and fulfills its mission for the Sisterhood. That mission is "to gain and acquire a unified global perception in every nation in the world." It is "advocacy work at all levels."[5]

SISTERHOOD MEMBERS

Sisterhood leader Amina Al-jaber is a professor within the Department of Chemistry and Earth Science at the University of Qatar.[6] She has a fascination with Brotherhood leader Sheikh Yusuf Al-Qaradawi and was eager to celebrate his birthday at the Ritz Hotel, even sharing the podium with him.[7]

Jaber even became a signatory to a campaign that condemns any and all of Qaradawi's critics.[8] Despite Qaradawi's anti-Semitic diatribes and support for suicide bombings, he is probably the most popular religious icon in the Sunni Muslim world. He has become the international liaison of the Muslim Brotherhood. In a 2009 speech that aired on *Al Jazeera*, Qaradawi said the following:

> "Throughout history, Allah has imposed upon the [Jews] people who would punish them for their corruption. The last punishment was carried out by Hitler. By means of all the things he did to them—even though they exaggerated this issue—he managed to put them in their place. This was divine punishment for them. Allah willing, the next time will be at the hands of the believers."[9]

The United States is not immune to the Sisterhood's influence. The group's male supervisor, Abdullah Alnoshan was the director of the Virginia office of the Muslim World League (MWL) and was ultimately deported after being charged with immigration violations.[10] The MWL is a group with significantly close ties to al-Qaeda.[11] Another male supervisor within the Sisterhood is Khaled Abou El Fadl.[12] Fadl is a UCLA Law professor whose resume includes an appointment by President George W. Bush to a position on the US Commission for International Religious Freedom. Daniel Pipes made the case as early as 2004 that El Fadl is a "stealth Islamist."[13] Despite his Brotherhood membership, El-Fadl's books are being promoted by the Council on American Islamic Relations (CAIR), which considers El-Fadl a Muslim scholar and has his book *The Great Theft, Wrestling Islam from the Extremists* on its reading list.[14]

MWL's financial arm—the defunct terror funding Rabita Trust—was initiated by former General Secretary of the MWL and notorious al-Qaeda godfather, Abdullah Omar Naseef.[15] Naseef played an integral role with both al-Qaeda and the Muslim Brotherhood.[16] He also had close ties to the most intriguing member of the Sisterhood—Saleha Abedin, the mother of Huma Abedin, the Deputy Chief of Staff for Secretary of State Hillary Clinton during the first term of the Obama administration

HUMA, HILLARY, AND WEINER

Prior to the twitter scandal involving sexual images posted by Weiner that became public, Huma Abedin lived in relative obscurity, especially when one considers she was the closest aid to the Secretary of State *and* married to a United States congressman from New York. While the sexting scandal's spotlight was directed squarely at Weiner, Huma could not escape its glare. In fact, without that scandal, what we learned about the Sisterhood would not have been discovered.

Fox News posted some facts about Weiner's wife as the scandal grew. Among them were that she was born in Kalamazoo, MI and moved to Saudi Arabia when she was two. She speaks fluid Arabic and first started working for then first lady, Hillary Clinton from 1996—2000 after returning to the United States to attend George Washington University.[17] We subsequently learned that Huma served on the Executive Board of the Muslim Students Association at GWU in 1997.[18] Here is a screenshot:

In The Name of Allah, Most Compassionate, Most Merciful

MSA Executive Board

Name	Position	E-Mail
Aisha Chaudary	President	aishac@gwis2.circ.gwu.edu
Syed Omair Hasan	Vice-President	omairh@gwis2.circ.gwu.edu
Ramzi Dalbah	Treasurer	brucelee@gwis2.circ.gwu.edu
Monna Shahna	Secretary-General	monnas@gwis2.circ.gwu.edu
Rabeea Janjua	Secretary	rabeea@gwis2.circ.gwu.edu
Usman Waheed	Head of Education Committee	umoney@gwis2.circ.gwu.edu
Salah Al-Rasbi	Head of Da'wah Committee	salah@gwis2.circ.gwu.edu
Souheila Al-Jadda	Public Relations Director	souheil1@gwis2.circ.gwu.edu
Huma Abedin	Head of Social Committee	pops@gwis2.circ.gwu.edu

[Main]|[Islam]|[Prayer]|[Board]|[Poems]|[Gallery]|[Events]|[Links]|

The *New York Times* identified Abedin as a "practicing Muslim" who was "raised in Saudi Arabia by an Indian father and a Pakistani mother."[19] Those very basic facts raised very bold red flags and caused us to dig deeper.

A noteworthy defender of Huma's marriage to Anthony Weiner was Imam Omar Shareef Abu Namous, the Imam at the Mosque of the Islamic Cultural Center in New York. The infamous Ground Zero mosque imam Feisal Abdul Rauf is a permanent trustee of that mosque. Namous' predecessor blamed the Jews for the 9/11 attacks.[20] When the sexting scandal broke, Namous publicly called for Huma to be patient with her husband and to start the healing process by "counseling" with Weiner.[21] Why would such a strict Islamist like Namous advocate for a practicing Muslim woman, Huma, to remain married to Weiner after this highly embarrassing, public scandal? He should have vehemently objected to the marriage in the first place. Weiner's indiscretions should have reinforced those objections. Instead, those indiscretions garnered Weiner an unlikely advocate.

By all accounts, Namous was a strict Islamic fundamentalist. Anecdotally, in addition to his ties to Rauf, he spoke alongside the director of the Islamic Society of North America (ISNA) at the First National Summit of Imams and Rabbis.[22] He was also quoted by the New York Times as saying there was no conclusive evidence that Muslims were responsible for the 9/11 attacks.[23]

Before we discovered *Muruna*, it simply made no sense that Namous would support Weiner, a Jew. After our discovery of Muruna, it made *perfect* sense. According to the strict interpretation of Sharia law, Huma would have been forbidden from marrying Weiner in the first place, unless the congressman converted to Islam. However, if Abedin was practicing *Muruna*, her marriage would have been considered a greater benefit according to the application of the *Doctrine of Balance*. Considering the fundamentalism practiced by Namous, Muruna is an intricate puzzle piece that fits perfectly.

Remember, according to the *Doctrine of Balance*, any evil committed by a Muslim that is traded for a greater "good" is an acceptable evil. Consider what Namous was quoted as saying in 2001:

> "A unified Muslim state would be the ideal instrument to convince the world that Islam is the last version of God's word. God meant his word to be obeyed."[24]

If Huma's marriage to Weiner furthered this goal, Namous' defense of Weiner amidst the public disgrace would have been justified by *Muruna*. I challenge any westerner to come up with a more logical explanation.

The Center headed by Namous has been a source of controversy in the US and is involved heavily in the collection of foreign funds. The Organization of the Islamic Conference (OIC), which represents multiple Muslim countries, has been at the forefront of fundraising for the center. At its Conference in 1983—held in New York—the call to build the center was answered by the OIC at its 16th Conference, held in Morocco in January of 1986.[25] The demand was that all represented Muslim nations must "contribute morally and financially to complete this project and to establish the Islamic Cultural Center in New York." Abu Namous thanked Kuwait for donating the lion's share.[26]

In subsequent research, we learned of extremist connections Abedin's parents—along with her male sibling—had with Islamic terrorist individuals and groups. Yet, somehow, Huma was able to become the Secretary of State's Deputy Chief of Staff and closest aid after working for the former first lady for several years.

Not so coincidentally, the Muslim Sisterhood gained access to the State Department. In a meeting brokered by Huma, Hillary met with Saleha Abedin and another Muslim Sisterhood member on a trip to a Saudi Arabian university where Huma's mother held a position of prominence.

Could JBTW be responsible? If Huma was a practicing Muslim with extensive familial ties to the Muslim Brotherhood, as several sources confirm, what would permit her to marry a Jewish congressman? The answer is the subject of another chapter in this book—*Welcome to Muruna.*

In 2010, Huma arranged for the Secretary of State to visit Dar Al-Hekma University in Jeddah, Saudi Arabia.[27] The Saudi newspaper *Al-Watan* mentions Saleha's relationship with Huma as being key to bringing secretary of State Hillary Clinton to Dar Al-Hekma:

> "Why did Secretary of State choose to visit Dar Al-Hekma College during her visit to the Kingdom last week and not Effat College or King Abdulaziz University? The reason is classic and simple; helping U.S. Secretary is Huma Abedin who knows the Dean of Admissions and Registration at Dar Al-Hekma—her mother. Dr. Abedin lived in the Kingdom for more than 3 decades, and therefore it was easy to arrange a visit and select Dar Al-Hekma."[28]

Huma's mother, Saleha, was the institution's Vice Dean at the time of the visit.[29] Clinton spoke alongside both Saleha and another Sisterhood member named Suheir Qureshi, who, like so many of her colleagues, holds a Ph.D.[30] Qureshi's educational accomplishments are typical of other Sisterhood members and debunk western claims that Islamists have no regard for the education of women.

Quershi's Ph.D is in Higher Education from Cambridge University; she holds a Masters degree from the United States University—International; she is an Administrative Development Graduate from Wharton Business College in Pennsylvania, PA, in Nov 1999; and she worked at a Pennsylvania Hospital in 1984 as a trainee and worked for the British Society on Eastern Studies.[31]

She is also a member of the IMMA alongside Saleha Abedin, a trusted private scheduler for Saleha at Dar Al-Hekma, and the Financial Officer for the IICWC.[32]

Saleha Abedin is not just the Vice Dean at Dar Al-Hekma; she is also one of the institution's founders.[33] That's not all. One of her colleagues—and Dar Al-Hekma co-founder—is a man named Yaseen Abdullah Kadi, a designated terrorist by the United States and a co-trustee with the bin Laden family.[34]

Are you still not convinced there is a problem created by Jihad-By-The-Word?

THE ABEDIN FAMILY

Though the MWL's financial arm in the United States—Rabita Trust—was shut down for its terror ties, it still exists under the name Rabita al-Alam al-Islami; Saleha Abedin is a member of this organization, which makes her part of the MWL.[35] Even the Anti-Defamation League (ADL) says the following about the MWL:

> "While the MWL has on several occasions condemned terrorism in general terms, it has a long history of providing financial support to terrorist groups or having organizational links to them, including to Hamas, Abu Sayyaf group, Moro Islamic Liberation Front, Jemaat al Islamiyya, and Al Qaeda."[36]

Abedin sits alongside MWL chairman, Dr. Abdullah Omar Naseef (mentioned earlier). It doesn't end there as Saleha's son, Hassan Abedin, has also served as a fellow on the board of the Oxford Center for Islamic Studies (OCIS) with Naseef, though his name is absent from the list now.[37] Naseef is listed as the chairman of the Board of Trustees there. Also serving as a trustee there was the aforementioned, Hitler-loving, Muslim Brotherhood advocate for *Muruna*, leader Sheikh Yusuf al-Qaradawi.[38]

As for Rabita Trust, litigation was filed in the District of Columbia relative to the September 11th terror attacks that named both Naseef and Rabita Trust as defendants in Case # 1:02CV01616(JR):

> 274. On October 12, 2001, President George W. Bush's Executive Order designated Defendant Rabita Trust as a Specially Designated Global Terrorist Entity and the Treasury Department froze its assets. Defendant Abdullah Omar Naseef founded the Defendant Rabita Trust in July 1988 and is currently its chairman. 275. Abdullah Omar Naseef (or "Naseef") also served as Secretary-General of the Muslim World League during the time he created Defendant Rabita Trust and has attempted to spread Muslim World League offices around the world. Part of his global efforts are found in his involvement in a SAAR Network charity.[39]

This reality makes Saleha Abedin and Abdullah Omar Naseef colleagues. Both are intimately involved with the MWL and, by extension have an historic link to Al Qaeda.

Saleha and her now-deceased husband, Syed Z. Abedin, were once believed to have founded the Institute of Muslim Minority Affairs (IMMA), established in both Great Britain and Saudi Arabia.[40] Through my Arabic research, much more about the forces behind the IMMA was learned. Translations of Arabic sources revealed that Naseef founded the IMMA with the backing of the House of Saud.[41] (**See Appendix A**) In Contemporary Discussions on Religious Minorities in Iran, Jorgen S. Nielsen writes of the relationship between the Abedins and Naseef on page 366:

> "Trained in social science and being of Indian origin, Professor Abedin (Syed Z.) was the founder of the Institute of Muslim Minority Affairs in Jeddah, Saudi Arabia, an institution that had the quiet but active support of the then General Secretary of the Muslim World League, Dr. Umar Abdallah Nasif."[42]

Huma was once listed on the IMMA website as being one of the group's Editors. Though the website currently lists both Huma's brother, Hassan Abedin, and her mother as editors, Huma's name was removed shortly before Hillary Clinton was named as Secretary of State. In essence, Huma left the IMMA after twelve years to work for Clinton as Deputy Chief of Staff beginning in 2009.[43]

Huma's mother Saleha still appears on the main Al-Azhar university website as a member of the *High Council for Islamic Matters* and participated in the 12th session regarding the Islamic Conference for the Islamic Uprising.[44] As such, she endorsed the mission of the Conference, which included representing the *Islamic Committee for Woman and Child* (ICWC); it stood for the decriminalization of rape within marriage.[45]

The IMMA Vice Chairman[46] is a man named Abu Bakr Bakader.[47] Bakader is also the Vice Chairman of the *International Islamic Committee for Woman and Child* (IICWC).[48]

Bakader isn't just connected to the Abedin family. He's also got a connection to three of the 9/11 hijackers. On one Arabic website, Bakader is seen with Saleh Al-Ghamdi.[49] Saleh is a relative of three of the nineteen terrorists, to include Saleh Al-Ghamdi, Hamza Saleh Al-Ghamdi, and Ahmed al-Ghamdi.[50]

The Abedin family has another disturbing connection to a leader within a radically Islamist group. His name was Maulana Muhammad Yusuf of Jamaat-e-Islami.[51] Yusuf reportedly joined the group after hearing the call from the movement's founder, Abu Al-Ala Maududi, whom he respected greatly.[52] Maududi was a Sunni of Pakistani origin who was influenced heavily by Muslim Brotherhood founder, Hassan al-Banna and perhaps even more so by al-Banna's successor, Sayyid Qutb.[53]

While with Jamaat, Yusuf was appointed Secretary-General and later elected Ameer of the group. He also presided over the printing of the Qur'an in several languages within India and was fluent in English, Arabic, and Urdu. Many credit him with introducing the radical Jamaat to the Arab world.[54]

In recent years, the Jamaat has expressed support for violent jihad against American forces and other non-Muslims in Iraq, Afghanistan, Palestine and elsewhere.[55] The organization also salutes the jihad of groups like Hamas, Hezbollah, and Hezbul Mujahideen in Kashmir.

THE ABEDIN-HELMY CONNECTION

As a Sisterhood leader, Saleha Abedin partners with co-leader Camellia Helmy.[56] Helmy also happens to be the wife of a prominent Muslim Brotherhood leader.[57] In the general elections, Helmy ran as a candidate representing one of twenty-four Sisterhood members. Siraj Al-Din Allboudi was accused and imprisoned for the primary role he played in establishing the International Women's Organization (Sisterhood) in 2002, which is confirmed by a Muslim Brotherhood announcement on April 6, 2010 that identified him as a "member representing the Muslim Sisterhood branch."[59]

Aside from being a member of the Sisterhood, Helmy is also the leader of the *International Islamic Committee for Woman and Child* (IICWC) and was found complaining that the "Women's Committee of the United Nations had declared war on Islam."[60] She confronted the United Nations and accused it of supporting "Gender Equality."[61]

Saleha Abedin and Camellia Helmy are key figures in the IICWC, about which, the Egyptian newspaper, Masr, reported:

"The *Islamic Committee for Woman and Child* condemns passing any law that imprisons a husband under the pretext of raping his wife or for having sex with her without her consent as prescribed under 'marital rape.' At the end of the workshop, which was held in Cairo, under the Charter of the Family in Islam, the Committee rejected any law that gives women the freedom to control her body or the recognition of illegitimate children. The committee is steadfast in stressing male superiority over women, including the necessity of a woman to obey her husband. It refuses to grant gays any rights or abolish differences between men and women". (Feb 22, 2009)[62]

"Our role is to apply pressure to the United Nations," said Camellia in an interview with Dr. Muhammad Saidi, during an installment of his program, entitled: "The Dialogue of Civilizations."[63] As is often the case with JBTW, the title of the program was not reflective of the true intent, which was nothing more than giving the Sisterhood a larger platform for the purpose of getting its message out. During the interview, Camellia explained the agenda of the Sisterhood relative to its dealings with the United Nations:

> "...we apply pressure in order to reject rulings that do not align with our religious beliefs; our main goal is to stop agreements [between nations] and to make known the Islamic position regarding such agreements."

She added:

> "The most dangerous of these is an international Bill of Rights for Women (CEDAW) as the most dangerous issue that was ever established...Within the United Nations exists a fifth column...these organizations apply daily pressure on governments which acts like a pincer. From one side the United Nations will apply pressure and from the other side these organizations apply pressure."

Those in the West who espouse feminism and whose natural inclination is to side with Islamists should perhaps rethink their ideological alliances. What the Muslim Sisterhood's leaders are advocating is antithetical to the stated goals of western feminists in this regard. Perhaps feminism isn't about equality at all. Maybe it leads to the same place the Sisterhood wants to go.

The elder Abedin and Helmy worked together in Egypt back in 2000. At that time, Abedin's intent was to obstruct any legislation that contradicted Sharia:

> "What Dr. Abdeen from the IICWC mentioned during the preparatory conference for the Special Session of the Assembly of the United Nations in Cairo was valid. She explained that the danger of Islamic silence about these international instruments is that they become binding upon the States, and enter into force upon signature by States".[64]

Besides Saleha Abedin's connections to Camellia Helmy, she also appears on the list of Sisterhood members with Dr. Fatima Naseef, who is the sister of Abdullah Omar Naseef. Like Abedin, Fatima was born in India. Her father—Sharaf Din Nurul—was the first to establish a printing press in India to publish

Islamic books. Fatima is an Islamic advocate and a professor at Um Al-Qura School of Sharia.

NAZI WOMEN

Official members of the Sisterhood include male supervisors with their wives/daughters acting as spies who proudly disclosed the heroic acts of their men during Israel's wars with Egypt. Others are Nazi-style propagandists; Nazi affiliates from the time of the Brotherhood's inception; Hijab advocates in Europe; prominent doctors; popular conspiracy theorists and media icons that closely emulate the Goebbels propaganda machine during Nazi Germany. This group has a span of influence over several international organizations from the United Nations to the United States to women's advocacy groups worldwide; that influence is immense. Overlooking this group's activities, to include those of Huma, is like ignoring Muhammad Atta's flight lessons prior to 9/11, with the hindsight of 9/11.

Try as they might, the doubters who dismiss the Sisterhood as a weak and symbolic entity exclusively, miss a critical point. The Sisterhood's goals and agenda mirror the goals found on the Brotherhood's official website.[65] This is also confirmed by Egyptian security services and top experts, including the Arab Center for Studies, headed by researcher Abdul Rahim Ali.[66]

Consider Sisterhood leader Najla Ali Mahmoud; she is supervised by her husband Mohammed Aidlmrsi (Mohammed Mursi).[67] Mursi was elected President of Egypt in 2012. This reality meant that Mursi's wife and Saleha Abedin were close personal colleagues. The mother of a woman with intimate access to State secrets of the United States had close connections to the wife of Egypt's Muslim Brotherhood president.

Mursi has served as both a member of the Guidance Bureau and the current leader of the Justice and Freedom Party (the Brotherhood's propaganda name).[68] He appeared on National television and explained why "Egypt needs to ban western dress" and how "no one with a full mental faculty can believe in the Trinity" (religious bigotry anyone?). He even condemned Egyptian monuments as "idols". The only difference between the Justice and Freedom Party and Taliban is a western propaganda machine.

Will Egypt's new rulers destroy the Sphinx like the Taliban destroyed the Buddha statue in Bamyan?[69] Will Egypt make a holocaust of Copts who are already portrayed as having a mental deficiency for believing in the Trinity?

And while this 'Gobbles' runs his propaganda machine, the naysayers demand evidence of Huma's membership with this notorious group. Would someone appoint the daughter of Magda and Joseph Goebbels as the Deputy Chief of Staff for Cordell Hull—the Secretary of State during World War II—arguing that she has no allegiance to the Nazi Party despite evidence to the contrary?[70]

We are not "racist" for comparing the Muslim Brotherhood to the Nazis. Consider that Hassan al-Banna, the grandfather of Tariq Ramadan (the man whose ban on entry into the United States was lifted by Huma's boss—Hillary), collaborated with my grandfather's associate and Hitler henchman, Haj Amin Al-Husseini, who became the Muslim Brotherhood leader after the war. These people have not repented; they still take pride in their collaboration with the Nazis.[71]

To promote a *Moderate* Muslim Brotherhood is like promoting "Capitalistic-Communism" to defeat Russia during the Cold War or even a "pro-Jew Nazism" during WWII. Hillary's "inclusion policy" brought in spies, and 'this' is how she plans to soften the Muslim Brotherhood!? Huma Abedin was never properly vetted and unless this diva answers some tough questions, ours is an ironclad case.

ASMA SA'AD EDDIN LACHIN

Sisterhood leader Asma Sa'ad Eddin Lachin, the daughter of Sa'ad Eddin Lacin, who was the leader of an official opposition group, has an agenda that closely mirrors the Nazi-style agenda.[72] The elder Lachin was a close associate of Muslim Brotherhood founder, al-Banna, who sought an alliance with Hitler; both shared a mutual hatred for the Jewish minority. In Egypt, this hatred is quite evident in Arabic and includes the portrayal of Christians as enemy conspirators during and after the Arab Spring uprising.

In English, Islamonline—one of the Brotherhood's favorite media outlets—reported that Mursi dismissed accusations by secular politicians that his Freedom and Justice Party would sideline Copts from the political life in post-Mubarak Egypt:

> "We want everyone to be reassured... that we want to see our Christian brothers elected in parliament."[73]

In Arabic, Mursi said that Egypt needs to "ban western dress" and that people who believe in "the Trinity" do not possess a "full mental faculty."[74] Do you still believe Islam is a tolerant religion? Does it not sound bigoted according to such a prominent practitioner of the religion? Is that not the quintessential example of JBTW from the Arab world and tone deafness on the part of the West? How would the people who drive around with "Coexist" bumper stickers respond?

One can see the writing on the wall; the Muslim supremacy over Christians in Egypt is a repeat of Nazism. The similarities between Hitler and the Brotherhood's founder, al-Banna, are more than palpable; they are undeniable. *Discover the Networks* writes:

> "Both movements sought world conquest and domination. *Both were triumphalist and supremacist: in Nazism the Aryan must rule, while in al-Banna's Islam, the Muslim religion must hold dominion.*"[75]

Whose side are *you* on? If you're lukewarm, guess which side will claim you.

ZAINAB ABDULAZIZ (The Chic, Female Professor)

When members of the Sisterhood speak English, messages about tolerance abound but when they speak Arabic, the audible emanations from their mouths are transformed into Nazi style propaganda. Consider the case of Sisterhood member Zainab Abdulaziz.[76]

Abdulaziz often appears in western dress while speaking several languages and teaches French civilization; she is also an avid conspiracy theorist…[77] (with translation)[78] who uses Nazi style propaganda which includes accusations that Vatican II is akin to the *Protocols of the Elder's of Zion*.[79] In Zainab's mind, the Vatican is conspiring with the Zionists to *"Christianize the Muslim world"* with the goal of *"completely uprooting Islam"* and *"making the Jews innocent through the blood of Jesus."* Al-Marsad, an Islamic media outlet, uses her propaganda worldwide. That propaganda includes horrendous and bloody depictions while calling on Muslims to resist Christianization.[80]

ILHAM SAAD ABDALBESER

Enter—if you dare—the mind of Ilham Saad Abdalbeser,[81] Sisterhood leader and spouse of released prisoner Mohi Hamid.[82] Hamid is a member of the "Guidance Bureau of the Muslim Brotherhood". In a video, Mohi can be seen communicating his vision with a photo of al-Banna on the wall behind him, next to a large plaque of the Brotherhood logo.[83] Hamid also appeared on Ikhwan TV (Brotherhood) where he discussed the short and long term vision of the Brotherhood. He called for "the Total Restitution" to "make Islam" not as a personal belief only but as "the total way of life everywhere," including governance with Sharia as a state and a "worldwide Caliphate," with Muslims ordained to become the "teachers for every nation on earth". It is this effort that will "bring about total happiness and utopia globally".

ZUHAIR LZIMAILI

Another Sisterhood leader, Zuhair Lzimaili sits on the board of *Al-Sabeel Newspaper* in Jordan.[84] One of its goals is to "expose the intrusion and assimilation attempts by the Zionist enemy".

AIDA AL-MUTLAQ

Aida Al-Mutlaq is another one of the infamous sixty-three Sisterhood members. She has provided the details of another Sisterhood conspiracy:

> "We assure that the danger to our national security is the American-Zionist project which aims to destroy our history, civilization and future..."[85]

Al-Mutlaq wants Jordan to become the...

> "...fortress and formidable gate to thwart the Zionist agenda, which threatens Jordan... and the entire Arab and Muslim world."

She so fears a Zionist conspiracy that she called for reducing the King of Jordan to nothing more than a figurehead, in a way not all that dissimilar from what the Nazis did with French General Philippe Pétain in Vichy, France during the second World War.[86]

As an aside, Pétain was a French General and war hero from World War I who was brought out of retirement in World War II to help beat back Nazi aggression. To say he failed would be an understatement. Pétain accepted the Nazis terms and became a figurehead who ruled over Vichy France. He was responsible for rounding up Jews for the Germans and ultimately convicted of treason after the war. The lesson is that figureheads are powerless and should be considered compromised goods. Perhaps Pétain won his own preservation for a finite period but he did so at the cost of his own legacy, which is as close to immoral as anything can come on the physical plane.[87] His sad story demonstrates both the intent of those who desire figureheads and those who acquiesce to their demands by meeting the need. Western leaders should learn from this but, unfortunately, most seem to be following the same path, at least at this moment in time.

Jawad Younis is not only a prominent attorney and Islamist activist but he's also my cousin.[88] He can be seen on the Brotherhood's website and is a leading figure who collaborates with Ahmad Al-Kafwin, a member of the Executive Office of the Muslim Brotherhood to overhaul the current Jordanian legal system; the movement is advanced under the guise of "Reformation."[89]

MANAL ABU HASSAN

The stated passion of Sisterhood member Manal Abu Hassan is "woman's activism". She actually ran as a Muslim Brotherhood candidate to help further it.[90] She is also a Professor at October Sixth Journalism University.[91] A link to her facebook page goes to a page with Muslim Brotherhood's logo.[92] Her daughter is Sondus Chalabi, also a Muslim Brotherhood activist who once expressed her hope that "Obama (will) open the door for (our) hope to advance political Islam."[93] Indeed he did. As a result of the Obama administration's support for the 'Arab Spring,' the Brotherhood took power of virtually the entire Middle East. During the Arab uprising that began in early 2011, the Sisterhood held its first conference in 60 years. The agenda included a plan of action for the group after the Brotherhood seized control of the Middle East.[94]

Decades earlier, a Sisterhood-like fervor for hateful ideology was also demonstrated by Hanna Reitsch, a committed test pilot for the Nazi Luftwaffe who was the only woman to earn the Iron Cross; she *worshipped* Hitler.[95] After Hitler's defeat, the Nazi Party was banned in Germany, its top leaders convicted.[96] In 1948, the Brotherhood was banned in Egypt and its founder (al-Banna) was killed by government agents in 1949.[97]

Unlike the Nazis, the Brotherhood has shown it can rise from the ashes.

In April of 2012, a Muslim Brotherhood delegation was welcomed by the Obama White House. The head of the delegation—Abdul Mawgoud Dardery— was accompanied by Sondus. Both appeared on CNN, as part of a panel discussion, and put on their best faces for western audiences.[98] In fact, Sondus was identified as Sondos Asem, not Sondus Chalabi. Her father, Asim Chalabi, is also a high ranking leader in the Brotherhood.[99] Sondus proceeded to contradict her own words from a few years earlier by advocating—in English—for Democratic rule in Egypt. Three years earlier, she professed that she wanted Obama to help "advance political Islam".

A noteworthy moment in the *CNN* exchange occurred when *The Blaze's* Will Cain asked both Dardery and Asem about doublespeak. Though he wasn't armed with specifics, the question posed by Cain did elicit an ironic response from Dardery, who identified charges of doublespeak as "conspiracy theories".[100] That's an interesting charge coming from the representative of a group that is rife with 9/11 Truthers.[101]

TYRANTS ON THE LOOSE

An Egyptian cleric named Miqdam Al-Khadhari recently extolled the Al-Azhar textbooks for teaching hatred of the Jews as well as for their ability to militarize students.[102] As the Mubarak regime was crumbling in Egypt, another prominent Egyptian cleric demanded that the "president of Egypt must be subordinate to Al-Azhar..."[103]

Such a scenario would grant significant power to any Sisterhood member who teaches there, including Sisterhood leader Makarim Dairi.[104] Dairi is the wife of Ibrahim Sharaf.[105] Sharaf was imprisoned in Egypt four times before his final release in 2000.[106] Dairi is also a teacher at the Al-Azhar school, which is Egypt's largest religious institution.[107] None other than Abdullah Azzam, al-Qaeda's founder, was a graduate and Muslim Brotherhood preacher.[108] The grandfather of al-Qaeda's number two man—Ayman al-Zawahiri—held one of the most coveted positions at Al-Azhar.[109] The institution also objected to Osama bin Laden's sea burial.[110]

JIHAN HALAFAWI

Jihan Halafawi is an officially recognized member of the Sisterhood.[111] She is also the wife of former Brotherhood leader Ibrahim Za'farani. Like Makarim Dairi, Jihan's husband was imprisoned along with several other members of the Muslim Brotherhood in attempting to bring the banned organization back into prominence.[112]

GROOMING YOUNG WOMEN

Consider Nahla Mohamed Allahita Yousef, wife of imprisoned Muslim Brother-hood leader Mohamed Amr Darraj or Afaf Fadl Al-Sisi, wife of Essam el-Erian.[113] Al-Sisi's husband was imprisoned for his membership in the Brotherhood in 1982 and is recognized as a leading voice for the group.[114] He is also the head of the Brotherhood's Political Bureau.[115]

The concoction that mixes passionate activism, high level education, and posi-tions of political influence can be dangerously powerful and such characteristics are very potent among Sisterhood members. For example, Nayla Najib Alrashdan is a lawyer who leads an advocacy group for Muslim women known as "Women's Association for Jerusalem," which calls for the funding of an effort to "liberate eastern Jerusalem from Jewish expansionism."[116] She was also influential enough to become a member of the House of Representatives in Jordan in 2002.

It is important to understand how tightly knit the familial ties to the Broth-erhood are. In much the same way that Nazi women were brought into the national socialist fold by being encouraged to raise Nazi children, the offspring of Brotherhood and Sisterhood members are indoctrinated into the zealous lifestyle of Jihadi activism, by their parents.

Kamel Sharif is on the list of Sisterhood supervisors.[117] His daughter, Maha Kamel Al-Sharif is one of the group's leaders.[118] This family's ties to the Nazis are quite literal. Kamel Sharif is the former Jordanian Waqf Minister who aided Hitler's closest Arab ally, Haj Amin al-Husseini.[119] He also led Muslim Brotherhood youth on "Jihad expeditions" that consisted of fighting in southern Israel.[120]

Espionage is a practice not foreign to Sisterhood members. Suheir Gelbana is a perfect example. She was the vice chairman of the Sinai expedition.[121] In her role there, Gelbana sent spies to the Sinai to give reports on Israeli military move-ments.[122] As president of the Association of Young Muslim Women,[123] she collaborated with the Muslim Brotherhood.[124] Amazingly, Gelbana met with John Crocker of the US Embassy to receive millions of dollars in aid for Northern Sinai.[125]

The modus-operandi for Sisterhood members is to be involved in child rearing like Doctor Badria Al Mutawa. Amal Nasir is another female "child rearing specialist" among Muslim women. She has written extensively about the "reasons for girls going astray."[126] Take note of the dress code required for the "Islamic Youth Conference" during the summer program she endorses.

العدد (١٥٦٧٧)

Nasir explains that girls should be careful because the reason young Muslim women go astray during summer vacation is "walking in the market place, speaking to friends and watching T.V." (insert Dragnet music here). Instead, while in the summer-vacation program, girls can learn "how to put up with marriage pressures in the future…" Nasir holds a series of bizarre events.[127] One course is entitled, "How to rear your children to support the Gaza Intifada."[128] The video presentations consist of the typical propaganda that is used to brainwash children.[129]

Suad Al-Jarallah is President of the Association of Women for Reform.[130] She is also involved with the International Conference for Women.[131] She is a supporter of the Gaza flotillas.

> "I am proud that my brother and his wife went on the journey [to Gaza], this is a right for the Islamic Umma [nation]. If I had my chance to go I would not hesitate."[132]

RANA SA'ADEH

Besides being a member of the Sisterhood, Rana Sa'adeh is a Member of the Women's Division of Jamaat-e-Islami, which is the Indian subcontinent's equivalent of the Muslim Brotherhood, as mentioned in a separate chapter. It has *extensive ties to Al-Qaeda and other terrorist groups.*

More recently, the Jamaat has expressed support for violent jihad against American forces and other non-Muslims in Iraq, Afghanistan, Palestine and elsewhere.[133] The organization also salutes the jihad of groups like Hamas, Hezbollah, and Hizbul Mujahideen in Kashmir.

Sa'adeh also runs *Women's Caucus for Palestinian Woman and Child* which includes the Lebanese Women's Council, Woman's Uprising Committee, Women's division of Hezbollah, the Lebanese Communist Party, the National Union of Lebanese Women's Baath Party, the Committee on Women's Work from Hamas, the Women's Bureau of Jemaah Islamiah, the Women's Movement, Women's Movement of the Palestinian Democratic Party, Office of Palestinian Women National Liberation Movement—Fatah, and the Central Council of the Association of Teachers for Primary Education.

The *Women's Caucus for Palestinian Woman and Child* has a mission statement that includes the following directives:

> Give full support to the struggle of our people in Palestine and help keep alive their courageous uprising and steadfastness.

> Support the Palestinian right to liberate the entire land and the establishment of the Palestinian state with its capital Jerusalem (Al Quds).

> Urge the international community to shoulder its full responsibility to protect the Palestinians, pressure the US government and the Zionist entity to stop the aggression against the Palestinian people.

> Call on all Arab governments to take a decisive stand against the arrogance of Zionism and cut off all ties with the Zionist entity, the closure of its embassies and condemn the hostile US position to our nation and the war waged against the Iraqi people.

> Urge the Lebanese government to prevent the US ambassador from interfering with the internal and political affairs of Lebanon.

> To call on all Lebanese parties and NGO's to boycott American goods as a form of resistance.

To call on all Palestinian factions to promote unity while escalating the intifada and the resistance until the defeat of the occupation is completed.

Ensure the return of refugees to their homes.

To call on the Palestinian Authority to stop any contacts with the Zionist entity and the announcement of the end of the settlement process in adherence to the demand of the Palestinian people in its resistance and its Intifada until victory and liberation and return.

We hail the Iraqi resistance, calling on the forces and all nationalities that live there to pressure their governments to withdraw there troops from Iraqi territories and guarantee Iraq's unity and freedom of people to choose their representatives.

We hail the steadfastness of Syria, Lebanon and Iran against in the U.S. and Zionist threats.[134]

This mission statement goes a long way in communicating the mindset of the Muslim Sisterhood. It is a group that isn't so much subservient to the Brotherhood as it is working in concert with it. The goals of each are not only perfectly aligned but the Sisterhood is much more active in furthering the Islamic agenda than was previously known.

FOOTNOTES

1. Arabic website. http://www.ikhwanwiki.com/index.php?title=%D8%AA%D8%B7%D9%88%D8%B1_%D9%82%D8%B3%D9%85_%D8%A7%D9%84%D8%A3%D8%AE%D9%88%D8%A7%D8%AA_%D9%81%D9%8A_%D8%AC%D9%85%D8%A7%D8%B9%D8%A9_%D8%A7%D9%84%D8%A5%D8%AE%D9%88%D8%A7%D9%86_%D8%A7%D9%84%D9%85%D8%B3%D9%84%D9%85%D9%8A%D9%86

2. Arabic website. http://www.ikhwanwiki.com/index.php?title=%D9%84%D8%A8%D9%8A%D8%A8%D8%A9_%D8%A3%D8%AD%D9%85%D8%AF

3. Spiegel Online International, *The Muslim Sisterhood, Visions of Female Identity in the New Eqypt,* by Dialika Krahe. http://www.spiegel.de/international/world/the-muslim-sisterhood-visions-of-female-identity-in-the-new-egypt-a-754250-3.html

4. Arabic website. http://hobaheba.blogspot.com/

5. Arabic website. http://hobaheba.blogspot.com/2010/01/blog-post_5903.html

6. Qatar University, College of Arts & Sciences. http://www.qu.edu.qa/arts sciences/about/committees/chemistry.php

7. Arabic website. http://www.ikhwan.net/forum/showthread.php?23427-%C7%E1%DE%D1%D6%C7%E6%ED-quot-%DD%ED%C7%E1%CB%E3%C7%E4%ED%E4-quot-%ED%D8%E1%C8-%C7%E1%D4%E5%C7%CF%C9

8. Arabic website. http://qaradawi.net/?cu_no=2&item_no=3430&version=1&template_id=116

9. Discover The Networks.org, *Sheikh Yusuf Al-Qaradawi*. http://www.discoverthe networks.org/individualProfile.asp?indid=822

10. The Washington Times, *U.S. deports Saudi director of Virginia Muslim charity*. http://www.washingtontimes.com/news/2005/dec/12/20051212-110500-7469r/

11. Discover The Networks.org, *Muslim World League (MWL)*. http://www.discover thenetworks.org/printgroupProfile.asp?grpid=7347

12. http://www.shoebat.com/blog/archives/1202

13. Daniel Pipes, Middle East Forum, *Stealth Islamist: Khaled Abou El Fadl*, by Daniel Pipes. http://www.danielpipes.org/1841/stealth-islamist-khaled-abou-el-fadl

14. CAIR Philadelphia, *Islam Reference List*. http://pa.cair.com/education/islam-reference-list/

15. Discover The Networks.org, *Rabita Trust (RT)*. http://www.discovertheneworks.org/printgroupProfile.asp?grpid=6411

16. History Commons, *Profile: Abdullah Omar Naseef*. http://www.historycommons.org/entity.jsp?entity=abdullah_omar_naseef_1

17. Fox News, *FAST FACTS: Huma Abedin, Anthony Weiner's Wife*. http://foxnews insider.com/2011/06/07/fast-facts-huma-abedin-weiner/

18. Walid Shoebat, *Well, Whaddya know? Huma Abedin was a Muslim Students Association Board Member*. http://shoebat.com/2012/08/15/well-whaddya-know-huma-abedin-was-a-muslim-students-association-board-member/

19. The New York Times, *Opposites in Many Ways, but Seemingly Melded Well*, by Ashley Parker. http://www.nytimes.com/2011/06/07/nyregion/wife-knew-of-online-past-but-not-photo-post-weiner-says.html?_r=4&

20. Discover The Networks.org, *Feisal Abdul Rauf*. http://www.discoverthenetworks.org/individualProfile.asp?indid=2462

21. Metro.us, *Report: Rep. Anthony Weiner's wife pregnant*, by Carly Baldwin. http://www.metro.us/newyork/local/article/882830--imam-to-rep-weiner-s-wife-stand-by-your-man

22. The Global Muslim Brotherhood Daily Report, *ISNA Builds Further Ties With U.S. Jewish Community.* http://globalmbreport.org/?p=374

23. The New York Times, *A National Challenged: The Imam; New Head of Mosque Wants Proof,* by Daniel J. Wakin. http://www.nytimes.com/2001/11/02/nyregion/a-nation-challenged-the-imam-new-head-of-mosque-wants-proof.html

24. The Radicalization of U.S. Muslims. *Inside U.S. mosques, American Muslims hear a message of fundamentalism,* by Marina Jiménez. http://www.rickross.com/reference/islamic/islamic38.html

25. http://www.moqatel.com/Mokatel/data/Wthaek/Wthaek/KhargiaMIslamy/AKhargiaMIslamy941_48-1.htm

26. Arabic website. http://www.kuna.net.kw/ArticleDetails.aspx?id=2147967&language=ar

27. Saudi Gazette, *Clinton warns of N-arms race,* by Hira Azharand Habib Shaikh. http://www.saudigazette.com.sa/index.cfm?method=home.regcon&contentID=2010021763651

28. http://www.alwatan.com.sa/News/newsPrinting.asp?issueno=3439&id=138354

29. Dar Al-Hekma College, National Accreditation (NCAAA). https://sisweb.daralhekma.edu.sa:8251/portal/page?_pageid=374,146513&_dad=portal&_schema=PORTAL

30. Arabic website. http://www.seraty.info/ar/?action=view&id=1670

31. Ibid

32. Arabic website. http://www.q11q.net/vb/q11q58716/

33. http://www.brookings.edu/~/media/events/2006/2/18islamicworld/20060218bios.pdf

34. The Global Muslim Brotherhood Daily Report, *Exclusive: Hillary Clinton Speaks At Saudi College Founded By U.S. Designated Terrorist.* http://globalmbreport.org/?p=2242

35. http://www.themwl.com/Bodies/Members/default.aspx?d=1&mid=473&l=AR

36. Anti-Defamation League, *Backgrounder: Muslim World League, Introduction.* http://www.adl.org/main_Terrorism/Muslim_World_League_Backgrounder.htm

37. Oxford Centre for Islamic Studies, Director and Fellows. http://www.oxcis.ac.uk/fellows.html

38. The Global Muslim Brotherhood Daily Report, *Exclusive: US State Department Adviser Visits UK Islamic Center Headed By Saudi Islamist Leader.* http://globalmbreport.com/?p=2641

39. http://www.deepcapture.com/wp-content/uploads/Terrorist-Lawsuit-5.pdf

40. Institute of Muslim Minority Affairs (IMMA). http://www.imma.org.uk/index.htm

41. The Abedin "Affairs" with Al Saud, by Walid Shoebat. http://www.shoebat.com/wp-content/uploads/2012/08/Abedin_Affairs_with_Al_Saud_0813123.pdf

42. Contemporary Discussions on Religious Minorities in Islam, by Jorgen S. Nielsen. http://lawreview.byu.edu/archives/2002/2/Nie8.pdf

43. Ordered Liberty, *Huma Abedin's Muslim Minority Affairs: Not Just a Journal,* by Andrew C. McCarthy. http://pjmedia.com/andrewmccarthy/2012/08/17/huma-abedins-muslim-minority-affairs-its-not-just-a-journal/?print=1

44. Anti-Mullah, Dedicated to the Removal of the Islamic Regime in Iran ---- I Prefer to Die on My Feet than Live on My Knees, *Huma Abedin – The Power Behind Hillary's Throne.* http://noiri.blogspot.com/2008/03/huma-abedin-power-behind-hillarys.html

45. Arabic website. http://www.masress.com/alshaab/15830

46. Arabic website. http://www.furat.com/index.php?Prog=book&Page=authorinfo&aid=8099

47. Arabic website. http://www.fikr.com/?Prog=book&Page=authorinfo&aid=7436

48. Arabic website. http://www.aawsat.com/details.asp?section=43&article=301911&issueno=9678

49. Arabic website. http://www.alwatan.com.sa/Culture/News_Detail.aspx?ArticleID=47894&CategoryID=7

50. Photo. http://www.globalsecurity.org/security/profiles/images/ahmed_al-ghamdi_3.jpg

51. Arabic website. http://www.al-islam.com/Content.aspx?pageid=1361&ContentID=2414

52. http://www.al-islam.com/Content.aspx?pageid=1361&ContentID=2414

53. Mideast Web, Encyclopedia of the Middle East, *Sayyid Abul A'la Maududi.* http://www.mideastweb.org/Middle-East-Encyclopedia/abul-ala-maududi.htm

54. http://www.radianceweekly.com/229/6299/jamaat-e-islami-hind-salt-of-the-soil/2010-11-07/cover-story/story-detail/a-few-jewels-of-jamaat-e-islami-hind.html

55. Arabic website. http://www.jamaat.org/new/english/news_detail/253

56. http://www.ikhwanonline.com/Article.asp?ArtID=11381&SecID=270

57. Muslim website. http://www.misrelgdida.com/index.php?print=1&news=8367

58. Arabic website. http://www.ikhwanwiki.com/index.php?title=%D8%A7%D9%84%D9%85%D8%B1%D8%B4%D8%AF_%D8%A7%D9%84%D8%B9%D8%A7%D9%85_%D9%8A%D9%88%D8%A7%D8%B3%D9%8A_%D9%85._%D8%B3%D8%B1%D8%A7%D8%AC_%D8%A7%D9%84%D9%84%D8%A8%D9%88%D8%AF%D9%8A_%D9%81%D9%8A_%D9%88%D8%A7%D9%84%D8%AF%D8%AA%D9%87

59. Arabic website. http://www.elbashayer.com/news-91899.html

60. http://www.moheet.com/show_files.aspx?fid=355417

61. http://www.islamonline.net/i3/ContentServer?pagename=IslamOnline/i3LayoutA&c=OldArticle&cid=1173695036284

62. Arabic website. http://www.islamonline.net/i3/ContentServer?pagename=Islam-Online/i3LayoutA&c=OldArticle&cid=1173695036284

63. Video in Arabic. http://www.prophecyinthenews.com/

64. Arabic website. http://webcache.googleusercontent.com/search?q=cache:0-6LgmXf3gMJ:www.iicwc.org/lagna/iicwc/iicwc.php%3Fid%3D537+%22%D9%83%D8%A7%D9%85%D9%8A%D9%84%D9%8A%D8%A7+%D8%AD%D9%84%D9%85%D9%8A%22+%22%D8%B9%D8%A7%D8%A8%D8%AF%D9%8A%D9%86%22&cd=1&hl=en&ct=clnk&gl=us&source=www.google.com

65. http://www.ikhwanhistory.org/index.php?title=%D8%A7%D9%84%D8%AD%D9%83%D9%85_%D8%A7%D9%84%D8%A8%D8%B9%D8%AB%D9%8A_%28%D8%A7%D9%84%D8%B9%D9%84%D9%88%D9%8A%29&diff=87650&oldid=87648

66. IKHWAN WEB, The Muslim Brotherhood's Official English web site, *Experts: Al-Qaeda New Generation becomes more vicious than Bin Laden and Al-Zawahiri*. http://www.ikhwanweb.com/article.php?id=23185

67. Arabic website. http://www.masress.com/almesryoon/64778

68. PipeLineNews, *Muslim Brotherhood's "Justice and Freedom Party," Will Discriminate Against Non-Muslims and Women*. http://www.pipelinenews.org/2011/may/12/Muslim-Brotherhoods-Justice-Freedom-Party-Will.html

69. USA Today, *Why the Taliban are destroying Buddhas,* by W.L. Rathje. http://usatoday30.usatoday.com/news/science/archaeology/2001-03-22-afghan-buddhas.htm

70. Michael Arditti, *Magda Goebels,* by Anja Klabunde. http://www.michaelarditti.com/non-fiction/magda-goebbels-by-anja-klabunde/

71. Arabic website. http://www.ikhwanwiki.com/index.php?title=%D8%A3%D9%85%D9%8A%D9%86_%D8%A7%D9%84%D8%AD%D8%B3%D9%8A%D9%86%D9%8A

72. Arabic website. http://hobaheba.blogspot.com/2010/01/blog-post_5903.html

73. http://www.islamonline.com/news/print.php?newid=511450

74. Arabic website. http://www.christian-dogma.com/vb/showthread.php?t=98586

75. Discover The Networks.org, *Hasan Al-Banna*. http://www.discoverthenetworks. org/individualProfile.asp?indid=1368

76. Arabic website. http://www.ikhwanwiki.com/index.php?title=%D8%AD%D9% 88%D8%A7%D8%B1_%D9%85%D8%B9_%D8%AF%D9%83%D8%AA%D9%88 %D8%B1%D8%A9_%D8%B2%D9%8A%D9%86%D8%A8_%D8%B9%D8%A8%D8 %AF_%D8%A7%D9%84%D8%B9%D8%B2%D9%8A%D8%B2

77. Video in Arabic. http://www.youtube.com/watch?v=KoMi_N3ZZAU

78. Video in Arabic, with Audio English Translation. http://www.prophecyinthe news.com/

79. http://mediastop4all.com/video/KoMi_N3ZZAU/%D8%A7%D9%84%D8%A3% D8%B3%D8%AA%D8%A7%D8%B0%D9%87-%D8%B2%D9%8A%D9%86%D8 %A8-%D8%B9%D8%A8%D8%AF%D8%A7%D9%84%D8%B9%D8%B2%D9%8A %D8%B2-%D9%88%D9%85%D8%AD%D8%A7%D9%88%D9%84%D8% A9-%D8%AA%D9%86%D8%B5%D9%8A%D8%B1-%D8%A7%D9

80. Video in Arabic. http://www.youtube.com/watch?v=uo7JaBCmeVk

81. Arabic website. http://hobaheba.blogspot.com/2010/01/blog-post_5903.html

82. Arabic website. http://magmj.com/index.jsp?inc=5&id=5990&pid=1369&ver sion=83

83. Arabic website with Video. http://www.ikhwantube.org/video/1657265/%25D8 %25AF-%25D9%2585%25D8%25AD%25D9%258A%25D9%258 A-%25D8%25AD%25D8%25A7%25D9%25B6%2585%25D8%25AF- -%25D8%25B9%25D8%25D9%2588-%25D9%2585%25D9%2583% 25D8%25AA5%25D8%25A8-%25D8%25A7%25D9%2584%25D8%25 A7%25D8%25B1%25D8%25B4%25D8%25A7%25D8%25AF -%25D9%2588%25D8%25B4%25D8%25B1%25D8%25AD -%25D8%25B1%25D8%25B3%25D8%25A7%25D9%2584%25D8%25 A9-%25D8%25A5%25D9%2584%25D

84. http://www.islamicpl.net/2010-05-22-23-17-54/82-2009-07-25-10-15-35.html

85. http://www.ikhwan.net/wiki/index.php?title=%D8%A7%D9%84%D8%AD%D8 %B1%D9%8A%D8%A9_%D9%82%D8%A7%D8%AF%D9%85%D8%A9

86. BBC, History, *Philippe Pétain (1856-1951)*. http://www.bbc.co.uk/history/ historic_figures/petain_philippe.shtml

87. The World at War, *Marshal Henri Philippe Pétain*. http://worldatwar.net/biog raphy/p/petain/

88. Arabic website. http://www.albalqanews.net/NewsDetails.aspx?NewsID=12351

89. http://wwwwww.ikhwanonline.com/new/Article.aspx?ArtID=29317&SecID=450

90. Arabic website with Video. http://www.ikhwantube.org/video/1656800/%25
D8%25AF-%25D9%2585%25D9%2586%25D8%25A7%25D9%2584-%25
D8%25A3%25D8%25A8%25D9%2588%25A7%25D9%2584%25D8%25AD%25D
%25B3%25D9%2586%25D9%2585%25D8%25B1%25D8%25B4%25D8%25AD%
25D8%25A9%25D8%25A7%25D9%2584%25D8%25A5%25D8%25AE%25D9%25
88%25D8%25A7%25D9%2586%25D8%25A8%25D8%25AF%25D8%25A7%25D8
%25A6%25D8%25B1%25D8%25A9%25D9%2585%25D8%25AF%25D9%258A%
25D9%25

91. Arabic/English website. http://manalabulhassan.blogspot.com/p/about-me.html

92. Arabic website. http://ar-ar.facebook.com/people/%D8%B1%D9%8A%D8%
AD%D8%A7%D9%86%D8%A9-%D8%A7%D9%84%D8%AC%D9%86%D9%
87/100002314243437

93. Arabic website. http://elgornal.net/

94. http://dailynewsegypt.com/2011/07/03/muslim-sisterhood-holds-first-conference-in-60-years/

95. Jewish Virtual Library, A Division of The American-Israeli Cooperative Enterprise, *Women of the Third Reich.* http://www.jewishvirtuallibrary.org/jsource/Holocaust/women.html

96. http://www.history.co.uk/encyclopedia/nazi-party.html

97. Jewish Virtual Library, A Division of The American-Israeli Cooperative Enterprise, *The Muslim Brotherhood.* http://www.jewishvirtuallibrary.org/jsource/Terrorism/muslimbrotherhood.html

98. Video: *Muslim Brotherhood Reverses Pledge.* http://www.youtube.com/watch?v=tz1LNI1VINM&feature=related

99. Arabic website. http://ikhwanonline.com/new/Article.aspx?ArtID=85649&SecID=290

100. Video: *Muslim Brotherhood Reverses Pledge.* http://www.youtube.com/watch?v=tz1LNI1VINM&feature=related

101. IKHWAN WEB, The Muslim Brotherhood's Official English web site, *Who's afraid of 9/11 conspiracy theories?* by Maidhc Ó Cathail. http://www.freemuslimbrotherhood.com/article.php?id=24071

102. The Middle East Media Research Institute, *Egyptian Cleric Miqdam Al-Khadhari on the Benefits of Al-Azhar Curricula: They are the Only Textbooks to Militarize the Students and Explicitly Teach Jihad and Hatred of Jews,* Excerpts from interview

with Egyptian cleric Miqdam Al-Khardhari. http://www.memri.org/report/en/0/0/0/0/0/0/5059.htm

103. IPT – The Investigative Project on Terrorism, *MB Wants Satellite Channel; Cleric Wants Nation*. http://www.investigativeproject.org/2623/mb-wants-satellite-channel-cleric-wants-nation

104. Arabic website. http://www.ikhwanwiki.com/index.php?title=%D9%85%D9%83%D8%A7%D8%B1%D9%85_%D8%A7%D9%84%D8%AF%D9%8A%D8%B1%D9%8A_%28%D8%B5%D9%88%D8%B1%29

105. Arabic website. http://www.ikhwanwiki.com/index.php?title=%D9%85%D9%83%D8%A7%D8%B1%D9%85_%D8%A7%D9%84%D8%AF%D9%8A%D8%B1%D9%8A

106. Arabic website. http://www.ikhwanwiki.com/index.php?title=%D9%85%D9%83%D8%A7%D8%B1%D9%85_%D8%A7%D9%84%D8%AF%D9%8A%D8%B1%D9%8A

107. FaithFreedom.org, *Al-Azhar University Curricula Encourages Extremism and Terrorism*, by Dr. Sayyid al-Qimni. http://www.faithfreedom.org/articles/islamic-jihad-articles/al-azhar-university-curricula-encourages-extremism-and-terrorism/

108. Discover The Networks.org, *Muslim Brotherhood (MB)*. http://www.discoverthenetworks.org/groupProfile.asp?grpid=6386

109. Old National Review, *The Egyptian Jihad on America, An unaddressed front of the war on terror*, by Steven Stalinsky. http://old.nationalreview.com/comment/stalinsky200404120847.asp

110. http://www.ansamed.info/ansamed/en/news/ME.XEF33040.html

111. http://www.elfagr.org/error.aspx?aspxerrorpath=/Portal_NewsDetails.aspx

112. IKHWAN WEB, The Muslim Brotherhood's Official English web site,*Dr. Ibrahim El Zafarani: Regime Still Adopts Despotic Policy*, by Maamon Ahmad. http://www.ikhwanweb.com/article.php?id=3673

113. Arabic website. http://ikhwanwiki.com/index.php?title=%D8%B9%D8%B5%D8%A7%D9%85_%D8%A7%D9%84%D8%B9%D8%B1%D9%8A%D8%A7%D9%86

114. Dialogue of Civilizations, *Divided Egypt*. http://egypt-dialogue.blogspot.com/2011/02/interview-with-dr-essam-el-erian-muslim.html#!/

115. The Global Muslim Brotherhood Daily Report, *Egyptian Supreme Guide Resignation Reports Trigger Media Speculation in the Middle East*, Report by Al-Ahram. http://globalmbreport.org/?p=1679

116. http://www.alrai.com/pages.php?news_id=325788

117. Arabic website. http://hobaheba.blogspot.com/2010/01/blog-post_5903.html

118. http://ikhwanwiki.org/index.php?title=

119. Arabic website. http://www.ikhwanwiki.com/index.php?title=%D8%A3%D9%85 %D9%8A%D9%86_%D8%A7%D9%84%D8%AD%D8%B3%D9%8A%D9%86%D9 %8A

120. Arabic website. http://www.palinfo.com/site/pic/

121. USAID, 2000 Report, *Non-U.S. PVO Executive Contact List, Local and International Private and Voluntary Organizations,* PDF File. http://pdf.usaid.gov/pdf_ docs/PNACQ036.pdf

122. http://webcache.googleusercontent.com/search?q=cache:Bu66NPTp8MQJ :www.trapeen.com/vb/showthread.php?7654-%C8%D8%E6%E1%C7%CA- %C8%CF%E6-%D3%ED%E4%C7%C1-%E1%E1%E3%D4%DF%DF%ED%E4- %E6%D6%DA%DD%C7%C1-%C7%E1%E4%DD%E6%D3+

123. WikiLeaks, *Development and Peace Key to Resolving North Sinai Problems,* Origin Embassy Cairo. http://wikileaks.org/cable/2010/02/10CAIRO249.html

124. Arabic website. http://www.al-akhbar.com/node/1675

125. Arabic website. http://98.130.162.161/news.php?id=4966&cat=4

126. Arabic website. http://www.wamy.ws/tawasol/showthread.php?t=9794

127. Arabic website. http://www.4shbab.net/vb/showthread.php?t=34014

128. Arabic website. http://www.inshad.com/forum/showthread.php?p=2761984

129. Video in Arabic with some English Subtitles. http://www.youtube.com/watch? v=W5KpoL3UNYO

130. http://www.eslah.com/new/nashat_only.php?ID=15

131. Arabic website. http://www.esh-wmn.org/test/nsa/content-6.html

132. Arabic website. http://www.alanba.com.kw/absolutenmnew/templates/local 2010.aspx?articleid=116868&zoneid=14&m=0

133. Arabic website. http://jamaat.org/ur/

134. http://webcache.googleusercontent.com/search?q=cache:-sLDbpxBkwIJ: www.nna-leb.gov.lb/archive/26-04-2004/JOU40.html+%22+%22&cd=57 &hl=en&ct=clnk&gl=us&source=www.google.com

SECTION

4

Resuscitation And Collaboration

CHAPTER

9

OTTOMAN CONNECTION

EMPIRE'S EMBERS GET SECOND WIND

*W*hen westerners hear the word 'ottoman' they typically think of putting their feet up but the word *should* put them on their toes. Though the Muslim Brotherhood was formed in Egypt, the inspiration for its creation was the reestablishment of the Ottoman Empire, which was centered in modern day Turkey. Like the dying embers of a fire, the empire was thought to have expired after WWI but like a hidden, stray hot coal, the hope of rekindling the flame was never extinguished. Four years after being dismantled, Hasan al-Banna began applying the bellows to that hot coal when he founded the Muslim Brotherhood.

After WWI, the Republic of Turkey was formed; it would become the most powerful, secular Arab ally of the West in the twentieth century. The country's first president was a man by the name of Mustafa Kemal Atatürk, who would usher in several decades that included a modernized and secularist Turkey. According to the *BBC*:

> He (Atatürk) launched a programme of revolutionary social and political reform to modernise Turkey. These reforms included the emancipation of women, the abolition of all Islamic institutions and the introduction of Western legal codes, dress, calendar and alphabet, replacing the Arabic script with a Latin one. Abroad he pursued a policy of neutrality, establishing friendly relations with Turkey's neighbours.[1]

Over the next several decades, Turkey would become home to multiple military coups that were intended to protect the country's secular form of government. Until 2007, those coups had been successful in overthrowing leaders who attempted to usurp or alter the Republic's Kemalist government. The last successful military coup d'état that secured the Republic occurred in 1997 when an Islamist coalition, headed by Necmettin Erbakan was successfully pressured to step down after the military feared the coalition was in the process of installing an Islamist-style theocracy.[2]

NAZIM EL KIBRISI

In order to lay the groundwork for what ultimately happened in 2007, let's go back to a packed stadium in Anvers, Belgium in 1994. A Sheikh named Nazim el Kibrisi was given the podium and spoke to an audience that included Erbakan and future Prime Minister of Turkey, Recep Tayyip Erdoğan. Some reports placed future president Abdullah Gül in the audience but unlike Erbakan and Erdoğan, Gül's presence is more difficult to confirm with the video.

Keep in mind that Kibrisi was a figure who longed for a time gone by; it involved a Turkey prior to 1924. Erdoğan and Erbakan had a front row seat as they were part of a raucous crowd that supported what Kibrisi had to say, which was all about motivating the youth in the audience to reestablish the Ottoman Empire:

> "This flood of people here is a small sign of the glorious rise of Islam. May they not think that this is the great sign. When the great sign appears, the world will shake (chants of 'allahu-akhbar'). Our forefathers made the world to tremble. While holding the flag of Islam, the world was made to tremble. This gathering is a memento from our forefathers. Today is showing that the youth are starting to take care of and protect the inheritance left over from our forefathers. Unfortunately, during these last 70 years, we could not be proper inheritors to the 600 year old legacy of our glorious forefathers who were carrying the flag of Islam. We find indolence and degradation upon us because we were not proper heirs. The ones who will change the indolence and degradation to dignity are you, o youth. You are the grandchildren of the Ottomans. It will be the Ottomans who make the world tremble again. If the Ottomans do not come back, the unbelievers will never be brought down to their knees (loud cheers)."[3]

Note that last sentence about the unbelievers never being "brought to their knees" unless the Ottomans arise from the smoldering fire. The implication is clear. Kibrisi spoke to a crowd sympathetic to bringing the unbelievers (westerners) to their knees; he then informed them that the formula for doing so was reviving

Ottoman hearts. Kibrisi was appealing to the youth in the audience; he was urging them to seize the mantle because their fathers and grandfathers had failed.

Kibrisi then closed thusly:

> "May Allah bring our dear president (Necmettin Erbakan), those who are serving, the youth, and all of you my young brothers, sons, and grandsons together under the same flag. History is made up of recurrences. Certainly, our glorious era will come. The day being born belongs to Islam...do not lose hope O, believers, turn your hearts to Allah. As long as Allah is with us, we will not need America, nor will we need the unbelievers of Europe, nor will we be servants to them, nor will we go on their path. This is enough to benefit us.

Clearly, Kibrisi spoke to a stadium filled with a receptive audience, about reinstalling the Ottoman Empire. It should be lost on no one that Turkey's then current and future Prime Ministers not only had front-row seats but sat next to one another. Three years later, the Turkish military forced the Erbakan government to resign out of concern that it was attempting to install an Islamist form of government.[4] As events played out in subsequent years, it would become apparent that Erdoğan would be more successful at dealing with attempts on the part of the military to prevent the overthrow of the Kemalist government. He would do so while wearing a suit and tie.

JUSTICE AND DEVELOPMENT PARTY (AKP)

In 1998, Recep Tayyip Erdoğan was jailed for inciting religious hatred. He did so while reciting a poem which would have surely made Kibrisi proud. Again, such incendiary rhetoric is reserved not for English speaking audiences but for Arabic or—in this case—Turkish ones. Here is the most noteworthy excerpt from that poem:

> "The mosques are our barracks, the domes our helmets, the minarets our bayonets and the faithful our soldiers..."[5]

Though sentenced to ten months, Erdoğan was released after serving approximately half that. In 2001, armed with the knowledge about how Erbakan was removed from power, Recep Tayyip Erdoğan founded the Justice and Development Party (AKP) along with none other than Abdullah Gül.[6] Like the poem

Erdoğan recited, Kibrisi likely would have approved of the Islamist party platform of the AKP as well.

Erdoğan would face what should have been a roadblock when he sought to become Turkey's Prime Minister in 2002. Instead, thanks in large part to Gül, that roadblock was essentially nothing more than a speed bump. According to Turkey's Constitution, no one with a criminal conviction was eligible for election. This prevented Erdoğan from running for office. From 2002-2003, Gül served as the Prime Minister and worked with Parliament to change the Constitution in that regard. When that change was successfully made, Erdoğan was elected to Parliament and Gül stepped aside. Soon thereafter, Erdoğan became Prime Minister.[7]

In what many viewed as an act of political reimbursement, the AK Party, headed by Erdoğan, nominated Gül for the presidency in 2007.[8] Some argue that Erdoğan nominated Gül for president so he could take Gül out of the decision making process that comes with being a Member of Parliament.[9] As you will soon see, there are significant differences of ideological opinion that exist between the two. When Gül won, he became the first Islamist president to hold the office since the fall of the Ottoman Empire. This greatly alarmed the secularist military, which had previously beaten back multiple attempts to overthrow Turkey's secular form of government.

With the rise of an Islamist government came a clearer line of demarcation between the secularist military and the AKP. Mistrust of the military on the part of the AKP leadership was high. In 2007, AKP seemed to throw down the gauntlet when it linked the discovery of multiple hand grenades and fuses in the attic of a house with what became known as the 'Ergenekon' conspiracy, an alleged attempt by Turkey's military to carry out another coup. Over 300 officers and military officials were detained as a result.[10]

Arrests and detentions continued as a result of the AK Party's conviction that the 'Deep State' (Ergenekon) had been secretly planning to overthrow the Islamist government with an operation known as 'Sledgehammer,' allegedly hatched in 2003. The showdown between the AK Party and the military seemed to end with the resignation of Turkey's military leaders, including its top commander, Gen. Isik Kosaner, a few short years after the discovery of those grenades. In essence, Turkey's Islamist government had been victorious over the military for the first time since the fall of the Ottoman Empire.[11] The *New York Times* quoted a writer for the Turkish daily newspaper Milliyet as saying the following:

"This is effectively the end of the military's role in Turkish democracy. This is the symbolic moment where the first Turkish republic ends and the second republic begins."[12]

Perhaps not so coincidentally, the birth of that second Turkish republic came shortly after the first Islamist was elected president of Turkey (Gül), who is also known as a Gülenist, not based on his own name but on that of Turkish Islamic scholar Fethullah Gülen, a very wealthy, politically connected JBTW artist who moved to the United States during the Clinton administration.

TURKEY'S LEADER IN AMERICA

Like Erdoğan, Turkish imam and scholar Fethullah Gülen said some things publicly that got him into some hot water with the Turkish authorities before the rise of AKP. Unlike Erdoğan, Gülen sought and found refuge by fleeing to the United States. For years afterward, he would live on a large estate in eastern Pennsylvania with his followers. Though some say Gülen's move to the US was about receiving medical treatment, his exodus from Turkey coincided with what were likely imminent indictments that were finally issued in 2000; Gülen had been secretly recorded giving quite incendiary sermons.[13]

In 1999, After Gülen had fled to the US, Turkish television aired some of his sermons. The content, originally in Turkish, was shocking:

> **You must move in the arteries of the system without anyone noticing your existence until you reach all the power centers...until the conditions are ripe**, they [the followers] must continue like this. If they do something prematurely, the world will crush our heads, and Muslims will suffer everywhere, like in the tragedies in Algeria, like in 1982 [in] Syria...like in the yearly disasters and tragedies in Egypt. The time is not yet right. You must wait for the time when you are complete and conditions are ripe, until we can shoulder the entire world and carry it...**You must wait until such time as you have gotten all the state power, until you have brought to your side all the power of the constitutional institutions in Turkey...Until that time, any step taken would be too early—like breaking an egg without waiting the full forty days for it to hatch. It would be like killing the chick inside.** The work to be done is [in] confronting the world. Now, I have expressed my feelings and thoughts to you all—in confidence...trusting your

loyalty and secrecy. I know that when you leave here—[just] as you discard your empty juice boxes, **you must discard the thoughts and the feelings that I expressed here.** [emphasis mine][14]

These words are not just dangerous to the West; they enunciate a strategy that fits perfectly with that of the Muslim Brotherhood. Think about the Muslim Students Association (MSA). Its primary goal is to teach Muslim students how to navigate upward through the political power centers of government. Is this not what Gülen was advocating in 1999?

In another sermon that caught the attention of the Turkish government, Gülen sounded very much like Kibrisi a few years earlier:

Now it is a painful spring that we live in. **A nation is being born again. A nation of millions [is] being born—one that will live for long centuries, God willing**...It is being born with its own culture, its own civilization. If giving birth to one person is so painful, the birth of millions cannot be pain-free. Naturally we will suffer pain. It won't be easy for a nation that has accepted atheism, has accepted materialism, a nation accustomed to running away from itself, to come back riding on its horse. It will not be easy, but it is worth all our suffering and the sacrifices. [emphasis mine][15]

A common theme among groups and individuals that buy into the Muslim Brotherhood's goal involves a high level of patience. Remember, the Ikhwan was started with a 100 year plan. When Gülen delivered these sermons, he knew that any such plan was decades away from coming to fruition. That knowledge is reflected in this excerpt from still another sermon:

The philosophy of our service is that we open a house somewhere and, with **the patience of a spider, we lay our web to wait for people to get caught in the web; and we teach those who do**. We don't lay the web to eat or consume them but to show them the way to their resurrection, to blow life into their dead bodies and souls, to give them a life.[16]

While in the US, Gülen filed for permanent residency based upon his being an educator and "an alien of extraordinary ability." The Department of Homeland Security under the George W. Bush administration denied the application but was overruled by a federal court ruling.[17]

While government entities were doing battle over Gülen's future in the US, the latter was hard at work, laying his web in the form of hundreds of charter schools, including more than one hundred inside the United States. The schools accept charges that they were inspired by Gülen while rejecting charges he's behind them. JBTW anyone? The *New York Times* reported that there are approximately 120 Gülen charter schools across the US. Many of the teachers and administrators have been imported from Turkey. The *Times* even reported on the possibility that the charter schools were receiving taxpayer dollars to help finance the Gülen movement.[18]

Gülen's influence in the United States has become substantial. For example, the Gülen Institute website proudly displays testimonials from former Secretaries of State Madeline Albright and James Baker, former Secretary-General of the United Nations Kofi Annan, US congresswoman Sheila Jackson-Lee, and others.[19]

According to the Gülen Institute's website, Albright said:

"In a world that lacks direction, there can be no doubt that a pathfinder is needed. It is much more likely to be found in the values that reside at the heart of **the Gülen Institute** and this luncheon series. These values include commitment to international dialogue, an understanding of cultural diversity, support for human justice and a love of peace." [emphasis mine]

Said Secretary of State Baker:

"Problems of the world would be easy to address if, on the global level, we develop ways of sharing respect for each other's religious perspectives. It is in this manner, **the Gülen Institute** and those who promote shared vision of interfaith dialogue provide truly invaluable leadership." [emphasis mine]

From Secretary-General Annan:

"I think it is extremely important to have institutions like **the Gülen Institute** bringing people together, getting them to understand that we all are in the same boat and in today's world you cannot be secure at the expense of the other, you cannot be safe and prosperous at the expense of other." [emphasis mine]

From Congresswoman Lee:

"The inspiration of **the Gülen Institute**, who understood the communicating the word of God, living for others, the spirit of devotion, sacrifice, fidelity and loyalty, was clearly the right path to take." [emphasis mine]

In a 2008 video message for the Third Annual Friendship Dinner at the Waldorf Astoria Hotel in New York, former president Bill Clinton delivered the following words to the Turkish Cultural Center Friendship Dinner:

"By being here tonight, you are contributing to lasting peace and security at home and abroad. You're contributing to the **ideals of tolerance and inter-faith dialogue**, inspired by Fethullah Gülen and his transnational social movement. You do it through your everyday lives and you are truly strengthening the fabric of our common humanity as well as promoting the ongoing cultural and educational ties that bind our world together." [emphasis mine][20]

The Gülenist schools conspicuously tout themselves as institutions of tolerance that teach secularist principles. Based on Gülen's professed objectives, these presumptions simply should not be made. Conversely, serious consideration should be given to granting domestic enemy status to Gülen, his followers, and his enablers.

There have been multiple reports that these charter schools are opened with American teachers but are eventually replaced with teachers who are imported from Turkey on H1B visas. The Philadelphia Inquirer reported on this very thing:

The visas are used to attract foreign workers with math, science, and technology skills to jobs for which there are shortages of qualified American workers. Officials at some of the charter schools, which specialize in math and science, have said **they needed to fill teaching spots with Turks**, according to parents and former staffers.

Ruth Hocker, former president of the parents' group at the Young Scholars of Central Pennsylvania Charter School in State College, began asking questions when popular, **certified American teachers were replaced by uncertified Turkish men who often spoke limited English and were paid higher salaries**. Most were placed in math and science classes. [emphasis mine][21]

In 2008, one Gülenist-inspired charter school in Minnesota named *Tarek ibn Ziyad Academy* (TIZA) was at the center of controversy—albeit not mainstream controversy—when it was learned that the school was using tax dollars to further the cause of Islam in the school.

Writing for the *Minneapolis Star-Tribune,* reporter Katherine Kersten uncovered some disturbing realities that existed within TIZA. For starters, there was a very real connection between the school and the Muslim American Society (MAS), a Muslim Brotherhood—affiliated group. Kersten wrote:

> Asad Zaman, TIZA's principal, declined to allow me to visit the school or grant me an interview. He did not respond to e-mails seeking written replies.

> TIZA's strong religious connections date from its founding in 2003. Its co-founders, Zaman and Hesham Hussein, were both imams, or Muslim religious leaders, as well as leaders of the Muslim American Society of Minnesota (MAS-MN).

> Since then, they have played dual roles: Zaman as TIZA's principal and the current vice-president of MAS-MN, and Hussein as TIZA's school board chair and president of MAS-MN until his death in a car accident in Saudi Arabia in January.

TIZA shares MAS-MN's headquarters building, along with a mosque.[23]

The connection to the MAS cannot be understated. In 2004, according to the website *Discover the Networks,* the Secretary-General of MAS proudly admitted that his organization had been founded by members of the Muslim Brotherhood.[24] This clearly shows a connection between the Muslim Brotherhood and Fethullah Gülen. Perhaps this is one of several facts that would explain why Gülenists are reticent to admit that their mentor is behind these schools. Instead, they say Gülen is the source of inspiration for them; he is not affiliated with them; it is quintessential JBTW. Consider the words of University of Oregon sociologist, Joshua Hendrick:

> "Gülen is both the reason behind his schools, and he has nothing whatsoever to do with them."[25]

In the spring of 2012, *CBS News' 60 Minutes* program aired a report on the Gülenist charter schools. Leslie Stahl opened her report by saying that Gülen "promotes (wait for it) tolerance, interfaith dialogue, and…education."[26] The conclusion reached by Stahl was that "incendiary" bloggers who expressed concern were probably just afflicted with "Islamophobia". After an unsuccessful attempt to interview Gülen for her report, Stahl credited Gülen with being the driving force behind a movement that installed a "moderate Islamic Democracy" in Turkey; she gave the schools a pass by concluding that while they were run by Islamists, Islam was not being taught.

Despite that conclusion flying in the face of what happened at the TIZA school in Minnesota, Stahl actually helped make the case she was trying to avoid making when she quoted Gülen as saying that the best way to further Islam is to do exactly what his movement is already doing:

> "...the Turkish imam Fethullah Gülen who tells his followers that to be devout Muslims they shouldn't build mosques—they should build schools; and not to teach religion, but science. In sermons on the web, he actually says: 'Studying physics, mathematics, and chemistry is worshipping God.'"[27]

In his 2005 book, *The Essentials of the Islamic Faith*, Gülen argues that science is an extension of magic and that Turks should use it to increase their power:

> "Jinn [demons] are conscious beings charged with divine obligations. Recent discoveries in biology make it clear that God created beings particular to each realm. They were created before Adam and Eve, and were responsible for cultivating and improving the world. Although God superseded them with us, he did not exempt them from religious obligations."

Gülen believes that God...

> "...uses angels to supervise the movements of celestial bodies, he allows humans to rule the Earth, dominate matter, build civilizations and produce technology."

If a Christian pastor spoke like that while having schools funded by taxpayer dollars, he would immediately be the subject of multiple left-wing news stories intended to impugn and pillory the character of any such pastor (assuming he wasn't indicted first). Shouldn't it be somewhat curious that the left in America chooses to ignore or whitewash the teachings of Fethullah Gülen? Gülen and his billions of dollars are even ignored while the schools inspired by his teachings, have in large part been given a pass.

60 Minutes' Stahl missed another rather obvious connection despite it being served up to her on a silver platter by Valerie Strauss of the *Washington Post*, who wrote just a couple of months earlier about what Gülenist insiders themselves told her:

> "...through education, we can teach tens of thousands of people the Turkish language and our national anthem, introduce them to our culture and win them over. And this is what the Gulen Movement is striving for."[28]

The facts are these. Fethullah Gülen was a source of tremendous concern for the secular Turkish government of the late 1990's. The government wanted him arrested for attempting to Islamize Turkey. After fleeing to the US, where he has been able to freely exercise his first amendment right of free speech while engaging in JBTW, Gülen has been an integral part of Turkey's conversion to an Islamist state that inches ever closer to embracing sharia law completely and overtly, with each Middle Eastern nation that falls to the Ikhwan; he does this while living in a foreign land and uses something antithetical to sharia law—the US Constitution—to do it. In fact, his movement does its part to incrementally push the US toward being more sharia compliant while also teaching our children.

Though Gülen lives in the US, he views Turkey as the center of a new caliphate uniting the Muslim world with a "Turkish renaissance" which will "ensure that religion and science go together and that science penetrates not only individual lives, but also social life."[29]

In short, Americans are being deceived in their own land, in their own country. The actions of a Turkish imam are radically changing the country he fled as well as the country he sought refuge in. Instead of revering the land he now sits on, Gülen spits on it while exploiting the children of its inhabitants; he even successfully denies that he has any connection to the brainwashing of America's children.

And he does it all with a two-faced smile.

WIKILEAKS

A look behind the curtain that hid diplomatic relations between the US and Turkey was provided courtesy of *Wikileaks*, when thousands of cables were released. While plausible deniability was likely sought by US diplomats when it came to the Gülenist movement, leaked cables would tell a different story. In particular, communications from US ambassador to Turkey, James Jeffrey, indicate a significant grasp of the issues. Prior to that, Americans who were interested saw behavior that was inexplicable on its face. *Wikileaks* cables proved that diplomats were far more informed than what they led the public to believe. Said Jeffrey:

> Gülen's purported main goal is to bolster interfaith dialogue and tolerance, but the notion is widespread among many circles in Turkey that his agenda is deeper and more insidious.[30]

In that one sentence, Jeffrey demonstrated that he understood exactly, the concerns of westerners who knew how to navigate the internet and who have been sounding the alarm bell relative to Gülen for years.

Another aspect of the cable that is beneficial has to do with the relationship between Gülen and Turkey's leaders. According to Jeffrey, President Abdullah Gül is considered to be a Gülenist while Erdoğan is not. This would indicate a schism in Turkey's leadership. Said Jeffrey:

> ...the political context for conversations about Gülen is complicated because President Gül is himself seen by almost all of our contacts as a Gülenist, while Prime Minister Erdoğan is not. Indeed, some of our contacts have argued that Erdoğan is so firmly outside the Gülen camp that Gülen loyalists view him as a liability.[31]

Reports are that Erdoğan is a follower of an older, Naqshbandi Sufi order while the Gülenists are partial to the teachings of a more contemporary Kurdish Islamist named Said Nursi. This ideological difference may be a significant source of any friction that exists between Erdoğan and the Gülenists, of which Gül is one.[32]

A SITTING TURKEY

Anyone who questions the desire of Turkey's political leadership to reestablish the Ottoman Empire should look no further than the words of Recep Tayyip Erdoğan himself. In late 2012, after several Middle Eastern / North African nations had essentially fallen to the Muslim Brotherhood, Syria's fate hung in the balance. As western leaders inexplicably bought into the lie that Turkey was still a moderate nation, Erdoğan publicly longed for Ottoman days.

In an article posted by *Hurriyet Daily News*, Erdoğan expressed not just an interest in his country's history but a desire for its resurrection:

> "We move with the minds of our Dumlupınar martyrs. We move with the spirit that founded the Ottoman Empire...We must go everywhere our ancestors

have been. We can not take [Atatürk's philosophy of] peace at home, peace in the world as passivity."[33]

Erdoğan made these comments at a time when Israel had reached a breaking point relative to Hamas rockets being indiscriminately fired into civilian neighborhoods; Israel had recently launched multiple airstrikes against Hamas strongholds in Gaza. The struggle for Syria was also at a fever pitch at that time; Turkey had a vested interest in seeing the fall of Bashar al-Assad.

Perhaps there has been no greater beneficiary when it comes to the 'Arab Spring' that began in early 2011 than Turkey. The world watched as dictators in Tunisia, Egypt, Libya and others were ousted. Westerners—particularly on the left—cheered at what they perceived to be the rise of Democracy in the Middle East. Western leaders seemed to implement policies that supported such views. Little, if any, regard was given to what would fill the vacuum.

Turkey's new Islamist leaders were very interested in filling that vacuum.

FOOTNOTES

1. BBC, History, *Kemal Atatürk (1881–1938)*. http://www.bbc.co.uk/history/historic_figures/ataturk_kemal.shtml

2. Historyguy.com, *Military Coups in Turkey (1960–1997)*. http://www.historyguy.com/coups_in_turkey.html

3. Video in Arabic with English Subtitles. http://www.youtube.com/watch?v=VhfnHKgF-yw

4. The Economist, Feeding the World 2013, *Turkey's Islamists: Erbakan's legacy, What a prime minister's funeral says about democracy and Islam.* http://www.economist.com/node/18289145

5. BBC News World Edition, *Turkey's charismatic pro-Islamic leader.* http://news.bbc.co.uk/2/hi/europe/2270642.stm

6. BBC News, Profile: Abdullah Gül, *Abdullah Gul's presidential ambitions have long alarmed Turkey's secular establishment.* http://news.bbc.co.uk/2/hi/europe/6595511.stm

7. BBC News World Edition, *Turkey's charismatic pro-Islamic leader.* http://news.bbc.co.uk/2/hi/europe/2270642.stm

8. Bianet News in English, *AKP Nominates Gul for Presidency.* http://bianet.org/english/politics/95121-akp-nominates-gul-for-presidency

9. Turkish Politics in Action, *Erdogan Versus the Gulenists?* http://www.turkish politicsinaction.com/2011/04/erdogan-versus-gulenists.html

10. The New York Times, Europe, In *Turkey, Trial Casts Wide Net of Mistrust,* by Dan Bilefsky. http://www.nytimes.com/2009/11/22/world/europe/22turkey.html? pagewanted=all&_r=1&

11. BBC News, Europe, *Turkey: Military chiefs resign en masse.* http://www.bbc.co. uk/news/world-europe-14346325

12. The New York Times, Europe, *Top Generals Quit in Group, Stunning Turks,* by Gul Tuysuz and Sabrina Tavernise. http://www.nytimes.com/2011/07/30/world/ europe/30turkey.html?_r=1&pagewanted=all

13. Middle East Forum, The Middle East Quarterly, *Fethullah Gülen's Grand Ambition,* by Rachel Sharon-Krespin. http://www.meforum.org/2045/fethullah-gulens-grand -ambition

14. Ibid, *U.S. Government Support for Gülen?* http://www.meforum.org/2045/fet hullah-gulens-grand-ambition#_ftnref47

15. Ibid

16. Ibid

17. USA Today, News/Education, *Court Orders U.S. to reverse immigration decision for Turkish intellectual,* by Osman Orsal. http://usatoday30.usatoday.com/news/ education/2008-07-18-scholar-religious_N.htm

18. The New York Times, Education, *Charter Schools Tied to Turkey Grow in Texas,* by Stephanie Saul. http://www.nytimes.com/2011/06/07/education/07charter.html? _r=1&pagewanted=all

19. Gülen Institute, *Testimonials.* http://www.guleninstitute.org/testimonials

20. Video, http://www.youtube.com/user/turkishcenter

21. Philly.com, *U.S. charter-school network with Turkish link draws federal attention,* by Martha Woodall and Claudio Gatti. http://articles.philly.com/2011-03-20/ news/29148147_1_gulen-schools-gulen-followers-charter-schools/2

22. Ibid

23. StarTribune, *March 9: Are taxpayers footing bill for Islamic school in Minnesota?—Group linked to Hamas,* by Katherine Kersten. http://www.startribune.com/ featuredColumns/16404541.html?page=all&prepage=1&c=y#continue

24. Discover The Networks.org, *Muslim American Society (MAS).* http://www.discover thenetworks.org/printgroupProfile.asp?grpid=6263

25. USA Today, *Objectives of Charter Schools with Turkish ties questioned,* by Greg Toppo. http://usatoday30.usatoday.com/news/education/2010-08-17-turkish final17_CV_N.htm

26. 60 Minutes, Video (Watch the Segment), *U.S. charter schools tied to powerful Turkish imam,* Lesley Stahl reports. http://www.cbsnews.com/8301-18560_162-57433131/u.s-charter-schools-tied-to-powerful-turkish-imam/

27. Ibid

28. The Washington Post, *Largest charter network in U.S.: Schools tied to Turkey,* by Valerie Strauss. http://www.washingtonpost.com/blogs/answer-sheet/post/largest-charter-network-in-us-schools-tied-to-turkey/2012/03/23/gIQAoa FzcS_blog.html

29. Asia Times Online, Middle East, *Fethullah Gulen's cave of wonders,* by Spengler. http://www.atimes.com/atimes/Middle_East/LF09Ak02.html

30. WikiLeaks, *Gulen – Turkey's Invisible Man Casts Long Shadow,* (Viewing cable 09ANKARA1722). http://wikileaks.org/cable/2009/12/09ANKARA1722.html

31. Ibid

32. Turkish Politics in Action, *Erdogan Versus the Gulenists?* http://www.turkish politicsinaction.com/2011/04/erdogan-versus-gulenists.html

33. Hurriyet Daily News, Leading News Source for Turkey and the Region, *Turkish PM talks Ottoman Empire, slams Turkish TV show.* http:// www.hurriyetdailynews.com/turkish-pm-talks-ottoman-empire-slams-turkish-tv-show--.aspx?pageID=238&nID=35405&NewsCatID=338

CHAPTER

10

COLLABORATION OF ISLAMIC SECTS

SUNNI / SHI'ITE NEXUS

$\mathcal{A}$ perception exists in the western world that Sunni and Shiite Muslims have a vehement hatred for one another. As evidence of this, experts point to Saddam Hussein, for example. The former Iraqi dictator sided with a Sunni minority that was brutally repressive to the Shiite majority. The wars between Iraq and Iran largely broke down along these lines as well. Still others point to Iran's hatred for Saudi Arabia based on the latter's treatment of Shiite clerics. In many ways, the hatred Iran's mullahs have for the House of Saud is greater than the former's hatred for Israel.

However, there are instances in which Sunni and Shiite Muslims work together. Consider the alliance between Hezbollah, which is backed by Shiite Iran, and Hamas, an arm of the Sunni Muslim Brotherhood.[1] What would make these two groups work together if each is supposed to consider the other as traitors to the real Islam?

To get to the answer, one almost has to zoom out from that epicenter of collaboration. Upon doing so, both Turkey and Iran begin to come into focus. If there is one common enemy of both countries, it is the nationalism found in places like Saudi Arabia and Iraq prior to Saddam Hussein's ouster. Additionally, as both Turkey and Iran continued to gain power after the turn of the century, each saw an opportunity to leverage the strengths of the other.

The Muslim Brotherhood was formed with the intention of restoring the Ottoman Empire. Turkey welcomes the idea of once again becoming ground zero for an Islamic caliphate. Iran sees Turkey as an ally in the fight against Saudi Arabia, which is hated by both countries. This alliance between Iran and Turkey serves as a nexus of collaboration between Sunni, Sufi and Shiite forces.

SEYYED HOSSEIN NASR

Seyyed Hossein Nasr is a University Professor of Islamic Studies at the George Washington University in Washington, DC. He is also one of the signatories to *A Common Word* (more on this later). Nasr, a Shi'ite, is also partly responsible for the expansion of Islamic and Iranian studies programs at institutions like Princeton, the University of Utah, and the University of Southern California (USC). Remember that the Muslim Students Association (MSA) was established to further the cause of the Brotherhood. Nasr seems to be someone the MSA could link up with.

Based on what is known about the intentions of the MSA, shouldn't westerners be somewhat curious about the agenda Nasr pushed at those universities?[2]

Nasr once gave a lecture entitled, "Islam and Modern Science," which was sponsored by the MIT Muslim Students Association. He opened his lecture thusly:

> "I feel very much at home not only at this university, but being the **first muslim student ever to establish a muslim students' association** at Harvard in 1954, to see that these organizations are now growing, and are becoming culturally significant. I am sure they play a very important role in three ways. Most importantly, in turning the hearts of good muslims towards God, Allah ta'allah. At a more human level to be able to afford the possibility for muslims from various countries to have a discourse amongst themselves, and third to **represent the views of muslims on American campuses** where there is so much need to understand what is going on at the other side of the world."[3]

Based on what is known about the intentions of the MSA, the fact that Nasr opened a chapter at Harvard in 1954 is more than just mildly disturbing, especially in light of the fact that his MSA chapter appears to have grown since he established it. There is another problem that Nasr demonstrates clearly in that excerpt from his lecture; it is one of assimilation. Note that in each one of Nasr's three examples of how Muslim groups are becoming "culturally significant," he espouses views that are antithetical to Muslim assimilation into western culture.

In *Dialogue with The Muslim World*, Nasr is quite revered. Here is a partial translation:

> "All the Islamic movements in Iran, including the religious reformers, considered Sayyed Hossein Nasr to be the greatest contemporary Islamic jurist. This

conclusion was thanks to his attack on the religious reformers and his stand for a fundamentalist interpretation of the Qur'an."[4]

Sayyed Hossein was recognized for having a fundamentalist interpretation of the Qur'an?! An Islamic fundamentalist with access to the highest levels of America's most prestigious learning institutions is recognized in Arabic for his allegiance to Sharia law which, again, cannot co-exist with the US Constitution.

Consider the example of Dr. Haddad Adel, the current spokesman for the Iranian Shura Council as a member of parliament.[5]

Adel's daughter married the son of Iran's Ayatollah Ali Khamenei, the Supreme Leader of Iran. Multiple sources report that this reality ingratiated Adel with senior Iranian leadership.[6]

Khamenei's new relative through marriage was also a proud student and follower of none other than Dr. Seyyed Hossein Nasr.[7]

In an article entitled "Fundamentalists Takeover Reformists," Iranian dissident Abdul Karim Soroush discussed a theoretical debate between himself and Dr. Seyyed Hossein Nasr in light of the unprecedented split between fundamentalist Islamists and reformers who face each other these days.

The Foundation for the Center for Dialogue of Civilizations, which aims to expand the dialogue between cultures, held a conference in Tehran on the theme of "Islam and Modernity". Several Iranian and foreign academics participated. In the theoretical debate, Soroush refused to derive all forms of politics and economics from the Qur'an. As he disclaims, he expresses support for democratic, secular Islamic forces that encourage separation between religion and the state to function in a parliamentary system.[8]

As Soroush was making reasoned arguments from Iran, Nasr's stand against reformation came from within the United States:

> "The strike against the reformers did not come from the traditional religious Muslim circles as expected, but from a thinker who graduated from Harvard University and Massachusetts Institute of Technology who was a researcher in Islamic science and enjoys a high status within Western academic circles that has no equal by any other Iranian scholar."

> Nasr objected, "the reconciliation between Islam and modernity is nothing more but to empty Islam from its contents."

In English, Nasr usually explains that he does support a reconciliation of modernity with Islam and then reverses it completely:

"...but this does not mean Islam is reconcilable with modernity," that "one of the main goals of the Quran is to, "find an Islamic society that prepares humanity to live under an Islamic government with its foundation stemming from Islamic Sharia laws in accordance to the Quran and the life (Sunna) of the glorified prophet."[9]

Nasr also accused Soroush of being, "...the type of second rate western scholar who doesn't understand either Islam or the West."[10]

On *Al-Jazeera*, Nasr explained away Islamic extremism thusly:

"...the reason for extremism is that a person is encapsulated as a turtle when he sees that his [Muslim] identity is threatened...people are despaired and lose hope when they see what happens in Chechnya, Palestine and Kashmir."[11]

That quote, translated from Arabic into English, serves to put Nasr even more on par with the Muslim Brotherhood, which has a history of using victimization and martyrdom to further its agenda.

THE ISMAILI SECT

One of the Islamic sects within a sect that is considered to be among the most innocuous to the casual observer is the Ismaili brand of Shi'ite Islam. The leader of this brand is referred to as the Aga Khan. In light of what we have learned about Seyyed Hossein Nasr, any affiliation he has with the Ismailis would be cause for further scrutiny of the Ismaili sect, not of Nasr.

Nasr is an advocate for Islamic fundamentalism and has very clear ties to the Muslim Brotherhood. One might think that based on this reality, the Ismailis would want nothing to do with someone like Nasr if they were as innocuous as they are portrayed.

On the contrary, Nasr is an integral part of the Ismaili movement. In fact, he is prominently featured on the Institute of Ismaili Studies website as a professor of Islamic Studies at George Washington University. If the Ismaili sect was as peaceful, harmless, or as innocuous as it as portrayed, why would it prominently feature a founder of a Muslim Brotherhood group?[12]

Additionally, Nasr was the first Aga Khan Professor of Islamic studies at the American University of Beirut. When coupled with his biography at the Ismaili

Studies website, this revelation places Nasr more firmly in the camp of an allegedly innocuous group. Unfortunately for that sect, the more closely it is associated with Nasr, the less innocuous it becomes.[13]

As further evidence that the Ismaili sect's views are more in line with those of the Ikhwan, consider the actions of Democratic Governor of Illinois, Pat Quinn. He announced the creation of the Muslim American Advisory Council (MAAC), which was created to help ensure Muslim participation in state government.

Perhaps more telling than what the members of the council hoped to accomplish are the names of the individuals on the list. Among them were Safaa Zarzour, security general of the ISNA and Ahmed Rehab, executive director of the CAIR-Chicago. Both of these individuals represent groups with very real ties to the Muslim Brotherhood and both groups were listed as unindicted co-conspirators in the Holy Land Foundation (HLF) trial.

There was another person of interest on the list of individuals who appeared on the MAAC. His name is Murad Moosa Bhaidani and that is significant because he was listed as the president, His Highness Prince **Aga Khan Shia Imami Ismaili Council** for the Midwestern United States. This is yet another connection between the Ismaili (Shia) sect and the Muslim Brotherhood.[14]

STEALTH COLLABORATION

While the Ikhwan and Sunni nationalists share a common view of Islam, the nationalism that separates them is an extremely significant bone of contention. In fact, the gap is so difficult to bridge that a Sunni / Shi'ite alliance is seen on one side. For all the differences that exist between Sunnis and Shia, there is one common goal at the heart of each movement—an Islamic caliphate. The desire of each sect to rid the world of national borders is strong; it trumps the Islamic brand each practices, especially in the case of Saudi Arabia, which is viewed as a prostitute of the West. The hatred both Sunnis and Shia have for nationalists allows for an alliance against those nationalists.

Moreover, if Sunnis and Shia can work together to deceive the West, they seem to do it gladly and at every opportunity. The Lowe's controversy serves as a perfect case in point.

LOWE'S CONTROVERSY

The Learning Channel (TLC) found itself at the center of controversy shortly after airing a program entitled, "All American Muslim" (AAM). The show focused on the lives of multiple Muslim families living in Dearborn, Michigan. The families were portrayed as being very westernized and the program was obviously intended to blunt anti-Muslim sentiment by demonstrating that Muslim Americans are really no different from ordinary Americans.

Lowe's, the home improvement giant, announced that it would be pulling its advertising from the program after a Christian group named the Florida Family Association (FFA) launched a campaign to get Lowe's to do just that. The resultant backlash from Muslim groups included the likes of CAIR, a Hamas front group. CAIR-Chicago's Ahmad Rehab levied charges of religious bigotry and Islamophobia against FFA and Lowe's.[15]

Rehab mocked FFA's reasoning, which was admittedly flawed because it lacked important evidence. FFA's argument was that TLC was portraying "…ordinary folks while excluding many Islamic believers whose agenda poses a clear and present danger…" Rehab indignantly interpreted this to mean that FFA was angry that TLC did not include terrorists in its portrayal of "normal" American Muslim families. While this was a distortion, it was effective because FFA put forth a somewhat easily assailable argument.

What would ultimately provide FFA the ammunition it needed to defend its position was the program's portrayal of a radical imam as a moderate one.

In the very first episode of AAM, a Shi'ite imam by the name of Husham Al-Husainy was prominently featured as a respected man of the cloth; he presided over the marriage of one of the Muslim women in the show, to a man who converted to Islam from Catholicism in order to marry the woman.

As part of my research into Al-Husainy's background, I discovered he was a signatory to an extremely anti-Semitic document known as the Jerusalem Document of 2009.[16] This document advocates for Jihad while expressing solidarity with Hezbollah and refers to the war against Zionism as one between "good and evil". The document also called on Iraqis living in the "diaspora," which includes Dearborn, to take note. Al-Husainy is himself an Iraqi Shi'ite Muslim who welcomed the removal of Saddam Hussain from power.

This alliance with Hezbollah made more relevant an interview Al-Husainy gave to Sean Hannity a few years prior to the Lowe's controversy. During that exchange, Hannity gave the imam multiple opportunities to denounce both Hezbollah and Iranian president Mahmoud Ahmadinejad. Al-Husainy obfuscated repeatedly and ultimately hung up the phone in anger without giving an answer.[17]

Moreover, Al-Husainy is the imam at Dearborn's Karbala Center. While he was featured alongside Muslim women donning westernized garb and colorful hijabs on the western television show, the way women are expected to dress inside the mosque is quite different. In the Karbala Center, all practicing Muslim women wear the full length, black hijab that covers everything but the face. These facts were not revealed on AAM, nor were the acts of self-flagellation among the men as part of a ceremony that memorializes the death of the Prophet Muhammad's grandson.[18]

In another *YouTube* video, Al-Husainy is seen speaking at the Saginaw Islamic Center in Michigan. During his talk, in which he mixes Arabic and English, the imam compared unnamed Zionists to Jeffrey Dahmer, Timothy McVeigh, and even Saddam Hussein.[19]

While Sunni terrorist groups like Hamas find themselves on the same side as Shi'ite terrorist groups like Hezbollah, individuals like CAIR's Rehab align with Hezbollah-sympathizers like Al-Husainy; this is another example of stealth Jihadists from two opposing sects coming together against a common enemy—the West.

As for claims that Lowe's caved to religious bigotry, the opposite appears to be true. Had Lowe's not pulled its advertising, it would have *fed* religious bigotry.

SUNNI SUPPORT FOR HEZBOLLAH

The Grand Mufti of Egypt, Sheikh Ali Gomaa, a Sunni, is that nation's government-appointed Muslim cleric. He is also a JBTW artist. In Arabic, Gomaa,[20] was not only a signatory to the *Basic Announcement of the World Campaign For Resistance to Aggression*[21] but one of its founders. That is a friendly title that no one who desires peace would object to, right?

It states:

> The Islamic nation is, in the recent period, subject to cruel aggression from the forces of oppression and tyranny, primarily the Zionist forces and the American administration, led by the extreme right, that acts to impose [their]

hegemony on the nations and on the peoples and to change their curricula and their social system [translation].

It is littered with inflammatory rhetoric that asserts the Zionists, with the American Administration…

…conspire to ease their supremacy over all peoples and nations, rob their resources, destroy their will, and change their social values [translation].[22]

Aside from Gomaa's hatred of the West, he supports Shi'ite terrorist group, Hezbollah. In fact, during the 2006 Israel-Hezbollah War, the *New York Times* reported that Gomaa and none other than Brotherhood leader, Yusuf al-Qaradawi were on the same page when it came to choosing sides:

Egypt's grand mufti, Sheik Ali Gomaa, the country's highest religious authority, issued a statement supporting Hezbollah, while Sheik Youssef Qaradawi, whose program on Al Jazeera makes him one of the Arab world's most influential clerics, defined supporting the guerrillas as a "religious duty."[23]

Unlike Qaradawi, Gomaa played the political game effectively enough to avoid exile. Official government clerics have been stigmatized by fundamentalists as being collaborators who do not bite the hand that feeds them. After browsing Arabic blogs, one can see the mistrust of Gomaa by the Muslim masses in the Middle East to the extent of his being called "The filthy dog of Egypt".

That was before the 'Arab Spring'.

Prior to the fall of Mubarak, Gomaa was between a rock and a hard place—he could either please the masses or please the Egyptian government. Now that even Qaradawi can set foot on Egyptian soil, Gomaa need not be so careful about playing both sides. In the past, one could always find contradictory statements that pleased both but one thing is certain—the Arabic rarely jibed with the English. Perhaps Gomaa's true colors will be further revealed in the post-Mubarak era and the west can stop seeking the issuance of his friendly fatwas. The good news could be that westerners will stop looking for love in all the wrong places.

Westerners who think that Gomma is an example of the fruits of western modernity fail to examine his statements in Arabic; they are among the most discussed topics about him. In Arabic, Gomma defends the custom of Prophet Muhammad's disciples enjoying the healing powers in drinking the prophet's urine. **Dubai, Arab Net, May 23, 2007.**[24]

There have also been conflicting statements relative to his support for or the denunciation of the mutilation of female genitalia; the fatwas switch depending on the audience he is addressing. Gomma can switch views to the extent of even supporting a unity between Shia and Sunni Islam; the one thing that remains constant is a hatred for Israel.

When it comes to the Shi'ite Hezbollah and the Sunni Hamas, Muslim fundamentalists unite in a common cause that is the defeat of Zionism. They also unite around another very common cause—the eradication of nationalism.

However, as Arabic nations fall to Universalist movements like the Muslim Brotherhood, the Ottoman revival, and Iran's Islamic Revolution, those Islamic forces will eventually square off against one another. Until then, the old adage that says, "the enemy of my enemy is my friend" will remain in effect.

IRAN'S ROLE IN 9/11 ATTACKS

Perhaps nothing more perfectly demonstrates the ability for Islamic sects to put aside their differences in order to fight against a common infidelic enemy than the implications of a ruling made by a federal judge in a US District Court in New York, just three days before Christmas in 2011.

On September 11, 2001 Fiona Havlish's husband was one of the thousands of victims murdered at the hands of Islamic jihadists who rammed hijacked commercial airliners into the World Trade Center towers; Donald Havlish died inside the north tower. A few short months later, Fiona led an action, joined by the families of other 9/11 victims, against those responsible for the attack.

No one could have predicted the outcome of that lawsuit. Judge George B. Daniels signed a 53 page document that consisted of 276 Findings of Fact and 35 Conclusions of Law; it asserted that Iran, Hezbollah, al-Qaeda, and several other Iranian agents / agencies were behind the 9/11 attacks.[25]

A relevant portion of the 9/11 Commission Report that was released in 2004 can be found on pages 240-241. Those pages highlight evidence that Iran and Hezbollah (Shi'ite) collaborated in some fashion with al-Qaeda (Sunni).

> ...senior managers in al-Qaeda maintained contacts with Iran and the Iranian-supported worldwide terrorist organization Hezbollah...[26]

The Commission concluded that what limited information it had about these connections warranted further investigation by the United States government.

That was not done. However, a law firm by the name of Mellon Webster & Shelly took the case and represented the plaintiffs in *Havlish, et al. v. Iran, et al.*

Janice Kephart, a former 9/11 Commission counsel who helped develop much of the information that pointed to an Iranian/Hezbollah connection, was also an expert witness in *Havlish.*

A key component in Havlish that helped Daniels arrive at the ruling he did involved an Iranian defector named Abolghasem Mesbahi, whose testimony had been deemed credible by two former undercover CIA officers and supervisors, according to Kephart.[27] Mesbahi was also found to be credible by the judge, in part, because the Iranian had testified in successful cases against Iranian and Hezbollah terrorists previously.[28]

According to Kephart, the groundwork for the plan that would ultimately come to fruition on September 11th first began getting laid in the 1980s with the participation of the same Ayatollah Khomeini that came to power during the Jimmy Carter administration. In fact, Kephart reports that Mesbahi had direct contact with Khomeini in the 1980s, during the time that Mesbahi helped to set up Iran's Ministry of Information and Security (MOIS).[29] Interestingly, MOIS also became a named defendant in *Havlish* as the case progressed.

Statement of fact #158 in the document Daniels signed, reveals that Mesbahi fled Iran in 1996 after being tipped off by a colleague named Saeed Emami, that the Iranian regime had put Mesbahi on a kill list.[30]

Among the most significant revelations relative to Mesbahi's testimony had to do with his claim that he was in receipt of three coded messages—from his sources inside Iran—over the course of the two months prior to the September 11th attacks. The first message came on July 23, 2001. That message came with three words: *"Shaitan dar Atash,"* which is Farsi for "Satan in Fire".[31] This phrase originated in the mid-1980s and described what happened on 9/11 from the Islamists' perspective. The plan to fly hijacked commercial airliners into the World Trade Center, Pentagon, and White House was not new; it had been crafted years earlier, thanks to a joint task force, which consisted of MOIS and the Islamic Revolutionary Guard Corps (IRGC), also a defendant in *Havlish.*[32]

Mesbahi testified that he received another coded message on August 13, 2001. In it, he was told that *Shaitan dar Atash* had been activated.[33] The third coded message Mesbahi received came through on August 27, 2001. In addition to confirming *Shaitan dar Atash* was still a go, it made reference to a German connection.[34] The 9/11 Commission determined that the terrorist cell which consisted of ringleader Mohamed Atta, was based in Hamburg, Germany.[35]

Additionally, Mesbahi testified that he informed Germany's State Investigation Bureau, *Landeskriminalamt*, two days after the 9/11 attacks that they were planned and coordinated by Iran.[36]

Another very important figure in *Havlish* was a man by the name of Imad Mughniyah, the terrorist operations chief for Hezbollah.[37] As the head of Hezbollah, this made Mughniyah an agent of Iran. Kephart writes that al-Qaeda began its relationship with Iran in Khartoum, Sudan in 1993. Citing expert affidavits from Havlish, Kephart explains that there was…

> …a meeting between Iranian and Hezbollah leadership with al Qaeda leadership to bridge the Shiite-Sunni gap and address common goals of defeating Israel and the United States. A direct working relationship was created between Iran's MOIS; Hezbollah's operational chief and key liaison with Iran, Imad Mughniyah; Osama bin Laden; and other senior al Qaeda leadership. Mughniyah himself was responsible for more than 100 terrorist incidents until his assassination in Syria in 2008.[38]

According to these same affidavits, Mughniyah met with both Ayman al Zawahiri and Osama bin Laden, along with other Iranian officials. The purpose of these meetings was to form a terror alliance; Mughniyah essentially became a key liaison between Iran and al-Qaeda.[39]

Based on the ruling in *Havlish*, if the Bush administration didn't err by going into Afghanistan, it most certainly erred by invading Iraq. When the United States removed Saddam Hussein from power, it rewarded Iran for its role in perpetrating the 9/11 attacks. It would have been like declaring war on China after Pearl Harbor was attacked in 1941.

Japan hit the United States while proudly displaying its Japanese *Zeroes* on the wings of its planes. It was an enemy that was easily identified. Iran helped to place its perceived opponents *inside* our *civilian* planes in order to attack us on our own soil. The result was that the United States did not identify our enemy effectively. Indications are that we attacked our enemy's enemy in Iraq.

Ancient Chinese warrior Sun Tzu wrote in *Art of War*:

> Know yourself and know your enemy.
> You will be safe in every battle.

> You may know yourself but not know the enemy.
> You will then lose one battle for every one you win.
> You may not know yourself or the enemy.
> You will then lose every battle.[40]

It's safe to say that after 9/11, the United States may have known itself but it assuredly did not know its enemy. As a result, US forces won the battle to remove Saddam Hussein but lost the battle for Iraq, which meant a victory for Iran.

Western civilization has accepted a narrative that says the Shi'ite and Sunni sects of Islam do not work together because they are mortal enemies. The willingness of each sect to align with the other against the West should be a lesson learned by those on whom Islamic fundamentalists have declared war.

This gets back to the essence of JBTW, which is deceit. Sun Tzu spoke of this as well

> Warfare is one thing.
> It is a philosophy of deception.[41]

Iran appeared to go to great lengths to avoid being connected to the September 11th attacks. It did so, according to the decision in *Havlish*, by using proxies and liaisons that were willing to take the fall for a greater cause. After all, promises of a martyr's legacy are quite intoxicating to the mind of a jihadist.

IRAQ AFTER SADDAM

Saddam Hussein was a Sunni Ba'athist who ruled Iraq with an iron fist but he was also a nationalist. Iraq's Universalist, Shi'ite majority population essentially had two reasons to hate him.

A very flawed Iraqi Constitution notwithstanding, the United States did the Shia majority an enormous favor by removing Saddam from power. By extension, this did Iran's Mullahs a favor as well. The Shi'ites believe in an Islamic caliphate devoid of national borders. With western-style Democracy being exported to Iraq, the country duly elected a Shi'ite Prime Minister named Nouri al-Maliki. As long as US troops were present there, the ability of Iran to annex its neighbor was greatly hindered. That all changed—and quickly—when the last of those troops left Iraq.

Shi'ite religious leaders welcomed the US-led invasion of Iraq in 2003 because it gave them an opportunity to fill any power vacuum left as a result of

Saddam Hussein's removal. That's exactly what al-Maliki's election as Prime Minister did for them.

HADI AL-AMERI

As the last of the US troops were leaving Iraq at about the same time that Judge Daniels had determined that Iran was culpable in the 9/11 attacks, the Obama administration welcomed an Iraqi delegation to the Oval Office. That delegation included al-Maliki, as well as his Transportation Minister, Hadi al-Ameri. Documents translated from Jordan's *Al-Malaf Net* show that al-Ameri has, for years, been a terrorist agent for Iran.[42] The fact that he holds such a prestigious position within the Iraqi government helps to make a very strong case for Iranian domination of that country.

Those same *Al-Malaf* documents identify al-Ameri as a high ranking member of Iran's Badr Organization, the armed wing of Iran's Supreme Council for Islamic Revolution in Iraq (SCIRI).[43] The documents show that al-Ameri wasn't just a powerful member of Badr; he was a top figure in its Central Authority. One of the documents published by *Al-Malaf* identifies the Central Authority as an entity that takes its orders directly from Iran's Ayatollah.[44]

A *YouTube* video of al-Ameri bowing and kissing the hand of his Fuhrer, Ayatollah Khameini, further bolsters the claim that the former's allegiance is to Iran's Universalist view, not Iraq's nationalist one.[45] With all of this evidence against al-Ameri, wouldn't Prime Minister al-Maliki, at the very least, jettison him from his administration?

Not only would that be an incorrect assumption but at about the same time al-Maliki was visiting the Oval Office with al-Ameri, a warrant for the arrest of al-Maliki's Vice President was being issued. Tariq al-Hashimi was charged with terrorism. He is also a Sunni who had the wrong "S" next to his name, relative to new Iraqi politics.[46] Charges against him notwithstanding, al-Ameri's career as a terrorist is notorious indeed. The Foreign Affairs Committee of the National Council of Resistance of Iran (NCR) reported that from between 1992-2003, al-Ameri had played...

> ...a principal role in the planning and execution of some 150 terrorist operations aiming the PMOI during the period 1992-2003 causing a large number of dead and wounded.[47]

Al-Ameri's alleged role in the 1996 Khobar Towers bombing is also a source of great concern, especially in light of his visit to the White House during the Obama administration. The bombing, which took place at the height of al-Ameri's terrorist days, killed 19 US Servicemen. *Fox News* reported on the back-lash caused by his visit:

> Linked to the attack through a federal indictment, al-Ameri was at one time the Commander of the Revolutionary Guard in Iran.
>
> Now, many, including FBI Director Louis Freeh and Congresswoman Ileana Ros-Lehtinen (R-FL.) have expressed concern over the visit.[48]

Translated documents show that al-Ameri was instrumental in torturing Iraqi prisoners during the Iraq-Iran war. His victims allege that he was the "cruelest" of their torturers. Al-Malaf reports that this cruelty is what helped al-Ameri gain credibility among the Iranians.[49] Someone as brutal as al-Ameri needs an Auschwitz to make his persona complete. Camp Ashraf may just fit the bill.

Ashraf is a camp in Iraq that consists of Iranians who oppose Iranian domi-nance in Iraq. The likes of al-Ameri consider these inhabitants to be worse than traitors. As a result, when US troops left Iraq, these defenseless prisoners faced the prospect of liquidation, a solution that al-Ameri reportedly supports.[50]

Despite this overwhelming evidence that an agent of Iran had reached a high level of power within the Iraqi government, US Secretary of Defense Leon Panetta said the following just one month prior to al-Ameri's Oval Office visit:

> "...my view is that the region largely rejects Iran and its intentions and I think Iraq is at the top of that list."[51]

In 2003, the United States invaded Iraq to depose Saddam Hussein because the former believed the latter possessed Weapons of Mass Destruction (WMD). Saddam was removed but as the US pulled out more than eight years later, Iran— a country with a nuclear weapons program, in search of Islamic hegemony— was moving in.

It should be noted that the differences are not necessarily about the Sunni/Shia divide in a post-Saddam Iraq, though that divide does exacerbate those differ-ences. The Shi'ites see a golden opportunity for Iranian domination in further-ance of a global caliphate. If that means throwing the Sunnis under the bus, it will be done.

Remember that CAIR's Ahmed Rehab defended TLC's "All American Muslim", despite the program's promotion of Shi'ite Muslims, including Al-Husayni. This demonstrates a willingness on the part of Sunnis and Shi'ites to align when it's expedient. When either side is no longer needed by the other that alliance is subject to termination, as Iraq's vice president can attest.

As events unfolded in Syria during the inaptly named 'Arab Spring,' we saw this phenomenon at work. The Syrian government, led by Alawite (Shiite) nationalist Bashar Al-Assad, fought Sunni rebels which consisted of Muslim Brotherhood elements. This pitted Hamas (Sunni) and Hezbollah (Shiite) against one another after the two terrorist groups had worked together for years to attack Israel.

FOOTNOTES

1. National Review Online, The Corner, *Hamas Is the Muslim Brotherhood,* by Andrew C. McCarthy. http://www.nationalreview.com/corner/258381/hamas-muslim-brotherhood-andrew-c-mccarthy

2. The Seyyed Hossein Nasr Foundation, *About Seyyed Hossein Nasr.* http://www.nasrfoundation.org/bios.html

3. http://msa.mit.edu/archives/nasrspeech1.html

4. Arabic website with English translation choice, [SEARCH] *Sayyed Hossein Nasr.* http://ar.qantara.de/wcsite.php?wc_c=11335

5. The Daily Star, Lebanon, *Shura Council: Lebanon ready for good relations with Syria,* by Rita Boustani. http://www.dailystar.com.lb/News/Politics/Oct/01/Shura-Council-Lebanon-ready-for-good-relations-with-Syria.ashx#axzz1X8FEat8n

6. http://www.iranian.com/main/2011/jun/gholam-ali-haddad-adel

7. http://www.metanexus.net/magazine/tabid/68/id/9833/Default.aspx

8. Arabic website with English translation choice, http://www.ahl-alquran.com/arabic/show_article.php?main_id=8700

9. Arabic website with English translation choice, http://www.ahl-alquran.com/arabic/show_article.php?main_id=8700

10. Ibid

11. Arabic website. http://www.al-jazirah.com/magazine/10122002/zj5.htm

12. The Institute of Ismaili Studies, *Seyyed Hossein Nasr.* http://www.iis.ac.uk/view_person.asp?ID=181&type=auth

13. http://www.rumiforum.org/luncheons/islam-science-muslimstechnology.html

14. IGNN—Illinois Government News Network, *Governor Quinn Announces Creation of Muslim American Advisory Council – Names Members to New Council During Religious Observance.* http://www3.illinois.gov/PressReleases/ShowPressRelease.cfm?SubjectID=3&RecNum=9697

15. Huff Post Religion, *Let's Face it: It's the Radical Right, not Islam, that is the Greatest Threat to the American Way,* Ahmed Rehab. http://www.huffingtonpost.com/ahmed-rehab/lets-face-it-its-the-radi_b_1144842.html

16. Arabic website. http://albadrion.com/news.php?action=view&id=35

17. Video. *"All-American Muslim" Imam says USA an Oppressor Nation",* will not condemn Hezbolla http://www.youtube.com/watch?v=DxTcRzARLZk *(Part 1),* http://www.youtube.com/watch?v=GMRUSAS4MPw&feature=player_embedded *(Part 2)*

18. Human Events, Powerful Conservative Voices, *All-American Muslim' Star: Shocking Truths & Lowe's Good Call,* by aandbenbarrack. http://www.humanevents.com/article.php?id=48166

19. Video (in English), Saginaw Islamic Center. http://www.youtube.com/watch?v=K2Z526dziIU&feature=player_embedded

20. Ali Gomaa, Grand Mufti of Egypt. http://www.ali-gomaa.com/

21. Arabic website. http://alarabnews.com/alshaab/GIF/02-05-2003/bayan.htm

22. Ibid

23. The New York Times, *Hostilities in the Mideast: The Muslim World; Hezbollah's Prominence Has Many Arabs Worried,* by Neil MacFarquhar; Mona el-Naggar contributed reporting from Cairo for this article, and Jad Mouawad from Mukhtara, Lebanon. http://query.nytimes.com/gst/fullpage.html?res=9E0CE1DC113FF937A3575BC0A9609C8B63&sec=&spon=&pagewanted=all

24. http://www.20at.com/

25. United States District Court, Southern District of New York. http://information.iran911case.com/Havlish_Findings_of_Fact_and_Conclusions_of_Law_Signed_12-22-11.pdf

26. The 9/11 Commission Report. http://www.911commission.gov/report/911Report.pdf

27. The Washington Times, *Kephart: What now? Court: Iran, Hezbollah partly responsible for 9/11,* by Janice Kephart. http://www.washingtontimes.com/news/2011/dec/30/what-now/

28. Havlish, et al vs. Osama Bin Laden, Iran, et al, *U.S. District Court Rules Iran Behind 9/11 Attacks.* http://www.iran911case.com/

29. The Washington Times, *Kephart: What now? Court: Iran, Hezbollah partly responsible for 9/11*, by Janice Kephart. http://www.washingtontimes.com/news/2011/dec/30/what-now/

30. Havlish, et al vs. Osama Bin Laden, Iran, et al, *U.S. District Court Rules Iran Behind 9/11 Attacks.* http://www.iran911case.com/p. 27

31. Ibid, p. 29

32. Ibid, p. 26

33. Ibid, p. 30

34. Ibid, p. 30

35. The 9/11 Commission Report. http://www.911commission.gov/report/911Report.pdf pgs. 160-169

36. United States District Court, Southern District of New York. http://information.iran911case.com/Havlish_Findings_of_Fact_and_Conclusions_of_Law_Signed_12-22-11.pdf p. 30

37. Ibid, p. 14

38. The Washington Times, *Kephart: What now? Court: Iran, Hezbollah partly responsible for 9/11*, by Janice Kephart. http://www.washingtontimes.com/news/2011/dec/30/what-now/

39. United States District Court, Southern District of New York. http://information.iran911case.com/Havlish_Findings_of_Fact_and_Conclusions_of_Law_Signed_12-22-11.pdf p. 17

40. Sun Tzu, *The Art of War,* Translated by Gary Gagliardi, p. 41, Clearbridge Publishing Seattle, WA 2003

41. United States District Court, Southern District of New York. http://information.iran911case.com/Havlish_Findings_of_Fact_and_Conclusions_of_Law_Signed_12-22-11.pdf p. 23

42. http://www.damasgate.com/vb/t230679/

43. Global Security.org, *Islamic Supreme Council of Iraq (ISCI),* http://www.globalsecurity.org/military/world/para/sciri.htm

44. Uruknet.info, *Hadi Al Ameri, Head of the Badr Brigades, blames Arabs for Iran's influence in Iraq,* Mustafa Amara, Azzaman. http://www.uruknet.info/?p=33567

45. *"Iraqi Minister of Transportation kissing the hand of Iran Supreme Leader Khamanae,"* http://www.youtube.com/watch?v=4dKIC-rsN7k

46. The Washington Post, Middle East, *Iraq issues arrest warrant for vice president on terrorism charges,* by Dan Morse. http://www.washingtonpost.com/world/middle

_east/iraqi-government-issues-arrest-warrant-for-vice-president-on-terrorism-charges/2011/12/19/gIQA7bbD5O_story.html

47. Foreign Affairs Committee of the National Council of Resistance of Iran, *Hadi al-Ameri, terrorist in charge of the Badr group of the Qods force accompany al-Maliki on US visit.* http://www.ncr-iran.org/en/ncri-statements/terrorism/11522-hadi-al-ameri-terrorist-in-charge-of-the-badr-group-of-the-qods-force-accompany-al-maliki-on-us-visit

48. Fox News Insider, *Terror Attack Victim 'Sick' Over Iraqi Minister Hadi al-Ameri's Visit to White House,* http://foxnewsinsider.com/2011/12/16/terror-attack-victim-sick-over-iraqi-minister-hadi-al-ameris-visit-to-white-house/

49. Uruknet.info, *Hadi Al Ameri, Head of the Badr Brigades, blames Arabs for Iran's influence in Iraq,* Mustafa Amara, Azzaman. http://www.uruknet.info/?p=33567

50. Foreign Affairs Committee of the National Council of Resistance of Iran, *Hadi al-Ameri, terrorist in charge of the Badr group of the Qods force accompany al-Maliki on US visit.* http://www.ncr-iran.org/en/ncri-statements/terrorism/11522-hadi-al-ameri-terrorist-in-charge-of-the-badr-group-of-the-qods-force-accompany-al-maliki-on-us-visit

51. Video, *Al-Amiri & Maliki vs Panetta on Iran, Iraq ties; White House guest, Iranian,* http://www.youtube.com/watch?v=lOG_4Vv_WHw&feature=related

SECTION

5

Spiritual Battlegrounds

CHAPTER

11
GROUND ZERO MOSQUE

THE IMAM

*W*hen it came to Imam Feisal Abdul Rauf's desire to erect a mosque near the site of the September 11th attacks in Manhattan, Americans began to focus on him; they wanted to understand his motives. He portrayed himself as a moderate but many began to question that premise. Before Rauf, Americans had been duped by another imam who was allegedly of the "moderate" persuasion. His name was Anwar Al-Awlaqi. Like Rauf, Al-Awlaqi condemned terrorism when speaking to American audiences. He even expressed support for "interfaith dialogue".

Just five months after the September 11th attacks, Awlaqi was invited to speak at a DoD luncheon as a moderate imam. Subsequently, he inspired a various number of jihadists, including Fort Hood shooter Nidal Malik Hasan, Christmas Day bomber Umar Farouk Abdulmutallab, Times Square bomber Faisal Shahzad, and others. After escaping to Yemen, Awlaqi became the number one target on the CIA's kill list. Then, in September of 2011, Awlaqi was killed in Yemen by two Predator drones armed with Hellfire missiles.[1] Prior to being exposed as an al-Qaeda leader, al-Awlaqi was successful in portraying himself as a 'moderate' Muslim.[2] Prior to being exposed, Awlaqi avoided sensitive questions about Hamas.

Similarly, Feisal Abdul Rauf decried extremism while saying that it's not easy to simply condemn Hamas because the issue is "complex."[3] This is nothing short of JBTW in English exclusively. While Rauf left himself enough wiggle room to avoid the perception that he endorsed the tactics of groups like Hamas and al-Qaeda, his equivocation on the issue indicated that he endorsed their goal—the establishment of Global Sharia. This was also a goal shared by al-Awlaqi.

Rauf didn't need to make multiple media appearances during the Ground Zero mosque controversy; he had the support of America's most powerful political leaders at the time. They included the president of the United States (Barack Obama), the mayor of the city that was attacked on 9/11 (Michael Bloomberg) and the speaker of the House (Nancy Pelosi). All ran interference for Rauf by telling Americans not to be alarmists, that Rauf should be judged by his "positive" accomplishments. A drawback to this way of thinking can, at times, be akin to ignoring a drop of cyanide in the punch bowl. Al-Awlaqi serves as the prime example. In 2001, he was considered moderate. In 2011, he was killed after rising to number one on America's kill or capture list.

Pelosi insisted that Rauf was moderate and that the 71% of Americans who opposed the mosque were: stereotypical, racist, divisive, inflammatory, hateful, Islamophobic, bigoted, ignorant and intolerant. She insisted that Rauf was all about reconciliation.

Conversely, no one could find Rauf's take on converts from Islam to other religions. Would he reconcile with them? Rauf was offered through FMU (Former Muslims United)—but refused to sign—a document that condemned the killing of converts from Islam to Christianity.[4] Rauf should have had no problem signing this, especially since president Barack Hussein Obama, an alleged convert from Islam to Christianity, supported Rauf.

The state department even sent Rauf as an envoy to discuss an "American-style Islam" and "Islamic democracy" in the Middle East. Will this American-style Islamic Sharia include interest banking since our whole capitalistic system depends on it? Will the Cordoba Initiative—the group behind the ground zero mosque—follow through with its promise of a swimming pool, lecture halls, sports centers and bridge-building classes include other religions? The name "Cordoba" was chosen to promote the golden age of Islam. Were Christians to be honored for accommodating a crescent in place of a cross? Were Christians supposed to be sensitive and not mention that the original Cordoba "Mosque" was built during the golden age of Christendom, not Islam?

Incidentally, more than two years after the controversy, an article in the *New York Post* seemed to indicate that a mosque would be all that the building once home to the Burlington Coat Factory would have to offer.[5]

Cordoba at WTC was supposed to be "an icon [Cordoba Mosque]". Americans began to ask: Is there no other place on God's green earth to build a mosque except next to the spot where Muslim hijackers killed thousands of people? During an interview that appeared on Arabic radio Hurytna, Rauf gave a romantic example of how Muslims should use dialogue with Christians and Jews to their advantage: "Deal with them as one courts a pretty girl he wants to date; stop thinking like a typical Muslim. Then you engage."[6]

Just what is a "typical Muslim?" Was this romantic technique used with Bloomberg?

In that same radio interview, Rauf was dumbfounded to hear that "Many American blogs print that Muslims want a Caliphate." It is an issue that Rauf needs to address. He should explain why Saudi Arabia is still Judenrein, which means "cleansed of Jews".

Westerners need to ask if Rauf's "American style Sharia" is any different from Anwar Al-Awlaqi's. And just how many versions of "Sharia" are there? Rauf says that Sharia is compatible with the US Constitution. As explained earlier, that argument is quickly debunked with Article VI, not the first amendment.

How are we supposed to verify Rauf's claims if every question meant to do so is quickly labeled as ignorant, stereotypical, and inflammatory regarding the Caliphate, beheadings, killing of converts, amputation of limbs or lashings for certain sins and infractions?

Even if we keep the discussion "civil", the following questions are apparently not allowed: Will "American Sharia law" protect marriage between Jewish men and Muslim women? Will inheritance be distributed equally to males as well as to females under "American Sharia law?" Will the sale of mosque properties be allowed to include setting up places of worship for other faiths?

Rauf, in his attempt at "reconciliation" stated: "We all worship the same God." So, can Christians salute Rauf: "we salute you in the name of Jesus Christ, the Son of the Living God, our Lord and yours, right?" If he says, "yes" then indeed, we would have reconciliation, for Rauf would have converted to Christianity. If he says, "no" then we have exposed Rauf as a liar and JBTW as a reality. He was never challenged, just accepted without being vetted by any government official. He had free reign to gain a foothold in the United States. How influential was he and what are the origins of the influence he acquired?

INFLUENCE ON GOVERNMENT

Feisal Abdul Rauf boasted in Arabic, on Egyptian radio, that Barack Obama's historic speech in Cairo was taken from a manuscript written by Rauf entitled, "The Blue Print". Its contents provide what he sees as the solution to the Islamic-American divide in Chapter 6. According to Rauf, it was the Cordova Initiative that engineered the entire speech.

Plans that included everything from US policy to Jewish and Christian relations with Muslims were enunciated as being part of Rauf's strategy. His boasting can be heard during the radio Hurytna interview:

"We have to look at it [as] how to engineer solutions. The Cordova Initiative, we think of ourselves as an engineering shop. We have an analytical approach. Our work has been that. In the book, chapter 6, I wrote about this blueprint as to what has to be done by the U.S. government, what has to be done by the Jewish community, what has to be done by the Christian community, what has to be done by the Muslim community, what has to be done by the educators and what has to be done by the media. In my book in the Arabic version pages 293 what did I write? What are the things that the United States had to do? In this chapter you will find that the entire speech in Cairo was taken whole from this section. This is an example of the impact of our work in a positive way to be used by the president. When you do a job that is very complicated. You ask yourself, what have you accomplished? All these problems can be solved but requires the will to solve it. It requires political will, resources and the right focus. The signs of how to go to the moon were known 200 years ago, but the political will and financial will for it happened during 1960-1961. When John Kennedy said that we will send an American to the moon before the end of the 60s, he established the financial resources and the political will."[7]

Further evidence of Rauf's influence, which he boasted about, was revealed again in his answer to a question about President Barack Obama's speech:

"...the speech was wonderful and wise in his choice of words. The Prime Minister of Malaysia, after the speech, disclosed to me that it is now easy for any president of a Muslim country to establish good relations with America, and I am not going to hide from you that one of those who participated in the writing of the speech transferred entire parts of my book 'A New Vision For Muslims and the West' in which he referred to US interests being compatible with top interests of the Muslim world". *(Quote from a written dialogue with Hani Al-Waziri of Egyptian radio Hurytna was published on Ahl Al-Quran (Quranic Society).*[8]

Rauf did not disclose the name of the speechwriter who incorporated the Imam's work into president Obama's historic address in Egypt. There is reason to believe that a man who would later become Barack Obama's envoy to the Organization of the Islamic Conference—Rashad Hussain—may have been intricately involved in crafting this portion of the speech.[9]

It is crucial to note that the Arabic version of Feisal Abdul Rauf's book was published in Malaysia under the title, *A Call to Prayer From The World Trade Center Rubble; Islamic Dawa [Summons to Islam] in the Heart of America Post 9/11.*

The prominent Imam was considered a peace messenger for the US State Department. If Americans understood Arabic and compared Rauf's Arabic with his English, the shocking conclusions they would arrive at with respect to Rauf's intentions would be trumped only by conclusions drawn about the state department's intentions as a consequence of the partnership.

After researching several interviews and articles in Arabic that featured Rauf, it is striking how different his focus becomes when speaking to different audiences. In Arabic, Rauf is much less concerned with spreading what's right with America. Instead, he speaks almost exclusively about how to spread *Islam* in America and how to incrementally move this country in the direction of being "Sharia Compliant" while adopting "American style Islam."

"So what must America do now to win the trust of both the Arab and Muslim world?" Rauf was asked.

> "America must do everything in its power to assist in the establishment of an Islamic world that is confidant in itself and fulfills the principles of an Islamic society, assisting in the development of an Islamic capitalistic democracy. Also, it must take on three of the most major issues in the Islamic world. They are: religion, Control of Government and the distribution of economic assets (re-distribution of wealth)."[10] *(Interview with Hani Al-Waziri in Al-Masri Al-Yaum (Egypt Today) on February 7th, 2010)*

As an aside, a man who pumped hundreds of thousands of dollars into Rauf's Cordoba Initiative—Saudi Prince Alwaleed bin Talal—has expressed views that would seem to align him with the idea of wealth re-distribution as well. In an interview with Charlie Rose, Talal explained that he believed America's debt woes necessitated higher taxes. Talal told Rose:

> "Taxes have to be raised. There is no doubt about that in my mind, across the board."[11]

Talal is also the same man who tried to give then New York City mayor Rudy Giuliani a $10 million relief check in the days after 9/11; Giuliani rightly refused to accept it. Ironically, Rauf accepted Talal's money in order to help construct the Cordoba mosque near ground zero. Reasons given by those who object to the idea of constructing a mosque so close to where America was attacked by Islamic terrorists often point to a lack of sensitivity on the part of the builders and the Cordoba Initiative. Using Giuliani's standard, Rauf displayed insensitivity simply by accepting Talal's money.[12]

TRANSLATING RAUF

Rauf stated—in his interview with Hani Alwaziri—that his goal was "To establish an American-style Islam in the United States". He explained how his aspiration of spreading Islam in America required flexibility and the molding of Islam in such a way that it can become palatable to the American culture while preserving the integrity of Islamic ideology:

> "If we look how Islam was spread from Hijaz (Arabia) to Morocco then Turkey, we note that Islam was shaped by the culture and society, hence showing a Muslim version of the architecture and culture and the arts, but with preservation of the framework of belief and worship. We need to provide a GLOBAL ISLAM in accordance with the nature of each society."[13] *(Interview with Hani Al-Waziri in Al-Masri Al-Yaum (Egypt Today) on February 7th, 2010)*

Rauf boasted about his towering structure as "an icon that will make Muslims proud, not only locally but globally". Remember his suggestion to Muslims in Egypt on how to deal with western Christians and Jews is to treat them like pretty girls you want to date before engaging. He also discussed how he courted Bloomberg and the Jewish Community boards, saying, "we have inroads with the Jewish Community Center".

When the grand plan of establishing the Ground Zero mosque was made public, media outlets scrambled to find out more about the mysterious mosque entrepreneur and began to ask about him. No one could find any dirty laundry on Rauf—besides a few statements that were soon to be dismissed as having been taken out of context.

When I first rushed to help this nation, knowing quite well that many Muslim imams practice JBTW, I scrambled to research Rauf, to be the first to break the bad news. I was finally granted an interview with Laura Ingraham on her radio program and was quickly scheduled that same night on the O'Reilly Factor; Ingraham was the guest host.

To be balanced, *Fox News* invited Reverend Barry Lynn to provide a counter-viewpoint. In that exchange, Lynn was not even able to say the Imam's name, referring to him as "Imam Raul" while criticizing my credentials instead of addressing the quotes I gave regarding "Raul's" statements in Arabic. Lynn denied them, although he never read them or heard of them and doesn't know a word of Arabic. The quote I gave at the time was an excerpt from an article entitled *"Sharing The Essence Of Our Beliefs"* by Feisal Abdul Rauf in *Al-Ghad* Newspaper in Jordan. In it, he states:

> "If someone in the Middle East cries out 'where is the law,' he knows that the law exists. The only law that the Muslim needs exists already in the Koran and the Hadith. People asked me right after the 9/11 attack as to why do movements with political agendas carry [Islamic] religious names? Why call it 'Muslim Brotherhood' or 'Hezbollah (Party of Allah)' or 'Hamas' or 'Islamic Resistance Movement'? I answer them this—that the trend towards Islamic law and justice begins in religious movements, because secularism had failed to deliver what the Muslim wants, which is life, liberty and the pursuit of happiness...The only law that the Muslim needs exists already in the Koran and the Hadith."[14] *(Translated from the Arabic by Walid Shoebat)*

The only thing more fascinating than the views held by western liberals is how they analyze facts. While they deny my credentials as a terrorist, they have never refuted my translations by showing an alternate word for word translation—ever. In an attempt to refute my translations, *Media Matters* spoke to Ahmad Moussalli and referred to him as:

> "...a widely quoted expert on Islamic movements and professor of Political Science and Islamic Studies at the American University of Beirut, to read the Arabic sources Shoebat cited on August 18 to evaluate his claim that they

show 'a straight support for terrorism' and for 'Hamas, Hezbollah, the Islamic jihad movement.'[15] Moussalli responded that Shoebat's remarks are a 'blatant misrepresentation of the denotation and connotation of Mr. Rauf's statements in Hadiyul-Islam and Al-Ghad newspaper. Rauf never expressed his support for the three organizations.' Omid Safi, professor of Islamic Studies at the University of North Carolina and expert on Sufism, also reviewed the Arabic articles and concluded that 'they do not show any support for terrorism.' Safi added that 'the accusation of 'Muslim double-speak' is one of the common accusations used by Islamophobes like Shoebat' and said: 'I would simply suggest dismissing what comes out of his mouth as much as I would dismiss anything David Duke would have to say about the essential nature of Judaism.' It's deeply unfortunate that *Fox News* presents Walid Shoebat, who hates Islam, as a credible authority on Islam, but it is downright reckless and irresponsible to provide a national platform for Shoebat's claim that Rauf endorsed terrorism in Arabic—an accusation that aside from being false, fuels distrust and perpetuates anti-Muslim platitudes. In doing so, Fox has again shown that informing its viewers is not the networks' priority and that it is more than willing to play dangerously close to bigotry."[16]

Though *Google* translate is not the best source for translating languages, the reader can cut and paste the articles and see for themselves; Rauf clearly shows moral support for Hamas and Hezbollah. Yet, even professional interpreters and professors play the game of JBTW. No one can refute that I provided a reasonable translation that would be accepted by expert translators of Arabic—unless that someone is a practitioner of JBTW.

It's clear that Rauf disclosed his views to Muslims right after 9/11—that Hamas, Hezbollah and Islamic Jihad were born as a result of the "Muslim hunger for Islamic law and justice". According to the Imam, secular laws do not appeal to a wide swath of Muslims and that "all the laws Muslims need are in the Qur'an and the Hadith". It is Islam and not the secular American Constitution that "offers life, liberty and the pursuit of happiness".

Westerners think that the goals of "extremists" like Anwar Al-Awlaqi and Rauf are different. While Al-Awlaqi has goals, he ultimately decided to achieve them through explosive acts. Rauf is no different; his goals are the same. His means are different.

Rauf enunciates his Trojan horse method for accomplishing this goal in the Hadiyul-Islam article:

> "So we advise that when there is a problem in the relationship between state and religious institutions in the form of the question you just asked, that people need to use peaceful means to advise the governors and government institutions and use peaceful means that are available to send their message out to the masses. And we also suggest to the governors and political institutions to consult [Muslim] religious institutions and [Muslim] personalities in the field so as to assure their decision making to reflect the spirit of Sharia"[17]

When it comes to religious dialogue, Rauf was quoted in an Arabic article entitled "The Most Prominent Imam in New York: 'I Do Not Believe in Religious Dialogue'" that appeared on the Cairo University's media department website, *Rights for All.* In it, Rauf said the following about religious dialogue:

> "…this phrase is inaccurate. Religious dialogue as customarily understood is a set of events with discussions in large hotels that result in nothing. Religions do not dialogue and dialogue is not present in the attitudes of the followers, regardless of being Muslim or Christian. The image of Muslims in the West is complex, which needs to be remedied."

As far as separation between religion and state, Rauf admonished Muslims on their openness:

> "[In the West] they have separation of church and state; this of course does not exist in any Muslim country. About 99% refuse to separate religion from state and many call for establishing an Islamic Caliphate."

When Rauf was asked what it means to separate religion from state in Islam, he replies:

> "For that, we collectively believe that the state that was erected by the prophet in Medina was the ideal model for an Islamic state. The challenge today in the Islamic world is how do we accomplish this in our current era? The challenge I was referring to is this; how do we call for the principles and standards that the prophet (peace be upon him) used to build the Islamic state in Medina [Arabia]? An Islamic state can be established in more than just a single form or mold; it can be established through a kingdom or a democracy. The important issue is to establish the general fundamentals of

[Islamic] Sharia that are required to govern. It is known that there are sets of standards that are accepted by [Muslim] scholars to organize the relationships between government and the governed."

He is then asked:

"...but when the rulers are ruling under traditional laws contrary to Islamic laws, what then should the Islamic institutions do?"

Rauf never wavers in any answer to the strict usage of examples from Islam's history:

"A time after the prophet (peace be upon him) arose certain new conditions that required the governors to institute new laws so long as they do not conflict with the Qur'an and the Sunna that were Sharia compliant as such followed in tribal laws. So in our modern era, governments that want to ensure the new laws as to not contradict Sharia rules—so they create institutions to ensure Islamic law and remove any that contradict with Sharia."

In another question, Rauf was presented with a dilemma: "No doubt that there are disastrous results if the Islamic world kept going under the principles that are used with religious issues and state, but what do we do on a personal level while in the midst of this low class system that is established in our Muslim states?" Rauf is clever and responds without wavering:

"First and foremost, we need to understand what Sharia requires from us. Second, we need to be a part of a larger group that is capable to give advice [to the government] as is done by lobbies in the West. Thirdly: We become an institutional group to provide benevolent needs in the society.[18]

At the height of the Ground Zero mosque controversy, Rauf appeared on *CNN's* Larry King Live with guest host Soledad O'Brien. While he spoke in a soothing, soft voice, Rauf's words spoke volumes. In response to a question from O'Brien about the overwhelming opposition to the mosque being built so close to Ground Zero, Rauf let his mask slip, speaking like someone who was holding America hostage:

"If we move from that location, the story will be that the radicals have taken over the discourse. The headlines in the Muslim world will be that Islam is under attack. And I'm less concerned about the radicals in America than I'm concerned about the radicals in the Muslim world.[19]

A short time later, Rauf said…

> "The concern for American citizens who live and work and travel overseas will increasingly be **compromised if the radicals are strengthened**. And if we do move, it will strengthen the argument of the radicals to recruit, their ability to recruit, and their increasing aggression and violence against our country."[20]

It should be clear to any objective observer what Rauf was suggesting. If the mosque's construction proceeded as he wished, Americans would be safer than if its progress was impeded. How is this not an Islamic spin on the old thuggish adage which says, 'do what we say and no one gets hurt'? It's amazing what one can get away with saying when he does so in soft, dulcet tones.

As if it were necessary after everything presented here, those who raised red flags about Rauf continue to be vindicated. A year after the Ground Zero mosque controversy first developed, during a trip to Edinburgh, Scotland Rauf told an audience at the Festival of Spirituality and Peace that Sharia law needed to be incorporated into the legal systems of the US and the UK; he didn't even hide it.[21]

ENVOY TO ORGANIZATION OF THE ISLAMIC CONFERENCE (OIC)

Mentioned earlier as having been the most likely person very involved in translating and incorporating portions of Rauf's book into President Barack Obama's Cairo speech was Rashad Hussain. The level of collaboration between Hussain and Rauf may also help to explain Obama's support for the mosque in light of Hussain's role within the Obama administration. In early 2010, Hussain was essentially promoted from White House lawyer to the administration's envoy to the Organization of the Islamic Conference (OIC).

Soon thereafter, Hussain, a Hafiz (someone who has memorized the Qur'an) was at the center of controversy over remarks he allegedly made at a 2004 Muslim Students Association (MSA) event. The fact that Hussain was speaking at an MSA event itself should have been controversial because MSA is a Muslim Brotherhood group—according to a 1991 document introduced as evidence in the Holy Land Foundation trial—but it was his reported support of convicted terrorist fundraiser Sami al-Arian that made news.

Worse still was the discovery that Hussain was caught attempting to cover up his comments.

In short, The *Washington Report on Middle East Affairs (WRMEA)* quoted Hussain in 2004 as saying that the prosecution of al-Arian was "politically motivated". The reporter who filed the story insisted Hussain made the comments despite the White House's charge that they were made by al-Arian's daughter, who was also present at the event, not Hussain. The relevant portion of the article had been deleted from the internet version of the story. The editor of the *WRMEA* said someone requested the comments be removed in early 2009 because they were misattributed to Hussain.[22]

Hussain was caught with his hand in the cookie jar and did not lose his job as envoy to the OIC. In a *POLITICO* story posted late on a Friday night, it was reported that an audio recording of Hussain speaking at the MSA event had surfaced. At that point, both the White House and Hussain admitted that the new OIC envoy had *not* been misquoted; he had been accurately quoted. Perhaps even more surprising was Hussain's late admission that it was he who complained to the *WRMEA* and requested that the quote be removed. The Obama administration stood by Hussain, who continued in his role after what was all but confirmed to be lying about his supportive comments for a convicted terrorist while at a Muslim Brotherhood event. There was no word on whether Hussain apologized to the reporter, whose credibility was called into question as a result of Hussain's actions.[23]

All of this speaks to the character of not only Hussain but of the Obama administration. In naming Hussain as OIC envoy, Obama himself said Hussain "has played a key role in developing the partnerships I called for in Cairo."[24]

How about JBTW? Is there any evidence that Hussain has engaged in it? Based on his actions and words relative to the 2004 MSA event, it's certainly a question worth asking. Research of Arab media shows that, in fact, Rashad Hussain boasted in Arabic to Al-Ahram Egyptian newspaper associate Yahya Ghanem of "having the largest share in the formulation of the famous speech of President Obama from the podium at the University of Cairo, which set the general framework for a new relationship between America and the Islamic world." (Al-Ahram, May 11th, 2010)[25]

This only serves as further evidence of a connection between Rauf and Hussain. If the latter was mostly responsible for the creation of Obama's Cairo speech and the former's Arabic work was incorporated into that speech, the likelihood that Hussain was instrumental in the inclusion of Rauf's work is strong indeed.

The interview between Ghanem and Hussain continued:

> **Ghanem:** "As an American Muslim, how do you feel about a possible military strike against Iran, and does the U.S. object if Tehran gains nuclear weapons?"

> **Hussain:** "The United States has no objection if Iran gains nuclear capability, but for peaceful use, this policy has been adopted by the Obama administration policy aimed at ensuring Tehran's right to obtain peaceful nuclear technology stressing our rejection [of Iran] to obtain nuclear weapons."

Then the code-speak began when Ghanem asked Hussain in direct fashion if he is a mover and shaker: "Part of your work covers Iran since it is part of the Islamic world. Have you made things happen on this level?" Ghanem noted in the article "Hussain refuses to talk." Then Ghanem insists: "Do you not think that a move on your part will have a positive impact on resolving the crisis?" Hussein responds: "I think so, but we will do so when the right opportunity comes."

Islamists like Rashad Hussain, under the guise of modernity, enter the establishment pretending to build bridges between the US and the Muslim world. His recorded comments on Sami Al-Arian, calling the convicted terrorist's prosecution "politically motivated," coupled with an attempt to cover up those comments demonstrates why character matters and why people like Rashad Hussain should be vetted.

FOOTNOTES

1. Fox News.com, *Two U.S.-Born Terrorists Killed in CIA-Led Drone Strike,* by Jennifer Griffin. http://www.foxnews.com/politics/2011/09/30/us-born-terror-boss-anwar-al-awlaki-killed/

2. Fox News.com, *Radical Muslim Cleric's Pentagon Lunch: Top DOD Lawyers, Executive Director of CAIR Invited,* by Catherine Herridge. http://www.foxnews.com/politics/2011/06/07/radical-muslim-clerics-pentagon-lunch-top-dod-lawyers-executive-director-cair/

3. New York Post, *Imam terror error—Ground Zero mosque leader hedges on Hamas,* by Tom Topousis. http://www.nypost.com/p/news/local/manhattan/imam_terror_error_efmizkHuBUaVnfuQcrcabL

4. FMU—Former Muslims United, *2009 Pledge Recipients*; Video "The Penalty for Apostasy Is Death" in Arabic with English sub-titles, also found on YouTube. http://formermuslimsunited.org/the-pledge/pledge-recipients/ http://www.youtube.com/watch?v=eqkxkqeCK8U&feature=player_embedded

5. New York Post, *No community programs at 'Ground Zero' mosque a year after the controversy*, by Isabel Vincent and Melissa Klein. http://www.nypost.com/p/news/local/manhattan/it_mosque_rade_E4bLtxvo3yIwrCnYm1fRLP

6. Shoebat.com, Feisal Abdul interview with Hani Al-Waziri on Egypt radio, fully Translated and Transcribed, *9/11 Mosque Imam Boasts: 'Obama's historic speech in Egypt came from me.'* http://www.shoebat.com/documents/911Imam.php

7. http://horytna.net/Articles/Details.aspx?TID=2&ZID=259&AID=20875

8. Arabic website, English available. http://www.ahl-alquran.com/arabic/show_news.php?main_id=8696

9. CNS News.com. *'Ground Zero Mosque' Cleric Says Parts of His Book Were Woven in Obama's Cairo Speech*. http://cnsnews.com/node/71750

10. Shoebat.com, Feisal Abdul interview with Hani Al-Waziri on Egypt radio, fully Translated and Transcribed, *9/11 Mosque Imam Boasts: 'Obama's historic speech in Egypt came from me.'* http://www.shoebat.com/documents/911Imam.php

11. http://www.charlierose.com/download/transcript/10825

12. WND—WorldNewDaily Exclusive, *The Fox News Connection to Ground Zero Mosque*. http://www.wnd.com/2010/08/195049/

13. Shoebat.com, Feisal Abdul interview with Hani Al-Waziri on Egypt radio, fully Translated and Transcribed, *9/11 Mosque Imam Boasts: 'Obama's historic speech in Egypt came from me.'* http://www.shoebat.com/documents/911Imam.php

14. Arabic website, Cited from *Sharing The Essence Of Our Beliefs*, by Feisal Abdul Rauf. http://www.alghad.com/index.php/article/456154.html Translated from the Arabic by Walid Shoebat.

15. Arabic website. http://www.alghad.com/index.php/article/456154.html

16. MediaMatters for America, *Latest bogus right-wing reason to oppose Park 51: Muslims have made no effort to promote tolerance*, by Jocelyn Fong. http://mediamatters.org/blog/2010/08/17/latest-bogus-right-wing-reason-to-oppose-park-5/169329

17. Arabic website. http://www.hadielislam.com/arabic/index.php?pg=articles/article&id=12025 Translated verbatim, From Rauf's interview on Hadiyul-Islam.com

18. Egypt Independent, Arabic website, English available. http://today.almasryalyoum.com/article2.aspx?ArticleID=243114&IssueID=1674

19. CNN Transcripts, CNN Lary King Live, *Interview With Imam Feisal Abdul Rauf*. http://transcripts.cnn.com/TRANSCRIPTS/1009/08/lkl.01.html

20. Ibid

21. Herald Scotland, *Ground Zero imam gives Scotland his recipe for successful multi-culturalism,* by Vicky Allan. http://www.heraldscotland.com/news/home-news/ground-zero-imam-gives-scotland-his-recipe-for-successful-multiculturalism-1.1120227

22. Fox News.com, *Obama's Islamic Envoy Quoted Defending Man Charged With Aiding Terrorists,* http://www.foxnews.com/politics/2010/02/16/obamas-islamic-envoy-disputes-report-quoting-defending-terror-convict/

23. Politico, *Islam envoy retreats on terror talk,* by Josh Gerstein. http://dyn.politico.com/printstory.cfm?uuid=E9590C34-18FE-70B2-A88C9208B93FC804

24. Washington Post.com, *Obama names U.S. envoy to Islamic Conference,* by Scott Wilson. http://www.washingtonpost.com/wp-dyn/content/article/2010/02/13/AR2010021303511.html

25. Arabic website. http://www.ahram.org.eg/163/2010/05/11/2/19751.aspx

CHAPTER

12

BEHIND THE VEIL OF
JIHAD BY THE $WORD

RAUF REDUX

*A*s we pointed out in another chapter, Feisal Abdul Rauf said the following in a moment of honesty, when he thought he was speaking solely to a sympathetic audience:

> *"...deal with them (westerners) as one courts a pretty girl he wants to date; stop thinking like a typical Muslim. Then you can engage."*

In order to fully appreciate what Rauf meant by this, it's important to understand how so many Muslims treat pretty girls (and boys) they want to date. Once this is understood, so can the true intentions of Rauf when he encourages similar treatment of westerners by Muslims.

HONEST MUSLIMS

It is necessary to debunk a portrait of the Islamic world that has, no doubt, been painted in the minds of some westerners. Not all Muslims engage in JBTW; some are very open about their beliefs. Generalizations only serve to alienate individuals who can help expose what's behind the curtain. Once individuals like this are located and given voice, it's like taking a trip behind the veil of JBTW.

For example, Saudi writer Dr. Zuhair Mohammed Jamil Kutby wrote (translated from Arabic) about the Arab world:

> The Arab Nation—according to scholars, jurists and intellectuals who desire one—think it is among the best of solutions, like no other in the universe. The fact is, however, that it went through periods of physical and moral degeneration, an embarrassment found in the pages of history.[1]

Kutby continues...

When we come back to read some pages of our own history—not the history written by Orientalists—we cannot say those pages are antagonistic; they belong to us. Our Arab history is full of conflict, crowded with a culture of lying, exposed by sexual and moral deviation...Was not the spread of corruption and sexual deviation in the corridors and palaces wrong when it existed during Arab rule? Plentiful were these [deviations] written in our history books, novels and stories. For example; The Abbasid Caliph, Harun al-Rashid, spent his nights with Al-Majin and the immoral poet Abu Nawas...Here are the verses that indicate sexual decadence and corruption in which Abu Nawas says:

> Adela blames my choice,
> a boy smooth as an Oryx ...
> leave me alone, I said
> do not blame me,
> I am committed to what you hate
> and until death do us part
> Did not the book of Allah instruct?
> To prefer boys over girls...[2]

Pedophilia stems from the Qur'an and the prophet Muhammad. Muslim doublespeak artists attempt to cover-up Muhammad's marriage to Aisha, his six year-old wife; they argue that he waited to consummate his marriage when she was nine. This waiting has nothing to do with Aisha's maturity but with payment:

...then Abu Bakr asked [the Prophet], "O Messenger of God, what prevents you from consummating the marriage with your wife?" The Prophet said, "The bridal gift (sadaq)." Abu Bakr gave him the bridal gift, twelve and a half ounces [of gold], and the Prophet sent for us. He consummated our marriage in my house, the one where I live now and where he passed away.[3]

Muhammad's companions and old geezers married underaged girls. Ali gave his daughter to Umar:

Umar asked Ali for the hand of his daughter, Umm Kulthum in marriage. Ali replied that she has not yet attained the age (of maturity)...Thus Ali gave his daughter Umm Kulthum a dress and asked her to go to Umar, who said, "Go and tell your father that you are very pretty..." With that, Ali married Umm Kulthum to Umar.[4]

The Summary for The Message of Prayer, How To Teach Our Children Prayer by Sheikh Yousuf Al-Asfuri AlBahreini, First Edition, 1989 is a book for the elementary schools in Bahrain. In it, the proper procedures for washing after ejaculation are issued. Page 53 discusses the necessity to cleanse oneself and the conditions for washing:

> 1. intercourse with the vaginal part of a woman...intercourse after ejaculating in her anus...intercourse after ejaculating in a boy's anus...after intercourse with an animal...

Moroccan journalist Hamid Tulist, while addressing the pedophilia problem in the Middle East, admits:

> Even the prince of the faithful Caliph Al-Amin, son of Caliph Harun al-Rashid, bought his eunuchs and dedicated them for his private use; he refused women and slaves and anguished over his love for a boy named Kauthar, and sang for him love songs and poetry. Caliph and Commander of the Faithful of Allah, al-Wathiq bin Khalifa Mu'tasim and Caliph Harun al-Rashid's grandson, longed for a boy called Mahj. Sweet and delicate poems were dedicated to him. Commander of the Faithful and Caliph al-Walid ibn Yazid ibn Abd al-Malik was even said to have enticed his brother to sodomize him.

Tulist doesn't refer to the Quran, Hadith or Islamic jurisprudence for a solution to the problem of pedophilia in the Arab-Muslim world; he goes to the Jewish faith:

> The first mention of a type of sexual perversion (homosexuality) stated in the first religious book known in the Arab East was Genesis, a Jewish book and the first book of the five books of the Torah. In the story of Lot, God punished sexual perversion. In fact, the Arabic word "Luat" (sodomy) came from the Hebrew "Lot" and not from the Arabic.

The truth is that human beings—including individuals who live in the Muslim world—possess a moral compass. The challenge is to find a way to get more people to follow it.

MISYAR MARRIAGES

Many of the social issues in the Muslim world need to be translated and presented to the West. Secular Arabic television stations address the issues of pleasure marriages and sex with infants and boys, especially amongst the Shia.

Sunnis may mock Shi'ites for pleasure marriages, of which many in the West are familiar but Sunnis have what is called *Misyar* marriages and they are rarely, if ever, discussed in the West. *Misyar* literally means 'traveler marriage,' in which women must agree to relinquish the care owed to them by a husband. Sheikh Ahmed al-Kubaissi from the United Arab Emirates thinks there is no formal problem with the *Misyar* marriage. After all, it meets the requirements of Islamic law. Wealthy Muslim men sometimes enter into *Misyar* marriages while on vacation, in order to have sexual relations with another woman without committing the sin of adultery. They usually divorce the women once their holiday is over.

However, if this is understood by both parties at the time the marriage contract ends (this is usually the case), it would constitute a pre-meditated, fixed time period (can you say prostitution?)

The Sheikh of al-Azhar Mosque, Muhammad Sayyid Tantawi, and theologian Yusuf Al-Qaradawi note—in their writings and in their lectures—that the majority of men who take a spouse within the framework of the Misyar marriage are already married men.

Many of these men would not marry a second wife within the framework of normal Islamic polygamy because of the heavy financial burdens, moral obligations and responsibilities placed on the husband as a result. The *Misyar* marriage, on the other hand, is a welcome option, especially when the theologians declare it to be licit.

According to a Fatwa from Ayatollah Sistani, a Shī'ah Sayyed, *Mut'ah* is permitted, but *Misyar* is considered to be prohibited by Shī'ah. While each sect condemns the other for immoral acts, *Mut'ah* and *Misyar* share much in common. Both require all the conditions applicable to Nikah (marriage) with the exception of a fixed date of expiration in *Mut'ah*. Every Sunni marriage requires two adult male witnesses whereas the two witnesses in Shī'ah marriages—in either nikah-e-Mut'ah or in ordinary marriage—may be just Allah and the Qur'an.

Websites in the English amount to a few thousand hits on *Misyar*, with the usual Muslim discussion groups but the Arabic has over a million hits with a litany of services that facilitate the process with blessings from the Kingdom of Saudi Arabia.[5]

It was rare during the Israeli occupation to hear of having multiple wives, even if it is was sanctioned in Bethlehem. With a high percentage of Christians, it was frowned upon, even by Muslims. I recall my teacher Sheikh Zakaria at Dar Jasser High School. He taught that a husband had to treat his wives equally; if he would have intercourse with one wife he had to satisfy the other. He would joke that, "the black snake had to enter two dens last night so please remain quiet while I take my snooze". He would fall asleep at his desk. The students laughed and each would simply do the homework required for the following day while Zakaria snored away.

It was usually religious Muslims who practiced polygamy; the second wife was usually a young girl. When the once young model began falling apart, another with fewer miles was purchased. I recall when my youngest uncle, Salameh, a man who taught biology, forced his daughter to marry a man older than him. Sana would be wife number two for the old, bald man who was well off. My cousin Eiad was detained in Canada for fraud, contraband, and working in the typical Middle Eastern network that involved siphoning western money; his father orchestrated the cartel from Bethlehem. Salameh decided to throw his older wife out. When Canada failed to have the FBI pick Eiad up—the web of crimes were mostly committed in the US—he was extradited back to Bethlehem and found his father married to a young girl from Hebron. Salameh could afford it but his children were upset and persuaded him to bring their mother back.

Of course, Salameh, being the mercifully kind man who was well-respected in his community, brought Tamam back. During all my youth, I recall Tamam consistently having to leave the home because she wasn't satisfying her husband. After her parents died, she had no one to go to, relegated to begging for the aid of her sons. The Middle East is a cruel place but not for everyone; the rich have it made and of course the religious man can get away with anything since he proclaims Allah's will.

In the Qur'an, whenever Allah proclaimed his will it was usually accompanied with, "Allah and His Prophet". Of course, "The Earth belongs to Allah and His prophet." Whatever the prophet wanted always seemed to come from Allah;

Muhammad was usually his partner. Yet, Islam proclaimed that *Shirk* is the unpardonable sin. *Shirk* means partnering with Allah. Likewise, the religious in the Arab world proclaim Allah's will which usually is their will also. Muslim holy men are better off proclaiming, "I am Allah".

FOOTNOTES

1. Arabic website, English available. http://www.alhares.org/site/modules/news/article.php?storyid=3037

2. Ibid

3. *The History of Al-Tabari: Biographies of the Prophet's Companions and Their Successors,* translated by Ella Landau-Tasseron, SUNY Press, Albany, 1998, Volume XXXIX, pgs. 171-173

4. *Tarikh Khamees,* Volume 2; *('Dhikr Umm Kalthum'),* p. 384; and *Zakhair Al-Aqba,* p. 168

5. Arabic website. http://www.msyaronline.com/

CHAPTER

13

CHURCH INFILTRATION

"CHRISTIAN" MOVEMENTS WORTH OPPOSING

The Church in America is divided when it comes to Judeo-phobia and the isolation of Israel as the leading entity in the world of evil. We have no problem opposing several "Christian" movements and individuals like Al-Sabeel, Abuna-Chakour, EMEU (Evangelicals For Middle East Understanding) Naim Ateek, Stephen Sizer, Colin Chapman, Bishara and Alex Awad of the Bethlehem Bible College, and Ron Brackin who all desire an end to Israel's lifeline by working with conduits to infiltrate major Christian media and churches.

EXPOSING MOSAB HASSAN YOUSEF

As much as it pained me, I even had to expose new convert Mosab Hassan Yousef (aka Son of Hamas), whom many on the Christian right got excited about when he should have been added to the mix of anti-Israel propagandists. Christians in the West are easily deceived. For example, *Christian Broadcasting Network* (*CBN*) was unaware that while it airs a major outreach program entitled, "Daring Question" that boasts some 20 million viewers in the Middle East, one installment aired a plea that repudiated anyone who turns in Hamas suicide bombers. This program was aired from *CBN*'s headquarters in Virginia Beach.[2]

CBN is unaware that the type of converts their Arab program produces is of the anti-Israel strain, which heavily influenced Mosab's conversion. Mosab was a product of *Al-Hayat* and *CBN*'s "Daring Question". In fact, Mosab himself—in English—stated that he wanted to set the record straight about the reason for his appearance on the program.[2] That reason was that *Al-Hayat* had been accused of being a Zionist entity and Mosab wanted to make it clear that while there are Arab Christians, many of them are staunchly anti-Israel, anti-Semitic, or both.

The *700 Club's* Pat Robertson was unaware that his program, "Daring Question" had a far more potent message in Arabic, tailored specifically to Middle Easterners. Mosab was clearly brought in to *Al-Hayat* to help clear the station of any charges that it was pro-Zionist because he collaborated with the Shin Bet. Perhaps the most shocking revelation from Mosab during the program came when he asked Arabs not to report terrorist activity. The host (Rasheed) asked a caller:

> **Rasheed**: "If you were in Mosab's position and have two choices: either someone from Hamas will be killed, or school children in a bus will be killed, will you report it?"

The anti-Israel Arab Christian caller vacillated, then Mosab spoke:

> **Mosab**: "If I was in your shoes, you should not report it to Israel. I do not encourage anyone to give information to Israel or collaborate with Israel...If anyone hears me right now and they are in relation to Israeli security I advise them to work for the interest of their own people—number one—and do not work with the [Israeli] enemy against the interest of our people. They should cooperate with the Palestinian Authority only."

Rasheed—a Christian convert himself—pardoned Mosab of any wrongdoing—not for his connection to Hamas—but for his collaboration with the Zionist enemy, excusing Mosab since his aid to Israel was during a time when he was still a 'Muslim' and not during 'his new life in Christ.'

At the end of the program, Rasheed reiterated Mosab's position when one of the last callers asked him about supporting Israel. Rasheed stated unequivocally that the Bible and everything he read is clear about this issue not to support Zionism; the mission was accomplished and both parties were cleared from the stigma of "Zionism".

Even Pat Robertson—apparently unaware that he was being duped—innocently interviewed Mosab, who communicated during that interview that "Israel tortures Palestinians."[3] I am all too familiar with this level of exaggeration. My recruiter—Mahmoud Al-Mughrabi—whom I met in one such Israeli prison, was a master at it.[4]

As an aside, Al-Mughrabi was actually a spy for the *Sunday Times* while being portrayed as an innocent civilian victim. Even prominent writers like Christopher Hitchens and Edward Said published the lies Al-Mughrabi told.[5] An Israeli raid in Operation Wooden Leg finally killed al-Mughrabi in Tunisia. He definitely wasn't there to smoke a Hukka or play cards in a café on the beach; Al-Mughrabi collaborated with me to bomb Bank Leumi branches in Israel.

Excited western Christians do not filter the 'Jezebels' from the 'Delilahs' when it comes to Arab converts supporting Israel. On Al-Arabia, Mosab declared to millions that he is not a traitor but a patriot whose goal is to infiltrate the life's blood of Israel—western Churches.[6]

Even Ron Brackin who co-wrote Mosab's story *Son of Hamas* is pro-Palestine and uses moral equivalency to justify his positions.[7] A Hamas supporter by the name of Alex Awad of Bethlehem Bible College had influenced Brackin; Awad is a notorious proponent for Hamas' legitimacy.[8]

In May of 2008, Awad attended Islamic terror supporting conferences hosted in Jakarta, Indonesia. Among the speakers at this event was Iranian Ayatollah Khomeini's daughter, *Zahra Mostafavi*, who had previously urged children to become suicide bombers.[9] Also included were representatives from the Hamas and Hezbollah terrorist organizations. (**Fredrick Töben,** *Indonesia holds a conference that dares to address the Palestinian tragedy of al Nakba* ISSN 1440-9828, July 2008, No. 392)

In hindsight, my views on Mosab have moderated a bit. I don't believe he is as nefarious as someone like Rauf. It's my view that Mosab is personally very conflicted and that his problems are more emotional than evil. In the Middle East, people often have huge personality swings and Mosab's behavior reminded me of such people. In either case, he is not someone who should be entrusted with converting the multitudes.

AWAD'S TACTICS SIMILAR TO MOSAB'S

In Arabic, Mosab hailed Hamas fighters as "heroes" and like Mosab, Awad uses conduits to spread the support for the Palestinian cause infiltrating some of the most influential churches in America. Prominent Pastor Wayne Cordeiro, the founding pastor of the Foursquare Church known as *New Hope Christian Fellowship* in Honolulu, allowed his church to be used as a platform to aid suffering terrorists.

After we contacted *New Hope* about a video posted to their site that consisted of an interview between Cordeiro and Awad, the video was removed. An ardent skeptic of our claims might be shocked by its contents. Mosab's JBTW was at least in Arabic. Cordeiro's interview with Awad was in English. It consisted of JBTW that didn't even go through the translation filter *into* Arabic.[10]

In the interview, Awad insisted on Hamas' right to rule and Cordeiro portrayed the protection wall (intended to thwart terror attacks) as being similar to the Berlin Wall, as if it was erected for the sole purpose of punishing Palestinians. As a result, Cordeiro ended up defending the suffering terrorists! Aside from the fact that the Berlin Wall was built to keep people in and the walls in Israel were built to keep terrorists out, the majority of Palestinians (Muslim and Christian) march in processions with suicide bombers.

Cordeiro's photo-ops alongside conservatives like Oliver North and Sean Hannity portray a facade of conservatism; he even uses the term "democracy" to argue that Hamas deserves recognition since it was elected through a democratic process. If democracy is the yardstick by which justice is measured, then Israel must be destroyed since the Islamists have democratically elected Hamas through a majority vote. In fact, a survey—taken by Al-Arabia Network during the election of Hamas—showed that 73.2% of Arabs supported Hamas and its goals to destroy Israel. Do we then honor such democratic choice?

Either Cordeiro is being deceptive or he's helping to achieve the same ends through his ignorance. The shepherd who barters with or acquiesces to the wolves is just as dangerous to the flock as one who is asleep as they prowl.

The type of peacemaking advocated by Awad and Cordeiro is also typical of the emergent church. They each expect Christians to confess the sins of their fathers without exposing the other side; such people and movements lament the crusaders' persecution of Muslims and ask Christians to humble themselves to Muslims, seeking their forgiveness. When will Christian churches finally demand that Muslims confess *their* sins of deceit?

HOW IT'S DONE

In order to deceive, the naïve must be convinced. When it comes to Judeo-phobia (fear of Jews) and its infiltration of Christian churches, focus must be narrowed to the four Gospels; this lowers the guard of the naïve who can then be more easily deceived by the Judeo-phobes. This is effective because it appeals to the heart strings and predispositions of Christians, who typically view the Gospels as the most important books of the Bible. By championing the Gospels, the Judeo-phobic infiltrators gain allies in much the same way that Islamists who champion the

Constitution are able gain Ron Paul supporters as allies—by appealing to the core of their beliefs.

Though the Gospels are a top priority for most Christians, isolating those books at the exclusion of others in the Bible is one way to get those Christians to passionately defend their own deceivers. Victims of such JBTW will passionately refute the truth-tellers, saying things like, "But he preached the Gospel!" There is nothing quite so thirst-quenching to a deceiver than seeing his victims defend him against his enemies. There's something quite vampirical about it all, isn't there?

Evil is effective because it isn't devoid of truth. If it were, it'd be rejected wholesale. Instead, it incorporates just enough truth to entice its victims into doing its bidding. This is part of evil's success formula. Judeo-phobic con artists who infiltrate Christian churches with an anti-Semitic agenda use Jesus as bait. Yes, they *use* Jesus. What can be more evil than that? They do so by intentionally ignoring Biblical doctrines that command support for Israel. Since these deceivers like to point to the Gospel, let us do the same. How about Mark 13: 5-6:

> 5 And Jesus, answering them, began to say: "Take heed that no one deceives you. 6 For many will come in My name, saying, 'I am He', and will deceive many.[11]

Of course, levying such a charge brings far more earthly wrath than do the deceptive techniques of those who warrant them. That brings us full circle relative to the reason why evil is so effective. Bible believers must ask themselves if their teachings are turning them away from the people Israel. If so, they are faced with a choice. They must either renounce the Old Testament or their newly ordained teachers.

The trick starts with the creation of a fictitious reality, one the Palestinian Christians advocate regarding the origin of the so-called "Palestinian" people. The desired narrative is that these Arab people are indigenous to the land that was stolen and occupied by evil colonialist Jews. This story begins with the falsification of historic facts regarding the origin of the Palestinians.

Alex Awad is not of Arabic origin and his ancestors did not "exist there for a thousand years" as he has claimed. His origin is well documented on our village's official pro-Palestine website, Beit Sahour's City Portal.[12] It includes family names, dates and countries of origin; all of our ancestors arrived during the eighteenth and nineteenth centuries. In our village, everyone knows that Awad's family was originally Egyptian.

Such claims made by the likes of Awad slip by, undetected by novices like Cordeiro, who know little about the real history. All they seem to know is what fanatic dreamers tell them about Palestinians being Arabs. Then again, what westerner is going to access archives written in Arabic?

ANTI-ZIONIST CHRISTIANITY

I am often asked about the bonafides of self-identified Christians like Mosab and Awad. It would be difficult for anyone to assess the salvation of others since this is God's department exclusively. It is also difficult to say that Mosab is still Muslim since he is openly critical of Islam but what *is* obvious is that Mosab adheres to "Christian Palestinianism," as evidenced by his statements and associations. The co-author of his book is none other then Ron Brackin, who speaks fondly of Alex Awad.[13] Both men are ardently anti-Israel while wearing a "Christian" label.[14]

Can a Christian claim the blood of Jesus, yet support homosexual marriage, abortion, or dividing the land of Israel? Can a true Christian support these things? Being labeled a bigot for answering "no" to any of those is something I have learned to wear as a badge of honor because it's what the Bible teaches and what I believe.

These are serious issues and while some might choose the first two as the worst infractions, God declares judgment against the ones who "divided up My land" (Joel 3). In Christian theology, Antichrist wants to "divide the land for gain" (Daniel 11) and Christ is against it. What side does a Christian think he is on if and when Antichrist divides the land? People enticed by silver-tongued converts who focus on the Gospels at the exclusion of other books should be careful.

The Bible tells God's story and teaches believers how to follow the Messiah, which is His will. Gay marriage and abortion are sadly becoming more acceptable by many in the fallen Church today, from Methodists to Presbyterians. Dividing His land is an automatic addition since nothing matters but "the Gospel", which is not a Gospel at all. Once the leaven gets in, "the whole batch is destroyed," as the Bible says (Galatians 5).

Silencing dissenters is another way to discourage sheep from engaging in politics; hot button issues like Israel and Zionism are prime examples. Liberal Christians always seem eager to claim that Christianity has nothing to do with politics. Yet, they themselves conflate the two whenever it's to their benefit. Take Jimmy Carter, who has always had a bone to pick with Israel. He then chastises anyone who interprets the Bible literally as being un-Christian. In an interview, Carter said he doesn't "dwell on Deuteronomy or Leviticus much."[15] Interestingly, the Book of Leviticus strongly rebukes the act of homosexuality (Lev 18) and Carter supports gay marriage.[16] If Carter is allowed to hold the view that gay marriage is ok because a book in the Bible that rejects it can be ignored, then we are allowed to hold the view that he's wrong while pointing to the book of Leviticus to prove it. Carter would have a difficult time arguing that Leviticus is not part of the Bible and that gay marriage is not a political issue.

Carter was very political in his book, *Palestine, Peace Not Apartheid*. Those who denounce the Palestinian state are often accused of being anti-peace and divisive because God is not interested in land. If so, why is the god of Cordeiro, Awad, and Carter so interested in establishing an Arab land called Palestine? As is the case with gay marriage, Christians should have no compunction about pointing to the Bible in defense of this "political" issue.

The effectiveness of JBTW is diminished in direct proportion to how much westerners reject double standards. It's really that simple but, unfortunately, double standards have become the norm.

Not only will real historians find laughable, such claims that Palestinians have a right to Israel's land but none of them will support the idea that Arabs ever ruled Israel on an imperial scale for more than one century. Neither are the Egyptian Copts or Lebanese Christians "Arab" as Awad claims. Just ask any of these peoples how they feel about being called Arabs—they don't like it. Rather, they will tell you that the Arab Muslims have always attempted to destroy their identity, culture and Christian heritage.

POPULAR FRONT TO LIBERATE PALESTINE

The main Palestinian Christian organizations collaborate primarily with Hamas, Fatah, Hezbollah and the Popular Front to Liberate Palestine (PFLP) to varying degrees. The PFLP was founded by an Arab Christian—George Habash—who took pride in the fact that his organization—unlike the Palestinian Authority—never collaborated with Israel. He refused to set foot in Palestinian territories because of Israel.[17] Perhaps the real reason was that Habash was afflicted with Judeo-phobia.

Do naïve Christian pastors know that it was this Palestinian brand of Christianity—an invention of socialist (leftist) revolutionaries—that produced the

PFLP or that it was founded by a Judeo-phobe like Habash? The PFLP is a group that still murders Jews wherever they are found. Yet, when you meet them, they profess that Christ was crucified. Their Jesus is always portrayed in Palestinian art work as a Palestinian revolutionary with barbed wire surrounding Him because He lived in a refugee camp (you know, a place where terrorists seem to thrive).

In fact, Awad once held a conference entitled, "Christ at the Checkpoint," in Bethlehem, partnering with the Holy Land Trust. Two of the speakers at the event were the spiritual counselors of Bill Clinton and Barack Obama—Tony Campolo and Joel Hunter, respectively. Awad attempted to refute charges that the conference was "anti-Semitic" while simultaneously conceding that there would be "criticism of Israel." There most assuredly was no such criticism of Palestinians.[18]

So what type of Biblical theology are they teaching at Awad's Bethlehem Bible College? Well, student Yousef Ijha (Joseph Ajeha), in his dissertation *Study on Christian Zionism*, wrote:

> (Theodor) Herzl established the first Zionist Congress in 1897, and succeeded in gathering the Jews of the world around him including the shrewdest of Jews to issue forth the most dangerous plan in the history of the world *The Protocols of the Elders of Zion* derived from sacred Jewish teaching, and from then the Jews articulated and organized themselves to move in stealth and shrewdness to fulfill their destructive goals which the results are in plain view today then judge the Jews their organizations and are moving accurately and subtle and insidious destructive to achieve their goals and results that are visible in our time.[19]

Awad was in attendance at Ijha's graduation.[20] While a student of Awad's, Ijha proclaimed his allegiance to the PFLP terrorist organization and honored the infamous terrorist Ahmad Sa'adat, the Secretary General of the PFLP terrorist organization:

> "All greetings to our comrade the General Council of Ahmad Sa'adat of the PFLP...and a red greeting drenched in the blood of the martyrs."[21]

Currently, Sa'adat is in Israeli custody for his involvement in the murder of former Israeli politician and Minister, Rehavam Ze'evi.[22]

Since we have clearly demonstrated that pastors such as Cordeiro have been duped, will we be thanked or treated like messengers bearing news the willfully ignorant doesn't want to hear? If the answer is the latter, it means that the likes of Cordeiro haven't been duped at all; they've been willing participants. Either that, or pride will have trumped the willingness to admit wrongdoing (we'll publish a revised edition of this book if our revelations are met with gratitude).

IMPETUS FOR EXODUS

Bethlehem was once made up of 80% Christians. Today, that number is closer to 10%. Who or what is responsible for this mass exodus? In the documentary film, *Holy Land: Christians in Peril*, it is revealed that not only are the Muslims to blame for forcing the Christians to flee but it was Palestinian terrorists who laid siege to the Church of the Nativity in 2002 after being surrounded by Israeli forces.[23]

Shockingly, western media outlets found a way to blame Israel for the Palestinian terrorists storming the church. The *BBC* reported:

> The Palestinian fighters faced random and sudden death—Israeli snipers were instructed to shoot at anyone in their sights seen carrying a gun.

> One young boy recalls lying among the pews at night, trying to sleep, watching the green laser beams of the Israeli snipers as they searched out targets in the church interior.[24]

Instead of identifying the terrorists as doubly despicable for seeking refuge in a Holy place they proceeded to desecrate, the *BBC* was all too content to identify the terrorists as victims while painting the Israelis as the devils who made them do it. The actual footage shows that Christian monks and priests were extremely grateful to the Israelis for rescuing them. Yet, the Jews were blamed. One of the first paragraphs in the *BBC* article is a fascinating point of study in liberal media bias:

> When Israeli troops and tanks rolled in to Bethlehem...they had no way of knowing that they were setting the stage for one of the most dramatic sieges in modern history.[25]

Israel set the stage for terrorism by *confronting* terrorism? That's like blaming the guy who turns on the light switch for making the cockroaches run in to the pantry!

Imagine the same paragraph written a different way:

> In response to Israeli troops and tanks that had rolled in to Bethlehem to arrest Palestinian militants, those militants unmasked themselves as terrorists—for the whole world to see—by laying siege to one of Christianity's holiest sites.

Since turning on the light makes the bugs run in to the pantry, not only does the man have the cockroaches cornered but his household is now convinced those cockroaches need to be dealt with; wording really is everything in the Middle East.

Former Israeli Prime Minister Golda Meir once famously stated:

"Peace will come when the Arabs love their children more than they hate us."[26]

A similar line of reasoning can be applied to Palestinian Christians who hate Jews more than they want to spread Christianity. If spreading the word of God takes a back seat to working toward the eradication of the Jews, the word of God is not being spread; it is being used as a means of deception and we all know where deceit comes from. Remember, JBTW is spoken with a forked tongue that includes the *use* of God instead of reliance *upon* Him.

Whether historically or biblically, there has never been a Palestinian civilization or culture. Yet, this premise is at the core of the Bethlehem Bible College's doctrine. Palestinianism—including the twisted brand of Christianity it incorporates—is designed to eradicate the Jewish presence first and foremost. Again, we are witness to more JBTW. The portrayal of anti-Semites as peaceful Christians is covertly trumped by anti-Semitism itself, with the hopes of a lowered Israeli guard.

The Christian emigration from Bethlehem and countless other places is a direct result of persecution by Muslim entities like Hamas and the Palestinian Authority. This *persecution* began with a program of *intimidation* and land grabs, including Christian centers that were turned into headquarters for terrorists and thugs. The birthplace of Christ, Joseph's Tomb, and Joshua's grave were all desecrated by Muslim terrorists. Palestinian Christians who reject the Old Testament or espouse "Replacement Theology" excuse such behavior because they sympathize with it.

JEKYLL FACE AND HYDE HEART

Inexplicably, many western Christians are eager to become signatories to peace deals with Islamic figures without examining the JBTW. When it comes to doublespeak in Islam, it is officially sanctioned. Al-Tabari's (d. 923) famous tafsir (exegesis of the Koran) is a standard and authoritative reference work in the entire Muslim world. Regarding Quran 3:28, he writes: "If you [Muslims] are under their [infidels'] authority, fearing for yourselves, behave loyally to them, with your tongue, while harboring inner animosity for them... Allah has forbidden believers from being friendly or on intimate terms with the infidels in place of believers— except when infidels are above them [in authority]. In such a scenario, let them act friendly towards them." Regarding 3:28, Ibn Kathir (d. 1373, second in authority only to Tabari) writes, "Whoever at any time or place fears their [infidels'] evil may protect himself through outward show."

As proof of this, he quotes Muhammad's close companion, Abu Darda, who said, "Let us smile to the face of some people [non-Muslims] while our hearts curse them." Another companion, al-Hassan, said, "Doing taqiyya is acceptable till the Day of Judgment [i.e., in perpetuity]." Source: **"War and Peace – and Deceit – in Islam" by Raymond Ibrahim /Pajamas Media February 12, 2009** [27]

Many Christian leaders have endorsed a JBTW initiative known as *A Common Word between Us and You.* The group's website lists hundreds of signatories, including JBTW artists such as former Ground Zero mosque Imam, Feisal Abdul Rauf, US Congressman Keith Ellison, Nihad Awad, the Executive Director of CAIR, and Ingrid Mattson, when she was the President of the ISNA. [28]

A primary objective of the group is to entice Christian organizations to endorse their initiative. By showing that Islam is willing to progress, the JBTW artists put the ball in the court of westerners. By appealing to a desire for "common ground," the JBTW artists hold the cards. In politics, this is often called "compromise." In Islam, as is the case in politics, there is a fine line between seeking compromise and *being* compromised.

The outreach that *A Common Word* seeks to engage in is known in many circles as "Chrislam." On the surface, it is an attempt to bring Muslims and Christians together with a premise that says both religions worship the same God. For Christians to subscribe to this idea, they must forego one of their most fundamental beliefs, that Jesus is the Son of the one and only Living God.

If such Christians are not engaged in JBTW, they are compromising their beliefs at minimum and committing blasphemy at maximum. Muslims who engage in JBTW stay true to *their* faith while lying to Christians, all in the name of interfaith dialogue. What kind of faith demands that its followers lie in order to stay true to that faith?

Saddleback Community Church founder, Rick Warren, seems to embrace the notion of Chrislam. He once addressed the ISNA and advocated that Christians and Muslims work together in a way similar to what A Common Word espouses.[29] In fact, Warren endorsed Christian and Muslim unity; the story appeared on the group's website.[30] Knowingly or not, Warren is herding sheep and leading them to the slaughterhouse. Either he is being deceived himself or is complicit in the tactic of JBTW. Unfortunately, the end result is the same.

RICK WARREN

Deception is not performed solely by evil men who intentionally lie in order to destroy what is good; it is also perpetrated by well-intentioned individuals who enable evil by acting as moderators between good and evil itself. *A Common Word*, the document Rick Warren embraced, was portrayed as an attempt to build bridges with the Christian world. This is what we who reside in the world of common sense call "bait".

Unfortunately, the famous pastor of Saddleback Church—along with other pastors—took that document seriously and willingly conceded to a stacked deck. *A Common Word between Us and You* is a work of deception. It attempted to get westerners to agree that Muslims and Christians all worship the same god. In typical sleight-of-hand fashion, the document was laced with doublespeak.

Nonetheless, supposed Christian leaders like Warren signed a document entitled *Loving God and Neighbor Together: A Christian Response to 'A Common Word Between Us and You'*. That document was the equivalent of a formal declaration of spiritual surrender.[31] It conceded the Muslim signatories' primary contention, that there is no god but Allah and Muhammad is his messenger. Not only that, but the document pleaded for Allah's forgiveness, saying:

> Before we "shake your hand" in responding to your letter, we ask forgiveness of the All-Merciful One (Allah) and of the Muslim community around the world.[32]

Did you catch that? Before Rick Warren—or any of his colleagues—would sign the "Christian Response," they asked "forgiveness" from Allah, the Unitarian god of Islam. Isn't that considered a *prayer* to Allah? In attempts to explain his position against accusations that he is a supporter of a new age religion known as Chrislam, Warren has twisted himself into knots.

In an interview with the *Christian Post*, Warren was asked if other religions worship the same God that Christians do. Here is the first part of Warren's response:

Of course not. Christians have a view of God that is unique. We believe Jesus is God! **We believe God is a Trinity: Father, Son, and Holy Spirit. Not 3 separate gods but one God.** No other faith believes Jesus is God. My God is Jesus. The belief in God as a Trinity is the foundational difference between Christians and everyone else.[33]

If Warren believed this, then why did he ask the god of Islam for forgiveness? Is this not a denial of the Trinity? As a Christian, shouldn't he apologize to the God of Abraham, Isaac, and Jacob for praying to a god he doesn't believe in while admitting he did wrong? Why would Warren agree with a premise that says Muslims and Christians worship the same god only to later deny it? What kind of message does this send to his flock? Is lying ok when it's politically expedient? Isn't it better to be hot or cold than it is to be lukewarm?

In a video posted by *Good Fight Ministries*, Pastor Joe Schimmel explains why what Rick Warren signed onto was so troublesome. Schimmel quotes from the Qur'an (Surah 4:171) to explain Islamic intent:

"Believe in Allah and say not, 'Trinity'; Cease! It is better for you. Allah is only one God. Far is it removed from His transcendent majesty that He should have a son."[34]

Again, why would Rick Warren pray to such a god for forgiveness? As a pastor, isn't he supposed to evangelize to people to get them to believe in *his* God and encourage them to pray for forgiveness, not to Allah but to Yahweh?

In another Surah, we learn where the signatories of *A Common Word* got their inspiration:

O People of the Book (Christians)! Come to a **common word between us and you**, that we worship none but Allah, and that we associate no partners (Trinity/Son of God) with Him, and that none of us shall take others as lords besides Allah." (Surah 3:64)

In Islam, it is blasphemous to say that Allah is part of a Trinity (Surah 5:73). In Christianity, it is blasphemy to *deny* the Trinity. Matthew 12 explains:

[31] "Therefore I say to you, every sin and blasphemy will be forgiven men, but the blasphemy against the Spirit will not be forgiven men. [32]Anyone who speaks a word against the Son of Man, it will be forgiven him; but whoever speaks against the Holy Spirit, it will not be forgiven him, either in this age or in the age to come.[35]

As we have stated previously, judging souls is not our department; warning them is another matter.

DECEIVING THE JEWS

Christians are not the only ones who are deceived. Like fish in a river, many Jewish organizations and philanthropists will bite—and swallow whole—the "dialogue" hook when it is dangled in front of them. One of the more attractive lures is the *"Olive Tree Initiative"* (OTI). It is a program that is billed as a "dialogue for peace" and is promoted throughout California State University.[36] In reality, this program is nothing more than an agenda that includes an "end" to "Israel." Shockingly, OTI is funded by taxpayers with monies provided by lured Jewish philanthropic organizations in California, Hillel and some Jewish Federations with public support by Yuli Edelstein, Israel's Minister of the Diaspora, Mark Regev from Israel's Foreign Ministry and Israel's Los Angeles Consulate.

Jewish youth get converted, in large part, thanks to the fiery, anti-Israel speakers whom OTI sponsors. OTI has welcomed the terrorist-cum-lecturer, Mazen Qumsiyeh to do multiple speaking tours on several University of California campuses.[37] Qumsiyeh is no stranger to 'the end-Israel' circle of lecturers; he is the co-founder of the virulently anti-Semitic group Al Awda.[38] Al Awda advocates for Israel's destruction "from river to sea" and Qumsiyeh is a practitioner of JBTW.[39] His activism in Arabic should even alarm the central left in the Jewish community. We translated what he truly believes according to his Arabic.

At the "Peace Center" in Beit Sahour-Bethlehem, Qumsiyeh lectured to large crowds. When he was asked by a member of the audience for his opinion on "other forms of resistance," in particular, "armed struggle," he expressed that "Armed struggle is a legitimate right for any people under occupation." He continued:

> "I am not against this form of response. Who am I to specify for every individual the form of resistance that he needs to adapt? Every individual needs to adapt to what he sees fit."

Is this not an overt call for anarchy? According to this precept, doing whatever anger leads you to do is a valid response, law and order should be damned. He further stated:

> "I am not a prophet but I am confident our people will use the form of resistance that suits them."[40]

It is worth noting at this point that this is the man OTI welcomed with open arms. Don't worry, there's more.

Qumsiyeh also participated as the main lecturer in a "Solidarity March for the Egyptian and Tunisian Revolutions." During the march, he spoke alongside Hussein Rahal of the Arab Liberation Front (ALF).[41] The ALF is significant because it gained notoriety during the al-Aqsa Intifada. ALF was a distributor of financial contributions from the Iraqi government, to families of "martyrs," with extra grants for the families of suicide bombers.[42]

It would seem that we've come full circle. Qumsiyeh, a man welcomed by OTI, was also welcomed by groups and individuals who support the extermination of an entire race of people. Shamefully, Jewish funders of OTI have not only been duped but have chosen a path that leads to the sacrifice of its own people, essentially to a foreign god.

Qumsiyeh's affiliation with Rahal is not simply a matter of "guilt by association". His Al-Awda (Right of Return) organization reflects his public support for terrorism. Qumsiyeh became signatory to The Declaration entitled, "Ajras Al-Awda" (Bells of Return)[43] It is a pledge to return the compass to call for the re-taking of the whole land of Palestine while stepping on the ashes of the Zionist Jews. We obtained damning evidence of his signed endorsement, which confirms the vision of the PFLP founder, George Habash:

> "We emphasize that the return is a sacred right (and) does not fall...our loyalty to our partner in struggle [PFLP] forces us to return our compass to Palestine, All of Palestine, which mandates that we re-issue a new national identity through building a new strategy that replaces the old, cowardly system that dwarfed our national project. The challenge is that we need to guard the dream of Naji Al-Ali, George Habash, and many others, to return and establish our Palestinian Democratic state over all the soil of Palestinian national lands on top of the ashes of the Zionist entity." (Signed Name: d. Mazin Qumsiyeh country: Palestine comment Date: 27/09/2010 06:48:36)

Shockingly, Jewish philanthropists are somehow magically duped into funding OTI, despite the group retaining Qumsiyeh to speak on its behalf. According to *FrontPage Magazine*, Qumsiyeh's presentations include rants that not only liken the Israeli government to a Nazi regime but charge Israeli collaboration with Hitler's Third Reich.[44]

Qumsiyeh was fired from Yale medical school when he used the University's email system to send out anti-Semitic emails before he moved back to Bethlehem. Qumsiyeh has also been arrested multiple times for participating in and organizing riots against IDF security forces for the Hamas-inspired International Solidarity Movement.[45] Yet, he continues to be considered a friend of OTI.

DR. ZUHDI JASSER

Self-described Islamic reformists are always interesting to engage because they have an extremely difficult time defending their positions. The very notion of Islamic reform must start with revisionist history. Dr. Zuhdi Jasser is a self-described reformist who honestly rejects violence.[46] The problem for him comes when he attempts to reject the idea that neither Muhammad nor Islam's founders exercised violence as the sunnah/hadith clearly describes.

Jasser promotes Muslim scholars to back his idea that Islam can be reformed. Yet, even such reformers confess that Muhammad conquered peoples with the sword. One such "reformist" who Jasser proudly cites when making his case is Muhammad Said Ashmawi.[47]

> "Arabs did not enter into Islam submitting and obeying as the Quran says, but they came as a result of the prophet's control and rule over them by the Muhajiroun and Ansar. So their view of governance came from Muhammad (governed by a governor) followers of a master and a king. This created a dangerous scenario on how to define the Caliphate." **(Al-Khilafa, M.S Al-Ashmawi, Pp 54.)**

You cannot reform Islam unless you deny the holy authority of the Quran and Muhammad; Jasser isn't prepared to go as far as Ashmawi does.

There is only one option left for the reformists. Ashmawi himself had to resort to the Hadith, after succumbing to Tahreef (textual corruption).[48] This is equivalent to telling devout Christians that the New Testament has been modified with insertions regarding the Kingdom of Christ, the hope of every devout Christian. Of course, Revelation 22:18-19 prohibits this exclusively so to attempt to reform Christianity by altering the Bible is tantamount to a rejection of Christianity.

If Muslims follow this path of reform, there is no hope left in keeping the faith. Islam is a Mohammedan religion just as Christianity is Christ's.

Removing Muhammad and his works from the equation is akin to removing Christ from Christianity. At that point, you don't have a reformed religion; you have a new one.

Consider the example of reform in Mormonism. By and large, Mormons moderated in the US; its original faith was similar to Islam's—warfare, concubines, execution of apostates, etc.—but it did not moderate of its own free will. It was defeated after the Utah War and the Mountain Meadow Massacre committed by Brigham Young. It was Mormonism's existence under President James Buchanan and the influence of Christianity that suppressed their movement and influenced it and toned it down. It was through textual changes and much abrogation that Mormonism reformed.

While Jasser prefers to look through an allegorical lens when interpreting the Quran, he follows the strict literal ruling that alcohol is forbidden, which is a literal interpretation. In so doing, he is in agreement with Islamic laws of abrogation because the consumption of alcohol was permissible in the early portions of the Qur'an; those verses were abrogated later. Therefore, if we apply Jasser's model, the peaceful verses he relies on for reform can also be abrogated. That explains Islamic terrorism and torpedoes Jasser's efforts.

Ashmawi, an authority whom Jasser loves to point to when making his Islamic reformation arguments, describes the intent of the caliphate, which was to build a spiritual entity on earth that mirrored Christianity (like Jesus established with Peter). While citing the Christian model as the one that got it right, Ashmawi contradicts himself by arguing that Muhammad never intended to have a successor, according to reformists.[49]

Jasser is to be commended for his stand against the Muslim Brotherhood front groups like CAIR, ISNA and others. However, his organization only has 1500 members with only 13% being Muslim. Yet, he stated on the *Dennis Prager Show* that 70% of all Muslims follow his style of Islam. Where did he get these numbers? If his brand was so attractive, why doesn't he have more followers? After all, he is one of the more prominent figures who advocate Islamic reform.[50]

In my view, there is no real significant evidence of reformation within Islam; Jasser gives a false sense of hope. Reformation begins with theologians, not medical doctors. We have no religious manuals in Islam that fit Jasser's views.

Even Sufi Muslims—frequently touted as moderates—are Mahdists. Guess what? If a Mahdi arrives, the world will have a fuhrer whose objective will be to destroy the Jews and Christians.

In a *Washington Post* article that featured Jasser, the Islamic reformist maintained that the problem is with people like me who "equate political Islam and sharia with Islam itself."[51] This advice, if followed, only serves to silence critics.

As Jasser proclaimed in another *Washington Post* article:

> "They [critics of Islam] cannot be on the frontlines in an ideological battle being waged, which demonizes the morality of the faith of Islam and its founder, the Prophet Mohammed."[52]

Jasser cannot have it both ways. That quote is reflective of the same argument made by CAIR, a group that Jasser rejects. How does he propose that such groups be dealt with by silencing their loudest and most informed critics? The argument here seems to be that by attacking CAIR, innocent Muslims will be alienated. Following this line of reasoning, doctors should not alienate smokers as engaging in self-destructive behavior, despite the fact that smoking kills. Should we be careful not to alienate heavy smokers for the sake of light smokers, rather than listen to the critics of smoking who might be able to get the moderates to quit instead of becoming more addicted?

Similarly, "moderate" Muslims believe in Sharia law and whatever strategy the West implements to deal with Sharia should never alienate freedom. Jasser almost seems willing to sacrifice the truth for strategy when he says things like:

> "Most should understand that strategically, identifying 'Islam as the problem,' immediately alienates upwards of one quarter of the world's population."[53]

What about alienating Christians? Fear of alienation never serves the truth, as the truth is almost always offensive. When Muslims curse the Trinity, are Christians not being alienated? Muslims who are "alienated" and choose the side of the fundamentalists suffer from a condition called intolerance and will eventually take their masks off anyway, when the inevitable lines are eventually drawn. Critics only speed up the process of determining who's on which side.

The fear of alienation is both defensive and destructive. Hinduism's reincarnation—if fully believed—is destructive since a baboon becomes someone's uncle. Do I alienate the Hindu by teaching him to kill wild baboons that ransack his village? Sati, the Hindu practice of burning widows was abolished—thanks to Christians like William Carey[54] and William Wilberforce.[55] Did these righteous Christians alienate moderate Hindus? No, they saved women from tortuous deaths. Did they do it by respecting Hinduism? No, Hinduism had its own 'Sharia' that needed to be defeated. It was the love of God and Biblical ethics that helped save women.

Islam rejects the Trinity and according to Christian theology, this is Antichrist (1 John 2:22). Does not Christian Scripture demonize and alienate Islam based on this verse? What side are *you* on? Are you willing to moderate Christianity in order not to alienate Muslims? Doing so is akin to drinking a luke-warm concoction designed to poison would-be, passionate Christians while inoculating moderate Muslims from true Christianity. Perhaps Christians should spit such a drink out of their mouths to avoid becoming the spat out drink themselves.

Jasser's argument presents a dilemma; he is against pointing to Islam itself when countering Islamists. The problem for Jasser is that everyone who objects to affixing the scarlet letter to Islam instead of "Islamism" is eventually caught flat-footed in the same way that people who attempt to make a distinction between Islam and "political Islam" do. Jasser himself states, "Political Islam has a viral recurrence in the form of an infection, which needs a Muslim counter-jihad in order to purge it."[56] Islam is political, so to say "political Islam" instead of Islam is ridiculous, counter-productive, and plays right into the hands of an enemy that has successfully achieved an advantage...all in the name of not sounding too "right wing". Are you beginning to understand why Jihadists love to demonize the right wing and find critics of Islam to be a greater threat to them than Jasser is?

Jasser has been de-clawed.

When is a strategy of denial better than one of truth? When do the ends justify the means? Moderates are not defined by denouncing violent Jihad or the subjugation of women. They choose to debate on a different playing field, one that deals with the issue of Sharia's civil aspects, including inheritance and marriage laws. Can a woman inherit equal portions of a man in Islamic Sharia? Can marriage between Muslim women and non-Muslim men be acceptable? Should a pastor be able to purchase a mosque in order to convert its use as a church?

Is Jasser willing to condemn Sharia? If so, how can he then face moderate Muslims who believe in it? Based on what we know about Sharia, "moderates" cannot accept Sharia, which means they're not moderate. Was the Northern Alliance of Afghanistan moderate when the US Military portrayed them as such? If you consider a position that advocates killing Islamic converts to Christianity as being moderate, they were. The argument is that the US needed the Northern Alliance and couldn't afford alienating that group against the Taliban.

How did that work out? It worked out in the short term but not in the long term, which is the perfect allegory for the larger war the West faces. It accepts the premise that groups like CAIR are moderate. In the short run, such a premise seems to make perfect sense. It makes perfect sense in the long term too—for CAIR.

For the West, such efforts simply create false hope based on a false premise. The problem lies in the literal interpretation of the Qur'an. The solution, according to Jasser, is to introduce a non-literal interpretation. The fact is that we only have a few choices. If Capitalism is considered an "extreme" solution to Communism then socialism is an agreed upon answer. But is it? Can we promote an oxymoron like "Communistic Capitalism"? When socialism is an agreed upon solution for compromise, then what? Doesn't it always lead to the greater tyranny that is Communism? Why wouldn't the same apply when attempting to find a middle ground with Islam? Muslim leaders want to seize the mantle of that middle ground, not as an end in and of itself but as a means to a greater end— Sharia. Jasser simply doesn't see it.

Reformation of Islam is impossible since no one with common sense could espouse to reform Communism or Nazism. Can we change Islamic inheritance laws without defeating Islam first? Until we admit that Islam itself is the problem, we are not addressing the root of that problem; we are dealing with tertiary arguments that Islam welcomes because such arguments are not only distractions but reveal dhimmitude, which gives Islam a sense of power and superiority. Will we succeed in allowing a glass of wine to be drunk and a pork chop to be eaten in Mecca without first defeating Islam? Will Zuhdi allow a Christian boy to marry a Muslim girl or allow a non-Muslim to marry his daughter?

What kind of return on investment can westerners expect by investing in Jasser's perspective? It is nothing more than a "feel good" investment that is high risk and low reward (other than the short term "feel good" return). Jasser has very few followers while the uncompromising Word of God found in the Bible won two thirds of Africa, which was two thirds Muslim less than than fifty years ago.

THE IRONY OF ISLAM

It is a myth to say that Christendom gained peace by allegorizing or moderating the Bible; such things actually cause people to fall away. The fact is that a Christian literalist is peaceful. No one can explain the Qur'an by avoiding the literal Hadith. No one can reverse the Qur'an—its violent Medina verses are its New Testament and the Meccan verses are its abrogated Old Testament. Self-deception is not viable either; reformation and Ijtihad have serious limitations.

No, the true Christian who denounces Islam does not do as Jasser suggests:

> "...dismiss our most powerful weapon against the militant Islamists—the mantle of religion and the pulpit of moderate Muslims who can retake our faith from the Islamists."[57]

When Jasser says that "(we need to) retake our religion," it falls under the myth that Islam was hijacked. When was it hijacked? Was it hijacked when Jews were exiled out of Arabia during the time of Mohammad, the Prophet of Islam? Was it hijacked when the Muslims sacked Jerusalem? Was it hijacked when the Muslims aligned with Hitler in WWII? Was it hijacked when Mein Kampf became a best seller in Turkey?

The issue of the massacre and exile of the Jews from Saudi Arabia was brought up in a debate with Jasser; he simply denied it, saying, "...it's impossible for a prophet to commit such a thing." He said this despite it being well documented in the Hadith of Al Bukari. This is how Dr. Jasser transforms from being an apologist for Jihad to becoming a holocaust denier by making excuses for the violence of the Prophet Mohammad. How is this any different from a modern day, well-intentioned Nazi trying to reform Hitler's image? Oskar Schindler did great things but his efforts didn't win the war; they bought time. If Jasser is driven to protect people from Muslim persecution, we commend him but he should not make the argument that his way is the way to problem resolution; it is not.

It's difficult to deny the bloody savagery perpetrated in the name of Allah when Omar ransacked Judea. If in doubt, read the works of Sophronius. Must Christians abandon history in order to endorse the reformation of a cult? Can a Muslim denounce Khalid bin Al-Waleed's blood thirst on Persians after the coagulation of their blood clogged a ravine? Will Dr. Jasser denounce Tareq bin Ziad's cooking of Christians in Caldrons in Spain? Will he denounce Ali's cry that, "we are a people who drink blood out of the goblets of the skulls of our enemies"? Will he denounce the drinking of the blood of Muhammad by his companions as it dripped from his shield? Will he denounce Muhammad's cry that "the trees and the stones will cry out, 'there is a Jew hiding behind me'?" Can Muslims cry out for the blood of the Martyrs of Cordoba as much as Christians continually confess murders committed by the Crusades?

The answer is yes, but this comes only through confession, which is the habit of Christians and Jews, not Muslims. Yet, it is Christians and Jews who are viewed as lower life forms by Muslims who are so culturally retrograde that they can't recognize their own sins.

Islamic irony is ironically, lost on far too many Muslims.

FOOTNOTES

1. PJ Media Daily Digest, *The Mosab Yousef Saga: Did Hamas 'Defector' Dupe All of Us?* by Walid Shoebat. http://pjmedia.com/blog/the-mosab-yousef-saga-did-hamas-%E2%80%98defector%E2%80%99-dupe-all-of-us/?singlepage=true

2. Son of Hamas. http://sonofhamas.wordpress.com/category/son-of-hamas/

3. Youtube.com, *Son of Hamas: Journey from Terror to Freedom—CBN News,* http://www.youtube.com/watch?v=YYjlcxOO_jM&feature=related

4. Arabic website. http://www.moghrabi-jerusalem.com/shohdaaa/mahmoud.htm

5. Palestine: Information with Provenance (PIWP Database), *Mahmud al-Mughrabi,* http://student.cs.ucc.ie/cs1064/jabowen/IPSC/php/authors.php?auid=17970

6. Arabic Video with English Audio Translation, *Mosab Hassan—His Goal To Infiltrate The Church.* http://www.youtube.com/watch?v=EeIrxROPYWk&feature=related

7. http://www.assistnews.net/Stories/2002/s02050064.htm

8. Alex Awad, *Why Christians Need to Support Palestinian Drive Towards Statehood,* by Alex Awad. http://www.alexawad.org/details.php?ID=26

9. New York, The Sun, *Islamic Leaders Urge Children To Be Bombers.* by Steven Stalinsky. http://www.nysun.com/foreign/islamic-leaders-urge-children-to-be-bombers/38023/

10. Video, Walid Shoebat Foundation, *Connecting Point.* http://www.shoebat.com/videos/connectingPoint.php.

11. BibleGateway.com, Mark 13:5-6, New King James Version. http://www.biblegateway.com/passage/?search=Mark+13&version=NKJV

12. Arabic website, with English available, *Beit Sahour City Portal.* http://beit-sahour.info/ar/story-of-beit-sahour?start=3

13. CanadianChristianity.com, *Rethinking the Middle East crisis,* by Ron Brackin. http://canadianchristianity.com/cgi-bin/bc.cgi?bc/bccn/0602/intrethinking

14. Crosswalk.com, *Whose Is The Palestine Deed? An Amendment,* by Ron Brackin. http://www.crosswalk.com/1141340/

15. http://www.beliefnet.com/Faiths/Christianity/Articles/Teaching-the-Bible-With-President-Jimmy-Carter.aspx?p=2

16. BuzzFeed, *Why Former President Jimmy Carter Supports Gay Marriage, Jimmy Carter comes out in support for gay marriage in his new book ABOUT THE BIBLE.* http://www.buzzfeed.com/mjs538/why-former-president-jimmy-carter-supports -gay-mar

17. BBC News, *Obituary: George Habash,* by Crispin Thorold. http://news.bbc.co.uk/2/hi/7211505.stm

18. http://frontpagemag.com/2012/02/20/christ-at-an-israeli-checkpoint-2/print/

19. *Study on Christian Zionism, Concept – inception – risks,* Joseph Ajeha, Summer 2009. http://translate.google.com/translate?hl=en&sl=ar&u=http://www.ppp.ps/pdfs/Deraseh.doc&ei=OqpTTKDYEYL-8AaDz6GuCA&sa=X&oi=translate&ct=result&resnum=9&ved=0CD8Q7gEwCA&prev=/search%3Fq%3D%2522%25D8%25A7%25D9%2584%25D9%258A%25D9%2583%25D8%25B3%2B%25D8%25B9%25D9%2588%25D8%25B6%2522%26hl%3Den%26sa%3DN

20. Arabic website, with English available. http://www.linga.org/local-news/NTgz

21. http://www.pflp.ps/arabic/solidarity.php?action=List&next=426

22. Jewish Virtual Library, *Background Information on Senior Prisoners in Jericho.* http://www.jewishvirtuallibrary.org/jsource/arabs/jerichoprison.html

23. Video in English, *Holy Land: Christians In Peril by Religion of Peace (Part 1 of 5).* http://www.youtube.com/watch?v=QWYqev6zfgI

24. BBC News World Edition, *The siege of Bethlehem.* http://news.bbc.co.uk/2/hi/programmes/correspondent/2029661.stm

25. Ibid

26. Jewish Virtual Library, *Golda Meir on Peace.* http://www.jewishvirtuallibrary.org/jsource/Quote/MeironPeace.html

27. Middle East Forum, *War and Peace – and Deceit – In Islam,* by Raymond Ibrahim. http://www.meforum.org/2066/war-and-peace-and-deceit-in-islam

28. A Common Word, *The Most Successful Muslim-Christian Interfaith Initiative in History.* http://www.acommonword.com/signatories/

29. Now The End Begins, *Chrislam Starts To Spread*. http://www.nowtheendbegins. com/blog/?p=1366

30. A Common Word, *The Most Successful Muslim-Christian Interfaith Initiative in History*. http://www.acommonword.com/?page=media&item=560

31. Yale Center for Faith & Culture, *Loving God and Neighbor Together, A Christian Response to 'A Common Word Between Us and You'*. http://www.yale.edu/faith /acw/acw.htm

32. Ibid (see Preamble)

33. The Christian Post, *Exclusive Rick Warren: 'Flat Out Wrong' That Muslims, Christians View God the Same,* by Alex Murashko. http://www.christianpost.com/news/exclu sive-rick-warren-flat-out-wrong-that-muslims-christians-view-god-the-same-70767/

34. Video, GoodFight Ministries, *Rick Warren, Emergents and Muslims,* by Pastor Joe Schimmel. http://www.youtube.com/watch?feature=player_embedded&v=iiMYRz FR2ZM

35. BibleGateway.com, Matthew 12:31-32, New King James Version. http://www.bible gateway.com/passage/?search=Matthew%2012:31-32&version=NKJV

36. Ha-Emet, *Bringing the War on Jerusalem to American Universities*. http://www. ha-emet.com/

37. Discover The Networks.org, *Mazin Qumsiyeh,* http://www.discoverthenetworks. org/individualProfile.asp?indid=933

38. Anti-Defamation League, *Al-Awda, The Palestine Right to Return Coalition, Back-ground and Ideology*. http://archive.adl.org/israel/anti_israel/al_awda/ide ology.asp

39. Al-Awda, The Palestine Right to Return Coalition, *About Al-Awda*. http:// www.al-awda.org/about.html

40. Arabic website. http://alrawwya.blogspot.com/2011/02/15.html

41. Arabic website. http://www.arabbab.com/?p=70537

42. http://webcache.googleusercontent.com/wiki/Suicide_bomber

43. Arabic website. http://www.ajras.org/?page=show_details&Id=3463&table= articles

44. Front Page Mag.com, *The 'Flytilla': Brought to You by Friends of the Olive Tree Initiative,* by Nichole Hungerford. http://frontpagemag.com/2011/nichole-hun gerford/the-flytilla-brought-to-you-by-friends-of-the-olive-tree-initiative/

45. *The International Solidarity Movement: Threat to America, Israel and the World,* by Lee Kaplan. http://www.usasurvival.org/docs/kaplan_rpt.pdf

46. AIFD, American Islamic Forum for Democracy. http://aifdemocracy.org/

47. Answers.com, *Muhammad Sa'id al-Ashmawi*. http://www.answers.com/topic/muhammad-sa-id-al-ashmawi

48. Ibid, pgs. 77-78

49. Ibid, p. 104

50. http://www.slantright.com/index.php?name=News&file=article&sid=3329

51. The Washington Post, *Islamic group asks DoJ to review police training,* by Jeff Stein. http://voices.washingtonpost.com/spytalk/2010/12/islamic_group_asks_doj_to_revi.html

52. The Washington Post, *An American Hajj,* by Eboo Patel. http://onfaith.washingtonpost.com/onfaith/eboo_patel/2007/12/an_american_hadj.html

53. BatesLine, *Juhdi Jasser: An interview with a moderate Muslim leader,* by Michael Bates. http://www.batesline.com/archives/2007/05/zuhdi-jasser-an.html

54. Wholesome Words, Worldwide Missions, *William Carey.* http://www.wholesomewords.org/missions/icarey.html

55. BMS World Mission, *Examples of people who have stood up to injustice throughout history.* http://www.bmsworldmission.org/news-blogs/blogs/justice-history-makers

56. BatesLine, *Juhdi Jasser: An interview with a moderate Muslim leader,* by Michael Bates. http://www.batesline.com/archives/2007/05/zuhdi-jasser-an.html

57. Walid Shoebat Foundation, *"Can Islam Reform?" Debate Featuring Walid Shoebat, Dr. Zuhdi Jasser and Robert Spencer.* http://www.shoebat.com/videos/CanIslamReform032211.php

CHAPTER

14

ISLAM, THE U.S. MILITARY, AND FOREIGN POLICY

INFILTRATION

Despite 9/11/01, the Fort Hood massacre, and various other Jihadist attacks, Muslim Scholars have not changed their intentions and western governments have not changed their policies. Consider the case of Louay Safi, a top official at the ISNA and a research director at International Institute of Islamic Thought (IIIT). Less than one month after the Fort Hood attack, Safi was still training US troops at Fort Hood about Islam at the behest of the US Defense Department (DoD). A man who belongs to organizations that shared Nidal Malik Hasan's objectives—if not his tactics—continued to have access to US troops after Hasan's jihadist rampage. Even if JBTW was the excuse for the continued breach, this was one time when it was an absolutely inexcusable one, especially in the wake of an act of war on a US military post.[1]

Safi's definition of an Islamic state seems to go hand-in-glove with what Ibn Khaldun calls "the right approach to the definition of an Islamic state". It ended with the following definition: "the Islamic State—is—the nation's power structures that guide political action and defined in accordance with the principles of Islamic political system." (Louay Safi, Religion and Politics p. 121)

As we have continued to maintain and demonstrate, when it comes to the JBTW artists, it's not about *living* under a secular government; it's about how to *use* that government as a vehicle of transport to a reality that will usher *in* Sharia.

In practically every way, Safi has repeatedly taken positions that would further the cause of the Muslim Brotherhood in America. As a leader within ISNA, this should be no surprise; ISNA is a member organization. Safi has supported talks between Washington and Iran's leaders; he has denounced raids on Islamic centers like those mentioned previously.

In an article written by Rowan Scarborough that appeared in *Human Events*, the author quoted from some of Safi's writings. Here are a couple of examples:

> "The war against the apostates [non-believers of Islam] is carried out not to force them to accept Islam, but to enforce the Islamic law and maintain order."

Or, how about…

> "It is up to the Muslim leadership to assess the situation and weigh the circumstances as well as the capacity of the Muslim community before deciding the appropriate type of jihad. At one stage, Muslims may find that jihad, through persuasion or peaceful resistance, is the best and most effective method to achieve just peace."[2]

When those two quotes are taken together, the intentions of a one Louay Safi are made quite clear. Islamic law is something that should be enforced and the method of doing so must be determined based on the circumstances that exist on the ground or in the lands where it is being enforced. These views are, most assuredly, 'Brotherhood-friendly.'

As a leader of ISNA, an approved Muslim Brotherhood group, that would make sense. Perhaps now is a good time to review one of the quotes from that 1991 Muslim Brotherhood document written by Mohamed Akram that called for destroying Western civilization from within.[3] Those words, along with Safi's access to US troops after the Fort Hood attack, should cause shockwaves, not something less than ripples.

They are the words of America's domestic enemies. Yet, America has not only refused to identify those enemies, it continues to embrace them. Safi's presence at Fort Hood *after* the jihadist attacks perpetrated by Nidal Malik Hasan may, in fact, be the most egregious example of dereliction of duty on the part of every American leader who has sworn allegiance to the following oath:

> I do solemnly swear (or affirm) that I will support and defend the Constitution of the United States against all enemies, foreign and domestic; that I will bear true faith and allegiance to the same; that I take this obligation freely, without any mental reservation or purpose of evasion; and that I will well and faithfully discharge the duties of the office on which I am about to enter: So help me God.[4]

Emblematic of this very problem were the words of General George Casey three days after the Hasan's jihadist rampage. At the time, Casey was the Army's Chief of Staff. While appearing on *ABC's This Week* with George Stephanopoulos, Casey focused on helping Muslims alienate Nidal Malik Hasan for public consumption, instead of pointing to the larger problem. Rather than take the opportunity to identify a Muslim Brotherhood problem, Casey actually warned viewers against doing so themselves:

> "Speculation could potentially heighten backlash against some of our Muslim soldiers and what happened at Fort Hood was a tragedy, but I believe it would be an even greater tragedy if our diversity becomes a casualty here. It's not just about Muslims, we have a very diverse army, we have very diverse society and that gives us all strength. But again, we need to be very careful about that."[5]

To be fair to Casey, he is not the problem. His public stance was merely symptomatic of a much larger one. Also, to be fair, Casey's words either originated with the Obama administration or had to be approved by it before they were uttered. In this regard, former President George W. Bush deserves more criticism than does Casey. Bush embraced Islamists immediately after 9/11 and had no one but himself to blame, if one believes the president should possess a 'buck stops here' mentality. Nonetheless, Casey's words indicate a systemic problem within America's leadership. Conversely, Islamists like Safi must have smugly smiled as they watched the US Army's top brass kowtow to them just three days after the deadliest jihadist attack on American soil since 9/11. The attack on Fort Hood should have been to Casey what the September 11th attacks were to George W. Bush. In 2009, after eight years of experience since 9/11, Casey's stance indicated the United States leadership was either just as ignorant *of,* or just as unwilling to *face,* the uncomfortable truth, a truth that involves a stealth Muslim Brotherhood invasion. There is more than enough evidence available to warrant an aggressive approach aimed at preventing that stealth invasion from being successful.

There are no excuses at this point.

On Arabic websites, Safi aspires to change Muslim societies as well. At the crux of this change is the introduction of a brand of modern thought to Muslims worldwide, not to *adapt* western-style secularism but to *use* it to further the creation of an Islamic state. In essence, as the west is being intimidated through political correctness, teachers like Safi are instructing Muslim students how to ratchet up that intimidation. When they see America's top leaders succumb to political correctness, such perceptions only fuel the fire. If the likes of Safi are the match that ignites fiery and hateful passions among his Muslim students, the acquiescence to Islam on the part of western leaders serves as the bellows that fan the flames.

This makes the actions of both Safi and Casey doubly dangerous for western civilization. Safi deceives westerners while emboldening Muslims. Casey and his ilk unwittingly do the same thing with words, actions, and inaction that collectively communicate weakness to both our foreign and domestic enemies.

As if Safi's English wasn't bad enough, his Arabic only serves up a far more dangerous dish. A translation of Louay Safi's Arabic more than proves that he supports the establishment of Sharia law and a single Islamic Nation (Umma) worldwide after engendering a commitment to the goals of Islamists. In short, Islam is the conception that, if carried to term, will see the birth of Sharia law:

> "The application of Sharia needs to build a public consensus by **developing an awareness and commitment to Islam before the imposition of Sharia law.** This vision is based...on two ideas. First: The relationship between persons is to obtain a goal (people are to be used)...Second: The political leadership represents the general purposes and common interests of the general public and is working to achieve them...the emergence of an Islamic nation within **that framework requires a society committed to the principle and standard of Islamists.** It requires the actual stability of the existing nation state being able to carry the aspirations of the Muslim community.
>
> Accordingly, if an Islamic state is conditional on the commitment of the nation selected prior to the Islamic regime approach to life, a discussion about the application of Sharia law in this nation is useless and meaningless. But it may suggest the support of the argument raised by some Muslim thinkers who argue for the gradual introduction of Sharia into Muslim countries in modern times, compared to the Covenant Prophet."[6,7]

Mr. Safi's words advocate the invitation to establish an Islamic state in this era by using the systems already in place. It's nothing short of political trickery. When the people of a nation choose to exercise their rights and affairs relative to political management, arguments for the provisions of Sharia's legitimacy will be far more powerful. When that happens, implementation of Sharia becomes the will of that nation and not implemented from the top, down. Gen. Casey displayed this principle perfectly.

A clear indication that this strategy may be working is when a country's people begins to deride its own constitution. Beginning in 2009, shortly after the election of Barack Obama, the United States experienced the rise of the Tea Party, which was nothing more than a call for the US to return to its founding principles. It was met with anger and disgust from a significant contingent of Americans. It is this kind of mindset among people within an existent nation that Islamists like Safi relish.

One of the most outrageous comments about the Tea Party came from none other than Rep. Andre Carson (D-IN) in 2011. Carson, himself a Muslim, said the following about the Tea Party:

> "Some of these folks in Congress right now would love to see us as second-class citizens. Some of them in Congress right now with this tea party movement would love to see you and me... hanging on a tree."[8]

Aside from the statement being out of bounds and completely without evidence, it only served to further divide America. Those who supported Carson aligned themselves with those who want to deconstruct the existing framework of the United States in order to replace it with Sharia law. Based on Safi's own words, Carson helped to further the cause of Sharia in America simply by attacking those who revere our founding documents.

On a larger scale, this mentality seemed to manifest itself in what became known as the *Arab Spring*, a movement in the Middle East that saw the overthrow of regimes in places like Tunisia, Egypt, Libya, and others. Despite the obvious reality at the time, that the vacuum left behind by the removal of those dictators would be filled by groups more sympathetic to the Muslim Brotherhood (if not the Ikhwan itself), the Barack Obama administration implemented policies that helped to further the *Arab Spring*.

Almost inexplicably, the United States seemed to come down on the side of the Muslim Brotherhood in nearly every instance, both diplomatically (Egypt) and militarily (Libya). In this regard, Safi's model seemed to be followed. By supporting the cause of Islam, the west was setting the stage for Sharia law in those regions.

As the Syrian regime of Bashar al-Assad faced a similar fate, it was discovered that Louay Safi was the head of a group called the *Syrian National Council*, which was formed in Turkey. The objective of the council was to bring all revolutionary forces together in united opposition to the Assad regime. It included secularists as well as Muslim Brotherhood members.[9] Following Safi's own words, the goal would be to use all of the Council's members to lay the groundwork for Sharia law—regardless of who in the Council desired it—once the regime fell.

COUNCIL ON FOREIGN RELATIONS

The Council on Foreign Relations (CFR), established in 1921, has become one of the most prominent foreign policy think tanks in modern history. In Independent Task Force Report No. 54, entitled *In Support of Arab Democracy: Why and How*, authors Madeline Albright, former Secretary of State under the Clinton administration, and Vin Weber considered the viability of promoting democracy in the Middle East:

> In its report, the Task Force asserts that over the long run, the development of democratic institutions in Arab countries "will diminish the appeal of extremism and terrorism, the risks of revolutionary upheaval, and the emergence of regimes openly hostile to the United States." From these important findings this Task Force report offers a comprehensive set of policy recommendations for the Bush administration to promote an "environment in the Middle East that is conducive to peaceful democratic change."[10]

In 2006, Hamas—a Muslim Brotherhood-inspired group—won a large majority when Palestinians were given the chance to elect a new parliament.[11] Some years later, the 'Arab Spring' demonstrated again, that when the Middle East is given the reigns to unfettered democracy, anti-Semitism and extremism increases. These realities ran counter to what the CFR asserted in its paper:

> Through a critical examination of regional developments and an assessment of U.S. options, the Task Force sought to answer two primary questions: First, does a policy of promoting democracy in the Middle East serve U.S. interests and foreign policy goals? Second, if so, how should the United States implement such a policy, taking into account the full range of its interests? The Task Force's answer to the first question is "yes." The United States should support democracy consistently and in all regions of the world. Although

democracy entails certain inherent risks, the denial of freedom carries much more significant long-term dangers. **If Arab citizens are able to express grievances freely and peacefully, they will be less likely to turn to more extreme measures. They will also be more likely to build open and prosperous societies with respect for human rights and the rule of law.**[12]

All of this was music to the ears of Feisal Abdul Rauf, who is listed in the paper as a member of the task force, which expressed to several Islamist agencies that an opportunity to introduce democracy was desirous and would usher in their long awaited goals. Are we to believe that someone with as much political experience as Albright got this all wrong? It's simply not plausible. Instead of accepting the premise that the likes of Albright are duped by the likes of Rauf, westerners need to entertain the possibility that Albright and Rauf are on the same page, especially when they're singing the same tune.

Islam's collaboration with the West to advance Islam is not new. Had it not been for the US aid to the Mujahideen in Afghanistan, the Taliban would not have been born. The gossip amongst the Arab population has always been that the Muslim Brotherhood and their sympathizers were CIA collaborators. But Islam allows for this in the *Doctrine of Balance* (Muruna), as a previous chapter that features the work of Qaradawi demonstrates. Westerners are not accustomed to *Taqiyya, Kitman, Muruna* and *Hudna*. As Muhammad, the prophet of Islam said, "*Al-Harbu Khid'a*" (war is deception). Yet, even Jihad—as Muslim apologists argue—is not simply about warfare; it is also fought with a pen, which Feisal Abdul Rauf always seems to have in his pocket.

The work of the CFR in this regard is akin to putting the cart flying the fortress's flag before the Trojan horse, which only further facilitates entry. Democracy in the Middle East is not only the cry of the Council on Foreign Relations; it is also the cry of the Muslim Brotherhood. Giving the Ikhwan what it wants would be like letting the Nazis in WWII have all of Czechoslovakia without consequence.

How about CFR's second question, the one about how the US would implement such a policy of Middle East democratization?

In answer to the second question, the United States should promote the development of democratic institutions and practices over the long term, mindful that democracy cannot be imposed from the outside and that sudden, traumatic change is neither necessary nor desirable. America's goal in the Middle East should be to encourage democratic evolution, not revolution."[13]

Albright and Company are either dupes who are operating from flawed premises or they are themselves deceiving westerners while the likes of Rauf can sit back and grin with his arms folded from a front row seat.

This CFR paper was written one year prior to the Palestinian voters decided to overwhelmingly sweep Hamas into power in 2006. It's fairly obvious that US policy relative to seeing that election take place was in line with what the CFR task force advocated. That policy decision was ultimately an unexpected—and quite large—black eye for the George W. Bush administration. According to an article that appeared in *The New Republic*, Bush demanded that Hamas be permitted to participate in the elections, despite the objections of those who knew better—like Israeli leadership.[14] Though Bush insisted that Hamas be on the ballot, he also insisted the US could not deal with them. This would be a strong indication that he in no way anticipated a Hamas victory.[15] This was not the only example of how the United States attempted to export western Democracy to the Middle East.

AFGHANISTAN CONSTITUTION

In response to the September 11th attacks, the United States led a coalition of countries into Afghanistan, which is where the repressive, Islamic Taliban regime had a stronghold. The objective of western forces was to uproot the Taliban and liberate the Afghan people. Ultimately, that liberation was supposed to conclude with western-style democracy. Unfortunately, geo-political correctness played far too much of a role in the strategy as the Judeo-Christian foundation of western culture was rejected and hypersenstitivity with respect to the country's Islamic past helped birth a Constitution in 2004 that placed Islamic law at its core.

After defeating the Taliban, the US had a tremendous opportunity to set the terms under which a future Afghanistan would operate. Instead, the newly installed Aghanistan government essentially used JBTW in its Constitution, beginning with the very first line of the Preamble, which states:

> With firm faith in God Almighty and relying on His lawful mercy, and Believing in the Sacred religion of Islam.[16]

Comparatively, this would be akin to Japan demanding that as part of its terms of surrender following World War II, the emperor would be allowed to continue to dictate the future of the country. Though the United States did permit Japan to keep an emperor, it was made clear in no uncertain terms that said emperor would be nothing more than a figurehead who would have to acknowledge the authority of the US Supreme Commander.[17]

Additionally, the United States permitted Afghanistan to put something in the very first line of *its* Constitution that is completely and totally antithetical to the content of the First amendment to the US Constitution—the freedom of religion. Essentially, instead of setting the terms for Afghanistan's surrender, the United States accepted the terms of the defeated.

That's not all. After the preamble, the first three Articles of the Constitution only serve to underscore this reality:

Article One
Ch. 1. Art. 1
Afghanistan is an Islamic Republic, independent, unitary and indivisible state.

Article Two
Ch. 1, Art. 2
The **religion of the state** of the Islamic Republic of Afghanistan is the **sacred religion of Islam.**

Followers of other religions are free to exercise their faith and perform their religious rites within the limits of the provisions of law.

Article Three
Ch. 1, Art. 3
In Afghanistan, **no law can be contrary to** the beliefs and provisions of **the sacred religion of Islam.** [emphasis mine][18]

A key point to make here is that when the west relents in the face of JBTW, it necessarily makes itself hypocritical. The introduction of western-style democracy into Middle Eastern countries should come with all that it entails, including its founding principles, like the freedom of religion, for example. In fact, it is the very first line of the very first amendment to the US Constitution that expresses this:

Congress shall make no law respecting an establishment of religion, or prohibiting the free exercise thereof; [19]

Does it sound like the United States was left holding the short end of the stick after defeating the Taliban? To the vanquished go the spoils! JBTW was most certainly effective when it came to the crafting of the Afghanistan Constitution.

There are two opposing examples that illustrate the willingness of the United States to reject its own principles while bending over backwards to respect the religious rigidity and fervor of Islamic fundamentalists.

CNN reported that the US Military confiscated and burned Christian Bibles in Afghanistan that were written in two of the more prominent Afghan languages. The official reason given by the military for the burnings involved troop safety as well as a rule that forbids soldiers from proselytizing while in Afghanistan. [20] Imagine a devout Christian being told that Bibles are being burned to protect him. To a Christian, the Bible represents the only thing that can *save* him. It sounds like a western version of doublespeak.

Approximately one year later, top US Commander in Afghanistan, General David Petraeus publicly reacted to a pastor in Florida named Terry Jones, who burned a Qur'an in protest of Islam. This is a portion of what Gen. Petraeus said in a video that appeared on the Wall Street Journal's website:

"...we condemn the action of an individual in the United States who burned a Holy Qur'an. That action was hateful, it was intolerant, and it was extremely disrespectful...we condemn it in the strongest manner possible." [21]

The implication was that nothing holy should be burned. Were the Christian Bibles not holy? Perhaps something far more intolerant than anything Jones did can be found in the case of Abdul Rahman, who converted from Islam to Christianity. Not long after the christening of the Afghanistan Constitution, he was arrested and charged with apostasy in that country. There was overwhelming sentiment that he would be put to death. Fortunately, international attention and pressure helped to prevent that and Rahman successfully fled to Italy. [22]

The wording of the Afghanistan Constitution allows for the application of both abrogation and the *Doctrine of Balance*; it is clear—based on sharia law— that it doesn't matter what the rest of the document says; Afghanistan is ruled by Islamic law and not western-style democracy.

IRAQI CONSTITUTION

As US Diplomats were working with Afghanis on the document that would ulti-mately be the supreme law of the land, the US Military had invaded Iraq and deposed Saddam Hussein. Like in Afghanistan, the goal was to install western-style democracy in that country as well. Also, as was the case in Afghanistan, the US Military did its job; it made quick work of Saddam Hussein but as was the case in Afghanistan, the defeated seemed to set the terms of their own non-surrender.

Very early in the new Iraqi Constitution, which was completed about a year after the Afghanistan Constitution, it was made clear that Islam and sharia law would rule the new day:

> Article (2): 1st - Islam is the official religion of the state and is a basic source of legislation:
> (a) No law can be passed that contradicts the undisputed rules of Islam.[23]

Quite ironically, the Christians in Iraq under Saddam Hussein were safer than they were in a post-Saddam era. According to the *USA Today*, various estimates show a reduction in the Christian population in Iraq since the US-led invasion to be approximately half a million just seven years later.[24]

JUDEO-CHRISTIAN ETHICS, ANYONE?

Unless the West introduces Judeo-Christian style ethics and western values, all that will result from the CFR's academic exercise is advancement of the Islamist cause. The Muslim world knows it. Yet, for years, the West devoured (and continues to devour) all the talk of peace in English, banking on wishful thinking and false hopes. If not ignorant, the CFR certainly portrays ignorance with verbiage like this:

> The United States must remain vigilant in opposing terrorist organizations.[25]

This CFR paper was authored at about the same time that Afghanistan and Iraq were completing their constitutions. Yet, the simplest of realities seemed to have been lost on one of the world's most powerful political think tanks. Terrorism is not simply an *explosive act* that involves guns, bombs, and passenger-filled airplanes used as missiles. It is also very political in nature. Pens can do with ink what bombs can do with fuses; they can change landscapes and the constitu-tions of the Middle Eastern countries the United States was supposed to liberate clearly demonstrate that terrorism can also manifest itself in the form of a *political act* of intimidation. Ground Zero mosque imam, Feisal Abdul Rauf did this when he threatened Americans with the wrath of physical terrorists if they didn't give him—the political terrorist—what he wanted.[26] Islamists like Rauf are always willing to play the role of a good cop who is warning virtual political prisoners that the bad cop is difficult to restrain.

Had the Council of Foreign Relations been "vigilant in opposing terrorist organizations," they would simply answer the question I always ask: What are the differences between the goals of Anwar Al-Awlaqi and Feisal Abdul Rauf? Answer: nothing, except means in furtherance of the same goal—Sharia. Drones hunted one while the other incubates unmolested inside a Trojan horse.

Islamists are also quite adept at exploiting the past sins of America while ignoring the logs in their own eyes. This is what we call the inverse comparison and it doesn't help that left wing westerners like Madeline Albright contribute directly to this technique by putting her name to it as a Co-chair on the CFR task force:

> "After all, the evolution of American democracy includes not only the majesty of the Declaration of Independence and the Constitution, but also the blight of slavery, a civil war, the denial of women's suffrage for well over a century, and the exclusion of African-Americans from formal participation until the enactment of landmark civil rights legislation in the 1960s."[27]

Perhaps this type of behavior helps liberal elitists like Albright feel like she's able to rise above the fray of nationalism. After all, it's a lofty goal to be able to see all sides of an issue, right? Westerners like Albright rarely seem interested in exploring why Islamists like her colleague on the task force, Rauf, never seem to offer such self-deprecating points of view to match, even when he has far more examples to highlight, like Islam's enslavement of blacks, endless civil wars, and the mistreatment of women.

Rigid secularism is rarely a match for rigid religious fundamentalism. Consider the increase in the Hijabization (wearing the Hijab) of women in the Islamic world. During the seventies, very few women were required to wear a Hijab. It was years of a slow brewing Islamic revolution, what Islamists call *"Thawarat Al-Masajid"* (The Mosque Revolution); it initiated a yearning for Islamic culture and law.

Egypt has already been Hijabized. Iran, Jordan, Syria, the Palestinians and Turkey are well on their way. Men in Egypt take great pride in their *Zebibas* (forehead marks from prostration during prayer). Extending the beard and trimming the mustache has become the trend in much of the Islamic world. In everything people do, they must always remember Islam is both a religion and a state. Secular democracies almost always yield to this reality. Inertia is the scientific principle which states that objects in motion tend to stay in motion and objects at rest tend to stay at rest. The rise of Islam—along with its persecution of non-Muslims—in the Middle East is very much in motion. The conditions of the minority Christian population are so severe that the West should be focusing on such persecution before even considering the appeasement of Islam. What Albright and her ilk are doing in collaborating with the Islamists while ignoring the victims of Islam would be like ignoring the Jews while collaborating with Nazis in order to bridge divisions between the West and Nazism.

The beauty of any nation can be found in how it treats minorities. In Muslim country after Muslim country, the persecution of Christian minorities is no longer just coming from the state; it is also coming from the Mosque Revolution.

Will the West ever face the mosque head on or will it simply pour more money into a lost cause that is a sinking ship of secular democratization in the Middle East? The only time the word "mosque" appears in the CFR report is in the bio of Feisal Abdul Rauf. His book title provides an added touch of irony in light of the fact that Albright seemed more interested in pointing out what's wrong with America:

> Imam of Masjid al-Farah, a mosque in New York City... His latest book, What's Right with Islam: A New Vision for Muslims and the West, ranked among the Christian Science Monitor's five best nonfiction books of 2004.

Does the Council on Foreign Relations ever investigate if whom they are dealing with is an Islamist or a secularist? Does it care? Rauf's book was originally written in Indonesian and entitled, *Seruan Azan Dari Puing WTC* (A Call to Prayer from the World Trade Center Rubble). Azan (summons for prayer) is only conducted from a minaret—a mosque. A mosque is hardly what's right with the Middle East; it is what is wrong with the Middle East, especially since the plan is to build one where thousands of Americans lost their lives. What the Middle East needs is fewer mosques and more hospitals and schools that allow religious dialogue that is devoid of religious bigotry and supremacy.

In an article published in the *Wall Street Journal* and posted to the *Religion News* blog, Albright's connection to an unindicted co-conspirator in the first World Trade Center attack in 1993 was shown to have served a purpose for the Islamist. Siraj Wahhaj was named as a co-conspirator by a US Attorney and when this point was highlighted years later, Wahhaj had a convenient and noteworthy defense; he pointed to the fact that in her role as Secretary of State, Albright hosted him and others for a dinner to celebrate the breaking of the Ramadan fast years after Wahhaj had been identified as a co-conspirator. Albright's spokesman declined to comment when asked about this charge.[28]

Wahhaj also carried the distinction of being the first Muslim to ever recite the opening prayer in front of the US House of Representatives. Two years later, the World Trade Center would suffer its first attack.[29]

So why do so many democrats and leftists seem blind to these obvious realities? Many Americans think that liberals are so cozy with Islamists because they are "useful idiots" or "naïve". While they are certainly useful, they are hardly naïve.

Albright, for example, has a career that is steeped in politics, diplomacy, and interactions with Islamist leaders. One is left to conclude that her ideology is more closely aligned with that of Islamists. It's not naiveté and it's certainly not the result of a lack of education. Even if it were, elitist westerners would never admit that; it'd be like the emperor admitting he has no clothes.

Islam has *Al-Ishtirakiya Al-Islamiya* (Islamic socialism), which tickles the ears of many liberals. In Islam, life does not begin at the moment of conception; that tickles the ears of abortionists. Islam has "Hima" (protection of environment); that tickles the ears of Al-Gore, who praised Islamic environmentalism. The Big Bang is also claimed to be in the Qur'an; this tickles the ears of the evolutionists. It would take volumes to cover the works of visiting Islamic scholars to the United States. Their accomplishments in American society are storied and make no mistake, they advance their agenda through liberals.

FOOTNOTES

1. National Review Online, *Somebody at Fort Hood Should be Walking the Plank,* by Andrew C. McCarthy. http://www.nationalreview.com/corner/191177/somebody-fort-hood-should-be-walking-plank-andrew-c-mccarthy#

2. Human Events, *FBI Partners With Jihad Groups,* by Rowan Scarborough. http://www.humanevents.com/2009/09/10/fbi-partners-with-jihad-groups/

3. IPT The Investigative Project on Terrorism, *An Explanatory Memorandum on the General Strategic Goal for the Brotherhood in North America,* by Mohamed Akram. http://www.investigativeproject.org/document/id/20

4. United States Senate, *Oath of Office.* http://www.senate.gov/artandhistory/history/common/briefing/Oath_Office.htm

5. ABC News, *Ft. Hood: Gen. Casey Doesn't Rule Out Terrorism,* by Jacqueline Klingebiel. http://abcnews.go.com/blogs/politics/2009/11/ft-hood-gen-casey-doesnt-rule-out-terrorism/

6. Arabic website with English available, Middle East Online. http://www.middle-east-online.com/?id=104290

7. WND Commentary, *The Emerging Muslim Union,* Exclusive: Walid Shoebat translates Arabic to discover ture goals of the Brotherhood. http://www.wnd.com/2011/02/259389/

8. The Washington Post, *Rep. Carson: Tea party wants to see African Americans 'hanging on a tree',* http://www.washingtonpost.com/blogs/2chambers/post/rep-carson-tea-party-wants-to-see-african-americans-hanging-on-a-tree/2011/08/30/gIQAFztmqJ_blog.html

9. The Global Muslim Brotherhood Daily Report, *Exclusive: U.S. Muslim Brotherhood Leader Central Figure in Newly Formed Syrian Opposition Council.* http://globalmbreport.com/?p=5046

10. Council on Foreign Relations, *In Support of Arab Democracy: Why and How,* Independent Task Force Report No. 43, pgs. xiii-xiv, by Madeleine K. Albright and Vin Weber. http://www.cfr.org/content/publications/attachments/Arab_Democracy_TF.pdf

11. Washington Post.com, Unrest in the Middle East, *Hamas Sweeps Palestinian Elections, Complicating Peace Efforts in Mideast,* by Scott Wilson. http://www.washingtonpost.com/wp-dyn/content/article/2006/01/26/AR2006012600372.html

12. Council on Foreign Relations, *In Support of Arab Democracy: Why and How,* Independent Task Force Report No. 43, pgs. 3-4, by Madeleine K. Albright and Vin Weber. http://www.cfr.org/content/publications/attachments/Arab_Democracy_TF.pdf

13. Ibid, p. 4

14. New Republic, *How Abbas's U.S. Gambit Empowered Hamas,* by Efraim Halevy. http://www.newrepublic.com/article/world/95274/abbas-un-gambit-empowered-hamas#

15. The Telegraph, *Terrorists Voted into power,* by Tim Butcher in Ramallah. http://www.telegraph.co.uk/news/worldnews/middleeast/palestinianauthority/1508974/Terrorists-voted-into-power.html

16. Afghanistan Online, *The Constitution of Afghanistan,* Year 1382. http://www.afghan-web.com/politics/current_constitution.html

17. BBC, *1945 Japan signs unconditional surrender.* http://news.bbc.co.uk/onthisday/hi/dates/stories/september/2/newsid_3582000/3582545.stm

18. Afghanistan Online, *The Constitution of Afghanistan,* Year 1382. http://www.afghan-web.com/politics/current_constitution.html

19. Cornell University Law School, Legal Information Institute, *U.S. Constitution, Bill of Right.* http://www.law.cornell.edu/constitution/billofrights

20. CNN World, *Military burns unsolicited Bibles sent to Afghanistan.* http://articles.cnn.com/2009-05-20/world/us.military.bibles.burned_1_bibles-al-jazeera-english-military-personnel?_s=PM:WORLD

21. The Wall Street Journal, *Petraeus Says Quran Burning Endangers War Effort,* by Yaroslav Trofimov and Maria Abi-Habib. http://online.wsj.com/article/SB10001424052748703806304576240643831942006.html

22. Fox News.com. *Afghan Christian Convert Flees to Italy.* http://www.foxnews.com/story/0,2933,189440,00.html

23. http://www.uniraq.org/documents/iraqi_constitution.pdf

24. USA Today, *Fear of jihad driving Christians from Iraq,* by Alice Fordham. http://usatoday30.usatoday.com/news/world/2010-11-12-iraqchristians12_ST_N.htm

25. Council on Foreign Relations, *In Support of Arab Democracy: Why and How,* Independent Task Force Report No. 43, p. 5, by Madeleine K. Albright and Vin Weber. http://www.cfr.org/content/publications/attachments/Arab_Democracy_TF.pdf

26. http://www.breitbart.com/breitbart-tv

27. Ibid, p. 9

28. Religion News Blog, *One imam traces path of Islam in black America,* by Paul M. Barrett. http://www.religionnewsblog.com/4820/one-imam-traces-path-of-islam-in-black-america

29. Discover The Networks.org, *Siraj Wahhaj,* http://www.discoverthenetworks.org/individualProfile.asp?indid=716

SECTION

6

Arab Thaw
And Geopolitics

CHAPTER
15

NORTH AFRICAN
DOMINOES

DRACULA LIVES

*P*erhaps there are no two words that better exemplify what we mean by JBTW than, "Arab Spring". To call it a misnomer is an insult to inaptly named events. Putting the movement in the proper context is more deserving of a Dracula metaphor in which the prince of darkness rises from the dead after having been banished from human consciousness.

In the 1969 film, *Dracula has Risen from the Grave*, the main character is awakened after having been frozen and forgotten. He is awakened when the blood of a priest with weak faith finds its way through the cracks of ice and into the mouth of Christopher Lee's character. After getting a sufficient amount of bloody sustenance, Dracula arises from his evil slumber and is angered when he learns that crosses have donned his castle.

Ladies and gentlemen, we introduce you to the Arab Spring.

TUNISIA

Self-Immolation is the act of setting oneself afire in some sort of protest. This happened on December 17, 2010 when Mohammed Bouazizi, a Tunisian, set himself ablaze after an encounter with police; he was severely burned. His protest generated such a spark that Tunisia's President, Zine el Abidine Ben Ali visited him in the hospital to assuage the public anger directed at Ben Ali. Bouazizi ultimately died from his burns on January 4th, 2011. Within ten days of Bouazizi's death, Ben Ali was in exile and had become the *former* president of Tunisia.[1]

Islamists saw opportunity. The protests in Tunisia—spawned partially by poor economic conditions—helped Islamists garner the support of leftists, a trick as old as time. Secular leftists joined with Islamists to call for the ouster of

Ben Ali. On January 14th, they got their wish when Ben Ali fled the country for Saudi Arabia.[2]

Upon Ali's exit, the founder of the Islamist Ennahda Party—Rachid Ghannouchi—soon made his way back to the country that had banned Ennahda, in much the same way that Egypt had banned the Muslim Brotherhood. Ghannouchi is very well connected to the Brotherhood too; he is a member of at least two organizations that are led by Yusuf al-Qaradawi.[3]

When post-revolutionary elections were finally held, Ennahda was the victor, capturing nearly 42% of the vote and 90 seats of a 217-member assembly, more than any other party.[4] A familiar pattern had emerged in the Middle East; Islamists attempted to assure people that they would not inflict their will on the country. *Reuters* reported at the time that Ghannouchi insisted—after 22 years of exile—that Islamic dictates would not be imposed on the people of Tunisia while at the same time saying that he would model his approach after that of strict Islamist and Turkish Prime Minister, Tayyip Recep Erdoğan.[5] More than a year after Ben Ali's regime fell, it was reported by *Tunisia Live* that the Turkish language would be taught in Tunisia's public schools a couple of months after a delegation from Turkey led by President Abdullah Gül visited Tunisia and suggested it.[6]

Moreover, Ghannouchi has not only called for the extermination of Israel but in 2002, according to the *Global Muslim Brotherhood Daily Report,* he co-signed a document to that effect, along with the Supreme Guide of the Brotherhood, the leader of the Syrian Brotherhood, the head of Hezbollah, and the spiritual leader of Hamas.[7]

Perhaps more shocking were the words of Hamadi Jbeli, the Secretary-General of the Ennahda Party, who said, after the election:

> "We are in the sixth caliphate, (Allah) willing."[8]

Again, the dysfunctionally deceptive relationship between Islamists and leftists cannot be overstated. Leftists always seem to align with Islamists before succumbing to them. Secularist Khemais Ksila, the head of an opposing party, said in response to Jbeli's outrageous flag-staking:

> "We do not accept this statement. We thought we were going to build a second republic with our partner, not a sixth caliphate."[9]

The use of the term "caliphate" in Arab politics is highly sensitive because it is a concept promoted by groups such as Hizb-ut-Tahrir, which is banned in many countries. The so-called "Moderate Islamist" movements such as Ennahda or Egypt's Muslim Brotherhood generally steer clear of the term because of these associations…and they use JBTW to hide their intentions. Jbeli allowed his mask to slip.

After his party won the election in October, Ghannouchi attended a Muslim Public Affairs Council (MPAC) event on Capitol Hill in Washington, D.C. In 1994, Ghannouchi was denied a visa after it was learned that he would speak at an event sponsored by none other than convicted terrorist fundraiser, Sami Al-Arian.[10]

So, to sum up, after an event in Tunisia lit the fuse of the Arab Spring, that country voted overwhelmingly for a party founded by a Muslim Brotherhood-friendly anti-Semite who wants to emulate the Prime Minister of Turkey and attempted to convince people that he doesn't want his will to be imposed on anyone. Of course, this is only what he says outwardly. What he believes inwardly—and speaks outwardly in a different language—is a far different matter; he is simply biding his time. The proverbial cherry on top is a Secretary-General who outwardly expresses his desire for a "sixth Caliphate."

Yet, western culture has set a high bar for impugning someone's motives; doing so before reaching that bar will get you impugned for jumping to conclusions. Westerners need to understand that Muslim leaders rarely mean what they say—unless they're speaking Arabic when they say it. Tunisia provides a case in point.

EGYPT

Mohammed Bouazizi in Tunisia seemed to inspire copy cat martyrs in Egypt; acts of self-immolation spread across that country like wildfire after Bouazizi's act provided the spark for revolution in Tunisia.[11] Though the Egyptian regime of Hosni Mubarak fell to a public uprising, it wasn't human flesh that was set afire; it was the social media networks. *The Wall Street Journal* reported after Mubarak's fall in February of 2011—one month after Ben Ali fled Tunisia—that the uprising had as much to do with a dozen tech-savvy activists who harnessed the power of facebook as anything else.[12]

One of those activists was Wael Ghonim, then a marketing executive with *Google*; he disappeared just as the protests were gathering momentum.[13] It was later learned that he had been detained by Egyptian police. In another article by the *Wall Street Journal*, it was reported that Ghonim set up the campaign website for former IAEA head, Mohamed ElBaradei, a man who would later come out in support of the Muslim Brotherhood after Mubarak's fall.[14] Nearly two years later, after the vacuum left by Mubarak had been filled by the Muslim Brotherhood, ElBaradei would sing quite a different tune as a non-Islamist who suddenly found himself on the wrong end of the Islamist power stick.[15]

It took little more than two weeks for Mubarak to step down. During that time, conflicting messages were sent both by his office as well as the White House. At one point, the protests appeared to have been dying down but two things seemed to give them new life. Vice President Omar Suleiman publicly stated that Egypt was not ready for Democracy and Ghonim was released.[16] Mubarak ultimately stepped down on February 11, 2011.

Ghonim was not just one of the faces of the social media revolution that led to Mubarak's overthrow. He was also a bright, young, naïve leftist ideologue who was either unwilling or unable to see the stealthy Muslim Brotherhood agenda that included using him as a tool to further that agenda. None other than CAIR Chicago's Executive Director Ahmed Rehab participated in the protests. At one point, he called in to Chicago radio station WBEZ from Cairo to give an on-the-ground report about the protests:

> "When I walked into Tahrir Square today and it was a site to behold, it was a lot more calmer (sic) in terms of no violence. When **we first stormed Tahrir Square** on Friday, we were facing.... dozens of tear gas bombs and rubber bullets, and police with batons."[17]

As a member of a Muslim Brotherhood front group, Rehab was working to further *its* goals, not the efforts of the likes of Ghonim. As a member of CAIR (one letter short of "Cairo"), he is part of an organization that seeks to dramatically and radically influence western media consumption. Muslim Brotherhood front groups were extremely effective in shaping public opinion in the United States about the overthrow of Mubarak, not because the removal of Mubarak was a good thing for Egypt but because it was a good thing for the Brotherhood.

One week after the fall of Mubarak, hundreds of thousands of Egyptians descended on Tahrir Square. What followed was an event so symbolic that it served as an allegory for the forces of the revolution as well as the forces of those who would benefit from it most. As Wael Ghonim prepared to take the stage, security guards prevented him from doing so; he was sent away in shame, with an Egyptian flag covering his head. The man who would steal the spotlight was none other than Muslim Brotherhood leader Yusuf Al-Qaradawi, who had been in exile for years prior to reaping the benefits of Ghonim's efforts.

Qaradawi subsequently gave a sermon in which he called on Arab leaders to heed the words of their people.[18] As the leader of the group that would eventually hold a majority of Egypt's power, Qaradawi wasn't exactly practicing what he preached. Then again, we *are* talking about JBTW.

In 1981, then vice president Hosni Mubarak became president of Egypt after the assassination of President Anwar Sadat during a military parade. Mubarak narrowly escaped with his life. The assassins were Muslim fundamentalists who resented Sadat's signing of the Camp David Accords, a peace treaty that recognized Israel in return for the Sinai Peninsula. Sadat's signature on that treaty was a primary reason why he was assassinated.

As the Mubarak regime was falling nearly thirty years later, Mort Zuckerman of *US News & World Report*, said the following in an interview with *CNN's* Piers Morgan:

> "How did Hosni Mubarak come into power? He was sitting next to Anwar Sadat, who was killed by the Muslim Brotherhood...These people are absolute; they are the radical Islamists...We have to make sure...that we don't get a reputation... where we make it possible for the radicals to take power. That would be a disaster for every interest the United States has."[19]

Perhaps not so coincidentally, the man convicted of orchestrating Sadat's assassination—Aboud al-Zumour—had been in prison for thirty years and was released after Mubarak stepped down. *The UK Telegraph* reported that he was also a close friend of al-Qaeda leader, Ayman al-Zawahiri.[20] Incidentally, al-Qaeda leadership, to include al-Zawahiri, formally endorsed the uprisings in an article entitled "Tsunami of Change."[21]

If former US President Jimmy Carter had a crowning achievement (hold your laughter), it was arguably the Camp David Accords. Yet, despite the Muslim Brotherhood's assassination of Sadat for signing it, Carter expressed support for the Brotherhood in the post-Mubarak era. During an interview with *America's Morning News*, Carter stated:

"...they (Muslim Brotherhood) assured me personally and they've made public statements accordingly that they will honor the peace treaty that I helped to negotiate back in 1979. They know it's very important to Egypt to maintain peace with Israel and I don't have any doubt that they'll carry out their promise to me."[22]

It is simply not believable that Carter didn't understand the intentions of the Brotherhood prior to that interview. In fact, it might be a bigger disgrace to his legacy if he *were* that ignorant; such a reality would indicate a level of stupidity that would make a changeling blush (information provided in Chapter 18 might help explain Carter's Arabic allegiances).

As the Arab Spring's poisonous blossoms bloomed, 2012 dawned. The Barack Obama administration seemed to echo Carter's sentiment as it became apparent that the Muslim Brotherhood would be a major player in the formation of Egypt's new government. *The New York Times* reported that Obama had begun to accept...

...the Brotherhood's repeated assurances that its lawmakers want to build a modern democracy that will respect individual freedoms, free markets and international commitments, including Egypt's treaty with Israel.[23]

By not standing with Mubarak the Obama administration was, to a significant degree, responsible for awakening the Muslim Brotherhood—a group banned under Mubarak. After the third and final round of Parliamentary elections, the Freedom and Justice Party (Muslim Brotherhood) had secured more seats in Parliament than any other party. The Brotherhood held 47% of the seats, with the more openly radical Salafist Party—Al Nour—holding the second most number of seats.[24] In essence, racist and radical Islamists with suits and ties had acquired a commanding majority of the first post-Mubarak Parliament. As if that weren't enough, the Secretary-General of the Freedom and Justice Party—Mohamed Saad Katatni—was chosen as the legislative body's Speaker.[25]

As the dust settled after the Parliamentary elections, Egypt began to shift its focus to the Presidential elections. Drama was in no short supply as candidates were disqualified based on things like prison records and citizenship status.

The official Muslim Brotherhood candidate was introduced after the Brotherhood had earlier pledged not to field a candidate for president at all (JBTW). His name was Khairat al-Shater and he got the group's endorsement.[26]

Ultimately, al-Shater's fate was sealed by Egypt's eligibility rules, which stated that no one can run for president if his prison sentence or pardon ended less than six years prior to running. Al-Shater was jailed five times and wasn't released from his most recent prison term until shortly after the fall of Mubarak, when he was pardoned, according to *Ahram Online*.[27] Once al-Shater exited the race, the Brotherhood quickly put up another candidate and Mohamed Mursi was the lucky winner.[28]

Egyptian cleric Safawat Higazi helped to launch the presidential campaign of Mursi. At a rally less than one month prior to the first round of presidential elections, Higazi assured those in attendance that if elected, Mursi would liberate Jerusalem and make it the Capital of the Islamic Caliphate. Mursi, who was seated directly behind Higazi, could be seen nodding in approval.[29]

Less than a week before Egyptians voted for their next president, an op-ed by former United States president George W. Bush appeared in the *Wall Street Journal*. It was troubling because it communicated a position that essentially concurred with that of both Jimmy Carter and Barack Obama. Though quite vague, Bush implied that the Middle East was lost and that the West should embrace the Arab Spring. It read like the voice of a man who wanted to preempt charges that his would be a surrenderous legacy by waving the white flag voluntarily before someone else could do it for him:

> Some in both parties in Washington look at the risks inherent in democratic change—particularly in the Middle East and North Africa—and find the dangers too great. America, they argue, should be content with supporting the flawed leaders they know in the name of stability.

> But in the long run, this foreign policy approach is not realistic. It is not within the power of America to indefinitely preserve the old order, which is inherently unstable. Oppressive governments distrust the diffusion of choice and power, choking off the best source of national prosperity and success.[30]

This is a far, far cry from what Bush told Americans shortly after the 9/11 attacks during a joint session of Congress:

> "From this day forward, any nation that continues to harbor or support terrorism will be regarded by the United States as a hostile regime."[31]

In 2001, Bush considered Mubarak an ally. In 2012, he seemed to be embracing Mubarak's demise at the hands of the Islamic terrorists he regarded as "hostile" just a decade earlier. Reading Bush's 2012 op-ed at face value leaves one with the impression that he didn't fully understand the Middle East or the Brotherhood's goals but if there's one thing *Wikileaks* demonstrated, it's that politicians are not nearly as ignorant as they would have the masses believe.

Had Bush been honest about how bad the 'Arab Spring' was, it would have served as a repudiation of his own doctrine during his tenure that ended in 2009. He and his legacy are tied to that doctrine. Denouncing the rise of the Muslim Brotherhood would be diametrically inconsistent with his own policies, if not his own words on 9/20/01:

> "We will starve terrorists of funding, turn them one against another, drive them from place to place, until there is no refuge or no rest. And we will pursue nations that provide aid or safe haven to terrorism. Every nation, in every region, now has a decision to make. Either you are with us, or you are with the terrorists."[32]

If one applies Bush's own words in 2001 to the 'Arab Spring' of 2012, the United States should have stood with Mubarak, a leader who stood against Muslim Brotherhood (al-Qaeda) terrorists. Yet, in 2012, Bush essentially advocated for standing with the Brotherhood. There is no other logical conclusion.

When Bush championed Democracy in Gaza, Hamas was voted into power. In Afghanistan, Democracy gave that country a very corrupt Hamid Karzai and a government that put Sharia law first. In Iraq, Democracy led to the election of a Shiite government that essentially became an arm of Iran. We are left to conclude that Democracy does not work in the Middle East.

If Bush had denounced the 'Arab Spring' he would have denounced what his administration had identified as freedom and Democracy. Ironically, the op-ed he wrote was self-indicting. George W. Bush went on record in 2012 as having conceded to the Muslim Brotherhood's rise in the Middle East, though he used western doubletalk to do it. He doubled down at a time when he may have been better served by 'fessing up' or even remaining silent.

In the first round of Egypt's presidential elections, no candidate received enough votes to declare outright victory but two men made it to the runoff. One was a holdover from Mubarak's regime, Prime Minister Ahmed Shafik. The other was the Brotherhood's candidate (Mursi). One candidate represented more of the same and the other represented something much worse.

Once again, the leftist revolutionaries did the heavy lifting to overthrow a dictator and were left holding the bag, as none of their candidates survived the first round.[33] It's a common theme in the Middle East that leftists never seem to learn.

Perhaps they should try a revolution based on Judeo-Christian principles.

In a shocking development two days prior to the runoff, Egypt's Supreme Constitutional Court ruled that the Muslim Brotherhood-dominated Parliament was to be dissolved. There were several things at issue but principally among them was an attempt by Parliament to rule Shafik ineligible and that the Brotherhood had claimed more seats than allowed by law. *The New York Times* reported that the court's ruling actually put Shafik's candidacy back on the table.[34] It smacked of the Brotherhood's eyes being bigger than its stomach. It had the Parliament but it wanted to guarantee itself the presidency. Had they discounted the power of the Superior Court? By attempting to rule Shafik ineligible, the Brotherhood seemed to overplay its hand. Egyptians were already skittish about the consolidation of the Brotherhood's power in Parliament. It was as if the Ikhwan was so close to capturing the golden ring that it had discarded discretion and savvy.

Another bone of contention had to do with the number of Parliamentary seats that would be reserved for Party loyalists. The court—whose members were appointed by Mubarak—essentially ruled that the Brotherhood cheated, by running its members as independent candidates for seats in Parliament that were designated specifically for non-political party candidates.[35]

In perhaps what many may have considered a throw-away line from the *Times'* piece, the most powerful revelation of the story may be found. It came in the form of a quote from Emad Gad, a leader among the Social Democratic Party. He was quoted as saying:

> "We can demonstrate against Shafik, but we cannot demonstrate against the Islamists."[36]

That twelve word sentence said it all. It was a statement that cried out for more questions. Why could Egyptians demonstrate against a Mubarak holdover and not against the Brotherhood? Had Mubarak known something they didn't? Were there forces at work that understood how to exploit the need for *some* change while always waiting for the moment when they could implement *radical* change? In a quest for freedom, Egyptians cheered Democracy and risked voting for something much worse than what they had grown used to.

Nonetheless, as a result of the Superior Court's ruling, Egypt once again found itself under martial law, with the military in full control. Meanwhile, on the day that all of this tumult unfolded, Vice President of the United States—Joe Biden—again extolled the virtues of the 'Arab Spring' by calling it a "democratic movement."[37] In reality, the democratic movement Biden was championing had resulted in martial law in Egypt.

Not all doubletalk is carefully calculated. Some of it is due to incompetence. After all, we are talking about Joe Biden.

With the new Parliament essentially in limbo, the runoff election went forward. After all the votes had come in, Mursi was reportedly the winner by a 52% - 48% margin (approx. 1 million votes).[38] Official results, which were slated to be announced a few days later, were postponed again by elections officials. The military was doing all it could to stave off what it knew would be bad for the entire region—an Egypt run by the Muslim Brotherhood.

As the runoff results remained unconfirmed, the Obama administration made it clear that it wanted the Egyptian military to back down and hand control over to the Brotherhood. The *Los Angeles Times* reported that both the Pentagon Press Secretary and the spokesman for the State Department were calling on the military to relinquish power to the Brotherhood.[39]

Incidentally, this was the same *Los Angeles Times* that refused, in 2008, to relinquish an allegedly very damaging video of Barack Obama speaking at an event for Rashid Khalidi in 2003. Khalidi is a former mouthpiece for Yasser Arafat's PLO and a virulent anti-Semite.[40] As you might expect, Khalidi also has a history of speaking of peace in English and hate in Arabic.[41] Viewed in this context, Obama's reverence for Khalidi would help explain his support for the Brotherhood in Egypt.

As the Arab Spring was descending on Egypt in 2011, Khalidi wrote an op-ed that appeared at the *Salon* website. It said, in part:

> The **unimpeded participation of the Muslim Brotherhood** and other groups in anticipated elections will be a crucial marker of change, but the most critical questions are whether there will be **genuine regime change**. This will require a dismantling of the police state...[42]

Once again, the dots connecting Obama's ideology to his un-American and bizarre foreign policy positions were not that far apart.

On June 24, 2012 Mohamed Mursi was declared the official winner of Egypt's presidential election. Barack Obama called Mursi to congratulate him.[43] The Democratic Party, to which Obama belonged, levied accusations of racism against Republicans with reckless abandon throughout Obama's tenure as president. Yet, Obama was expressing support *for* and congratulations *to* an unabashed racist.

Consider the words of another prominent Democrat and future Secretary of State, Senator John Kerry (D-MA) after Mursi's victory:

> "Obviously American concerns about the Muslim Brotherhood's past statements and positions are widely shared and well understood. But **it would be a mistake for us to pull back from our engagement with a free and democratic Egypt**," the senator said. **"This is a time to test intentions not to prejudge them.** All parties must come together to build a better future for the Egyptian people and I will continue to monitor Egypt's political transition with great interest."[44]

This is the same John Kerry who, in testimony before the Senate Foreign Relations Committee in 1971, impugned his fellow countrymen and brothers in arms who were still fighting overseas in Vietnam. Kerry said the following about American soldiers:

> "They told the stories at times they had personally raped, cut off ears, cut off heads, tape wires from portable telephones to human genitals and turned up the power, cut off limbs, blown up bodies, randomly shot at civilians, razed villages in fashion **reminiscent of Genghis Khan**, shot cattle and dogs for fun, poisoned food stocks, and generally ravaged the country side of South Vietnam..."[45]

In 1971, Kerry likened American soldiers to Genghis Khan. In 2012, he was willing to give a pass to a group that would make Genghis Khan blush.

After the dawn of the 'Arab Spring', the devolution of Egypt grew increasingly obvious on a day-to-day basis, despite Kerry's desire for the Brotherhood to get a fair shake. Reports of ghastly and gruesome crimes began to surface in the summer of 2012. In one case, a man allegedly beat his pregnant wife to death because she didn't vote for Mursi.[46] This is but one in a long line of horrid and macabre examples.

Consider the words of Biblical prophet Isaiah in Chapter 19:1-4:

1 See, the Lord rides on a swift cloud and is coming to Egypt.

The idols of Egypt tremble before him, and the hearts of the Egyptians melt with fear.

2 **"I will stir up Egyptian against Egyptian—brother will fight against brother, neighbor against neighbor, city against city, kingdom against kingdom.**

3 The Egyptians will lose heart, and I will bring their plans to nothing; they will consult the idols and the spirits of the dead, the mediums and the spiritists.

4 **I will hand the Egyptians over to the power of a cruel master, and a fierce king will rule over them,"** declares the Lord, the Lord Almighty.[47]

Though it's quite difficult to tell if Mohammed Mursi is the "cruel master" Isaiah refers to, he certainly seems to possess some of the characteristics.

In perhaps one of the more salient allegories with respect to Egypt, Mursi's pen belied his words, upon signing the new Egyptian Constitution as westerners were celebrating Christmas. In the wake of his signature appearing on the Sharia-inspired document, Mursi both publicly acknowledged that he made mistakes relative to the process and attempted to ameliorate them by calling for 'dialogue'.[48]

It was clearly Mursi's attempt at a two-for-one bargain. In exchange for an ironclad document that he wanted, he would both apologize for nondescript mistakes and extend a hand of friendship in the interest of 'dialogue'.

How can the people be mad at a contrite leader who wants to talk? In reality, the ink did all the talking while the mouth gave lip service to make the victims of the pen look intolerant if they didn't accept Mursi's peace offering.

That's JBTW indeed.

Weeks later, six US Senators—John McCain among them—traveled to Cairo to meet with Mursi. One of the things reportedly discussed was the resurrection of a video from 2010 that featured Mursi saying that Jews were "the descendants of apes and pigs". McCain issued a statement that said the topic came up and the Senators made their objections known to Mursi but that the conversation was "constructive".

One of the other Senators present—Chris Coons (D-DE)—opened up to *Foreign Policy* and gave readers a look at the man behind the doublespeak curtain. It wasn't just readers who were shocked; it was also every Senator in the room, according to Coons:

> Morsy told the senators that the values of Islam teach respect for Christianity and Judaism, and he asserted repeatedly that he had no negative views about Judaism or the Jewish people, but then followed with a diatribe about Israel and Zionist actions against Palestinians, especially in Gaza.
>
> Then Morsy crossed a line and made a comment that made the senators physically recoil in their chairs in shock, Coons said.
>
> "He was attempting to explain himself...then he said, 'Well, I think we all know that the media in the United States has made a big deal of this and we know the media of the United States is controlled by certain forces and they don't view me favorably,'" Coons said.[49]

It's important to understand what happened at that meeting. It was as if these six Senators got a look at the duality that exists inside an Islamist's mind. In the same meeting, Mursi said he harbors no ill will toward the Jews while simultaneously blaming unidentified Jews for taking his comments about them being 'descendants of apes and pigs' out of context.

The reason those Senators recoiled was because the mind of a JBTW artist was on full display for all of them to see. Each one was a witness to the Islamic version of multiple personality disorder.

LIBYA

It was uncanny how, less than one week after Mubarak stepped down, protests against Libyan dictator Muammar Gadhafi's government began in the country that bordered Egypt to the west. Bouazizi was portrayed as the catalyst for the uprising in Tunisia. The arrest of a human rights activist is credited with giving rise to anti-government protesters in Libya but make no mistake; there were forces at work looking for any excuse they could find to replicate successful uprisings elsewhere.[50]

The Libyan dictator was at a distinct disadvantage internationally; he had made many enemies. The Lockerbie bombing of Pan Am Flight 103, for which he was found responsible, hadn't been forgotten by the West.[51] It was relatively easy for Muslim Brotherhood loyalists to pit the evil Gadhafi against the repressed masses, in part, because the Libyan dictator was the enemy the West knew; the rebels represented the enemy it didn't know. Confusing matters further were the consequences of Gadhafi's economic tentacles. He had economic power that enticed unlikely allies—like China, Russia, and Turkey—to support him.[52]

Gadhafi proved to be a much more formidable opponent for revolutionaries than was Mubarak in Egypt. While the idea of toppling the Libyan dictator seemed like a "no-brainer" to many Americans, the western media was again missing in action when it came to being objective about the forces that sought to fill the vacuum Gadhafi's absence would leave behind. The Brotherhood had member groups and sympathizers in the US with influence in both the media (CAIR at CNN) and the Obama administration (Huma Abedin at the State Department) and it became a self-evident truth—unless your name was Republican Senator John McCain—that such influence was used.

It soon became apparent that relying on a social network revolution (like in Egypt) would be like shooting spitballs at a battleship in Libya. Gadhafi's power base was much more consolidated and he didn't have to fend off the overwhelming number of people that Mubarak did. If Gadhafi was going to fall, rebel forces would need help. Despite the United States already being engaged in wars in Iraq and Afghanistan, McCain and fellow Republican Senator Lindsay Graham (R-SC) called for the removal of Gadhafi using NATO forces. It was this type of bipartisan support that helped President Barack Obama get away with "limited Military action in Libya" without Congressional approval, despite what's known as the War Powers Act of 1973.[53] This law requires any president to get the approval of Congress for continued military action after 60 days.[54]

In a political game of Three Card Monty, the Obama administration asserted that its efforts in Libya did not violate this Act because NATO was leading the operation and America's involvement did not constitute "full-blown hostilities."[55] Despite the fact that the US essentially *is* NATO, Obama hid behind a UN Resolution that authorized force against Gadhafi.[56] The War Powers Act was essentially neutered from the bully pulpit and Congress did little to assert its authority.

Republicans that sided with the President didn't help. The offensive against Gadhafi continued.

While Gadhafi was widely regarded by the West as a very bad guy, little consideration seemed to be given to a viable replacement. During a trip to Benghazi, Senator McCain told a reporter that the Libyan rebels were his "heroes," indicating that the Senator had no clue about who would replace Gadhafi.[57] Would McCain really prefer that Americans consider him this ignorant? If yes, it says quite a bit about why he wasn't willing to be truthful.

About two weeks prior to McCain's visit to Benghazi, reports of human rights atrocities perpetrated by forces sympathetic to the rebels were quite prevalent. *The Daily Caller* reported that the atrocities had a racial component to them, with the majority of victims being "black Africans and dark-skinned Libyans."[58] In one of the most repulsive examples, a video was posted online that showed a black man being hung upside down outside Benghazi's main courthouse. The video shows his attackers screaming, 'Allahu-Akhbar' as the man's head was sawed off for allegedly being a Gadhafi loyalist.[59] Hate crime anyone?

Despite this, John McCain walked past the courthouse during his visit, looking completely oblivious to the Islamo-Klan behavior that took place there only days earlier. Residents gathered around and cheered McCain, who smiled and waved to chants of—you guessed it—'Allahu-Akbar.'[60] Lost not only on McCain but on opportunistic Democrats back home who were always eager to play the race card, was the notion that a black man was lynched and beheaded in Libya. Yet, sentiment among the power structure in the United States was to support those who did it. Meanwhile, in America, the slightest hint of racist sentiment is snuffed out by the political correct police. Double standards are very close cousins to doubletalk.

Consider the example of Hillary Clinton senior adviser Alec Ross. While speaking at a summit in London, Ross sang the praises of the 'Arab Spring.' During his presentation, Ross communicated a very ignorant position when it came to the forces behind the leftists who helped to overthrow dictators:

> "The overarching pattern that I think you can see in all of this is the redistribution of power from governments and very large institutions to individuals and small institutions."[61]

In hindsight, this view was childish naivete at best and nefarious deception at worst. These "small institutions" Ross spoke about were quickly overtaken by Islamic forces that made up the Muslim Brotherhood, an entity that is all too familiar with seizing a power struggle from the weak, which is exactly what happened in Egypt. As Ross spoke, Libyan dictator Gadhafi had not yet fallen but it was clear that Ross was advocating such an outcome.

If there was any doubt about where the State Department stood when it came to Libya's rebels, Secretary of State Hillary Clinton expunged it; she was in Jamaica speaking to an audience that included the Jamaican Prime Minister as Ross was speaking in London. It was clear that part of Clinton's agenda included making the case for NATO's involvement in Libya.

Hillary essentially sought to demonize anyone who disagreed with her policy:

> "...the bottom line is, whose side are you on? Are you on Qadhafi's side or are you on the side of the aspirations of the Libyan people and the international coalition that has been created to support them? For the Obama Administration, the answer to that question is very easy."[62]

Considering that the rebels were connected to the Muslim Brotherhood, didn't it make sense to question Clinton's advocacy for the rebels in light of the fact that her Deputy Chief of Staff and closest aid—Huma Abedin—had such strong familial connections to the Brotherhood? Conflict of interest allegations were more than warranted but in short supply.

After several months, Gadhafi finally met his end when he was captured and executed by rebel forces.[63] Many westerners cheered as a murderous nemesis of the United States was killed. Unfortunately, those who cheered didn't know what they would be getting in the future—except for those in the West who seemed eager to welcome whatever alternative reared its head.

Less than one month after the fall of Gadhafi, an al-Qaeda flag was spotted flying over the Benghazi courthouse.[64] Less than one year after Gadhafi had been killed the al-Qaeda flag waving had become much more prevalent; it was waved proudly from vehicles in parades in Benghazi. The purpose was to call for Sharia law.[65] Are we to believe that the power brokers in the West did not see this coming? The relative silence from western leaders indicated that they knew all too well and chose the wrong side either for some dastardly reason or out of cowardice.

In the summer of 2012, Libya held elections and the man who served as the interim Prime Minister—Mahmoud Jibril of the National Forces Alliance—did surprisingly well. Though Jibril was himself a Muslim, the left was eager to tout his western education and secularist leanings as a repudiation of those who sounded alarm bells about the Brotherhood replacing Gadhafi. After the fall of Gadhafi, Jibril seemed to be a good enough placeholder to garner himself a better-than-expected showing in the election.[66]

That is a bit of a rosy interpretation. In an interview with the *Daily Beast*, Jibril made two eyebrow-raising claims. First, he asserted that he believed a "governing alliance" could be formed with the Muslim Brotherhood. This was done, the *Beast* speculates because out of the 200 Parliamentary seats up for election, only 80 are assigned based on party affiliation; the remaining 120 are independent candidates. It is this dynamic that was expected to give the Brotherhood an edge in Parliament.[67]

Perhaps the best indicator that Jibril was more interested in playing both sides of the fence than in real change is his deference to sharia law:

> "Sharia law, when it was understood in the proper way, managed to create one of the great civilizations in human history. The problem is not with Sharia or Islam; the problem is with the interpretation of Sharia."[68]

How much of a reformer could he be? His willingness to assert that Sharia law is not the problem was a problem. That is an interesting strategy in light of a news report from *Gulf News*; reports about why Jibril's party did so well in the elections reached conclusions one wouldn't expect.

> Some have attributed what seems to have happened in Libya to the personal standings of liberal leader Jibril and his good performance as prime minister in the immediate aftermath of the revolution.
>
> Others have looked to large number of women who were worried that they might lose the high standing that they held under Muammar Gaddafi's dictatorial but secular regime.[69]

There's a shock. Women were motivated to vote *against* Sharia law. If the report is true, women didn't just vote *against* Sharia; they voted *for* a man who thought the problem with Sharia was one of "interpretation".

The western left sang the praises of Jibril because they believed that his victory was a victory for secular humanism over the radical brand of Islam that was sweeping across the Middle East. It was a victory that was supposed to silence those on the right who warned of Muslim Brotherhood dominance in the region.[70]

Consider Marc Ginsberg—Deputy Senior Advisor to the President for Middle East Policy during the Carter administration and U.S. Ambassador to Morocco during the Clinton administration. In an interview on *MSNBC*, Ginsberg said the following:

> "The Obama administration's approach in Libya has yielded the type of results that could, in effect, stop the monopolization of the Muslim Brotherhood across North Africa as well as into the rest of the Middle East. And if you have a leader like Mahmoud Jibril, who emerges and is able to, in effect, eliminate some of the fighting that still goes on around the country; this is the type of foreign policy success we...should be proud of."[71]

This would prove to be wishful thinking and a hope that would be short-lived.

9/11 ALL OVER AGAIN

On the afternoon of September 11, 2012, the eleventh anniversary of the 9/11 attacks, reports came in about attacks on US Embassies in the Middle East. In Cairo, Islamists stormed the US Embassy there en masse and replaced an American flag with an Al-Qaeda flag. The reason given for the siege was some obscure anti-Muhammad video on *YouTube*.[72] Yes, an act of war was allegedly perpetrated against the United States in response to a video; that would be speech.

That evening, the US Consulate in Benghazi—later identified as a Special Mission Compound (SMC)—came under assault by Islamists. Four Americans were murdered during the attack and several more wounded. Tyrone Woods and Glen Doherty, Navy SEALs who had been contracted by the Central Intelligence Agency (CIA), US Ambassador to Libya J. Christopher Stevens, and Foreign Information Services Officer Sean Smith all perished during the attack. Woods and Doherty died defending the CIA Annex compound where survivors of the Consulate attack had been transported.

Soon after the Benghazi attacks, the narrative that the anti-Muhammad video—the same one allegedly responsible for the siege on the US Embassy in Cairo—was applied to the attacks on the SMC and Annex. A statement from

Hillary Clinton dated 9/11/12 did just that. In fact, according to Terence P. Jeffrey of *CNS News*, that statement was published before Doherty and Woods had died in the line of duty.[73] The relevant excerpt of that statement read:

> Some have sought to justify this vicious behavior as a **response to inflammatory material posted on the Internet.** The United States deplores any intentional effort to denigrate the religious beliefs of others. Our commitment to religious tolerance goes back to the very beginning of our nation. But let me be clear: There is never any justification for violent acts of this kind.[74]

Two days later, Clinton seemed to imply that the video was responsible for violence all across the Middle East. In a video statement, she said:

> "I also want to take a moment to address a **video circulating on the internet that has led to these protests** in a number of countries. Let me state very clearly, and I hope it is obvious, that the United States Government had absolutely nothing to do with this video."[75]

That evening, Clinton would celebrate a Muslim Holiday inside the Ben Franklin room in Washington, D.C. Present with her was a man named Ali Sulaiman Aujali, Libya's Ambassador to the United States, who resigned from that position under Gadhafi in early 2011 but became Libya's Ambassador to the US again in August of that year.

Clinton then graciously introduced Aujali.[76]

The Secretary of State's judgment when it came to Libya's Ambassador left much to be desired, especially two days after an attack in that country left four Americans dead. *AllGov* had the following to report about Aujali's past:

> In September 2009, he defended the transfer of convicted Lockerbie bomber Abdel Baset al-Megrahi from Scotland to Libya by explaining that most Libyans thought Megrahi was falsely convicted.[77]

In July of 2011, one month before he became ambassador again, Aujali spoke at the annual Islamic Society of North America (ISNA) convention. Not only that but he was introduced by none other than Council on American Islamic Relations Chicago (CAIR-Chicago) Executive Director Ahmed Rehab.[78]

One day prior to his appearance with Hillary and one day after the attack, Aujali appeared alongside ISNA President Mohamed Magid and Haris Tarin, the director of the Muslim Public Affairs Council (MPAC) in Washington, DC.[79]

Why was so much attention paid to pushing a false narrative, that a video was responsible for the attack in Benghazi while the head of the State Department appeared to be far too cozy with the Libyan ambassador, who had quite a checkered past?

One day later—on September 14th—Secretary Clinton was on-hand at Andrews Air Force base to welcome the four caskets of the Americans murdered at the hand of Islamists in Benghazi. During her speech, she said the following:

> This has been a difficult week for the State Department and for our country. We've seen the heavy assault on our post in Benghazi that took the lives of those brave men. **We've seen rage and violence directed at American embassies over an awful Internet video** that we had nothing to do with.[80]

Later, in a radio interview with talk show host Lars Larson, Charles Woods, the father of Tyrone Woods, said that when he met Secretary of State Clinton at Andrews, she told him that the man behind the video would be arrested and prosecuted.[81]

Ultimately, an Accountability Review Board (ARB) established by Clinton, found that there was no protest outside the SMC. Claims of a protest were central to the argument that the attacks in Libya resulted from the anti-Muhammad video. They did not. The ARB likewise found no one at State responsible for the egregious lack of security in Benghazi and recommended no disciplinary action be taken.[82]

THE ANTI-MUHAMMAD FILM

The attack on the US Embassy in Cario had nothing to do with the *Innocence of Muslims* video unless seen through the prism of it being a tool of exploitation. It had more to do with the old story of the Muhammad cartoons and the failure of Muslims to prosecute internationally, the culprits who drew them. It was another attempt to change speech laws globally. This is what added to the disturbing nature of the Obama administration's attempt to pin the Benghazi attacks on the video. It put the administration on the same side as the Islamists in one regard.

Shortly after 9/11, we identified two persons of interest when it came to the attention drawn to *Innocence of Muslims*. Their names were Wisam Abdul Waris of Dar Al-Hekma (House of Wisdom) and Nader Bakkar, a spokesman with the Salafist Nour Party, which publicly announced that it would be demonstrating in support of Dar Al-Hekma. The demonstration was about making it a crime to criticize Islam.

In a *YouTube* video posted two days *before* 9/11, Wisam reiterated his call to push for the passage of laws to be placed in the Egyptian Constitution—as well as internationally—that would make it illegal to criticize Islam.

Here is a translation of Wisam's words taken from that video:

> "We have moved to review with Mr. Rifai all the legal procedures today by which we created The Voice of Wisdom Coalition (I'itilaf Sawt al-Hekma); **it will hold accountable everyone who insults Islam locally and internationally, in accordance with every country's laws.** We all know the problems Yasser Al-Habib had in London and after that in Berlin...in Germany, an extremist group was allowed to publicize cartoons that insult the prophet in front of the Salafist Mosque in Berlin, through a legal decision. So what we did was to ask Sharabi Mahmoud to reject this legal decision on behalf of the Egyptian people who are Muslim; for this reason, we created this coalition. We also made an official request from the Church in Egypt to issue a public announcement, to state it has nothing to do with this deed."[83]

The embassy attack in Cairo may have been about calling for the release of Omar Abdel Rahman (The 'blind Sheikh')—who was convicted for this role in the first World Trade Center bombing in 1993—but it was also definitely about creating havoc to apply pressure that would lead to a change in Egyptian Constitution by Nour. The Nour Party publicly announced its partnership with Wisam:

> Salafi Nour Party officially joined the Commonwealth of 'voice of wisdom' with Wisam Abdul Waris, as well as with Nader Bakkar, the party's official spokesman and Dr. Ahmed Khalil Khairallah, member of the supreme body.[84]

The attack on the US Embassy in Cairo was not about the video; it was about exploiting a crisis created. It was about intimidating countries into implementing laws designed to extinguish free speech rights. The Obama administration's decision to push the narrative that *Innocence of Muslims* was responsible for the Benghazi attacks was incredibly suspicious in this regard.

On September 16th, five days after the attacks, UN Ambassador Susan Rice appeared on five separate Sunday shows and made the charge that the attacks in Benghazi arose spontaneously from protests in response to the video. Clinton's own ARB debunked that claim. It had to; claims to the contrary had already become politically radioactive.

Ultimately, the demonstrably false information given by Rice on those shows caused her to withdraw her name from consideration as the next Secretary of State.[85]

Nonetheless, she was not the only administration official to blame the video for the Benghazi attacks. Barack Obama himself did so several times, including two days later during an appearance on the David Letterman show, where he said the following:

> "Extremists and terrorists used this (video) as an excuse to attack a variety of our embassies, **including the consulate in Libya.**"[86]

One week later, on September 25th, Obama said the following at the United Nations:

> "...what we saw play out in the last two weeks, as a **crude and disgusting video sparked outrage throughout the Muslim world.** Now, I have made it clear that the United States government had nothing to do with this video, and I believe its message must be rejected by all who respect our common humanity."[87]

There is something Obama said during the Letterman interview that we agree with. The president referred to the man behind *Innocence of Muslims* as a "shadowy character".[88] Our research not only led us in that direction as well but we also learned that the man known as Nakoula Basseley Nakoula—a professed Coptic Christian—had a lengthy relationship with my first cousin, Eiad Salemeh, a Muslim fundamentalist mentioned in another chapter. I can personally attest to the fact that Eiad despises Coptic Christians.

It is our view that the background of Nakoula has not gotten enough attention.

WHO'S IN CHARGE?

During a September 13th appearance on Sean Hannity's television show to discuss the Benghazi attacks, Republican Senator John McCain became defensive when the subject of Libya's post-Gadhafi government came up. While Hannity was absolutely correct, he didn't have the necessary facts to refute McCain's claim that the new Libyan government was moderate.

When Hannity—who had rightfully predicted that the Muslim Brotherhood would fill the power vacuum left by an ousted Mubarak in Egypt—attempted to get the Senator's take on the rise of the Muslim Brotherhood there while chastising the Obama administration for not knowing it would happen, McCain refused to accept Hannity's premise. The Republican senator immediately took a defensive posture while pointing to Libya's recent elections in which the Muslim Brotherhood was defeated by the secularists, in order to make his case.[89]

Here is a partial transcript of the exchange:

> **Hannity:** I don't view the Muslim Brotherhood as Democracy. They want sharia law implemented now, in Egypt.
>
> **McCain:** First of all, that's not clear that that's true but also it was you and people on Fox that said, 'in Libya, we didn't know who they were and let's not help these people.' They had an election and they elected moderates. They rejected Islamists and yes, there are al-Qaeda factors and there are extremists in Libya today but the Libyan people are friends of ours and they support us and they support Democracy. So you were wrong about Libya.
>
> **Hannity:** I don't think I was wrong about Libya at all.
>
> **McCain:** Yes...I know you were. I know you were. They had a free and fair election and a Democratic, non-Islamic government was elected, so you were wrong.[90]

McCain's defensiveness revealed willful ignorance at minimum. In hindsight, he was wrong to dismiss the charge that the Muslim Brotherhood would implement sharia law in Egypt; it did. While McCain was right about a secular government being elected in Libya, he was wrong to assume that the power lied with that government. It didn't.

In supporting the removal of Gadhafi, the Obama administration essentially signed on to an arrangement that left forces loyal to Al-Qaeda in charge of security at the US embassy in Tripoli from 2011 through at least the spring of 2012.

The National Transitional Council, which represented the political apparatus that opposed Gadhafi in 2011 and served as the interim government after his removal, made an extremely curious appointment in August of 2011. That appointment was none other than Abdel Hakim Belhaj, an Al-Qaeda ally and 'brother'. Here is a copy of that letter (translation beneath it):

الـمـجـلـس الوطـنـي الإنـتـقـالـي لـيـبـيـا
National Transitional Council - Libya

التاريخ : 2011/8/30 م
اشارتنم : 270-2011

السيد عبدالحكيم الخويلدى بالحاج

بعد التحيه، ،،

نود افادتكم بان قد تقرر تكليفكم بمهام رئاسة المجلس العسكري لمدينة
طرابلس وذلك لاتخاذ كافة الاجراءات الكفيلة بتامين وسلامة العاصمة من
مواطنين وممتلكات عامة وخاصة ومؤسسات وبعثات وسفارات دولية واقليمية ،
والتنسيق مع المجلس المحلى لمدينة طرابلس واللجنة الأمنية العليا وشئون
الدفاع على المستوى الوطنى.

والسلام عليكم، ،،

مصطفى محمد عبدالجليل
رئيس المجلس الوطنى الانتقالي

صورة : للحفـــــظ

Translated, the document reads:

National Transitional Council—Libya

8/30/11

Code: YGM-270-2011

Mr. Abdel Hakim Al-Khowailidi Belhaj

Greetings,

We would like to inform you that you have been commissioned to the duties and responsibilities of the military committee of the city of Tripoli. These include taking all necessary procedures to secure the safety of the Capital and its citizens, its public and private property, and institutions, to include all international embassies and to coordinate with the local community of the city of Tripoli and the security assembly and defense on a national level.

Mustafa Muhammad Abdul Jalil

President, National Transitional Council—Libya

Official Seal of National Transitional Council

Copy for file.

As for Belhaj's bonafides as an Al-Qaeda ally, consider the words of the notorious Ayman al-Zawahiri. In a report published one day prior to the date on the memo above, *ABC News* quoted the Al-Qaeda leader as saying the following—in 2007—about the man the NTC put in control of Tripoli in 2011:

> "Dear brothers...the amir of the mujahideen, the patient and steadfast Abu-Abdallah al-Sadiq (Belhaj); and the rest of the captives of the fighting Islamic group in Libya, here is good news for you," Zawahiri said in a video, using Belhaj's nom de guerre. "Your brothers are continuing your march after you... escalating their confrontation with the enemies of Islam: Gadhafi and his masters, the crusaders of Washington."[91]

The *ABC* report went on to explain that the Libyan Islamic Fighting Group (LIFG), an entity the US State Department had designated as a terrorist organization, was founded by Belhaj.

Now, how about a level of JBTW so obvious that referring to it as such is practically a misnomer? In a *BBC* report from one month earlier—on July 4, 2011—a man named Al-Amin Belhaj was identified as an NTC spokesman and said the following:

> "Everyone knows who Abdel Hakim Belhadj is. He is a Libyan rebel and a moderate person who commands wide respect."[92]

Abdel Hakim Belhaj had been identified in a video report embedded in the *BBC* article as...

"...about the most powerful man in Tripoli."

Abdel Hakim Belhaj is many things but moderate is not one of them. According to a report by the Jamestown Foundation in 2005, the man who applied the 'moderate' label to Abdel Hakim Belhaj was actually a leader with the Libyan Muslim Brotherhood:

This last week Al-Amin Belhadj, head of the Libyan Muslim Brotherhood, issued a press release on the Arabic language section of Libya-Watch, (Mu'assasat al-Raqib li-Huqquq al-Insan) calling for urgent action on behalf of 86 Brotherhood members imprisoned since 1998 at Tripoli's Abu Salim prison and on hunger strike since October 7.[93]

So, the leader of the Libyan Muslim Brotherhood refers to the founder of another Muslim Brotherhood group as 'moderate' and the West is supposed to accept it?

Let's take a look at someone mentioned earlier in this chapter. Libyan Ambassador to the United States, the same guy who spoke next to Hillary Clinton two days after the Benghazi attack—Ali Sulaiman Aujali—had the following to say about Belhaj according to an *ABC News* report:

"(Belhaj) should be accept(ed) for the person that he is today and we should deal with him on that basis...people evolve and change."[94]

Really? How many times do westerners have to fall for this line before they trip over it? Aujali represents one individual who is willing to bridge the gap between Al-Qaeda and the Muslim Brotherhood.

CLINTON TESTIFIES

More than four months after the attack on Benghazi, Secretary of State Clinton finally testified in front of both the Senate Foreign Relations and House Foreign Affairs committees. During her testimony in front of the Senate committee, Clinton's toughest questioner was Rand Paul (R-KY). In addition to telling Clinton she would have been fired had he been president during the Benghazi attack, Paul confronted the former first lady on a very sensitive subject about why there was a need for a CIA Annex in Benghazi:

Here is the relevant portion of that exchange:

Paul: Is the US involved with any procuring of weapons, transfer of weapons, buying, selling, anyhow transferring weapons to Turkey out of Libya?

Clinton: To Turkey? I will have to take that question for the record. Nobody's ever raised that with me.

Paul: It's been in news reports that ships have been leaving from Libya and that they may have weapons and what I'd like to know is the Annex that was close by, were they involved with procuring, buying, selling, obtaining weapons and were any of these weapons being transferred to other countries—any countries—Turkey included?

Clinton: Well, Senator, you'll have to direct that question to the agency that ran the Annex. I will see what information is available and...

Paul: You're saying you don't know?

Clinton: I do not know. I don't have any information on that.[95]

Of course, one of the other countries Paul was likely referring to was Syria, home to the next target of the 'Arab Spring'. After Iraq, Afghanistan, and then Obama's overreach in backing NATO's efforts to remove Gadhafi, his political capital when it came to another military action, was all but gone. This led many to find credible, reports of gun running out of Benghazi.

One such person was Retired Army Lt. Gen. William G. Boykin, an original member of the US Delta Force as well as the group's commander. In an interview with Terence Jeffrey of *CNS News*, Boykin appeared convinced the the CIA Annex was used to funnel weapons to Libyan rebels to help overthrow Gadhafi and that US Ambassador Stevens was leading in that effort.

Boykin then expressed what he thought was going on at the Annex after the fall of Gadhafi and it is in line with Paul's question to Hillary:

"More supposition was that he (Stevens) was now funneling guns to the rebel forces in Syria, using essentially the Turks to facilitate that."[96]

In either case, it strains credulity to believe that Clinton did not know the answer to Paul's question. If she *did* know the answer—regardless of what it was—perjury was likely committed when she said she *didn't* know.

Almost immediately after the fall of Gadhafi, attention shifted toward Syria. Many of the same players who backed the overthrow of the Libyan dictator also called for the removal of Bashar Al Assad, with little regard for what was going to fill the power vacuum in Libya. The problem was that the same evil that was unleashed in a post-Gadhafi Libya would be released in a post-Assad Syria. The rebels in each country had the same aspirations as well as the support of the Muslim Brotherhood.

They also had something else—the media narrative. When it came to the propaganda war, Assad was successfully assailed as the brutal dictator and the rebels as the innocent and out-gunned victims. In reality, the brutality of the rebels was far worse.

JBTW is a key component of any successful propaganda campaign as well. Once Syria fell to the rebels, Jordan would be next on the list.

TERROR IN ALGERIA

One week prior to Clinton's testimony, Islamic terrorists hijacked a natural gas plant in Amenas, Algeria and took dozens of people hostage. Amenas sits approximately 30 miles from that Northern African country's eastern border with Libya. Reports were that the terrorists launched the attack in response to assistance given to neighboring Mali—which borders Algeria to the southwest—by France. The Malian government had been fighting off Islamists in the northern part of that country and needed military help.[97]

Moktar Belmoktar, the man who claimed responsibility for the attack in Algeria, blamed the French action in Mali as the reason for the attack. A problem with that claim had to do with how long the attack on the gas plant had been planned. *CNN* cited multiple regional analysts who said the attack was far too sophisticated to have been planned after the French airstrikes in Mali.[98] That declared reason was also belied by attempts by the hijackers to exchange two hostages for the same 'blind Sheikh' whose release was demanded by Egyptians at the US Embassy in Cairo a few months earlier.[99] JBTW comes in all forms.

Like so many other African nations, Mali had also been a victim of the 'Arab Spring' when its president was overthrown in a coup. Islamists flourished after that coup and were the ones France was helping Mali fight near the Algerian border. *CNN* reported that these Islamists want to establish Sharia law in Mali.[100]

Ultimately, 38 hostages from multiple countries lost their lives; three of them were Americans named Victor Lynn Lovelady, Gordon Lee Rowan and Frederick Buttaccio.[101] In the days after the siege ended, reports surfaced that indicated a Libyan connection. The *UK Telegraph* reported that most of the weapons used in the attack actually came from Libya.[102]

Perhaps even more troubling was a report that came out which placed Egyptians involved in the Algerian attack at the attacks in Benghazi on 9/11. According to a report by Adam Nossiter in the *New York Times*, three of the

Algerian attackers were captured and gave specific details about Egyptians involved in both attacks.

MAGHREB

As complicit entities in the West cheered the fall of Tunisia and Libya, Islamic forces that rebelled in those countries saw a much bigger picture. They didn't aspire to the reestablishment of those countries; they sought the reassembly of the Maghreb, a conglomeration of territories in northwest Africa that consisted of countries that are today Libya, Tunisia, Morocco, Algeria, and Mauritania.[103] Based on the violence in Mali, that nation could be annexed by the Maghreb as well.

Barely a month had passed since the fall of Gadhafi when Morocco's Parliamentary elections granted a majority to the Islamic Justice and Development Party (PJD)[104]

Algeria was a different story. Though that country also held elections in the wake of the Arab Spring, the Islamists didn't win; the military did.[105] This was clearly an anomaly in the Arab Spring but in light of the forces at work who insist on the reestablishment of the Maghreb, the military rulers of Algeria have an uphill climb, as the Islamists in northern Mali, the instability in the entire northern part of the continent, and the terrorist attack in Amenas all demonstrate.

Mauritania, a country that borders Morocco and Algeria to the southwest (Mali sits to Mauritania's east), was not insulated from the Arab Spring. In fact, that country saw its people rally around a self-immolation perpetrator as well.[106] The *UK Guardian* reported that al-Qaeda in the region (AQIM) was a source of great concern:

> The rise of al-Qaida in the Maghreb is also attracting attention. While there is no evidence that it has infiltrated Mauritania's uprising, regional instability means there is always potential for the extremist group to make its presence felt.[107]

What the West either refused to admit to itself or validate publicly was the fact that simply removing dictators of countries within the Maghreb didn't take place in a vacuum. Forces were at work to consolidate the leadership of these nations under one umbrella. In the case of Tunisia, Libya, Morocco, and Mauritania those efforts appeared to be successful to some degree. Though secularist liberals did much better in Libya's elections than they did in Egypt or Tunisia, the truth about who is in power there is much less encouraging. While Algeria was able to beat such movements back in the short term, the desire to reestablish the Maghreb will eventually overwhelm the Algerian military and any secular movement that might emerge in places like Libya. Any setbacks suffered by the Brotherhood in this region will be ones that they will most assuredly overcome. If there is one thing we've learned with the gift of history, it's that the secular left is no match for the Islamic fundamentalists, especially in times such as these.

It is the consolidation of these North African nations that should alarm western leaders. Yet, these leaders inexplicably seem to be more interested in feeding the Islamic movement. It is a testament both to the stupidity of such leaders as well as to the steadfastness of the Brotherhood's ability to infiltrate and influence the offices of said leaders with deceit.

BARBARY PIRATES LIVE

In much the same way that Dracula was revived in that 1969 film, the Arab Spring seemed to revive the Barbary Pirates. In the late 1700s, the North African coast was known as the Barbary Coast because it was home to barbaric Muslim pirates who hijacked merchant vessels for ransom. A leader of the North African region known as Maghreb was Khair ad Din, or Barbarossa. Once he demonstrated his power, Barbarossa pledged allegiance to the Ottoman Empire, which all but ceded domain of Maghreb to the Turks.[108]

Pirating ships that sought passage through the Mediterranean was common fare for the Barbary Pirates for centuries during the Ottoman Empire. It wasn't until the resolve of America's third president—Thomas Jefferson—was tested, that the pirates backed down from demanding "tribute" from American vessels that sought passage.[109] There were two Barbary Wars. The first was from 1801-1805; the second was a protracted campaign that relied on the superior Navy of the United States in 1815. In both cases, American leaders stood up to Muslim intimidation.

In the years after the 'Arab Spring', American leaders seemed content to watch the Barbary Pirates reconstitute in the form of Islamic nations on the North African coast. Countries that once were part of an Empire, openly sought a resurrection of that empire so that they could have more power.

Whether westerners knew it or not, nations that once were sovereign were suddenly coagulating in order to honor the wishes of the Brotherhood; those wishes included a return to the Ottoman Empire.

FOOTNOTES

1. TIME, *Bouazizi: The Man Who Set Himself and Tunisia on Fire,* by Rania Abouzeid. http://www.time.com/time/printout/0,8816,2044723,00.html

2. Encyclopedia Britannica, *Zine al-Abidine Ben Ali.* http://www.britannica.com/ EBchecked/topic/60277/Zine-al-Abidine-Ben-Ali

3. The Global Muslim Brotherhood Daily Report, *Global Muslim Brotherhood Claims Victory In Tunisia.* http://globalmbreport.org/?p=5186

4. France 24 International News, *Moderate Islamist Ennahda party wins Tunisian vote.* http://www.france24.com/en/20111027-moderate-islamist-ennahda-party-wins-tunisian-vote-assembly-constitution

5. Reuters, *Islamists claim win in Tunisia's Arab Spring vote,* by Tarek Amara and Andrew Hammond. http://www.reuters.com/article/2011/10/24/us-tunisia-election-idUSTRE79L28820111024

6. http://www.reuters.com/article/2011/10/24/us-tunisia-election-idUSTRE79 L28820111024

7. The Global Muslim Brotherhood Daily Report, *Global Muslim Brotherhood Claims Victory In Tunisia.* http://globalmbreport.org/?p=5186

8. khilafa.com, *Tunisia Islamist causes outcry with "caliphate" talk,* by Tarek Amara. http://www.khilafah.com/index.php/news-watch/africa/13041-tunisia-islamist-causes-outcry-with-qcaliphateq-talk

9. Ibid

10. IPT The Investigative Project on Terrorism, *MPAC Proud to Host Radical Tunisian Leader,* http://www.investigativeproject.org/3311/mpac-proud-to-host-radical-tunisian-leader

11. The Guardian, *Mohamed ElBaradei warns of 'Tunisia-style explosion' in Egypt,* by Jack Shenker. http://www.guardian.co.uk/world/2011/jan/18/mohamed-elbaradei-tunisia-egypt

12. The Wall Street Journal, *Fall of Mubarak Shakes Middle East,* by Charles Levinson, Margaret Coker and Matt Bradley (Cairo) and Adam Entous and Jonathan Weisman (Washington). http://online.wsj.com/article/SB10001424052748703786804576137543866154926.html

13. CBS News, *Google Exec Reported Missing in Egypt,* by Stephen Smith. http://www.cbsnews.com/8301-503543_162-20030204-503543.html?tag=contentMain;contentBody

14. The Wall Street Journal, *Google Executive Emerges as Key Figure in Revolt,* by Margaret Coker (Cairo), Nour Malas (Dubai) and Marc Champion (Alexandria).

http://online.wsj.com/article/SB1000142405274870398950457612762171
2695188.html

15. The Daily Caller, *White House silent as Egypt's president grabs power, moves toward Sharia Islamic law,* by Neil Munro. http://dailycaller.com/2012/11/26/white-house-silent-as-egypts-president-grabs-power-moves-toward-shariah-law/?print=1

16. The Wall Street Journal, *Fall of Mubarak Shakes Middle East,* by Charles Levinson, Margaret Coker and Matt Bradley (Cairo) and Adam Entous and Jonathan Weisman (Washington). http://online.wsj.com/article/SB1000142405274870378680457 6137543866154926.html

17. WBEZ 91.5, *Chicagoan Ahmed Rehab provides an update from Cairo, (short article or download story)* by Worldview. http://www.wbez.org/episode-segments/chi cagoan-ahmed-rehab-provides-update-cairo

18. HindustanTimes, *Egypt protest hero Wael Ghonim barred from stage.* http://www.hindustantimes.com/world-news/Africa/Egypt-protest-hero-Wael-Ghonim-barred-from-stage/Article1-663996.aspx

19. Video, *Did the Muslim Brotherhood kill Anwara Sadat?* http://www.youtube.com/watch?v=5LDakIYho1Y

20. The Telegraph, *Aboud al-Zumour, Islamic Jihad mastermind of Sadat's murder, comes in from the cold after Egypt election,* by Richard Spencer. http://www.tele graph.co.uk/news/worldnews/africaandindianocean/egypt/8933537/Aboud-al-Zumour-Islamic-Jihad-mastermind-of-Sadats-murder-comes-in-from-the-cold-after-Egypt-election.html

21. The Guardian, *Al-Qaida leaders welcome Arab uprisings, says cleric,* by Jason Burke. http://www.guardian.co.uk/world/2011/mar/31/alqaida-leaders-welcome-arab-uprisings

22. The Examiner, *Jimmy Carter: I trust Egypt's Muslim Brotherhood,* by Paul Bedard. http://washingtonexaminer.com/article/350336

23. The New York Times, *Overtures to Egypt's Islamists Reverse Longtime U.S. Policy,* by David D. Kirkpatrick and Steven Lee Myers. http://www.nytimes.com/2012/01/04/world/middleeast/us-reverses-policy-in-reaching-out-to-muslim-brotherhood.html?_r=0

24. Bloomberg Businessweek, *Egypt's Islamists Dominate First Parliament of Post-Mubarak Era,* by Mariam Fam and Abdel Latif Wahba. http://www.business week.com/news/2012-01-22/egypt-s-islamists-dominate-first-parliament-of-post-mubarak-era.html

25. The Los Angeles Times, *Muslim Brotherhood party official tapped for Egypt's Parliament speaker.* http://latimesblogs.latimes.com/world_now/2012/01/islamists-brotherhood-leader-parliament-speaker.html

26. http://news.yahoo.com/egypt-brotherhood-candidate-says-sharia-main-goal-061230332.html;_ylt=Ah6Cvj3kISNe2TXe2rqImHysONUE;_ylu=X3oDMT NpYTVldmcwBG1pdAMEcGtnA2FjZjNjMmUxLWJkY2QtM2JiZS1hZWUyLThjN2ViMz A4Mzc2YQRwb3MDMDNwRzZWMDbG5fTGF0ZXN0TmV3c19nYWwwEdmVyAzhjZmQ2N

27. Ahram Online, *Is Brotherhood candidate El-Shater legally eligible to run for presidency?* by Salma Shukrallah. http://english.ahram.org.eg/NewsContent/36/122 /38401/Presidential-elections-/Presidential-elections-news/Is-Brotherhood-candidate-ElShater-legally-eligible.aspx

28. Al Arabiya News, *Egypt's Muslim Brotherhood presidential candidate Mursi,* by Yasmine Saleh. http://www.alarabiya.net/articles/2012/04/17/208502.html

29. The Jerusalem Post, *Egypt Islamist vows global caliphate in Jerusalem,* by Oren Kessler. http://www.jpost.com/MiddleEast/Article.aspx?ID=269074&R=R1

30. The Wall Street Journal, *George W. Bush: The Arab Spring and American Ideals,* by George W. Bush. http://online.wsj.com/article/SB100014240527023041927045 77406612351805018.html

31. Encyclopedia Britannica Profiles: The American Presidency, *George W. Bush: Declaration of War on Terrorism.* http://www.britannica.com/presidents/article-9398253

32. Ibid

33. CNN U.S., *Protests erupt as runoff set for Egypt's presidential election,* by CNN Wire Staff. http://articles.cnn.com/2012-05-28/middleeast/world_meast_egypt-election_1_prime-minister-ahmed-shafik-mubarak-regime-tahrir-square?_s=PM: MIDDLEEAST

34. The New York Times, Middle East, *Blow to Transition as Court Dissolves Egypt's Parliament,* by David D. Kirkpatrick. http://www.nytimes.com/2012/06/15/ world/middleeast/new-political-showdown-in-egypt-as-court-invalidates-parliament.html

35. Ibid

36. Ibid

37. CNS News.com, *Biden Praises Arab Spring on Same Day Egypt Dissolves Its Parliament,* by Patrick Burke. http://cnsnews.com/news/article/biden-praises-arab-spring-same-day-egypt-dissolves-its-parliament

38. The Australian News, *Muslim Brotherhood candidate Mohammed Mursi wins Egypt's presidential election.* http://www.theaustralian.com.au/in-depth/middle-east-in-

turmoil/muslim-brotherhood-candidate-mohammed-mursi-wins-egypts-presidential-election/story-fn7ycml4-1226398451851

39. The Los Angeles Times, *U.S. officials 'deeply concerned' by Egypt military decree.* http://latimesblogs.latimes.com/world_now/2012/06/us-officials-deeply-concerned-by-egypt-military-decree.html

40. National Review Online, *The L.A. Times Suppresses Obama's Kahlidi Bash Tape,* by Andrew C. McCarthy. http://www.nationalreview.com/blogs/print/226104

41. The Jewish Policy Center, *Rashid Khalidi, Campus Watch & Middle East Studies,* by Cinnamon Stillwell. http://www.jewishpolicycenter.org/457/rashid-khalidi-campus-watch-middle-east-studies

42. Salon, *The promise of real democracy in Egypt,* by Rashid Khalidi. http://www.salon.com/2011/02/11/rashid_khalidi_egypty_democracy/singleton/

43. The White House, *Readout of the President's Call with President-Elect Morsi of Egypt.* http://www.whitehouse.gov/the-press-office/2012/06/24/readout-president-s-call-president-elect-morsi-egypt

44. PJ Media, *Kerry: Don't 'Prejudge' the Muslim Brotherhood,* by Bridget Johnson. http://pjmedia.com/tatler/2012/06/24/kerry-dont-prejudge-the-muslim-brotherhood/?utm_source=twitterfeed&utm_medium=twitter

45. http://old.nationalreview.com/document/kerry200404231047.asp

46. A; Arabiya News, *Egyptian beats pregnant wife to death for not voting for Mursi,* by Yasmin Helal and Al Arabiya. http://english.alarabiya.net/articles/2012/06/24/222413.html

47. The Bible Gateway.com, Isaiah 19:1-4. (NIV) http://www.biblegateway.com/passage/?search=Isaiah%2019&version=NIV

48. The New York Times, *Morsi Admits 'Mistakes' in Drafting Egypt's Constitution,* by David D. Kirkpatrick. http://www.nytimes.com/2012/12/27/world/middleeast/morsi-admits-mistakes-in-drafting-egypts-constitution.html?hp&_r=0

49. Foreign Policy, Membership Required, *Exclusive: Morsy Implies Jews control the American media.* http://thecable.foreignpolicy.com/posts/2013/01/23/exclusive_morsy_implies_jews_control_the_american_media?wp_login_redirect=0

50. The Guardian, *Libyan protesters clash with policy in Benghazi,* Reuters. http://www.guardian.co.uk/world/2011/feb/16/libyan-protesters-clash-with-police

51. BBC NEWS South Scotland, *Colonel Gaddafi 'ordered Lockerbie bombing'.* http://www.bbc.co.uk/news/uk-scotland-south-scotland-12552587

52. The Telegraph, *Libya: western leaders call for Nato to target Gaddafi,* by Toby Harnden. http://www.telegraph.co.uk/news/worldnews/africaandindianocean/libya/8471337/Libya-western-leaders-call-for-Nato-to-target-Gaddafi.html

53. The White House, *President Obama Authorizes Limited Military Action in Libya.* http://www.whitehouse.gov/photos-and-video/video/2011/03/19/president-obama-authorizes-limited-military-action-libya#transcript

54. Pro Publica, *What Exactly Is the War Powers Act and Is Obama Really Violating It?* by Marian Wang. http://www.propublica.org/blog/item/what-exactly-is-the-war-powers-act-and-is-obama-really-violating-it

55. The New York Times, *White House Defends Continuing U.S. Role in Libya Operation,* by Charlie Savage and Mark Landler. http://www.nytimes.com/2011/06/16/us/politics/16powers.html

56. The Telegraph, *Libya: UN approves no-fly zone as British troops prepare for action,* by Robert Winnett, Jon Swaine (New York) and Richard Spencer (Tripoli). http://www.telegraph.co.uk/news/worldnews/africaandindianocean/libya/8389565/Libya-UN-approves-no-fly-zone-as-British-troops-prepare-for-action.html

57. Fox News.com, *McCain Calls for More Military Support to Anti-Qaddafi Forces During Libya Visit.* http://www.foxnews.com/politics/2011/04/22/mccain-travels-libya-meet-rebel-forces/

58. The Daily Caller, *John McCain celebrated Libyan rebellion at site of rebels' public beheading, videos show,* by John Rosenthal. http://dailycaller.com/2011/09/15/john-mccain-celebrated-libyan-rebellion-at-site-of-rebels%E2%80%99-public-beheading-videos-show/

59. Video, Sign-in Required. http://www.youtube.com/verify_age?next_url=http%3A//www.youtube.com/watch%3Fv%3DvrAqcd5WgHY%26skipcontrinter%3D1

60. The Daily Caller, *John McCain celebrated Libyan rebellion at site of rebels' public beheading, videos show,* by John Rosenthal. http://dailycaller.com/2011/09/15/john-mccain-celebrated-libyan-rebellion-at-site-of-rebels%E2%80%99-public-beheading-videos-show/

61. The Guardian, *Hillary Clinton adviser compares internet to Che Guevara,* by Josh Halliday. http://www.guardian.co.uk/media/2011/jun/22/hillary-clinton-adviser-alec-ross

62. U.S. Department of State, *Remarks With Jamaican ForeignMinisterKenneth Baugh and St. Kitts and Nevis Deputy Prime Minister Sam Condor.* http://www.state.gov/secretary/rm/2011/06/166752.htm

63. The Guardian, *Muammar Gaddafi is dead, says Libyan PM—Former Libyan dictator reportedly killed as government forces overrun home town of Sirte,* by James Meikle. http://www.guardian.co.uk/world/2011/oct/20/gaddafi-dead-says-libyan-pm

64. The Telegraph, *Libya: Al Qaeda flag flown above Benghazi* http://www.telegraph.co.uk/news/worldnews/africaandindianocean/libya/8861608/Libya-Al-Qaeda-flag-flown-above-Benghazi-courthouse.html

65. Press TV, *Sharia guardians reviving Islamic revolution in Libya*. http://presstv. com/detail/2012/06/08/245246/sharia-guardians-reviving-libya/

66. Euronews, *Ex rebel chief Jibril early leader in Libya poll*. http://www.euronews. com/2012/07/10/ex-rebel-chief-jibril-early-leader-in-libya-poll/

67. The Daily Beast, *Libya's Optimistic Leader: Mahmoud Jibril Poised for Historic Election Victory*, by Jamie Dettmer. http://www.thedailybeast.com/articles/2012/07/ 09/libya-s-optimistic-leader-mahmoud-jibril-poised-for-historic-election-victory.html

68. Ibid

69. Gulfnews.com, *Libya elections point to a different trend*. http://gulfnews. com/opinions/editorials/libya-elections-point-to-a-different-trend-1.1047138

70. CBS News, *Pro-Western parties gain in Libyan elections*. http://www.cbsnews. com/8301-202_162-57468308/pro-western-parties-gain-in-libyan-elections/

71. MSNBC.com, Video. http://video.msnbc.msn.com/martin-bashir/48141099#4814 1099

72. USA Today, *Cairo protesters scale U.S. Embassy wall, remove flag*. http://con tent.usatoday.com/communities/ondeadline/post/2012/09/11/cairo-us-embassy-protesters-prophet-mohammad/70000126/1#.UP3d1vKThdg

73. CNS News.com, *Clinton Publicly Linked Benghazi to Video Before Woods and Doherty Were Killed*, by Terence P. Jeffrey. http://cnsnews.com/blog/terence-p-jeffrey/clinton-publicly-linked-benghazi-video-woods-and-doherty-were-killed

74. U.S. Department of State, *Statement on the Attack in Benghazi*, Hillary Rodham Clinton. http://www.state.gov/secretary/rm/2012/09/197628.htm

75. Video, *U.S. Secretary of State Hillary Clinton condemns anti-Islam video*. http://www.youtube.com/watch?feature=player_embedded&v=qXYdb57P7T4

76. U.S. Department of State, *Remarks at Reception Marking Eid ul-Fitr*, Hillary Rodham Clinton. http://www.state.gov/secretary/rm/2012/09/197735.htm

77. AllGov, *Libya's Ambassador to the U.S. Resigns: Who is Ali Aujali?* http://www. allgov.com/news/appointments-and-resignations/libyas-ambassador-to-the-us-resigns-who-is-ali-aujali?news=842252

78. Video, *Former Libyan Ambassador Ali Sulaiman Aujali Speaks ata ISNA about Revolution*. http://www.youtube.com/watch?v=qvplv72VKAI&feature=player_ embedded

79. The Jewish Daily Forward, *Jews Condemn Anti-Muslim Video and Violence*, by JTA. http://forward.com/articles/162759/jews-condemn-anti-muslim-video-and-violence/

80. Video, *President Obama and Secretary Clinton Delivery Remarks at Andrews Air Force Base.* http://www.youtube.com/watch?v=fjHzEHGzHYA&feature=player_embedded

81. News.Gather.com, *Tyrone Woods' Father Speaks out about His Son,* by Renee Nal. http://news.gather.com/viewArticle.action?articleId=281474981721497

82. Unclassified. http://i2.cdn.turner.com/cnn/2012/images/12/18/202446.pdf

83. Video in Arabic. http://www.youtube.com/watch?feature=player_embedded&v=Hn57YxuwLJI

84. Arabic website. http://elbadil.com/parties-and-movements/2012/09/10/63414

85. Daily Nation, *Susan Rice gives up US secretary of state bid,* by AFP. http://www.nation.co.ke/News/world/Susan-Rice-gives-up-US-secretary-of-state-bid/-/1068/1643676/-/410k82/-/index.html

86. FactCheck.org, *Benghazi Timeline—The long road from "spontaneous protest" to premeditated terrorist attack.* http://www.factcheck.org/2012/10/benghazi-time-line/

87. The White House, Remarks by the President to the US General http://www.whitehouse.gov/the-press-office/2012/09/25/remarks-president-un-general-assembly

88. Huff Post, *Obama On Anti-Islam Film Creator: 'A Shadowy Character'.* http://www.huffingtonpost.com/2012/09/19/obama-anti-islam-film-shadowy-character_n_1896671.html

89. The Global Muslim Brotherhood Daily Report, *Muslim Brotherhood Loses One in Libya.* http://globalmbreport.org/?p=6499

90. MediaITE, *John McCain Clashes With Hannity: You And Fox News 'Were Wrong About Libya',* by Andrew Kirell. http://www.mediaite.com/tv/john-mccain-clashes-with-sean-hannity-you-and-fox-news-were-wrong-about-libya/

91. ABCC The Blotter, *Former Terror Group Founder to Libyan Rebel Military Commander,* by Lee Ferran and Rym Momtaz. http://abcnews.go.com/Blotter/terror-group-founder-libyan-rebel-military-commander/story?id=14405319#.UJCK5o7_SQJ

92. BBC News Africa, *Profile: Libyan rebel commander Abdel Hakim Belhadj.* http://www.bbc.co.uk/news/world-africa-14786753

93. The Jamestown Foundation, *Libya Arrests al-Qaeda Suspects,* by Stephen Ulph. http://www.jamestown.org/programs/gta/single/?tx_ttnews[tt_news]=251&tx_ttnews[backPid]=237&no_cache=1

94. ABC The Blotter, *Former error Group Founder to Libyan Rebel Military Commander,* by Lee Ferran and Rym Momtaz. http://abcnews.go.com/Blotter/terror-group-founder-libyan-rebel-military-commander/story?id=14405319#.UJCK5o7_SQJ

95. Courier-Journal.com, *Sen. Rand Paul to Secretary of State Hillary Clinton: 'I would have relieved you of your post'*, by James Carroll. http://blogs.courier-journal.com/politics/2013/01/23/sen-rand-paul-to-secretary-of-state-hillary-clinton-i-would-have-relieved-you-of-your-post/

96. CNS News.com, *Former Special Forces Commander: Was U.S. Running Guns to Syrian Rebels Via Benghazi? Cia: No,* by Terence P. Jeffrey. http://cnsnews.com/news/article/former-special-forces-commander-was-us-running-guns-syrian-rebels-benghazi-cia-no

97. CNN, *At least 37 hostages killed in Algeria gas plant standoff, prime minister says,* English and Arabic with translation, from Amir Ahmed. http://www.cnn.com/2013/01/21/world/africa/algeria-hostage-crisis/index.html

98. Ibid

99. Daily News, *Islamist hostage takers in Algeria demand release of 'Blind Sheikh', Omar Abdel-Rahman, '93 WTC bomber, in exchange for two Americans,* by Corky Siemaszko. http://www.nydailynews.com/news/world/algeria-hostage-crisis-continues-fighting-article-1.1242432

100. CNN World, *Fance continues Mali airstrikes; residents frantic,* by Katarina Hoije and Greg Botelho. http://www.cnn.com/2013/01/17/world/mali-unrest/

101. USA Today, *Americans killed in Algerian attack are identified,* by Jabeen Bhatti. http://www.usatoday.com/story/news/world/2013/01/21/algeria-hostages-militants-gas-plant/1850707/

102. The Telegraph, *Algeria hostage crisis: Most weapons used in attack came from Libya,* by Mélanie Matarese. http://www.telegraph.co.uk/news/worldnews/africaandindianocean/algeria/9814510/Algeria-hostage-crisis-Most-weapons-used-in-attack-came-from-Libya.html

103. The Word MAGHREB. http://www.maghreb-studies-association.co.uk/en/all home.html

104. The Telegraph, *Islamist party wins power for first time in Morocco,* by Nabila Ramdani. http://www.telegraph.co.uk/news/worldnews/africaandindianocean/morocco/8919096/Islamist-party-wins-power-for-first-time-in-Morocco.html

105. The New York Times, *Algerians Belittle Elections, but Not Enough to Protest*, by Adam Nossiter. http://www.nytimes.com/2012/05/19/world/africa/in-algeria-belittling-elections-but-no-arab-spring.html?pagewanted=all

106. AlJazeera, *Mauritania's overlooked uprising.* http://stream.aljazeera.com/story/mauritanias-overlooked-uprising-0022010

107. The Guardian, *Mauritania's 'overlooked' Arab spring,* by Sharif Nashashibi. http://www.guardian.co.uk/commentisfree/2012/may/26/mauritania-overlooked-arab-spring

108. Global Security.org, *Barbary Wars.* http://www.globalsecurity.org/military/ops/barbary.htm

109. About.com, *The United States Fought Wars Against North African Pirates in the Early 1800s,* by Robert McNamara. http://history1800s.about.com/od/american wars/tp/barbarywars.htm

SECTION

7

How Did The West Get Here

CHAPTER

16

DISTURBING THE NEST...
BY LEAVING

BOTH SIDES OWN IT

*T*he degree to which the western left and right are responsible for enabling the rise of Islamic fundamentalism is certainly up for debate. What is *not* disputable is that leaders on both sides have played significant roles in that rise, going back decades.

Perhaps no two incidents better illustrate this reality than what happened in Beirut, Lebanon and Mogadishu, Somalia respectively, within ten years of one other.

In those two cases—for both similar and divergent reasons—decisions were made to cede moral and literal ground. Strategically, while the decisions to retreat *were* calculated, they were also *not* inconsequential. By retreating, the United States emboldened the Muslim world.

BEIRUT AND SOMALIA

In the early morning hours of October 23, 1983, a suicide bomber drove a truck into the US Marines barracks in Beirut, Lebanon. The massive explosion killed 241 Marines. The attacks were believed to have been committed by an Islamist group that was in its infancy at the time; that group was Hezbollah.

President Ronald Reagan met with his advisers and the response was supposed to involve an attack on the Sheik Abdullah barracks in Baalbek, Lebanon, home to Iranian Revolutionary Guards who were training Hezbollah fighters. Then Secretary of Defense Caspar Weinberger is said to have talked Reagan out of such a plan because of how it might harm US relations with Arab nations.[1] One could infer that Weinberger was concerned about enflaming the Middle East. If true, Weinberger could not have been more wrong.

The subsequent pullout of US troops from the region served to embolden the likes of Osama bin Laden, who used the incident to identify the United States as a "paper tiger."[2] The bombing also served as a blueprint for future bombings in the Middle East because of how effective it was perceived to have been. Instead of being decimated while in its infancy, Hezbollah grew.[3]

Ten years later, the US had a military presence in Somalia as a result of a program known as 'Operation: Restore Hope,' which was an effort to help feed a starving population caught between warring Islamic factions. According to multiple reports, over 300,000 Somalis died of starvation as an estimated 80% of food provided internationally was being stolen by rival warlords. Restore Hope was put into place at the end of the George H.W. Bush administration and continued into the Bill Clinton administration; it included armed US forces to help ensure that food made it to those who needed it most.[4]

Mohammed Farah Aidid was the most powerful warlord in the region at the time. Violence had been escalating. American troops were being injured and in some cases, killed, as a direct result of forces loyal to Aidid. This led to the Battle of Mogadishu, which was the subject of the film "Black Hawk Down." During that battle—on October 3, 1993—18 Americans were killed, as were hundreds of Somalis. Clinton decided to withdraw US troops from Somalia days later.[5]

How does this relate to JBTW, you ask? Something had obviously penetrated the minds of Somalis to get them to believe that the Americans were there to do them harm when, in actuality, they were there to *help* them against Aidid.

Interestingly and perhaps not coincidentally, strong evidence exists that Osama bin Laden sent al-Qaeda operatives to Somalia to train indigenous forces to defeat the Americans. In a 1997 interview bin Laden granted to *CNN*, the al-Qaeda leader said:

> "With Allah's grace, Muslims over there cooperated with some Arab muja-hedeen who were in Afghanistan ... against the American occupation troops and killed large numbers of them."[6]

One year later, bin Laden reportedly met with Imad Mugniyah, the alleged mastermind behind the 1983 Marine barracks attack in Lebanon. Indications are that the two collaborated to some degree and undoubtedly shared their common experiences relative to Beirut and Somalia.[7]

Though these two very historic events do not represent the starting points for the left and the right when it comes to confrontations with Islamic fundamentalism, both events are emblematic of those confrontations. In both cases, the left and the right chose what they thought was strategic retreat but in both cases, both were mistaken.

FOOTNOTES

1. Frontline, *Terrorists attacks on Americans, 1979-1988, Hostages taken at the U.S. Embassy in Tehran.* http://www.pbs.org/wgbh/pages/frontline/shows/target/etc/cron.html

2. The Foundry, *The 1983 Marine Barracks Bombing: Connecting the Dots,* by James Phillips. http://blog.heritage.org/2009/10/23/the-1983-marine-barracks-bombing-connecting-the-dots/

3. History Commons, *Hezbollah was a participant or observer in the following events:* [see Article]. http://www.historycommons.org/entity.jsp?entity=hezbollah

4. Operation Restore Hope/Battle of Mogadishu. http://novaonline.nvcc.edu/eli/evans/his135/Events/Somalia93/Somalia93.html

5. Ibid

6. Wayback Machine, *Scant evidence shown to link bin Laden to GI deaths in Somalia,* from Phil Hirschkorn. http://web.archive.org/web/20010808075823/http://www.cnn.com/LAW/trials.and.cases/case.files/0012/embassy.bombing/trial.report/trial.report.04.20/index.html

7. History Commons, *Hezbollah was a participant or observer in the following events:* [see Article]. http://www.historycommons.org/entity.jsp?entity=hezbollah

CHAPTER

17

ISLAM AND THE RIGHT

MUSLIMS LIKE IKE

On June 28, 1957 the Islamic Center of Washington was opened. Republican President Dwight Eisenhower was on-hand during the dedication ceremony.[1] This would be the same mosque that George W. Bush would visit in the days after the 9/11/01 attacks. Lost on both presidents was the true purpose of that mosque's construction.

According to the Islamic Center website, the land the mosque now sits on was purchased on April 30, 1946—the first anniversary of Adolf Hitler's death—by the Washington Mosque Foundation. The cornerstone was laid on January 11, 1949.[2] Though that date may not be significant, January 12th is; it is recognized as Muhammad's birthday and Mecca is eight hours ahead of the Eastern Time zone.[3]

The Islamic Center attributes the following quotes to Eisenhower during his speech at the dedication ceremony:

> "America would fight with her whole strength for your right to have here your own church and worship according to your own conscience. This concept is indeed a part of America, and without that concept we would be something else than what we are."

And…

> "As I stand beneath these graceful arches, surrounded on every side by friends from far and near, I am convinced that our common goals are both right and promising. Faithful to the demands of justice and of brotherhood, each working according to the lights of his own conscience, our world must advance along the paths of peace."[4]

It is noteworthy to consider that barely more than one decade after the end of WWII, an American hero in that war who had been elected president, would embrace a religion that sided with Hitler in his desire to see the extermination of the Jews.

President George W. Bush returned to the Washington, D.C. mosque for the RE-dedication ceremony in 2007, fifty years after Eisenhower did it originally. The man who introduced Bush was the mosque's director, Abdullah M. Khouj, who began his tenure there in 1984. According to the *Weekly Standard's* Stephen Schwartz, Saudi officials took over the mosque in 1983 and Khouj was subsequently appointed. Khouj has been a representative for the Muslim World League (MWL):

> Khouj represented the Muslim World League (MWL), founded in Saudi Arabia in 1962 as an international agency for the propagation of Wahhabism. In 2006, relief branches of the MWL in Southeast Asia would be designated by the U.S. Treasury as financing fronts for al Qaeda. In addition, Khouj was admitted to the United States as a diplomat, allegedly serving as an attaché at the Saudi Embassy, but actually dedicated to advancing the most radical interpretation of Islam in history.[5]

The MWL is significant for many reasons but one such reason is its involvement as the umbrella organization for the Institute of Muslim Minority Affairs (IMMA). This is the same IMMA where Secretary of State Hillary Clinton's Deputy Chief of Staff, Huma Abedin, worked as an assistant editor for at least twelve years until leaving in 2009, to work for Clinton at the State Department. The man responsible for launching the IMMA was none other than Abdullah Omar Naseef, who was the Secretary General of the MWL when Khouj became the Director of the Washington mosque.

ACCESS TO THE PRESIDENT

A signatory to *A Common Word* is a man named Dr. Muzammil Siddiqi. He gained access to President George W. Bush in 2001. Before we delve into the background of Siddiqi specifically, let's look at some history of his associations and what he was able to accomplish in the wake of the September 11th attacks; it is shocking.

Siddiqi once served as the president of the Muslim Brotherhood's Islamic Society of North America (ISNA) from 1997—2001.[6] It was in his capacity as president of ISNA that Siddiqi was able to visit the White House just weeks after the September 11th attacks. Yes, the head of a Muslim Brotherhood group was granted inside-access to the President of the United States and, in particular, the George W. Bush administration, only days after the worst attack on American soil.

In hindsight, if there was an enemy the United States should have identified after 9/11, it was the Muslim Brotherhood. Instead, the enemy identified by the Bush administration was a *tactic* employed by Ikhwan-affiliated groups; that tactic was terror. As a result, men like Siddiqi were viewed as agents for peace. Ostensibly, the thinking was that leaders like Siddiqi could appeal to other Muslim leaders in order to avoid a greater conflict. The problem for the Bush administration was that it had decided to deal with leaders who shared the *objectives* of al-Qaeda, if not the group's means.

In an article written by Franklin Foer that appeared in the *New Republic* on November 1, 2001, some shocking details were brought to light.[7]

Two other prominent Muslim leaders in attendance with Siddiqi were Dr. Yahya Basha, then president of the American Muslim Council (AMC), and Salam Al-Marayati, Executive Director of the Muslim Public Affairs Council (MPAC). All three men had alarmingly close associations with terrorists and terrorist groups. AMC itself was founded by a man named Abdurahman Alamoudi, who would be convicted of terrorist fundraising and sentenced to 23 years in prison just two years after the leader of the group he founded had met with Bush.

Perhaps even worse is the fact that one year prior to his September 26, 2001 meeting, Bush—along with then-Senatorial candidate Hillary Clinton—had each returned $1000 in campaign contributions they had received from Alamoudi because of the AMC founder's defense of both Hezbollah and Hamas.[8]

At the time, Alamoudi was actually employed by the US State Department and continued to serve on the board of the AMC. If Bush was willing to return campaign contributions to a board member and founder of AMC one year *before* 9/11, why would he agree to meet with that organization's president two weeks *after* 9/11? Was Basha properly vetted?

Just a few short hours after the September 11th attacks, MPAC's al-Marayati appeared on a Los Angeles radio program and suggested the Israelis may have been behind the attacks. He would meet with the President just two weeks later. Like Alamoudi, al-Marayati is on record as having defended both Hamas and Hezbollah.[9]

That's not all. President Bush stood alongside Muslim leaders *six days* after September 11th inside the Islamic Center of Washington discussed earlier. One of those leaders was none other than CAIR Executive Director, Nihad Awad, who had expressed support for Hamas less than ten years earlier. Here is some of what Bush said at a podium while speaking inside the mosque:

> "Like the good folks standing with me, the American people were appalled and outraged at last Tuesday's attacks...This is a great country. It's a great country because we share the same values of respect and dignity and human worth. And it is my honor to be meeting with leaders who feel just the same way I do. They're outraged, they're sad. They love America just as much as I do."

In addition to such a statement being demonstrably false, it was harmful to the greater cause of identifying America's true enemies. Such events were seized upon by Muslim groups as something to bolster their credibility. CAIR's national headquarters was still citing Bush's words ten years after he uttered them.[10]

KARL ROVE

There is a photo of George W. Bush and the man who would be his closest, most trusted adviser—Karl Rove—meeting with Alamoudi circa 2000. In that photo, Rove can be seen holding a book, obviously given to him by the delegation also seen in the photo. It's entitled, The Cultural Atlas of Islam and was written by a man named Ismail Al Faruqi in 1986.

Now, obviously, Karl Rove cannot be held accountable for accepting a book from a group he met with; it happens all the time. In fact, in 2009, Barack Obama accepted a far left-wing book from Hugo Chavez. That made news because Chavez wanted to make a public spectacle of himself.

However, there were red flags raised by the Secret Service and Intelligence officials relative to both Alamoudi and Sami Al-Arian, another individual who would later plead guilty to charges related to terrorism. Yet, Bush and/or Rove met with them on more than one occasion after this book was put into Rove's hands. If there were suspicions about Alamoudi prior to these meetings, wouldn't it have been prudent to investigate the author of material this group felt was important enough to put into Rove's hands?

Newsweek had reported on Alamoudi's connections being known years earlier:

> ...Alamoudi and the AMC had been previously criticized for their ties to Hamas and other militant groups and figures (see March 13, 1996). Bush and/or Rove will meet with Alamoudi on other occasions (see July 2000, June 22, 2001, September 14-26, 2001). US intelligence learned of ties between Alamoudi and bin Laden in 1994 (see Shortly After March 1994);[11]

Yes, Alamoudi visited the White House after 9/11. As it turns out, Al Faruqi is identified as the founder of one of the Muslim Brotherhood front groups listed as unindicted co-conspirators in the Holy Land Foundation trial (HLF). That group is the Association of Muslim Social Scientists of North America (AMSS). Here is what *Discover the Networks* says about AMSS:

> Established in 1972 by Temple University professor Ismail Raji al-Faruqi and University of Pennsylvania graduate student Abdulhamid AbuSulayman, the Association of Muslim Social Scientists of North America (AMSS) is a constituent organization of the Islamic Society of North America (ISNA) and a sister organization of the International Institute of Islamic Thought.

> AMSS describes itself as "an independent membership-based organization that encompasses the United States and Canada." It has no corporate, legal or financial relationship with any organization bearing the name of AMSS in any other country. Its mission is "to provide a forum through which Islamic positions on various academic disciplines can be promoted, with an emphasis on the social sciences and humanities"; to further "the continuity of the Islamic intellectual heritage"; and "to serve the interests of the larger Muslim community by bringing together Muslim and non-Muslim scholars in an academic setting to examine and define Islamic perspectives on issues of global concern that contribute to the prosperity of Muslims around the globe and the betterment of humanity."

> AMSS collaborates with the International Institute of Islamic Thought to publish the American Journal of Islamic Social Sciences (AJISS), which is distributed in more than 50 countries around the world. Launched in 1984, AJISS is an interdisciplinary publication of scholarly research on all facets of Islam and the Muslim world: politics, history, economic philosophy, metaphysics, psychology, religious law, and Islamic thought.[12]

So, the author of the book given to Rove in 2000 was closely affiliated with the Muslim Brotherhood, a group that has pledged to work toward the destruction of the United States. The International Institute of Islamic Thought (IIIT), another unindicted co-conspirator in HLF also lists al-Faruqi as its founder.

Are we to believe that the Bush administration did not know of the nefarious intentions of these individuals and groups?

According to Foer's *New Republic* piece mentioned earlier, Rove was confronted about the very questionable individuals both he and the President were meeting with:

> Days later, after a conservative activist confronted Karl Rove with dossiers about some of Bush's new friends, Rove replied, according to the activist, "I wish I had known before the event took place."[13]

For a conservative activist to know this information while Rove and the president were ignorant is simply not believable.

THE DIARY OF WILLIAM MURRAY

In the weeks after September 11, 2001 the chairman of the Religious Freedom Coalition—William Murray—wrote a journal about his experiences after the attacks. It was a firsthand account of someone who lived near *to* and worked *in* Washington, D.C. Murray was someone who worked near the Capitol Building and knew Congressmen and Senators personally.

Had Murray been listened to then, the rise of Islam across the Middle East, Europe, and here in America since, may have been significantly reduced, if not outright prevented. His observations at the time were so spot-on from someone who had much less information than Bush's inner circle did that this is not an issue of Monday morning quarterbacking. The Bush strategy after 9/11 was fatally flawed and his administration chose the path of least resistance. In short, the administration lied to Americans and to itself before ever going into Iraq.

Upon reading Murray's words in the days and weeks after 9/11, one is left face to face with the painfully obvious reality that everything Murray wrote had to have been known at the highest levels of the Bush administration too. It's simply not possible to believe otherwise.

The following are some excerpts from Murray's journal.

Wednesday, September 12th—By mid afternoon on Wednesday I was convinced that not only was the United States a victim of Islamic Jihad, but that the attack had been perpetrated by an organization controlled by a Saudi citizen and that most of those involved were Saudi, and that furthermore the attack was financed for the most part by Saudi businessmen and members of the Saudi royal family.

At the end of the day I made the following statement to my wife:

"These attacks were planned, financed and carried out by Saudi nationals and as a result the real culprits will never come to justice. We will bomb some third world nation like Afghanistan and our government will say our "moderate" Islamic friends with all the oil were not involved. Worse, we will put a handful of people in jail like we did the last time the World Trade Center was bombed. The Islamic fanatics will think a trade off of four or five in jail getting three meals a day, versus thousands of Americans dead, is a great deal.

So far, Murray accurately identified what the Bush administration would do with respect to Afghanistan. We also know that based on the fact that al-Qaeda financier—Abdullah Omar Naseef—was not held to account for his role in funding al-Qaeda, there were some "moderate" Islamic friends who escaped American wrath over 9/11. Naseef was once the Secretary General of the Muslim World League (MWL), which is funded by the Saudi Royal family.[14] He also founded the Rabita Trust, an entity that was identified by the U.S. Treasury Department as one that financed al-Qaeda; it was listed as a terrorist organization and its assets frozen one month after 9/11.[15]

Wednesday, September 13th—As I talked to congressmen and Senators my worst fears were realized. I carried documents with me showing clearly that most funding for Osama Bin Laden's terror network came from moderate states like Saudi Arabia. While the Saudi government itself claims that it has no ties to these terror organizations, each year the government gives $10 billion to fundamentalist Islamic organizations, many of them located in the United States.

When I confronted one well known Senator about the millions of dollars going to Bin Laden's terror network from Saudi businessmen, he said to me, "Yes, but they are coerced into giving it to him."

I responded to this by saying, "Maybe those millionaire Saudi businessmen should be more fearful of us than they are of Bin Laden."

Later that day almost the identical conversation took place between myself and a member of the House leadership and then again with someone within the Bush Administration. It was made clear to me that none of the wealthy Saudi Arabians who finance Islamic terror would meet the wrath of the United States for fear of angering the "friendly" state of Saudi Arabia. This was made clear to me by members of the House and Senate, both Democrat and Republican as well as by some in the Administration. I was appalled.

Murray was quite correct about those "moderate" Islamic friends facing no consequences. Perhaps the most chilling excerpt from the author was found in his account of what he witnessed the next day:

Thursday, September 14th—My stomach churned as I watched Muzammil Siddiqi, the Imam for the Islamic Society of North America, stand on stage with President George W. Bush in the National Cathedral. Imam Siddiqi is a radical extremist who has participated in anti-American demonstrations in front of the White House as recently as October of 2000. He has in the past called for a Jihad or holy war against this nation. While the Christian and Jewish leaders at the event prayed for our nation and for the dead and dying from the attack, Imam Siddiqi did not do so. At no time did he condemn the acts of the terrorists nor did he pray for America or for the families of those who lost their lives in the Jihad attack against the United States...

As the service closed I felt the chill of the presence of the awesome power of God. I was clearly reminded of the very first of the Ten Commandments, THOU SHALT HAVE NO OTHER GODS BEFORE ME (Exodus 20:3). The National Cathedral had been defiled... Our Christian President had bowed his head to prayers offered to other gods, prayers that may have been for those who would destroy our nation and enslave our children to an alien religion. At that moment the hand of protection of the true God was removed from our nation.

Since the Jihad attack on the United States on September 11th the President has surrounded himself with and sought advice from radical Islamic leaders who have openly called for the violent overthrow of the government of the United States. In addition, the President has invited six of the seven Islamic nations known to sponsor terror into his "coalition against terror".

By late Friday it became apparent to me that our nation was in fact not going to fight a war on terrorism, but rather follow the same old track of "punishing those who actually committed the crime." This was not a "crime;" it was an act of war.

Sunday, September 17th—A sharp line began to form in Washington between those of us willing to tell the truth about what had happened on September 11th and those who wish to continue to live in the fantasy world of pluralism. The ACLU began a campaign to stop "oppression" of Muslims in the United States. They began the campaign by signing up organizations to protect the "civil rights" of Muslims.

Meanwhile the "moderate" Islamic organizations had a word of their own for Muslims in America: DO NOT HELP THE FBI. Internet sites warned Muslims that: "The FBI has a history of harassing and harming minority and immigrant communities. Some people are spending a long time in jail because they or their friends talked to the FBI."[16]

All of this begs an answer to a very simple question: How is it that a man with far less information at his disposal in the days after 9/11 was able to more accurately diagnose who hit the United States than was the Bush administration, which had far more at its disposal?

The answer to that question did not involve a mis-diagnosis; it involved turning a blind eye to the problem instead of treating it. The follow-up question is why?

Read on. (**See Appendix B**)

GROVER NORQUIST

Was JBTW really so powerful that it deceived the president of the United States and his administration *after* 9/11?

During the election campaign of 2000, the Bush team had become familiar with Yahya Basha because his AMC was one of four groups that joined together to form the American Muslim Political Coordination Council (AMPCC), which endorsed Bush's presidential run against Gore. The other three groups that made up the AMPCC were the Council on American Islamic Relations (CAIR), the American Muslim Alliance (AMA) and MPAC, the group headed at the time of the September 26, 2001 meeting by al-Marayati.[17]

This would indicate that Bush was somewhat beholden, at least to some degree, to these Islamic groups. However, perhaps in the aftermath of 9/11, he would need some extra persuasion to welcome such individuals into the White House. If there was such an individual, Grover Norquist certainly fit the bill.

Norquist, the presumed conservative head of a group known as Americans for Tax Reform (ATR), was largely responsible for the Bush administration's decision relative to Muslim outreach and embracing leaders like Siddiqi, al-Marayati, and Awad.[18]

During the September 26th meeting at the White House, Siddiqi was one of 15 Muslim leaders to appear with President Bush, who said the following publicly:

"...the teachings of Islam are teachings of peace and good."[19]

In 2011, CAIR California honored Siddiqi for his receipt of the "Community Leader Award" and extolled his "Strong Leadership and Commitment to Bridge-building." On CAIR's website, they were sure to make reference to Siddiqi's appearance with Bush in the days after the September 11th attacks.[20]

According to Foer in his *New Republic* article, Bush's most trusted adviser—Karl Rove—was approached with some disturbing facts about the Islamic leaders with whom the administration had aligned; Rove feigned ignorance. Such a stance would ring hollow in light of Norquist's continued access and Bush's continued outreach to Islamists; the president would return to the same mosque at which he stood with Islamists six days after the September 11th attacks, little more than one year later to celebrate a Muslim holiday.[21]

NORQUIST'S PALESTINIAN WIFE

A very interesting element to this particular dynamic is who Norquist is married to. Her name is Samah Alrayyes, a Palestinian Muslim with an Egyptian name. It is a violation of Sharia law for a female Muslim to marry a non-Muslim man, right? Though Grover reportedly would not admit or deny a conversion to Islam in order to marry Alrayyes, this question would later come up in the wake of the scandal involving Congressman Anthony Weiner (D-NY) in the summer of 2011. Weiner married a Muslim woman named Huma Abedin, who was also the Deputy Chief of Staff for Secretary of State Hillary Clinton.

Like Abedin, Alrayyes landed a job inside the US Government, working as a Public Affairs Specialist for Arab and Muslim outreach at the Bureau of Legislative and Public affairs at USAID.[22] The question about any conversion to Islam by Norquist or Weiner so their marriages would be legal according to Sharia law is one that can be answered by the Muslim Brotherhood's Sheikh Youssef al-Qaradawi and his endorsement of *Muruna*, a tactic that allows Muslims to violate their most sacred prohibitions if doing so serves a higher calling. Nonetheless, the influence wielded by both Alrayyes and Abedin has been significant at the highest levels of the US government.

SUHAIL KHAN

The saga of Suhail Khan provides another example which demonstrates that the infiltration of America's political system by Islamists is not done exclusively through the Democratic Party. Khan has also been a colleague of Norquist over the years. Known as a fiscal conservative, Norquist had access to the Bush White House and apparently leveraged it in order to allow Khan to have access through the front door.[23]

Eventually, as part of the George W. Bush administration, Khan gained enough influence to become what David Horowitz described as a "White House gatekeeper for the Muslim community." In that capacity, Khan was involved in the post 9/11 meetings that took place between the administration and groups like ISNA and CAIR. Khan also brokered a White House meeting with none other than Sami al-Arian, who was later convicted of charges related to financing terrorism.[24]

As a veteran of the Bush administration, Khan has portrayed himself as a conservative. As of this writing, he is still listed as a member of the American Conservative Union's (ACU) Board of Directors, along with Norquist.[25] In fact, at the Conservative Political Action Conference (CPAC), the annual event sponsored by the ACU, Khan was one of the featured speakers in 2011, though not without some controversy. At about the same time, videos had surfaced that showed Khan receiving an award from none other than Abdurrahman Alamoudi. Another video showed Khan speaking in front of the Islamic Society of North America (ISNA) in 1999. During that speech, Khan tearfully extolled the virtues of Muslim jihadists who martyred themselves.[26]

With the controversy about these videos swirling around CPAC in 2011, Khan was confronted during a panel discussion at the event. In a video, the *United West's* J. Mark Campbell can be seen asking Khan about outreach to the Muslim Brotherhood in the United States. Khan's answer was a bald-faced lie. Said Khan:

"There's no Muslim Brotherhood in the United States."[27]

Such a claim was beyond brash, especially when one factors in Khan's upbringing. His father was a man named Mahboob Khan, who is credited with helping to found Muslim Brotherhood groups in the United States in the 1960s— the Muslim Students Association (MSA) and the Islamic Society of North America (ISNA) are among them; these groups have only grown since Khan's father helped them get their sea legs in the US. By denying the existence of the Ikhwan in the United States, Khan denied the work of his own father.[28] It takes a special brand of *muruna* to deny your father's supposedly righteous work.

While the Khan clan lived in California in the 1970s, Mahboob founded an organization known as the Islamic Society of Orange County (ISOC). After resigning from his position there, the vacancy was filled by none other than Muzammil Siddiqi. Yes, that Muzammil Siddiqi.[29]

TWO FACES OF SIDDIQI

Dr. Muzammil Siddiqi is head of the Fiqh Council and the American Society in California. I am personally familiar with both as a result of time I spent with my Syrian Imam Abdul Qader Al-Najjar, prior to my conversion to Christianity. I would chat with Najjar about how the Saudis purchased an entire block in Garden Grove California where I resided in 1980. In English, he would tell my Jewish girl-friend the virtues of Islam; this ultimately led her to convert to Islam. However, in Arabic, he preached Friday sermons in which he declared that Allah cursed the US for the mishaps that happened in Operation Eagle Claw, the botched rescue attempt of American hostages in Iran.

Siddiqi, like Najjar, knows how to impress Jews with words in English. After all, he was able to get inside access to the White House shortly after 9/11. Hannah Rosenthal—Special Envoy to Monitor and Combat Anti-Semitism Bureau of Democracy, Human Rights and Labor US Department of State—made the following statement in support of Dr. Siddiqi:

> "Dr. Siddiqi and his wife traveled with me to Dachau and Auschwitz last
> summer and helped author a strong statement condemning Holocaust denial
> and all other forms of anti-Semitism. The group we traveled with looked to
> Imam Siddiqi as a leader, as the group memorialized the six million exter-
> minated by the Nazis, he led the group in a historic prayer next to the 'Never

Again' sign at Dachau concentration camp. He is a kind and generous man who deserves praise for his leadership, caring and condemnation of all forms of hatred."[30]

Once one gains the ability to read in Arabic, it becomes obvious that these Islamists are engaged in extreme levels of deception. One of his supporters is Dr. Abdullah Al-Qadri Al-Ahdal, who had the opportunity to interview Siddiqi. I have translated, from Arabic, Al-Ahdal's notes from his discussion with Muzammil Siddiqi:

"T met with him later in North America—California in Los Angeles at the home of the Saudi Consul-General Abdul-Majid on 10/11/1405 H [1985]. During the interview, he discusses what he calls 'Islamic penetration' with "Blacks" in the U.S. in which Muzammil explains: 'The reason for low penetration of white Americans with Islam is the whites' fanaticism and sense of superiority and sovereignty over other nationalities. Unlike blacks, who have a need for Islam to excel over the whites, who despise blacks. The whites have a great spiritual vacuum."[31]

The racist remarks of Muzammil went unchecked by the interviewer of the Islamic Muslim web news agency. He then documented Muzammil's plan on campus:

"I asked him 'Do you have a plan to Islamize non-Muslims?' He responded: 'In my job at the university, we have work to invite Muslims and non-Muslims. I taught at the university, and most students are non-Muslims, and I have taught at the university five years, and converted five students and four hundred non-students.'"

The Fiqh Council, of which Siddiqi is member, was under the scrutiny of The US government after another Fiqh Council member and Chairman was accused of maintaining links to terrorist financiers in Northern Virginia. That other member was none other than Taha Jaber Al-Alwani. Court documents showed that Alwani also funded Islamic Jihad front groups in Tampa. None other than Abdurrahman Alamoudi, who is a former trustee of the Fiqh Council, was named by the Treasury Department as having been a financier for al Qaeda. He also founded a group that had access to George W. Bush.[32]

In 1998, Fiqh Council member Sheikh Muhammad al-Hanooti turned his ire toward both the United States and Great Britain when he delivered a speech in which he excited the audience with rhetoric like, "Allah will curse the Americans and British" and "the curse of Allah will become true on the infidel Jews and on the tyrannical Americans."[33]

Keep in mind the types of people who had access to the George W. Bush administration after 9/11; one of them—Siddiqi—shared much of this sentiment. As for Siddiqi, in 1995, the former ISNA president gave a speech in which he expressed passionate support for suicide bombers:

> "Those who die on the part of justice are alive, and their place is with the Lord, and they receive the highest position, because this is the highest honor."[34]

Al-Ahdal himself is no moderate either. We examined his quotes in Arabic and they are littered with references to Americans as "Zionists," "conspiratorial," and "crusaders". In "For Your Honor O Mujahideen," al-Ahdal describes his goals for the US thusly:

> "The opportunity has come to manage the American crusaders and the dispersed bunch of Zionist Jews implementing their old conspiracy plans to destroy Islam everywhere."

and…

> "The American Constitution has a terroristic slant that needs to be destroyed by warplanes and intercontinental ballistic missiles until their strands break and their seeds disperse."

According to the site that posted these quotes, al-Ahdal was sent by the Islamic University in Medina by Abdul Muhsin bin Hamad bin Abad to report on the Muslim community of North America to attend the Islamic Conference in Indianapolis.[35]

Al-Ahdal first documents the misery of Muslims in America. He cites the story of a Nigerian Muslim woman who "married an American Christian and brought him four children. She escaped with her children in order to rescue them from the filthy and corrupt Christian faith." As a former Muslim whose parental unit consisted of a Christian mother and a Muslim father, this account is quite opposite from mine.

TWO FLORIDA GOVERNORS

In 2006, a South Florida pastor named O'Neal Dozier, was forced to resign from his position on the Judicial Nominating Commission for comments he made on a radio show during an interview about his fight against the construction of a mosque in his church's neighborhood. The man who appointed him in 2001—Governor Jeb Bush—was also the man who forced Dozier to step down.

Dozier's concerns were more than well-founded. The group that was attempting to build the mosque near his church—the Islamic Center of South Florida (ICOSF)—was owned by the North American Islamic Trust (NAIT), a group identified in evidence produced in the Holy Land Foundation trial as being a Muslim Brotherhood front. Yet, Dozier's governor offered him no assistance while demanding he resign.

CAIR BANQUET

In 2005, Governor Jeb Bush was invited to the CAIR-Orlando's annual banquet. Though he didn't attend, Bush sent a letter to the group that was effusive in its praise for CAIR:

> "It is a great pleasure to extend greetings and best wishes to all attending the Florida Chapter of the Council on American-Islamic Relations (CAIR-FL) annual banquet...I commend your contributions to the protection of civil rights and freedom of religion...Once again, congratulations on your accomplishments and my warmest greetings and best wishes on your continuing success."[36]

Then Florida Attorney General Charlie Crist—a Republican at the time—was also invited to the banquet. Like Bush, he didn't attend but extended "best wishes for a wonderful event".[37] Crist would later be elected Governor of Florida. During his tenure, a shocking revelation came to light thanks to *Breitbart's* Patrick Poole. Imam Muhammad Musri, the Imam of the Islamic Society of Central Florida (ISOCF) was also on one of Crist's Advisory Councils as well as the Governor's Sunshine Census Committee in 2010. Thanks to an undercover video, it was learned that Musri hosted a fundraiser for Hamas in his mosque in 2009.[38]

Siding with virulent anti-Semites had become preferable to presenting a united front against them.

A NEW JERSEY GOVERNOR

Not long after Republican Chris Christie was sworn in to office as Governor of New Jersey in 2010, conservatives warmed up to him for turning his bombastic style on teachers unions; it was red meat *after* the election. Unapologetic conservative Glenn Beck was smitten with Christie's penchant for yelling at reporters and shortly thereafter, unionized schoolteachers; the talk show host had been won over in what many deemed a true "bromance".[39]

There's a law in physics that says for every action, there's an equal and opposite reaction. As much as he may have ingratiated himself with conservatives in his first year as Governor of New Jersey, Christie seemed to wipe a significant amount of that support away one year later among those who understand the threat of Islamic fundamentalism. Any confidence such patriots may have had in Christie's ability to articulate their concerns seemed to wither away in front of those who were paying attention.

The Chris Christie brand of double*talk* involved going after teachers unions and reporters initially and then standing with questionable Islamic figures.

APPOINTMENT OF SOHAIL MOHAMMED

In the summer of 2011, Christie appointed a man named Sohail Mohammed to a Superior Court judgeship in Passaic County. This was a source of controversy as Mohammed had a history which included defending an Imam by the name of Mohammed Qatanani, who had been convicted by Israel for involvement with Hamas.[40] Qatanani also reportedly railed against Jews and called for the funding of Hamas in the same speech. As an attorney, Mohammed had also represented the American Muslim Union (AMU), which has extremely questionable ties, and defended Sami Al-Arian, a convicted terrorist financier. As Mohammed racked up such cases, it became apparent—according to Steve Emerson and Daniel Pipes—that he was "one of them".[41]

On the day of Mohammed's swearing-in ceremony,[42] Christie addressed the media and seemed to re-direct his righteous ire toward conservatives who rightly saw Islamic fundamentalism as a legitimate threat. He was asked about what was behind the criticism of his appointment of Mohammed and responded thusly:

> "Ignorance. Ignorance is behind the criticism of Sohail Mohammed. Sohail Mohammed is an extraordinary American who is an outstanding lawyer and

played an integral role in the post-September 11th period in building bridges between the Muslim-American community in this state and law enforcement. I was there for it. I saw it personally and the folks who criticize my appointment of Sohail Mohammed are ignorant, absolutely ignorant of that..."[43]

It didn't end there. Christie's declamatory nature was revealed when answering a follow-up question that involved concerns about Sharia law:

"Sharia law has nothing to do with this at all! It's crazy! It's crazy, the guy's an American citizen...this Sharia law business is crap! It's just crazy, and I'm tired of dealing with the crazies!"[44]

Subsequent questions about Qatanani were not answered by Christie. However, one year later, Christie's comments at the Governor's mansion spoke volumes. It was then that the Governor held an Iftar dinner, at which Qatanani was in attendance.[45] During his speech, Christie referred to Qatanani as a "friend" before playing the race card, saying that the entire episode points to a:

"...gaze of intolerance that's going around our country that is disturbing."[46]

It is indeed noteworthy that nothing of substance about this issue was uttered or written by Christie until a video, which was assuredly captured and posted against his will, exposed the Governor's true allegiance. As of this writing, the video is no longer available, listed as "private".

NYPD SURVEILLANCE IN NEW JERSEY

In early 2012, the Christie administration launched an investigation into tactics used by the New York Police Department (NYPD) inside New Jersey. Those tactics included the surveillance of Muslim establishments. After a three month investigation, Christie's Attorney General—Jeffrey S. Chiesa—concluded that no wrongdoing had taken place. Christie's main bone of contention was that NYPD had not informed him of its plans.[47]

This ruling angered Muslim leaders. Then, as reported by Ryan Mauro several months later, Christie had appointed four Islamists—to include Qatanani—to his Muslim Outreach Committee. This Committee was formed after Chiesa had concluded that the NYPD had done nothing wrong.[48]

Soon after his Outreach Committee was put together, it was learned that Attorney General Chiesa paid a visit to a Newark mosque that had been listed by the NYPD in their investigation. The purpose of Chiesa's visit, during which he attended prayer services, was to reassure worshippers.[49]

Christie was appointed as a US Attorney in New Jersey by President George W. Bush in 2002.[50]

RON PAUL REVOLUTION

Widely viewed as a libertarian masquerading as a Republican, US Congressman Ron Paul had become quite effective when it came to generating a very passionate, youthful following. In large part, he did this while championing fiscal responsibility, a reduction of the federal government, mandatory spending cuts, returning to the gold standard, and a protectionist/isolationist foreign policy that calls for the closure of foreign military bases as well as a return of all US troops to the homeland.

Many Americans view Paul's domestic policies as sound and logical but see his foreign policy ideas as irrational and sympathetic to the Muslim world because they begin with a premise that says the Muslim world hates westerners as a result of our own actions; we're viewed as occupiers who have meddled in Middle Eastern lands for too long. During an interview with *CNN's* Larry King about the motivations of the Christmas Day bomber, Umar Farouk Abdulmutallab, Paul claimed that the infamous "underwear bomber" attempted to blow up a commercial airliner descending into Detroit because the United States had bombed Yemen. Paul asserted that Muslim terrorists hate the United States, generally, because "we're occupiers."[51]

Not long after the 9/11 attacks, a belief began to take root amongst Paul's supporters; it led to the vilification of the Bush administration over the attacks. Cries that 9/11 was an "inside job" began to take hold with the help of controversial talk show host Alex Jones. This belief was fueled by a mistrust of government (which can be a good thing) that subjugated the actual threat and as time went on, the actual Islamic threat became increasingly diminished in the eyes of Paul's supporters. Conspiracy theories became commonplace among them. Advocates for what was called "9/11 Truth," these supporters became known as "Truthers."[52] Islamists eventually learned how to exploit this mindset to their advantage. *Accuracy in Media's* Cliff Kincaid explored the possibility that Jones was actually an Agent Provocateur for the Russians.[53] At the very least, a consequence of Jones' following is that a significant percentage of Americans all but ignores the Islamic threat to western civilization. This undeniably benefits Muslim fundamentalists.

A consequence of believing that the 9/11 attacks were perpetrated by the United States government is that the Muslim world avoided a huge dose of accountability while the government of the country it attacked became the target of such conspiracies. Ron Paul became associated with this movement through sheer numbers; if you were a Truther, you were likely a Paul supporter (and vice versa). Paul's name almost became synonymous with the movement.

During the 2012 presidential campaign, a video surfaced of Paul explaining why he wouldn't publicly come out in support of the 9/11 Truth movement. His answer was not that he denounced it as conspiratorial; he said he didn't want to deal with the controversy.[54] It was practically an overt admission that he believed it but didn't want to publicly make that belief known.

In an interview with *CNN's* Sanjay Gupta about the Cordoba Initiative's right to construct the ground zero mosque, Paul drew a comparison between Islam and Christianity by pointing to Oklahoma City bomber Timothy McVeigh:

> "...McVeigh probably was a Christian and he bombed the Oklahoma federal building but does that mean that a Christian church can't be built near there and Christianity is blamed, no I don't like that broad brush..."[55]

Why did Paul say that McVeigh *"probably"* was a Christian? Is it because Paul knew that McVeigh was not a Christian at all? McVeigh's official biographers—Lou Michel and Dan Herbeck—both relayed that he was "agnostic."[56] They also quoted McVeigh as saying that, "Science is my religion."[57] Are we to believe Paul was unaware of a biography about McVeigh printed nearly ten years earlier that disqualified the bomber as a Christian by his own admission? If Paul was oblivious to such an important fact, why didn't he issue a correction when he learned that there had been such an admission?

Beyond that, whenever the multiple terrorist attacks perpetrated by Muslims are brought up, the default position for their apologists always seems to be that Timothy McVeigh neutralizes any preponderance of Muslim terrorists. With his assertion, Paul joined that crowd. Despite the fact that McVeigh is the anomaly in a sea of Muslim terrorists, the lie that he was a Christian is perpetuated in order to convey balance. What is Paul's excuse? Why would he do all of this when the subject of Islamic extremism is brought up? The list of Muslim extremists who use this argument is extensive and even includes Nation Of Islam leader Louis Farrakhan.[58] Why is Paul echoing the egregiously false arguments of Islamists and their sympathizers?

At a campaign stop in Iowa during one of his presidential runs, a man asked Paul to address his concerns about the threat of radical Islam. Paul replied thusly:

> "I don't see Islam as our enemy...I see that motivation is occupation and those who hate us and would like to kill us, they are motivated by our invasion of their land, the support of their dictators that they hate."[59]

The most well known Islamist in Great Britain is a Salafist named Anjem Choudary. He expressed a different point of view to an interviewer in 2006, who asked him why he wouldn't condemn the 7/7 terror attacks in 2005. Choudary responded to a question about whether the innocent victims deserved to be killed:

> "As a Muslim, you must have allegiance where the sharia says that you have allegiance. You must hate and love for the sake of Allah... As a Muslim, I must support my Muslim brothers and sisters... I must have hatred towards everything which is non-Islam."[60]

According to Choudary's own admission, Islamic anger has nothing to do with the western occupation of Muslim lands; it has everything to do with the desire of Islam to occupy western lands. Yet, Paul seems more interested in dismissing people like Choudary while blaming his own country for stoking Islamic hatred against the United States.

Another very curious aspect to Ron Paul has been his stance on Iran being allowed to acquire a nuclear weapon. In presidential debates, Paul expressed radical positions that seemed to sympathize with a mad man in Mahmoud Ahmadinejad. In a *Fox News* debate, Paul conceded to moderator Bret Baier that when it comes to dealing with the threat of a nuclear Iran, he considered himself to be "left" of Barack Obama.[61] Baier followed up with Paul on a question about lifting sanctions on Iran if there was ironclad intelligence that Iran had a nuclear weapon and sought clarity on Paul's position relative to Democratic President Obama:

> **Baier:** "...as the GOP nominee would (you) be running left of President Obama on this issue?"

> **Paul:** "Yes. All we're doing is promoting their (Iran) power to have it (nuclear weapon)...It makes more sense to work with people."

In the days following that debate, Paul dug in his heels and actually defended Iran's desire for nuclear weapons:

> "...if I were an Iranian, I'd like to have a nuclear weapon, too, because you gain respect from them."[62]

Throughout the 2012 campaign, Paul made no secret about his support for Iran getting a nuclear weapon if it chose to do so. His rationale seemed to do with the concept of Mutually Assured Destruction (MAD) that kept the United States and Soviet Union from attacking one another during the cold war. This was a clear indication that, at minimum, Paul did not understand the Jihadist mindset of martyrdom.

"ANTI-ISRAEL"

During Paul's 2012 presidential campaign, the media took great interest in newsletters printed in the 1990s that bore his name. The newsletters contained anti-Semitic and racist writings. Paul distanced himself from the newsletters by saying they were published under his name but that he didn't write them or read them at the time.[63]

In an article that appeared at the *American Spectator*, it was reported that none other than extreme racist and anti-Semite David Duke had announced he would vote for Paul. The author of the piece—Quin Hillyer—made the argument that one of the reasons Duke voted for Paul was likely an act of reciprocation for support Duke received from Paul in one of the Texas Congressman's 1990 newsletters.[64]

As for Paul's support of anti-Semitic candidates, one need look no further than 2008, when he endorsed four candidates after refusing to endorse the Republican Party's nominee—John McCain. One of those candidates was virulent anti-Semite Cynthia McKinney, who provided support for Hamas in the latter's attempt to break an Israeli blockade of Gaza as part of a Free Gaza Movement flotilla.[65]

On the 2012 campaign trail, Paul said he would give serious consideration to appointing far left Democrat Dennis Kucinich to his cabinet if elected president.[66] As Daniel Pipes pointed out in an article of his that appeared on the *Investigative Project on Terrorism* website, Kucinich has been very cozy with Muslim groups, including CAIR. Both Paul and Kucinich were two of five no votes on a Resolution affirming Israel's right to defend itself against Hamas.

As for Hamas, the *Yid with Lid* blog posted a video of Rep. Paul speaking on the House floor in 2009. During that speech, the congressman from Texas actually attributed the creation of Hamas to Israel.[67]

One of the more damaging accusations levied against Paul during the 2012 Presidential campaign came from his former Senior Aide, Eric Dondero. In an article that appeared on the *Right Wing News* website, Dondero made some explosive claims about Paul. While he asserted his belief that Ron Paul wasn't a "racist" or an "anti-Semite," Dondero didn't mince words when it came to what he believed Paul's views about Israel were:

> He (Paul) is... most certainly Anti-Israel, and Anti-Israeli in general. He wishes the Israeli state did not exist at all. He expressed this to me numerous times in our private conversations. His view is that Israel is more trouble than it is worth, specifically to the America taxpayer. He sides with the Palestinians, and supports their calls for the abolishment of the Jewish state, and the return of Israel, all of it, to the Arabs.[68]

Of course, if Dondero was being truthful, would not Paul be the one engaged in some form of JBTW? In fact, one of Dondero's charges was that Paul "engaged in conspiracy theories" about the 9/11 attacks. In subsequent days, while appearing on *ABC's This Week*, Paul was asked about this charge by host Jake Tapper and became visibly defensive while scoffing at the sheer notion that Tapper would bring it up.[69] A curious thing didn't happen, however. Paul didn't lose the "Truthers." Why not? Hadn't he discredited them and impugned their credibility on national television? This phenomenon is very common in the Muslim world too. It's a brand of political expediency that comes with a wink and a nod. Some refer to it as a "non-denial" denial.

COURTING THE MUSLIM VOTE

Up to this point, we've presented evidence that shows Ron Paul is against Israel but does that mean he's in support of Israel's enemies?

Let's take a look at an article from Joel Richardson entitled, "Ron Paul's Saul Alinsky" that appeared on *World Net Daily*. The central figure of the article is a man by the name of Robert Pape, whose views are featured prominently on Paul's website. Those views provide a great insight into Paul's views about why Islamists attack America; it involves a "blame America first mentality."[70]

Interestingly, Pape has a curious connection to CAIR. According to the *Investigative Project on Terrorism*, Pape—a University of Chicago political scientist— engaged the Hamas front group and reached a deal with the group that would have CAIR chapters across the country purchase Pape's books in bulk to boost sales. Such a scenario would obviously make Pape beholden to CAIR. According to *IPT*, Pape used the fact that his book trumpeted CAIR's agenda as a selling point to entice CAIR to purchase copies.[71]

In an article written by Kenneth Timmerman that appeared on the *Accuracy in Media* website during the 2012 presidential campaign, readers learned that the government of Iran had warmed up to Ron Paul. In the article, Timmerman chronicled the multiple examples of how Iran's *PressTV*, which is a media arm of the Iranian government, provided glowing reports of Paul compared to all of the other candidates.

> The Iranian government channel portrays Ron Paul as an American hero, and brings on conspiracy theorists masquerading as political "analysts" to laud him for "challenging the American establishment" and the "corporate neo-conservative Zionist consensus," that cabal of Jews, banksters, and Reagan Democrats who in Tehran's eyes (and in the eyes of these Ron Paul supporters) run the world.[72]

Consider the example of a man named Yousef al Khattab, co-founder of a hateful Islamic website known as *Revolution Muslim*. Khattab, a former Jew named Joseph Cohen, founded the website with a man named Younus Abdullah Muhammed, who was previously known as Jesse Curtis Morton. Younus pleaded guilty and was convicted of using the Internet to solicit murder and encouraging violent extremism.[73]

In 2008, the *Revolution Muslim* website and its content was the subject of a *Fox News* report. In particular, a link to a puppet show that mocked the beheading of Daniel Pearl was featured on the site. Khattab defended the video and referred to Pearl as a:

> "...convicted spy that was murdered and he was punished by the punishment of death...This man was convicted, he was tried, and he was killed."

Reporter Rick Levanthal ended the report by quoting Khattab as saying he completely rejects the US Constitution and the country's founders.[74]

Fast forward about four years. On his *YouTube* channel, Khattab gave an empassioned plea for his fellow Muslims to throw their support behind Ron Paul's presidential campaign, in part, because he felt that Paul would be inclined to pardon his friend, Morton. Suddenly, Khattab loved the Constitution:

> "I think our only way forward in the United States right now, realistically, is to vote for Ron Paul, who stands for everything that we said and I hope that when Ron Paul is elected, and I really, really, really do pray that he is... I really think that's the way forward. I love the first amendment of the United States..."[75]

This is the quintessential example of how JBTW works. Khattab knows that the hot button for Paul's supporters is talk in support of the Constitution. In this regard, he was able to align with those supporters by claiming to be a proponent of their most important issue—their "sacred cow" (everybody has one). In many ways, this actually serves to divide Americans. In fact, the U.S. Army Field Manual deals with this very technique in its section on Psychological Operations (PSYOP):

> Deception (military or political) includes manipulating, distorting, withholding, or falsifying evidence available to an opponent. History has shown **that it is far easier to deceive by reinforcing an opponent's existing preconceptions than it is to persuade him to change his mind**. PSYOP personnel should encourage the opponent that the most likely way of achieving the objective will in fact be adopted (thereby diverting his attention from an alternative plan). Given two options, one of which reinforces our existing point of view, people are more likely to believe what they already suspect. **Psychologically, they are gratified by evidence that confirms their preconceptions. People generally attach undue importance to evidence supporting their point of view and reject that which does not. PSYOP personnel should avoid deception that requires persuading a target audience of something it is not already predisposed to believe.** — U.S. Army Field Manual FM 33-1-1, Psychological Operations Techniques and Procedures, Appendix A, "Deception Operations."[76]

Whether intentionally or not, the approach taken by Khattab—to appeal to Paul's supporters by championing the Constitution while secretly despising it (unless he had a major conversion not demonstrated by even his most current statements)—can actually encourage Paul's supporters to embrace Islamists, not because they agree with Islam's teachings but because they see Islamists espousing the same core beliefs. A consequence of this reality is that Paul's supporters, in many instances, can come across as defending Islamic doublespeak artists who welcome the assistance.

This leads to a disturbingly curious act on the part of Ron Paul volunteers in Dearborn, Michigan during the 2012 Republican primary in that state. Paul's regional volunteer coordinator for Dearborn had flyers made that included one side in English and the other side in Arabic. The English side touted seven of Paul's domestic policy agenda items. The Arabic side included three of those, plus a pledge to end foreign wars—including support of Israel. That volunteer explained his decision:

> "When I got involved with the Ron Paul campaign, I felt that it was kind of an untapped voter base by the other GOP candidates and even the Democratic candidate, so I really thought it was a great area to pursue especially with Ron Paul's standing with foreign policy and civil liberties."[77]

Those who understand the agenda of Islamists would have nothing to do with such a strategy but again, ends-justifies-the-means thinking is very powerful. Paul's supporters were so passionate in what they believe that so many of them were willing to align with those who would impose a system far worse than what they fear from their own government.

Shockingly, none other than Yahya Basha—mentioned earlier in this chapter—was quoted in the *Yahoo News* article above as saying, "As a group, we like Ron Paul." As a member of the American Muslim Council (AMC), Basha is someone whom Americans should be rejecting in every regard.[78]

Then again, he knows how to tickle the ears of the Ron Paul supporters. After all, ends justify the means in Islam.

FOOTNOTES

1. British Pathé, *News Flashes – Eisenhower Opens Mosque In...1957.* http://www.britishpathe.com/video/news-flashes-eisenhower-opens-mosque-in-washington

2. The Islamic Center, *History*. http://theislamiccenter.com/about-us/history/

3. Front Page Mag.com, *Is World War II Still Being Fought?* by Walid Shoebat and Ben Barrack. http://frontpagemag.com/2012/walid-shoebat-and-ben-barrack/is-world-war-ii-still-being-fought/

4. The Islamic Center, *History*. http://theislamiccenter.com/about-us/history/

5. The Weekly Standard, *The Mosque and the Imam,* by Stephen Schwartz. http://www.weeklystandard.com/Content/Public/Articles/000/000/015/850orgbk.asp

6. ISNA, *Muzammil Siddiqi, Past President.* http://www.isna.net/ISNAHQ/pages/Muzammil-Siddiqi.aspx

7. ce399 research archive, *Radical Islam and the Republican Party, Grover Norquist's Strange Alliance with Radical Islam.* http://ce399.typepad.com/weblog/2005/04/radical_islam_a.html

8. http://articles.nydailynews.com/2000-10-31/news/18151135_1_abdurahman-alamoudi-american-muslim-council-muslim-activist

9. Discover The Networks.org, *Salam Al-Marayati.* http://www.discoverthenetworks.org/individualProfile.asp?indid=1402

10. CAIR, *What They Say About CAIR, Interfaith, Law Enforcement, Elected Officials and Others (July 2011).* http://www.cair.com/Portals/0/pdf/WhatTheySayAbout CAIR.pdf

11. History Commons, *Context of 'June 22, 2001: Bush Adviser Karl Rove Meets with Suspected Supporters of US-Designated Terrorist Groups'.* http://www.historycommons.org/context.jsp?item=a062201alarianrove#a062201alarianrove

12. Discover The Network.org, *Association of Muslim Social Scientists of North America (AMSS).* http://www.discoverthenetworks.org/printgroupProfile.asp?grpid=7418

13. New Republic, *Fevered Pitch,* by Franklin Foer. http://www.newrepublic.com/article/politics/83799/norquist-radical-islam-cair#

14. Klein Online, *Huma Directly Tied to Al-Qaida Charity Front-Man: Radical Islamic web grows for Hillary's chief-of-staff,* by Aaron Klein. http://kleinonline.wnd.com/2012/07/26/huma-directly-tied-to-al-qaida-charity-front-man-radical-islamic-web-grows-for-hillarys-chief-of-staff/

15. Discover The Network.org, *Rabita Trust (RT).* http://www.discoverthenetworks.org/printgroupProfile.asp?grpid=6411

16. Religious Freedom Coalition, *Journal of 911 events posted in October, 2001,* by W.J. Murray. http://www.religiousfreedomcoalition.org/2012/08/12/journal-of-911-events-posted-in-october-2001/

17. Belief Net, *Bush's Muslim Backing,* by Ira Rifkin. http://www.beliefnet.com/ News/Politics/2000/11/Bushs-Muslim-Backing.aspx?p=1

18. Americans for Tax Reform, *Who is Grover Norquist?* http://www.atr.org/grover-nor quist-a3016

19. ce399 research archive, *Radical Islam and the Republican Party, Grover Norquist's Strange Alliance with Radical Islam.* http://ce399.typepad.com/weblog/2005/ 04/radical_islam_a.html

20. CAIR, *CAIR-LA Congratulates Dr. Siddiqi on 'Community Leader Award'.* http://ca.cair.com/losangeles/news/cair-la_congratulates_dr._siddiqi _on_community_leader_award

21. Free Republic, *Bush Marks End of Ramadan, Visits Mosque (Islam brings hope and comfort),* by Scott Lindlaw. http://www.freerepublic.com/focus/news/801595/ posts

22. Daniel Pipes, Middle East Form, *Is Grover Norquist an Islamist?,* by Daniel Pipes. http://www.danielpipes.org/blog/2005/04/is-grover-norquist-an-islamist

23. Front Page Mag.com, *A Troubling Influence,* by Frank J. Gaffney Jr. http://archive.frontpagemag.com/readArticle.aspx?ARTID=15084

24. IPT The Investigative Project on Terrorism, *Individual Terrorists, Sami Al-Arian.* http://www.investigativeproject.org/profile/100

25. http://www.conservative.org/about-acu/board-of-directorsstaff/

26. Front Page Mag.com, *Who is Suhail Khan?* by Paul Sperry. http://frontpagemag. com/2011/paul-sperry/who-is-suhail-khan/

27. PJ Media, Video: *ACU's Suhail Khan declares that there is no Muslim Brotherhood in the United States.* http://pjmedia.com/tatler/2011/02/12/video-acus-suhail- khan-declares-that-there-is-no-muslim-brotherhood-in-the-united-states/

28. Discover The Networks.org, *Mahboob Khan.* http://www.discoverthenetworks.org/ individualProfile.asp?indid=2509

29. Ibid

30. CAIR, *CAIR-LA Congratulates Dr. Siddiqi on 'Community Leader Award'.* http://ca. cair.com/losangeles/news/cair-la_congratulates_dr._siddiqi_on_community _leader_award

31. Arabic website, with English. http://www.al-rawdah.net/r.php?sub0=allbooks& sub1=r_malysia&p=54

32. American Spectator, *A Phony Fatwa,* by Christopher Orlet. http://spectator.org/ archives/2005/08/03/a-phony-fatwa

33. WND, *U.S. Muslims' Anti-Terror Fatwa 'Bogus',* Steven Emerson. http://www.wnd.com/2005/07/31534/

34. American Spectator, *A Phony Fatwa,* by Christopher Orlet. http://spectator.org/archives/2005/08/03/a-phony-fatwa

35. Arabic website. http://www.al-rawdah.net/r.php?sub0=allbooks&sub1=1&p=11&key=%C3%E3%D1%ED%DF%C7

36. CAIR Florida, *Annual Orlando Banquet and Letters.* http://www.americansagainsthate.org/OrlandoLettersCAIR.htm

37. Ibid

38. Front Page Mag.com, *Charlie Crist's Ally Hosted Hamas Fundraiser,* by Patrick Poole. http://frontpagemag.com/2010/patrick-poole/key-charlie-crist-ally-hosted-hamas-fundraiser/

39. Hot Air, *True bromance: Glenn Beck can't get enough of the sweet, sweet Chris Christie porn,* by Allahpundit. http://hotair.com/archives/2010/07/30/true-bromance-glenn-beck-cant-get-enough-of-the-sweet-sweet-chris-christie-porn/

40. Radical Islam, *Four Islamists on Gov. Christie's Muslim Outreach Committee,* by Ryan Mauro. http://www.radicalislam.org/analysis/four-islamists-gov-christies-muslim-outreach-committee

41. IPT The Investigative Project on Terrorism, *Chris Christie's Islam Problem—He has repeatedly sided with some nasty characters,* by Danie Pipes and Steve Emerson. http://www.investigativeproject.org/3560/chris-christie-islam-problem

42. State of New Jersey, Governor Chris Christie, *Swearing In.* http://www.state.nj.us/governor/media/photos/2011/20110726b.shtml

43. Video. *Governor Christie Talks About Superior Court Judge Solail Mohammed.* https://www.youtube.com/watch?v=y83z552NJaw

44. Ibid

45. Radical Islam, *NJ Gov. Christie Hosts Radical Imam; Reaffirms Support.* http://www.radicalislam.org/news/christie-hosts-radical-imam-reaffirms-support

46. Family Security Matters, Video, *Christie Says "Bigots" Attacking Him on Radical Islam,* by Ryan Mauro. http://www.familysecuritymatters.org/publications/detail/video-christie-says-bigots-attacking-him-on-radical-islam

47. AP, *NJ Official: NYPD Muslim Surveillance Legal,* by Samantha Henry. http://bigstory.ap.org/content/nj-official-nypd-muslim-surveillance-legal

48. Radical Islam, *Four Islamists on Gov. Christie's Muslim Outreach Committee,* by Ryan Mauro. http://www.radicalislam.org/analysis/four-islamists-gov-christies-muslim-outreach-committee

49. http://articles.washingtonpost.com/2012-11-30/national/35584971_1_nypd-attorney-general-jeffrey-chiesa-mosque

50. U.S. News & World Report, *10 Things You Didnt Know About Chris Christie*, by Caitlin Huey-Burns. http://www.usnews.com/mobile/articles_mobile/10-things-you-didnt-know-about-chris-christie-2

51. Hot Air, *Ron Paul on the airline plot: "They're terrorists because we're occupiers!"*, by Allahpundit. http://hotair.com/archives/2009/12/29/ron-paul-on-the-airline-plot-theyre-terrorists-because-were-occupiers/comment-page-3/

52. Huff Post Politics, *9/11 "Truthers" a Pack of Liars*. http://www.huffington post.com/michael-shermer/911-truthers-a-pack-of-li_b_84154.html

53. Accuracy in Media, *Agents Provocateurs and the Tea Parties*, by Cliff Kincaid.

54. http://www.verumserum.com/?p=35707

55. Video, *On Ground Zero Mosque Issue – Ron Paul on Sanjay Gupta's Show*. http://www.youtube.com/watch?v=VJ2wil9kx7E

56. CNN.com Transcripts, *Authors Lou Michel and Dan Herbeck on their book about Timothy McVeigh*, http://www.cnn.com/COMMUNITY/transcripts/2001/04/04/michelherbeck/

57. http://www.michaelmedved.com/pages/mcveigh

58. The American View, *McVeighNo Christian; Worshipped Himself; Said "Science is my Religion"*, by John Lofton. http://archive.theamericanview.com/index.php?id=1189

59. 2012 Iowa Caucuses, *Ron Paul says U.S. intervention motivated 9/11 attacks*, by Josh Haffner. http://caucuses.desmoinesregister.com/2011/08/27/paul-says-u-s-intervention-motivated-911-attacks/

60. Video, *Anjem Choudary talks of 7.7*. http://www.youtube.com/watch?v=C73ePf_2KVw&feature=player_embedded

61. Video, *Ron Paul Republican Iowa Debate on Iran*. http://www.youtube.com/watch?feature=player_embedded&v=8xwfANcK8gs

62. The Los Angeles Times, *Ron Paul: Sanctions against Iran are 'Acts of War'*, by Paul West. http://articles.latimes.com/2011/dec/29/news/la-pn-ron-paul-sanctions-act-of-war20111229

63. CBS News, *Report: Paul signed off on racist 90s newsletters*, by Jerry Markon and Alice Crites. http://www.cbsnews.com/8301-502223_162-57367601/report-paul-signed-off-on-racist-90s-newsletters/

64. American Spectator, *Ron Paul Praised David Duke*, by Qin Hillyer. http://spectator.org/blog/2012/01/14/ron-paul-praised-david-duke

65. The Palestine Telegraph, *Former U.S. Congresswoman speaks from jail in Israel,* by Cynthia McKinney. http://www.paltelegraph.com/palestine/gaza-strip/1261-former-us-congresswoman-speaks-out-of-her-jail-in-israel

66. CBS News, *Ron Paul: I'd consider putting Dennis Kucinich in my cabinet,* by Lucy Madison. http://www.cbsnews.com/8301-503544_162-20109638-503544.html

67. The Lid, Video, *Ron Paul 2009 Video – Israel Created Hamas.* http://yidwith lid.blogspot.com/2011/12/ron-paul-claim-in-2009-israel-created.html

68. Rightwing News, Statement from former Ron Paul staffer on Newsletters, *Anti-Semitism,* by Eric Dondero. http://www.rightwingnews.com/election-2012/state ment-from-fmr-ron-paul-staffer-on-newsletters-anti-semitism/

69. ABC News, *Ron Paul Calls 9/11 Conspiracy Charge 'Nonsene',* by Jake Tapper, http://abcnews.go.com/blogs/politics/2012/01/ron-paul-calls-911-conspiracy-charge-nonsense/

70. WND Commentary, *Ron Paul's Saul Alinsky?* by Joel Richardson. http://www.wnd.com/2012/01/ron-pauls-saul-alinsky/

71. IPT The Investigative Project on Terrorism, *CAIR, Academic Scheme to Inflate Book Sales.* http://www.investigativeproject.org/2226/cair-academic-scheme-to-inflate-book-sales

72. Accuracy in Media, *Tehran TV Loves Ron Paul,* by Kenneth R. Timmerman. http://www.aim.org/special-report/tehran-tv-loves-ron-paul/

73. The FBI, *Leader of Revolution Muslim Pleads Guilty to Using Internet to Solicit Murder and Encourage Violent Extremism.* http://www.fbi.gov/washingtondc/press-releases/2012/leader-of-revolution-muslim-pleads-guilty-to-using-internet-to-solicit-murder-and-encourage-violent-extremism

74. Video, *Yousef al Khattab on FOX News.* http://www.youtube.com/watch?feature= player_embedded&v=SeRUAvMDhkY

75. The Jawa Report, *Former al Qaeda Supporter & Terror Suspect Now Supports Ron Paul.* http://mypetjawa.mu.nu/archives/211119.php

76. Sipsey Street Irregulars, *Sipsey Street Exclusive: Deception Plan. The Gunwalker Conspiracy was not, and is not, primarily an ATF scandal, although you are meant to think it is.* http://sipseystreetirregulars.blogspot.com/2012/02/sipsey-street-exclusive-deception-plan.html

77. Yahoo! News, *Muslims and Arab Americans in Michigan aren't getting attention from Republican presidential candidates,* by Chris Moody. http://news.yahoo.com/blogs/ticket/republican-candidates-avoid-direct-outreach-michigan-muslims-arab-134539124.html

78. Ibid

CHAPTER

18

ISLAM AND THE LEFT

THREE DEMOCRATIC PRESIDENTS

*C*ountless Islamic scholars have figured out that it's easier to align with leftist entities than it is to find allies on the right. While there are certainly exceptions, the more secular an individual or institution, the more liberal or "left-wing" that entity tends to be. Islamists have historically made significant inroads by appealing to the secularists of the West. Though they have attempted to penetrate the conservative right, and not without success (see previous chapter), alliances with left-wing individuals, groups and institutions have been much easier to come by; it's the low-hanging fruit for Islamists.

Anti-Semitism is a trait endemic to Islamists and can be found in far greater abundance among secularists in the West than on the right. Consider three consecutive Democratic (left-wing) presidents in the United States—Jimmy Carter, Bill Clinton, and Barack Obama. Each administration helped to further the Islamic agenda while simultaneously endangering the nation they swore an oath to protect.

JIMMY CARTER

The legacy of the Carter administration as it relates to Iran is one of his many crowning failures. By not backing the Shah of Iran in 1978, Carter set the stage for the Islamic revolution in that country, which was completed in 1979 with the Shah's overthrow. Ironically, however, it was the socialist left in Iran that was instrumental in facilitating the Shah's demise. The Ayatollah Khomeini essentially did what the Ikhwan would do in Egypt more than three decades later; he filled the vacuum left vacant by the overthrow of a dictator.[1]

Since Carter's irresponsible decision not to back the Shah, Iran has become one of the world's greatest threats due to its quest for nuclear weapons. In practically every respect, Carter's position made no sense from a western perspective. The prospect of a vehemently anti-Semitic, nuclear Iran always seems to come up whenever international geopolitics is debated. Carter's presidency shoulders a tremendous amount of that responsibility. Yet, since losing his bid for reelection in 1980, Carter has continued to take positions that support Israel's enemies.

In fact, Carter's positions are so consistently and totally anti-Semitic that the former US President was excoriated by self-proclaimed, lifelong liberal, Alan Dershowitz, who all but accused Carter of being bought and paid for with Arab money:

> Carter and his Center have accepted millions of dollars from suspect sources, beginning with the **bail-out of the Carter family peanut business in the late 1970s by BCCI, a now-defunct and virulently anti-Israeli bank indirectly controlled by the Saudi Royal family**, and among whose principal investors is Carter's friend, Sheikh Zayed. Agha Hasan Abedi, the founder of the bank, gave Carter "$500,000 to help the former president establish his center...[and] more than $10 million to Mr. Carter's different projects."

> Carter gladly accepted the money, though Abedi had called his bank, ostensibly the source of his funding, "the best way to fight the evil influence of the Zionists." BCCI isn't the only source: Saudi King Fahd contributed millions to the Carter Center "in 1993 alone...$7.6 million" as have other members of the Saudi Royal Family. **Carter also received a million dollar pledge from the Saudi-based bin Laden family**, as well as a personal $500,000 environmental award named for Sheikh Zayed, and paid for by the Prime Minister of the United Arab Emirates. It's worth noting that, despite the influx of Saudi money funding the Carter Center, and despite the Saudi Arabian government's myriad human rights abuses, the Carter Center's Human Rights program has no activity whatever in Saudi Arabia.

Dershowitz also wrote about an instance in which the source of money Carter accepted was so blatantly anti-Semitic that even Harvard University refused to accept it.

> Jimmy Carter was, of course, aware of Harvard's decision, since it was highly publicized. Yet he kept the money. Indeed, this is what he said in accepting

the funds: "This award has special significance for me because it is named for my personal friend, Sheik Zayed bin Sultan al-Nahyan." Carter's personal friend, it turns out, was an unredeemable anti-Semite and all-around bigot.

In reading Carter's statements, I was reminded of the bad old **Harvard of the nineteen thirties, which continued to honor Nazi academics after the anti-Semitic policies of Hitler's government became clear. Harvard of the nineteen thirties was complicit in evil. I sadly concluded that Jimmy Carter of the twenty-first century has become complicit in evil.**[2] [emphasis mine]

As if to underscore questions about Carter's allegiances, the man behind the September 11th attacks—Osama bin Laden—recommended three books for westerners to read in 2009. One of those books was penned by Jimmy Carter, entitled *Palestine: Peace Not Apartheid*. A former US President had become a source of propaganda for the enemies of his own nation.[3]

BILL CLINTON (AND AL GORE)

Twelve years after Carter left office, Bill Clinton was sworn in as president. The name Abdurahman Alamoudi became well known to the Clinton administration. Alamoudi, who would be convicted on terrorism charges in 2004, became an adviser for the administration and then a "goodwill ambassador" for the Clinton State Department in 1997.[4] Again, one of the defenses politicians always seem to retreat to when questions about their decisions are raised involves plausible deniability and either silence or pleas of ignorance. Such a tack in response to questions about appointing Alamoudi to a position at the State Department in 1997 is made much more difficult when one considers that Alamoudi said this publicly to a Hamas-affiliated group in Chicago—the Islamic Association of Palestine (IAP)[5]—in late 1996:

> I think if we are outside this country, we can say oh, Allah, destroy America, but once we are here, our mission in this country is to change it. There is no way for Muslims to be violent in America, no way. We have other means to do it.[6]

According to the website *Discover the Networks*, Alamoudi had quite the anti-Semitic track record before his stint as "goodwill ambassador" with the State

Department. In 1994, he asserted that Hamas was not a terrorist group and he expressed solidarity with Hamas leader Mousa Abu Marzook in 1996. He also contributed heavily to the Democratic Party after Clinton was elected president.[7]

The Department of Defense (DoD) under Clinton is responsible for launching the program designed to vet and endorse Muslim chaplains for the US Military, discussed in another chapter of this book. One of those entities certified by DoD was Alamoudi's American Muslim Armed Forces and Veterans Affairs Council (AMAFVAC). Another was the Graduate School of Islamic and Social Sciences (GSISS), which is currently headed by virulent anti-Semite, Taha Jaber Al-Alwani, mentioned earlier.[8] The US Military is still feeling the repercussions of these policy decisions years after Clinton left office.

Moreover, Bill Clinton's wife Hillary wielded a great deal of political power as first lady. *Investigative Project on Terrorism's* (IPT) Steve Emerson chronicled her outreach to radical Muslim groups and traced the origins of that outreach back to 1996.[9] Coincidentally, that was the same year that a woman with strong familial connections to the Muslim Brotherhood began work for Hillary. Huma Abedin, who would later become Hillary's Deputy Chief of Staff, raised bold red flags after I stumbled onto an Arabic blog. We detail Abedin's affiliations in much greater depth in another chapter but it is noteworthy that Hillary Clinton's outreach to radical Islamist groups seemed to coincide with Abedin's arrival.[10]

Shortly before Bill Clinton left office in early 2001, he recorded a video message for the 37th Annual Convention for the Islamic Society of North America (ISNA)—a Muslim Brotherhood group—in which he said the following:

> "I'm so glad to have this opportunity to join you in recognizing the **wonderful contributions the American Muslim community has made in the progress of our nation and to the strength of our communities**. For nearly four decades now, **ISNA has served America's Muslims and its more than 300 community and professional organizations with distinction**. Working for better schools and better programs, building bridges not just between one another but to the larger American community but that's nothing new to the nearly 7 million Muslims in America…You've always been at the forefront of progress, helping to bring the values of hard work, faith, and family to the forefront of our nation…**all Americans owe you our respect and our heartfelt thanks**. The Qur'an tells us that we are made into nations and tribes, that we may know each other, not that we may despise

each other. American Muslims are living proof that people of different backgrounds can coexist peacefully in a diverse world as one community. **We must all learn to celebrate, not just to tolerate, our diversity**. No one should have to face discrimination or fear violence because of the way they speak, the way they look, or the way they worship God. Your work helps move all of us closer to that elusive, one America. [11]

Are we to believe that after all of the Islamic terror attacks suffered by the United States during Clinton's tenure as president—coupled with the extensive intelligence that had been gathered on Osama bin Laden—the administration did not have enough information about who the ISNA was? Clinton took a lot of heat for not dealing with bin Laden when he had the chance to do so on multiple occasions but the greater sin may just be his coziness with groups that shared bin Laden's goals. Remember that Clinton delivered a similar message to the Turkish community, in which he lauded the work of Fethullah Gülen in 2008, long after the time when he should have known better. [12]

By publicly showing an alliance with the ISNA as well as with the man who inspired the like-minded Gülenist movement, Bill Clinton aligned with the Muslim Brotherhood on multiple fronts. *Newsmax* reported in 2003 that the Arkansas state trooper who guarded the Clintons for years—Larry Patterson—attested to the Clintons' anti-Semitism. Patterson also revealed that Bill Clinton was fascinated with Adolph Hitler:

> Clinton's interest in Hitler was not based on the fascist leader's anti-Semitism, but the great leadership skills of Hitler, according to Patterson.
>
> Clinton, Patterson remembered, was intrigued that Hitler "had so much power over these people and that it had just been a short period of time since World War I where they'd been defeated, and this man had come forward and had rallied the German people." [13]

Consider Clinton's vice president, Al Gore, a man who would lose the 2000 presidential election to George W. Bush by the narrowest of margins. By several accounts, this defeat embittered Gore. In fact, while accepting the Nobel Peace Prize, Gore conveyed that bitterness when he referenced his 2000 defeat. [14] It was a highly contested election and though he won the popular vote, he lost the electoral vote. A few short years after that defeat, Gore would travel to a foreign land and deride his own nation.

In 1947, Sir Winston Churchill was credited with the following quote:

"When I am abroad, I always make it a rule never to criticize or attack the government of my own country. I make up for lost time when I get home."[15]

In 2006, Al Gore performed the equivalent of spitting on this rule while speaking in Jeddah, Saudi Arabia. He didn't just criticize the government of his own country; he demonized it in front of an audience whose nation had more blood on its hands than any other, relative to the September 11th attacks, which had only occurred five years earlier.

According to multiple sources, Gore's team never did provide a full transcript of the speech.[16] While in Jeddah, Gore accused the United States of "terrible abuses" against Arabs after September 11th. He also charged that Arabs had been "indiscriminately rounded up" and maintained that the circumstances under which they were held were "unforgiveable."[17] These were lies and the former vice president of the United States was pandering to an Arab audience for some reason.

An article penned by Lowell Ponte at *FrontPage Magazine* helped shed some light on why Gore would be so overtly anti-American while standing on Saudi Arabian sand. At the time, the former vice president was heavily invested in Occidental Petroleum according to Ponte. In addition to the company having oil interests in several Muslim countries to include Yemen, Libya, and Pakistan, its leader was the son of the founder of the Communist Party USA (CPUSA).[18]

According to the founder of *Jihad Watch*, Robert Spencer, Iranian Hassan Nemazee also had some close financial ties with both Al Gore and Bill Clinton:

Nemazee is an influential figure with many friends in high places in groups such as the American-Iranian Council (AIC), the National Iranian American Council (NIAC), and the Iranian-American Bar Association (IABA). Nemazee's name is also well known in Democratic Party circles. He was a prominent contributor to Bob Torricelli's New Jersey Senate campaign. **The multimillionaire entrepreneur also contributed $50,000 to his friend Al Gore's Recount Fund (and $250,000 to the Gore campaign), $60,000 to Bill Clinton's legal defense fund, and over $150,000 to the Democratic National Committee.** [emphasis mine][19]

Often, speculation about motives is all one has but in light of the extremely strained relations between Iran and Saudi Arabia, it's at least conceivable that Gore might pander so pathetically to a Saudi Arabian audience, in part, to compensate for his cozy relations with an Iranian donor.

What's that saying about tangled webs? When looking that up, be sure not to confuse it with the metaphor about spiders and webs put forth by Fethullah Gülen.

After losing the election, Gore seemed to gravitate toward the pseudo-science known as *global warming*, which was renamed *climate change* after evidence of *global cooling* began to surface. The optics of Gore testifying in front of Congress about global warming during a snow storm didn't help either.[20] His film, entitled *An Inconvenient Truth* was a hit among the environmental left-wing movement and shockingly won an Academy Award.[21] Al Gore has also praised Islamic environmentalism:

> The central concepts of Islam taught by the Qur'ân —*Tawheed* (unity), *khalifa* (trusteeship), *akharah* (accountability)—also serve as the pillars of the Islamic environmental ethic. The earth is the sacred creation of Allah." (Al Gore, *Earth In The Balance*, Page 260)

World renowned environmentalist (sniff, sniff, cough) Al Gore swallowed Islamic environmentalism hook, line, and sinker from the Al-Qaeda supporter Dr. Abdullah Omar Naseef, secretary general of the *Muslim World League during the Muslim declaration on Nature in 1986.*

Naseef wrote:

> So unity, trusteeship and accountability, that is tawhid, khalifah and akhirah, the three central concepts of Islam, are also the pillars of the environmental ethics of Islam. They constitute the basic values taught by the Qur'an. It is these values which led Muhammad, (peace be upon him), the Prophet of Islam, to say: 'Whosoever plants a tree and diligently looks after it until it matures and bears fruit is rewarded',...Environmental consciousness is born when such values are adopted and become an intrinsic part of our mental and physical make-up."[22]

The website entitled *Future Islam*, created after the US led invasion of Iraq also seemed to endorse much of Gore's agenda. On its "About" page, Future

Islam makes it quite clear that its interests lie in seeing a new global world order come to fruition:

> Future Islam is intended to **emerge as a global forum** where best minds of the world will participate in shaping a better future. Upholding the last Revelation and determined to pull down all the misgivings of interpretations, here is a **forum inviting us all to plug into God and His Prophet**. As the situation has never been so ripe as today we believe that **the time has come to fulfill the promise of a truly international world order** — the mission statement of all the Prophets — to be accomplished in full measure by those who have the guts and courage to accept the challenge of the Last Revelation. [emphasis mine][23]

In an article posted to *Future Islam*, entitled "Winning the Struggle Against Global Warming," authors Brendan Mackey and Song Li reference Gore's work early on and make the case that the world must band together to fight the nebulous foe known as global warming:

> If global warming is the mother of all environmental problems—as Al Gore's film "An Inconvenient Truth" suggests...then we must find a solution soon. Addressing the root causes of global warming will require a level of national and international cooperation not seen since the Allied nations' response during World War II.[24]

The environmental agenda of Al Gore and the Muslim world was mutually enjoined but what would motivate an Islamic website with prominent Muslim contributors to help further a narrative that likens a war on "global warming" to the West's war against the Nazis? Remember, the Muslim Brotherhood aligned with the Nazis; it is an alliance that the Islamic world no doubt wants to keep suppressed as long as possible. As long as attention is deflected away from the descendants of Hitler's allies the subsequent deception is made effective. An added benefit is certainly a willingness on the part of the West to use less of its own resources. Al Gore's wealth and his political influence would certainly help further this agenda.

Among the list of contributors on *Future Islam's* website is none other than ISNA leader Louay Safi, which shows a direct connection between the Muslim Brotherhood, this website, and the global warming agenda. While we're on the topic of Islam's alliance with the left, far left *PBS* news personality Bill Moyers is also listed as a contributor.[25]

For those still unsure about the true intention of the global warming movement in general and *Future Islam's* professed interest in it, have a look at another excerpt from the "About" page on the website:

> The debacle in Afghanistan followed by illegal and unethical war on Iraq and the bullying of other muslim countries by America, **left the Ummah with no choice but to ponder why it is was happening to us and where could we find refuge**? Has God really forsaken the best of nations, the khair-e-Ummah, who otherwise were supposed to lead history till End Time?[26] [emphasis mine]

A little bit later, the "About" page revealed the type of thinking that would cause *Future Islam* to seek an alliance with the likes of Al Gore:

> **Submitted souls around the globe regarded it a matter of urgent concern to save the world from civilizational fascism** which, if not immediately checked, may eventually turn the entire world into a Guantanamo Bay. Long before it was eventually launched in September 2004 the editor of Future Islam and his friends came to the conclusion that different civilizational units of the world have to do enough homework so as to **forge a loosely structured council of thinking individuals, policy makers and intellectually beaming minds across the globe**.[27] [emphasis mine]

Gore's agenda was getting significant traction in the liberal mainstream media, as well as on the international stage, at about the same time the next Democrat would be elected president of the United States. Gore had the ear of that president very early on and Barack Obama's connection to the Muslim world would prove much more extensive than any president before him. As President-elect, Obama showed solidarity with Gore and the climate change agenda; he made it clear that it would be a high priority within his administration.[28]

While seated in between Gore and Vice President-elect Joe Biden, Obama said the following to the press in talking about his administration's plans to pursue Gore's agenda:

> "The time for delay is over; the time for denial is over."[29]

While environmentalism is a matter of faith in Islam, the secularist west is persuaded more through science, which is how the climate change movement was sold to western audiences. This is what Obama said in the press conference:

> "We all believe what the scientists have been telling us for years now, that this is a matter of urgency and national security, and it has to be dealt with in a serious way."[30]

In this setting, terms like *tawheed, khalifa,* and *akharah* were not used. Instead, the language of science was obviously assumed to be more effective to western audiences. The Islamic world could live with this because, well, the environmental agenda was being championed. Why quibble over motives? Are you beginning to see how the *Doctrine of Balance* works?

The pseudo-science known as Anthropogenic (man-made) Global Warming (AGW) was dealt a tremendous blow about a year after Obama took office. Thousands of emails from the University of East Anglia's Climate Research Unit (CRU) in Great Britain were leaked and cast widespread doubt on the notion of AGW; the emails pointed to a hoax.[31] The timing of the release—days before the United Nations climate change conference in Copenhagen—could not have been worse for the movement and was widely accepted to be intentionally timed for that reason. Two years later, just prior to the same conference, this time scheduled to take place in Durban, South Africa, even more damning emails were released. These emails truly blasted the movement when it was already reeling.[32]

It's worth noting that much of the Muslim world lined up with the AGW movement of Al Gore. Allegedly, they did so because Gore espoused many of the same beliefs about the environment that Islam did. Yet, the AGW movement was exposed as fraudulent. If Islamists were truly critical thinkers, they would begin to question their precepts based on this reality.

CURRENT TV SAGA

In 2005, Gore co-founded an entity known as *CURRENT TV.* In 2011, the network shifted gears and decided to compete with *MSNBC* for viewers, even hiring former far left *MSNBC* host, Keith Olbermann. This proved ineffective and the network was sold to *Al Jazeera* amidst a confluence of hypocrisy on January 1, 2013.

For the last two months of 2012, a term known as the 'fiscal cliff' was constantly in the news. It referred to the expiration of the Bush tax cuts enacted years earlier. Unless a deal was done, everyone's taxes would go up. Gore, a staunch critic of everything Bush, attempted to close the sale before the end of the year to avoid paying an additional $8.8 million in extra taxes.[33] Poetic justice prevailed as the deal wasn't finalized until January 1st.[34]

Of course, in addition to Gore's history of making gobs of money through his investments in Occidental Petroleum, *CURRENT TV* was sold to an entity whose primary funder is a member of OPEC (Qatar).[35] Gore reportedly made $100 million when the network was sold to *Al Jazeera*. He did all this while sounding alarm bells about global warming, which was allegedly being caused by the burning of…fossil fuels (oil).

One year earlier, conservative talk show host Glenn Beck reportedly offered to buy Gore's network but was rejected. According to *POLITICO*, a source close to the situation said the reason why Beck's offer was not entertained was because…

> "…the legacy of who the network goes to is important to us and we are sensitive to networks not aligned with our point of view."[36]

That response must necessarily have meant that *Al Jazeera*'s point of view aligns with that of Al Gore's network.

In a 2003 article that appeared on the *New York Magazine* website, Michael Wolf relayed Israel's sentiment that *Al Jazeera* was instrumental in fueling the violent intifada. At one point, *Al Jazeera* featured an interview with David Duke—of KKK/American Nazi Party fame—in which Duke suggested the Mossad knew that the 9/11 attacks were going to happen in advance and warned the Jews.[37]

If one would like to debate whether *Al Jazeera* is in total alignment with Al Gore's vision for *CURRENT TV*, we'll concede the point in exchange for a concession on the following point; *Al Jazeera* is more aligned with Al Gore than is Glenn Beck.

This is an indictment of Gore, not of Beck.

The history of *Al Jazeera* is a matter of public record. It was a mouthpiece for Osama bin Laden after 9/11 and should have been declared an official enemy of the United States. However, as time evolved, *Al Jazeera* evolved and formed *Al Jazeera* English in 2006.[38] When comparing *Al Jazeera* English with its Arabic counterpart, it's easy to see a contrast. One network is for western consumption and another for Arabic consumption. Some might argue that the difference has to do with demographics and bottom lines. That would be a logical conclusion—without factoring in JBTW.

Both *Al Jazeera* and *Al Jazeera* English are headquartered in Doha, Qatar. Guess who else is headquartered there and actually has his own show on the Arabic speaking network? Yusuf Al Qaradawi. That would be the same Qaradawi who espouses *Muruna*.[39]

Consider too that *Al Jazeera* interviewed Musa Ismail Obama—the cousin of Barack Obama—in 2011. (**See Appendix C**) During that interview, done in Arabic, Musa explained that the Mama Sarah Obama Foundation (run by the step-grandmother of Barack) was using the contributions of unsuspecting western contributors to fund the Wahhabi education of Kenyan students who were sent to Saudi Arabia to learn the most virulent strain of fundamentalist Islam. Musa later explained that there was such an influx of students from Kenya to Saudi Arabia that he was put in charge of managing the overflow, which was sent to Qatar, the home of the government-run *Al Jazeera*.[40] Why did Musa feel so comfortable divulging such sensitive information to *Al Jazeera*? Why did *Al Jazeera* not report this story on its English network? This was quite the omission of information very relevant to the English-speaking world, was it not? In fact, Musa's account implicated the foundation in the commission of a fraud that *Al Jazeera* did not report to its English audience, despite the fact that most of those who were allegedly defrauded were westerners. Why?

If doublespeak artists say one thing in English and another in Arabic, why couldn't entire news networks do the same? Are they not made up of individuals?

BARACK OBAMA

No president in US history personifies the nexus between socialism and Islam better than Barack Hussein Obama, Jr. From the day he was born, Obama's influences consisted primarily of Socialists, Communists, Marxists, and Muslims. Though Obama maintains that he is a Christian, such a claim should have posed a significant problem for him in the Muslim world because his father, Barack Hussein Obama, Sr., was a Muslim, albeit a non-practicing one. According to sharia law, any child born to a Muslim father is automatically a Muslim himself, regardless of how devout that father may be.[41]

By asserting that he'd never been a Muslim, the younger Obama showed disrespect to the Islamic faith. Yet, no one from the Muslim Brotherhood condemned him for it. Based on the *Doctrine of Balance*, this should be a red flag to westerners. Remember, according to Qaradawi, even blasphemy in Islam is permitted if it is committed in furtherance of a greater good (this will be an important consideration as we review Obama's record as president and the degree to which his policies hindered or aided the cause of Islam). If blasphemy is permitted under the *Doctrine of Balance*, why wouldn't apostasy be?

Islamic expert Daniel Pipes performed a great deal of research into Obama's upbringing relative to Islam and though the man who would be president was all but abandoned by his Muslim father, his stepfather was also Muslim. From 1967—1971, the young Obama lived in Indonesia and was registered in a Catholic school as a Muslim.[42] Though Pipes' research concluded that Obama did attend a mosque in Jakarta with his stepfather, the visits were not necessarily frequent. Nonetheless, Obama told Nicholas Kristof of the *New York Times* what he thought of the Islamic call to prayer:

> Mr. Obama recalled the opening lines of **the Arabic call to prayer, reciting them with a first-rate accent**. In a remark that seemed delightfully uncalculated (it'll give Alabama voters heart attacks), Mr. Obama described the call to prayer as "**one of the prettiest sounds on Earth at sunset**." [emphasis mine][43]

Again, based on Islamic law, Obama is a Muslim; that is non-negotiable. Pipes made the argument that because Obama converted from Islam to Christianity as a child, it is a lesser offense. Instead of being considered an *apostate* or a *murtadd* who warrants the death penalty in Islam, Obama's sentence would not include such a penalty because he would have converted to Christianity before reaching puberty. Nonetheless, Islam considers Barack Hussein Obama, Jr. a Muslim.[44]

Pipes draws the logical conclusion that because, by any Islamic standard, Barack Obama, Jr. was born a Muslim and necessarily must have converted away from the faith if he claims to be anything else, which makes him an *apostate* or *murtadd*. Pipes implied that by electing such a man president of the United States, Americans would be posing quite a problem for themselves with the Muslim world:

> ...if Obama once was a Muslim, he is now what Islamic law calls a murtadd (apostate), an ex-Muslim converted to another religion who must be

executed. Were he elected president of the United States, this status, clearly, would have large potential implications for his relationship with the Muslim world.[45]

In reality, the opposite happened. Obama embraced and endorsed Muslim causes like the controversial Ground Zero mosque, for example.[46] Indications are that the Muslim Brotherhood is perfectly willing to overlook Obama's apostasy as long as he is helping them get closer to their goal of a global caliphate. Take note that US Middle Eastern policy under the Barack Obama administration has been a boon to the Muslim Brotherhood in practically every way. Egypt, Tunisia, Libya, Morocco, and others have all seen the overthrow of dictators and the Ikhwan has all but filled each power vacuum.

Circa 1971, the young Obama returned to Hawaii and was introduced to a Marxist with strong ties to the Communist Party USA (CPUSA), Frank Marshall Davis. From 1944—1963, the FBI had been following Davis, who had amassed a file of more than 600 pages.[47] Davis, a friend of Obama's maternal grandfather, had repeated access to the young Barack until the latter left for college about ten years later, in 1981. Davis also wrote graphically pornographic books.

An interesting side note on Davis is that before he left Chicago for Hawaii in 1948, he had been a colleague of Communist, Vernon Jarrett, the father-in-law of the woman who would become Barack Obama's closest adviser in the White House, Valerie Jarrett.[48]

After leaving Hawaii, Obama attended Occidental Community College in Los Angeles, CA. According to an article that appeared in *Newsmax*, written by Ronald Kessler, it was reported that Obama's roommate was a man from Pakistan, named Mohammed Hasan Chandoo. While a sophomore at Occidental, Obama met with a man named John C. Drew who, at the time, was also a socialist. In the years since, Drew became more of a conservative.

According to Kessler, Drew told him that Obama, with Chandoo at his side, spoke of a Marxist revolution in America:

"He (Obama) was arguing a straightforward Marxist-Leninist class-struggle point of view, which anticipated that there would be a revolution of the working class, led by revolutionaries, who would overthrow the capitalist system and institute a new socialist government that would redistribute the wealth."[49]

Of course, in one of the more oft-cited excerpts from Obama's book, *Dreams From My Father*, he references his affiliations with Marxists:

> To avoid being mistaken for a sellout, I chose my friends carefully. The more politically active black students. The foreign students. The Chicanos. The Marxist professors and structural feminists and punk-rock performance poets. (Dreams from my Father, p. 100)[50]

According to an *Associated Press* report that appeared in the *Seattle Times*, the Obama campaign admitted in 2008 that between the time Obama attended Occidental and then Columbia University in New York, he traveled to Pakistan with another friend from the region—Wahid Hamid—and visited Chandoo's family for approximately three weeks. Upon his return and subsequent attendance at Columbia, Obama picked himself up another Pakistani roommate, whose name was Sohale Siddiqi, a friend of Hamid and Chandoo.[51]

The *AP* also reported that both Hamid and Chandoo were Obama's single largest fundraisers during the 2008 campaign; each raised between $100,000—$200,000 in campaign contributions.[52]

From 1988—1991, Obama attended Harvard Law School after spending some time in Chicago as a Community Organizer upon leaving Columbia.[53] That fact is not necessarily important to the subject matter of this book but the circumstances around which he got into Harvard and then became president of the institution's Law Review in 1990 very much are.

In a video, posted to *World Net Daily*, Percy Sutton, a Harlem attorney whose clientele list once included Malcolm X, appeared on a television program before Obama was elected President of the United States and made some shocking claims. Sutton, who had some high-ranking contacts at Harvard, told the host that he received a call from a man named Khalid Abdullah Tariq al-Mansour, who told Sutton that he was raising money for Obama and asked the Harlem lawyer to write a letter of recommendation for Obama to Sutton's contacts at Harvard. Sutton asserted that his letter is what helped get Obama into Harvard and potentially put him on the inside track as editor of the *Harvard Law Review*.[54]

In an article that appeared in *Newsmax*, Ken Timmerman said al-Mansour confirmed that he was a close adviser to Saudi Prince Alwaleed bin Talal.[55] Sutton even made reference to this by saying that al-Mansour was "the principal adviser to one of the world's richest men." This almost necessarily has to be a reference to Talal. Further bolstering that conclusion is the fact that Talal has invested tens of millions of dollars in Harvard according to Timmerman.[56] The Saudi prince also established the Prince Alwaleed Bin Talal Islamic Studies Program. This demonstrates that bin Talal has a history of funding projects at Harvard. Was Obama one of those projects? Sutton's claims make that a logical conclusion. A quote from Talal sits atop the Overview page of the site:

> "I am pleased to support Islamic studies at Harvard and I hope that this Program will enable generations of students and scholars to gain a thorough understanding of Islam and its role both in the past and in today's world. Bridging the understanding between East and West is important for peace and tolerance."[57]

Clearly, thanks to Sutton's comments, coupled with facts already known about the people he mentioned, there is just cause to demand further information about the extent of these relationships. If president Obama was personally beholden to a Saudi Prince, it would mean Obama was beholden to a man who is loyal to the furtherance of an Islamic agenda.

In 2012, a blogger named Frank Miele uncovered an amazing find. It was a column penned by none other than Vernon Jarrett in 1979. The contents of the piece included details of an interview between the author and none other than Khalid al-Mansour.[58]

Miele writes about the discovery of Vernon Jarrett's 1979 column that appeared in the *St. Petersburg Evening Independent*. In the column, Jarrett quotes heavily from the interview he did with al-Mansour. What were they talking about? Well, funneling Saudi money to black college students, of course:

> So far as I know, this 1979 column has not previously been brought to light, but it certainly should be because it broke some very interesting news about the "rumored billions of dollars the oil-rich Arab nations are supposed to unload on American black leaders and minority institutions." The columnist quoted a black San Francisco lawyer who said, "It's not just a rumor. Aid will come from some of the Arab states."
>
> Well, if anyone would know, it would have been this lawyer — Donald Warden, who had helped defend OPEC in an antitrust suit that year and had

developed significant ties with the Saudi royal family since becoming a Muslim and taking the name Khalid Abdullah Tariq al-Mansour.

Al-Mansour told Jarrett that he had presented the "proposed special aid program to OPEC Secretary-General Rene Ortiz" in September 1979, and that "the first indications of Arab help to American blacks may be announced in December." Maybe so, but I looked high and wide in newspapers in 1979 and 1980 for any other stories about this aid package funded by OPEC and never found it verified.

You would think that a program to spend "$20 million per year for 10 years to aid 10,000 minority students each year, including blacks, Arabs, Hispanics, Asians and native Americans" would be referred to somewhere other than one obscure 1979 column, but I haven't found any other word of it.

Of course, what this means is that if Khalid al-Mansour, Percy Sutton, and Vernon Jarrett are all to be taken at their word, then their accounts—which span over nearly 30 years—all make sense when taken together. The other thing it would mean is that Barack Obama was beholden to Saudi money in a very personal and substantial way. It would have meant the Saudis helped put him in the White House and such a deal doesn't come without steep payment.

The words of al-Mansour and Jarrett in 1979—coupled with the words of Sutton in 2008—also suggest that if a man so beholden to the Saudis ever became president, the rise of fundamentalist Islam all over the Middle East and an administration hostile toward Israel would become manifest.

In an article that appeared in the *Canada Free Press*, author Lawrence Sellin concluded that Obama's relationship with al-Mansour helped the future US president align left-wing and Islamic views:

> It was Obama's friendship with Khalid Abdullah Tariq al-Mansour and his sponsorship of Obama as a prospective Harvard law student...that probably helped merge Obama's Islamic, leftist and black nationalist anti-American views.[59]

Years later, in 2007, Obama would go to Kenya and campaign for a Marxist named Raila Odinga, who was running for president there. In a deal with Muslim leaders, it was widely reported that Odinga agreed—through a signed Memorandum of Understanding (MOU)—to make Islam "...the only true religion."[60]

It would seem politically unwise for Obama to go out of his way to publicly support such a man at a time when the Senator from Illinois was gearing up for a presidential run. Interestingly, according to Timmerman's article, al-Mansour boasted that he had introduced bin Talal to "51 of the 53 leaders of Africa."[61] As a result, al-Mansour was likely quite familiar with the politics in the various countries on that continent. If, indeed, Obama was beholden to al-Mansour and bin Talal, Odinga would likely have been their preferred choice for president of Kenya. Did Obama campaign for Odinga at the behest of al-Mansour and, by extension, a Saudi Prince?

The examples showing common cause between Islam and the left are bountiful. Let's consider two close acquaintances of Barack Obama from the latter's days in Chicago after returning from Harvard. Bill Ayers, a self-professed Marxist and Rashid Khalidi, a Muslim and former PLO member at a time when it was listed as a terrorist organization, both knew Obama quite well, despite Obama's attempts to distance himself from each man. During a presidential debate with Hillary Clinton, Obama attempted to dismiss Ayers as simply "a guy who lives in my neighborhood"[62] and during a town hall at a Florida synagogue, Obama admitted to knowing Khalidi but seemed to dismiss any notion of a close friendship by suggesting they became closer acquaintances than they otherwise would have, as a result of their children going to school together.[63] These two instances also demonstrate that it is not desirous for Marxists and Islamists in the west to reveal the truth about their intentions until the time is right. Had Obama been honest about his relationships with Ayers and Khalidi, it would have torpedoed his presidential campaign.

Obama came to know Khalidi when the latter was a professor at the University of Chicago. In 2003, Khalidi took a position with Columbia University. At his farewell dinner, both Obama and Ayers were in attendance. The left-wing *Los Angeles Times* was in possession of a videotape of that event but refused to release it as the election that would make Barack Obama president drew closer.[64]

According to an article at *World Net Daily*, the Arab American Action Network (AAAN) was a group co-founded by Khalidi. The Woods Fund—an organization on whose board both Obama and Ayers served—issued grants to the AAAN totaling close to $100,000 during their tenure there together. [65] The *New York Sun* reported that the AAAN was responsible for sponsoring the 2003 dinner all three men attended.[66]

As for connections to Nazism, consider that Khalidi was a spokesman for Yasser Arafat, who had extensive ties to the Muslim Brotherhood, which closely allied with Hitler during WWII. Ayers, according to sworn testimony from Larry Grathwohl, the only man to successfully infiltrate the Weather Underground for the FBI, insists that Ayers sought the elimination of "25 million people" who could not be successfully "re-educated into the new way of thinking" after the overthrow of the US government.[67]

The vice president of the AAAN—Ali Abunimah—wrote in 2007 that he'd had conversations with Obama about their mutual support for the Palestinians but seemed less than pleased when Obama appeared to cast aside that support in order to get elected:

> If disappointing, given his historically close relations to Palestinian-Americans, Obama's about-face is not surprising. He is merely doing what he thinks is necessary to get elected and he will continue doing it as long as it keeps him in power.[68]

It would seem that Abunimah was not in support of the use of JBTW in this instance.

Another Marxist with whom Barack Obama was closely affiliated was his pastor of twenty years, Jeremiah Wright, a proponent of black liberation theology and head of the Trinity United Church of Christ in Chicago. Obama only left the church when remaining a member became a significant political liability after video clips of Wright's shocking sermons began to surface before the election. In a way similar to how he attempted to distance himself from Ayers and Khalidi, Obama actually argued that in the twenty years he attended Wright's church, he never heard his pastor say any of the things available in abundance on video, recorded on different dates.

Wright expressed vehemently anti-Semitic views time and time again in his sermons but perhaps the most damning indictment of him was the result of something he published in his church's bulletin, not anything that came out of his mouth from the pulpit. Nearly a year before Obama left the church, Trinity's bulletin included a column by Mousa Abu Marzook that had appeared in the *Los Angeles Times*. Marzook's byline listed him as the "deputy of the political bureau of Hamas." Other outlets referred to the editorial as the Hamas "manifesto."[69] Incidentally, the AAAN's Abunimah praised Marzook's *Los Angeles Times* op-ed as well.[70]

At about the same time Wright was showing this very public alliance with the work of Marzook, who is identified as a senior political leader of Hamas, the US government was in the process of prosecuting the Holy Land Foundation and listed Marzook as one of several co-conspirators. According to the *Investigative Project on Terrorism*, Marzook was also an HLF founder.[71] It cannot be overstated that Hamas is the Muslim Brotherhood. After being deported from Jordan, Marzook is believed to have moved to Syria, where he likely had grand aspirations that included the overthrow of Bashar al-Assad so that the Ikhwan could rise to power there.[72]

During his first year in office, Barack Obama gave a speech at the University of Cairo (Al-Azhar) in Egypt. In another chapter, we discuss the alleged involvement of Feisal Abdul Rauf and Rashad Hussain in crafting that speech.

At the beginning of the speech, Obama extended an Islamic greeting by saying "assalaamu alaykum." According to *Jihad Watch's* Robert Spencer, that is a greeting reserved only for Muslims when communicating to other Muslims. Spencer explains what Obama should have said:

> According to Islamic law, a Muslim may only extend this greeting—Peace be upon you—to a fellow Muslim. To a non-Muslim he is to say, "Peace be upon those who are rightly guided," i.e., Peace be upon the Muslims.[73]

In light of the controversy over Obama's religious loyalties, the Muslim world should have been greatly offended by such a greeting. After all, Obama has maintained that he was *never* a Muslim. Since Obama was born Muslim according to Islamic law, it *should* have been more offensive to Muslims to hear *him* utter such a greeting than to have it come from the mouth of an Islamophobic infidel. Why no outrage? As an apostate, Obama's greeting should have been perceived as a tremendous slap in the face to Islam. Again, think *Doctrine of Balance*.

Along these lines, Obama later said the following in his speech:

> I am a Christian, but my father came from a Kenyan family that includes generations of Muslims.

Spencer again makes a salient point in response:

Note that he avoids saying his father was a Muslim, which would open him to charges of apostasy.[74]

Obama continued in Cairo:

...I consider it part of my responsibility as President of the United States to fight against negative stereotypes of Islam wherever they appear.[75]

In light of Obama's history, this assertion seems a bit curious. Where in his words can one find an equal amount of defense for Jews and Christians?

At another point in the speech, Obama relied on inflated figures when referring to the number of Muslims in America:

*The dream of opportunity for all people has not come true for everyone in America, but its promise exists for all who come to our shores—and that includes **nearly 7 million American Muslims in our country today** who, by the way, enjoy incomes and educational levels that are higher than the American average.*[76] [emphasis mine]

Perhaps as much as any other excerpt of Obama's speech, that one in particular points directly to a Muslim Brotherhood influence. As Daniel Pipes points out, the figure of 7 million Muslims in America is not only inflated but touted by the likes of CAIR and the ISNA.[77]

Why would Obama's speech contain figures so obviously endorsed by the Muslim Brotherhood?

Arif Alikhan was appointed as assistant secretary for the Office of Policy Development at the Department of Homeland Security in 2009, prior to Obama's Cairo speech.[78] Less than two weeks before that appointment, Alikhan joined the Muslim Public Affairs Council (MPAC) for a fundraiser.[79] MPAC is virulently anti-Semitic and has distinct ties to CAIR which, coincidentally, endorsed Alikhan's appointment at DHS.[80] It is simply not believable that the Obama administration did not know of these connections.

Kareem Shora was appointed to Barack Obama's Homeland Security Advisory Council despite his ties to the very anti-Semitic group known as the American-Arab Anti-Discrimination Committee (ADC).[81] There are at least two glaring problems with Shora's ties to the ADC that should have prevented his hiring by the Obama administration. First, the organization has a history of running interference for Hamas by not denouncing it as a terrorist organization. Second,

ADC's ties to the Holy Land Foundation (HLF) include running ads for the group in the ADC's publication, the *ADC Times*.[82]

Dalia Mogahed was appointed to Obama's Advisory Council on Faith-Based and Neighborhood Partnerships.[83] Mogahed's ties to the Muslim Brotherhood are unmistakable; she has been a staunch defender of both CAIR and ISNA.[84] Mogahed is also a student of Dr. John Esposito of Georgetown University, according to the *Global Muslim Brotherhood Daily Report.* The *Investigative Project on Terrorism* cites Esposito as being a staunch defender of none other than Yusuf al-Qaradawi, the quintessential voice of *Muruna*.[85] According to Esposito's bio, he is the Founding Director of the Prince Alwaleed bin Talal Center for Muslim-Christian Understanding in the Walsh School of Foreign Service.[86] Esposito's role as Editor-in-Chief with Oxford Center for Islamic Studies Online raises flags we address in another chapter. Again, though, if Percy Sutton's words about being approached by al-Mansour, who was a close adviser to bin Talal, are true, appointments like Mogahed would make sense.

As was the case with Alikhan, CAIR was quite pleased with the Mogahed appointment. The following statement came courtesy of Executive Director Nihad Awad:

> Congratulations to Ms. Mogahed on this well-deserved appointment. Her knowledge and expertise will be an asset to this important council. The American Muslim community can feel confident that she will be a balanced and valuable resource on the vital issues the council must address.[87]

In a sane world, when the head of an organization listed as an unindicted co-conspirator in the largest terrorism financing trial in American history—the Holy Land Foundation trial—congratulates someone for being appointed by the President of the United States to head an advisory council, sane people would question such an appointment.

In an article that appeared on the *Mother Jones* website, staunch leftist David Corn pilloried the conservative Reverend Franklin Graham for the latter's claim that the Muslim Brotherhood had infiltrated the US Government. First, here is what Graham said:

> The Muslim Brotherhood is very strong and active in our country. It's infiltrated every level of our government. Right now we have many of these people that are advising the US military and State Department on how to

respond in the Middle East... We've brought in Muslims to tell us how to make policy toward Muslim countries. And many of these people we've brought in, I'm afraid, are under the Muslim Brotherhood.[88]

There is more than enough evidence—many of it presented here—that validates Graham's concerns. There is also more than enough evidence that leftists like Corn are more interested in running interference for the Muslim Brotherhood than they are in honest journalism. Here is what Corn said in response to the Graham quote he had a problem with:

> *Infiltrated every level of our government*—that's quite a claim. Yet Graham did not name a single Muslim Brotherhood infiltrator or cite a specific Obama administration decision that has been manipulated by these crafty behind-the-scenes Islamists.[89]

Oh, he wants names? Aside from the ones we've already listed throughout this book, there is one about whom there is an entire report at the end of this book; her name is Huma Abedin.

If there is an individual Barack Obama is beholden to most when it comes to his ascendancy to the White House, it just might be far left billionaire George Soros, who not only worked hard to get him elected to the US Senate in 2004 but threw his support behind Obama instead of Hillary Clinton in 2008.[90] Buzz Patterson, the man who carried the 'nuclear football' for Bill Clinton, asserted that if not for Soros, Obama likely wouldn't have made it out of Chicago. As it is, Obama was elected President of the United States and Soros' agenda almost seemed to become Obama's agenda, regardless of any significant disagreements that may have arisen after the inauguration.[91]

What makes the Soros agenda relevant to this discussion is his reverence for none other than the Muslim Brotherhood. That support manifested itself in Soros' support for a series of revolutions across the Middle East, designed to overthrow nationalist dictators.

At the dawn of the inaptly named 'Arab Spring,' Soros wrote an op-ed that appeared in the *Washington Post*. With the gift of hindsight, it's foolish not to conclude that either Soros is a liar or he was so egregiously wrong that he should consider leaving the public eye in total shame. After referring to Israel as "the main stumbling block," Soros wrote:

> The Muslim Brotherhood's cooperation with Mohamed ElBaradei, the Nobel laureate who is seeking to run for president, is a hopeful sign that it intends to play a constructive role in a democratic political system.

Again, it is simply not believable that Soros is ignorant of the Muslim Brotherhood's goals. Despite that, Soros closed his op-ed by excitedly supporting the Ikhwan:

> ...in the case of Egypt, I see a good chance of success. As a committed advocate of democracy and open society, I cannot help but share in the enthusiasm that is sweeping across the Middle East. I hope President Obama will expeditiously support the people of Egypt. My foundations are prepared to contribute what they can.[92]

The policies of the Obama administration, relative to the 'Arab Spring,' had the effect of furthering the cause of the Muslim Brotherhood, which seemed to fall right in line with the goals of George Soros, who once called for better relations with Hamas while simultaneously deriding Israel as the problem.[93] The goals of the left and Islam are again, one and the same, regardless of how many leftists realize it.

The Soros-funded Center for American Progress (CAP), an organization *TIME Magazine* referred to as the Obama administration's "idea factory" found itself defending anti-Semitic emails when CAP's editor-in-chief, Faiz Shakir, had to respond to revelations published by the *Jerusalem Post*, that one of his bloggers, Zaid Jilani, referred to "Israel-firsters" who continued to give money to Obama.[94]

Andrew McCarthy seemed to encapsulate perfectly, the dynamic that facilitates the alliance between Islam and the left in his book, *The Grand Jihad*.

> Revolutionaries of Islam and the Left make fast friends when there is a common enemy to besiege. Leftists, however, are essentially nihilists whose hazy vision prioritizes power over what is to be done with power... Islamists, who have very settled convictions about what is to be done with power, are much less so. Even their compromises keep their long-term goals in their sights. Thus do Leftists consistently overrate their ability to control Islamists. **(Andrew McCarthy, The Grand Jihad: How Islam and the Left Sabotage America, Encounter Books, 2010, p. 169)**

Providing another explanation for why Islamists and leftists seek to align with each other comes courtesy of Cliff Kincaid. In an article, he relayed what former Soviet KGB officer Konstantin Preobrazhensky told him:

> "The communists have considered Islam their ally from the very beginning because in the early 20th century, Islam was the religion of the 'oppressed people,' of 'the oppressed nations.' Support of Islam was considered part of Russian-based anti-colonialism. It is very significant that Vladimir Lenin in 1917 addressed his second message to the 'Muslim toilers of Russia and the Whole World.' So they considered Muslims a reservoir of people for the world communist revolution."[95]

In short, the left in the West seems to allow its hatred for the right to overpower its ability to use reason when it comes to Islam. In a word, it is pride. Denial of Islam's true intentions overpowers any inclination the left might have to even remotely listen to the right's alarm bells.

In the 1987 film *Wall Street*, the seasoned capitalist, played by Hal Holbrooke, had some words of wisdom after the film's hero Bud Fox—played by Charlie Sheen—had come face to face with the consequences of his illegal actions before deciding to do the right thing:

> "Man looks into the abyss; there's nothing staring back at him. At that moment, man finds his character and *that* is what keeps him out of the abyss."

Whether leftists understand their predicament or not makes little difference; they're in it and they're face to face with the abyss. Unless leftists find their character and realize who they're aligning with, they will fall into that abyss simply because they rejected the humility necessary to avoid it.

Speaking of the abyss, the left continues to identify Christian conservatism as the straw man it must defeat. Unfortunately, that straw man is nothing more than a baited hook, which the left chooses to identify as antithetical to righteousness.

A 17th Century French philosopher named Blaise Pascal illustrated this type of thinking perfectly with one sentence:

> We run heedlessly into the abyss after putting something in front of us to prevent us from seeing it.[96]

Each of three Democratic presidents, starting with Carter and ending with Obama—who got progressively worse when it came to protecting the US from the creeping threat of Islamic fundamentalism—placed right-wing, conservative Christian values in front of the abyss. The Islamic abyss cares not about *how* it sucks its victims into itself, only that it *does* so.

OTHER SHARED AGENDAS

Major environmentalist and population control fanatic, Harvard (there's that University again) professor Peter Singer, who champions infanticide and euthanasia in the name of saving the environment, romanticizes about Islam as an environmental remedy:

> Muslims clearly understand nonhuman animals to have souls. **(In defense of animals, By Peter Singer, Page 74)**

Muhammad, according to Singer, was also an environmental hero, a man who...

> ...compared the doing of good or bad deeds to other animals to similar acts done to humans.[97]

As for the Qur'an, Singer writes that...

> Qur'an 17:44 notes that nonhuman animals and the rest of nature are in continuous praise of Allah, although humans may not be able to understand this.[98]

Singer asserts that America should contribute more to world poverty, saying "America is taking far more than our fair share;"[99] and that population growth will ruin the environment. In all of his writings, Singer portrays the Christian Bible as a foe.[100]

In an article entitled "Heavy Petting," Singer comments:

> In the Judeo-Christian tradition—less so in the east—we have always seen ourselves as distinct from animals, and imagined that a wide, unbridgeable gulf separates us from them. Humans alone are made in the image of God. Only human beings have an immortal soul.[101]

In his work *A Companion to Ethics*, it reads:

> Christian ethics is intolerant and breeds intolerance.[102]

Islam has many attributes that are right in line with western-style environmentalism. Muhammad commanded his followers to care for the earth "Even when the Day of Judgment comes" and that "if any one has a palm-shoot in hand, he should plant it." Muhammad established himas (environmental laws) in Arabia.[103]

For years, Muslim scholars have been courting western educators by adapting Islam and making it palatable to evolutionists. The left's ideological agreement with much of Islam is no accident. These scholars have been planting these seeds for decades. B.A. Masri writes that *himas* (protected areas) were established by Muhammad…

> …some 14 centuries ago, and covers not only forests but also wildlife. According to these laws, certain areas, called *haram* or *hima*, are set aside and protected. This code of ecological conservation has its origins in the life and sayings of the Prophet Muhammad. One of the latter, reported by Bukhari and Muslim, the most reliable compilers of Muhammad's deeds, states that, "Whoever plants a tree and looks after it with care, until it matures and becomes productive, will be rewarded in the Hereafter."[104]

Even the phrase 'survival of the fittest' has become a common saying in the Muslim world. One Muslim professor explains:

> In the [Muslim] students' bridge models, microevolution and the concept of "the survival of the fittest" appeared on the accepted side of the equation. Students reasoned that it is impossible to deny the logic and empirical backing of these concepts. They also connected microevolution to theistic evolution, the idea that God has guided the adjustments in his creatures. Several students accepted the Big Bang and believed that the Qur'an contains references to both the Big Bang and evolution theory. **(Islam And Evolution. From Al-Bab, An Open Door To The Muslim World. Quote from Farida Faouzia Charfi, a science professor at the University of Tunis)**

Dr Khalid Anees, president of the Islamic Society of Britain confirms:

> There is no contradiction between what is revealed in the Koran and natural selection and survival of the fittest. **(Creationism: Science and Faith in Schools, Wednesday 7 January 2004, guardian.co.uk)**

Evolution is not a new discovery; Muslims worldwide claim that Allah revealed it in the Qur'an. In promoting Theistic Evolution, Muslim academics like Adnan Oktar, a Turkish-born Islamist who goes by the pen name of Harun Yahya,[105] seeks to gain merit with modern western thinkers by pushing the narrative that Islam has contributed greatly to explaining the origin of the universe. Here is the corresponding text to a *YouTube* video that claims to be inspired by Oktar:

> The universe, then, is a more complex and impressive creation than mankind himself. Modern scientific findings support the Big Bang Theory, which proposes that the universe took shape out of nothingness after a massive explosion, and that particles resulting from this blast came together to form planets, stars and entire galaxies. Similar reference is made in the Qur'an: "Do the Unbelievers not see that the heavens and the earth were joined together, before We clove them asunder?" (Qur'an 21:30); and, "Then He turned to the heaven when it was smoke: He said to it and to the earth: 'Come together, willingly or unwillingly.' They said, 'We do come together, in willing obedience.' (Qur'an 41:11)"[106]

Qur'an 21:30 and 41:11 are primary sources for major arguments by so many Muslim scholars, academics and apologists who fight for Islam and science to enjoin in order to satisfy modern audiences while arguing for the miracle of the Qur'an. This all sounds like agenda-driven brainwashing, doesn't it?

Islam at its most basic is socialist. Muslims use many examples when Islam immigrated to Medina and shared the wealth between Al-Muhajirun (immigrants) and the Ansar (supporters). Pakistan, under the rule of Zulfiqar Ali Bhutto established a social government. Today, the Pakistan People's Party (PPP), under the guidance of President Asif Ali Zaradi advocates a system based on Islamic socialism. Muammar Gadhafi of Libya established an Islamic socialist state in 1969. Even the Iranian constitution contains collectivist views.

In *Al-Takaful Al-Ijtimai And Islamic Socialism*, Sami Hanna, considered to be a trailblazer in the area of Islamic socialism,[107] wrote in 1969:

> ...the common themes among the revolutionary regimes in Egypt, Syria and Iraq, may be traced back to the days of the Prophet Muhammad (PBUH) himself and his successors. This concept was expressed one way or another by **the single call for social justice among the Muslims**. But perhaps the most overt call came from Abu Dharr al-Ghifari who knew **the Prophet and**

witnessed the remarkable social changes which took place in the new Muslim empire, especially during Uthman's reign **when Abu Dharr issued his warning against the accumulation of wealth in the hands of the few** whom the Caliph had appointed to rule the conquered regions. [emphasis mine][108]

Jamal al-Din al-Afghani, the Muslim theologian, philosopher and political leader, has examined western socialism and suggested that Islamic socialism (*ishtirakiyya*) is far better.

Mustafa al-Sibai, whose book *Ishtirakiyyat al-Islam* (Islamic Socialism) could be considered the most widely acclaimed work on the subject by Egyptian authorities. He quotes from the Qur'an: "The believers are brethren." (S. 49: IO)

He continues:

> To declare brotherhood among the individuals of any society necessitates *al-takaful* among them, not only in eating, drinking and bodily needs but also in every other necessity of life. The acknowledgment of brotherhood between two persons is an acknowledgment of *al-takaful* and *al-tadamun* (solidarity) between them in sentiments and feelings, in demands and needs, and in status and dignity. This is the truth of al-takaful al-ijtimai in Islamic socialism."

Islamic socialism, like the old Soviet-style Communism, wants a universal utopia in which the poor 'have-nots' clean the coffers of the rich 'haves'—Islam's universal *Ummah* in which dissident Jews and Christians are taxed with Jizzya by the Muslim have-nots. After the Bolsheviks took over Russia, Vladimir Lenin stole all of the land owned by the church "for the benefit of the community" and was "to be distributed in equal shares." The private ownership of land was to be "abolished forever."[109]

Similarly, Muslims conquered Spain and Church property was placed under the control of the *Ummah*; Christians were thereby forced to comply with the *Pact of Umar* that guaranteed the Islamic enforcement over Christian lands. In the document it reads:

> We shall not build, in our cities or in their neighborhood, new monasteries, Churches, convents, or monks' cells, nor shall we repair, by day or by night, such structures that have fallen in ruins or are situated in the quarters of the Muslims." **(Islam: Truth or Myth? Pact of Umar, (probably drafted during**

the time of Umar b. Abd al Aziz who ruled 717- 720 AD) from Al-Turtushi, Siraj al-Muluk, pgs. 229-23)

The Islamic philosopher Said Qutb wrote of capitalism:

...the exploitation of individuals and nations due to greed for wealth and imperialism under the capitalist systems are but a corollary of rebellion against God's authority... Look at this capitalism with its monopolies, its usury and whatever else is unjust in it; at this individual freedom, devoid of human sympathy and responsibility for relatives except under the force of law...**(Sayyid Qutb's Milestones, Elmer Swenson, Last Updated: 6-27-2005, From pgs. 11 and 139)**

Qaradawi, the world renowned Muslim scholar who is regularly greeted with a red carpet by leftist European leaders, said that capitalism:

...is based on usury and securities rather than commodities in markets... it is undergoing a crisis and... our integrated Islamic philosophy—if properly understood and applied—can replace the Western capitalism.[110]

So the left and Islam both tend to exploit the poor masses in the name of fairness. Wealth that would otherwise support those masses through capitalist principles and free economies is hoarded by those who claim to be the custodians of wealth and protect it from falling into the hands of the greedy few. In reality, the self-anointed protectors are the greedy hoarders.

This leads to a Bible verse that may help to explain why Islamists and Socialists so vehemently reject Christianity.

The name Judas Iscariot has become synonymous with betrayal, which is the disgraced disciple's most widely understood characteristic but Judas had another, very undesirable trait that is at the core of socialism; he was a thief who exploited the poor so he could enrich himself.

When Jesus was reclining at table with Lazarus, whom he had raised from the dead, Mary Magdelene arrived with expensive perfume. She anointed the Son of Man's feet with it and wiped them with her hair. Judas objected and what happened next is told in John 12:4-6:

4 But one of His disciples, Judas Iscariot, Simon's son, who would betray Him, said, 5 "Why was this fragrant oil not sold for three hundred denarii[b] and given to the poor?" 6 **This he said, not that he cared for the poor, but**

because he was a thief, and had the money box; and he used to take what was put in it. [111]

Socialists and Islamists lie, as a matter of course, not as the result of a perceived weakness. Perhaps this is why they each reject the Judeo-Christian mindset so completely. They lie and deceive in order to enrich themselves while pretending to be the protectors of the public purse, the paragons of justice who are ostensibly looking out for the best interests of the masses. In reality, it is all a ruse designed to do the exact opposite, to turn the masses into pawns against any manifestation of wealth until the holder of that wealth places his coins into the public purse, which is held by the selfish with an agenda.

In essence, while true capitalists seek the fruit-bearing fulfillment of self-interests, socialists and Islamists seek the fulfillment of self interests exclusively at the expense of others. A clearer line of distinction between good and evil you will be hard pressed to find.

ISLAMIC PRESENCE IN US CONGRESS

Another signatory to *A Common Word* is a key member of the Fiqh Council and lecturer-Scholar-in-Residence for the Zaytuna Institute; his name is Zaid Shaker. In Arabic, Shaker shares his story about how he changed his name from Ricky Mitchell and converted to Islam during his service in the United States Air Force in 1977. Zaid studied Islam in Syria and Morocco; he then served as the Imam of the Connecticut Mosque from 1988—1994. This is how he expressed his dream and goal in Arabic:

> "To make the United States of America an Islamic state governed by Islamic Sharia law which must be accomplished through persuasion and non-violent means." [112]

Shaker and Rep. Keith Ellison (D-MN) share at least two things in common; both are Muslim and both were signatories to *A Common Word*. Shaker has openly called for the replacement of the US Constitution with Sharia law (remember, the two cannot co-exist). Ellison, a Muslim, who took an oath to defend the US Constitution, was also a signatory. Shouldn't Ellison have to answer for being affiliated with such a group? In 2006, Ellison became the first Muslim elected to US Congress. Democrat Andre Carson of Indiana was the second, in 2008.

Shaker expressed his hatred for the US military brass. Again, this should be a problem for Ellison, who joined with ISNA one day after the Fort Hood shootings to denounce the act of violence and murder. Using twisted logic, Shaker's condemnation of Nidal Malik Hasan's Fort Hood Massacre, in reality, actually served to blame the US:

> "I firmly believe there is no legitimate reason for the deaths of the hundreds of thousands of Iraqi and Afghani civilians who have perished as a result of those two conflicts. Even though I disagree with the continued prosecution of those wars, and even though I believe that the US war machine is the single greatest threat to world peace."[113]

Ellison became a signatory in 2008.[114]

Additionally, Rep. Carson joined Ellison at the press conference with the ISNA and MPAC one day after the jihadist attack at Fort Hood to denounce the shootings. At first blush, there doesn't appear to be anything wrong with such a gesture but once the goals of the ISNA are understood, it becomes obvious the move was entirely political. Thanks to that 1991 document penned by Mohamed Akram, the ISNA was listed as an organization that seeks the overthrow of the US Government. The presence of Ellison and Carson at that press conference was indeed disturbing. Groups that hold press conferences designed to show respect for those they view with disgust can be nothing but political.[115]

On a side note, for those who assert that Islam and socialism aren't natural bedfellows, the only two Muslims in the US Congress—Ellison and Carson—together made up two of 70 members of Congress who were registered members of the Democratic Socialists of America caucus as recently as 2009.[116]

Despite the egregious nature of these words and the complete lack of respect they reveal for the US Military, what the DoD itself is responsible for may be far worse.

FOOTNOTES

1. *The Islamic Republic and the Iranian Left,* by Yassamine Mather and David Mather. http://www.critiquejournal.net/iran32-33.pdf
2. Campus Watch, Frontpage Magazine, *The Real Jimmy Carter (Dershowitz on Harvard and the Zayed Foundation),* by Alan Dershowitz. http://www.campus-watch.org/article/id/3267

3. The New York Times, *Bin Laden's Reading List for Americans,* by Sharon Otterman and Robert Mackey. http://thelede.blogs.nytimes.com/2009/09/14/bin-ladens-reading-list-for-americans/

4. Newsmax.com, *The Clintons, Abdurahman Alamoudi, and the Myth of "Moderate" Islam,* by Lawrence Auster. http://archive.newsmax.com/archives/articles/2000/11/6/170946.shtml

5. Discover The Network.org, *Islamic Association for Palestine (IAP).* http://www.discoverthenetworks.org/printgroupProfile.asp?grpid=6215

6. Newsmax.com, *The Clintons, Abdurahman Alamoudi, and the Myth of "Moderate" Islam,* by Lawrence Auster. http://archive.newsmax.com/archives/articles/2000/11/6/170946.shtml

7. Discover The Networks.org, *Abdurahman Alamoudi.* http://www.discoverthenetworks.org/individualProfile.asp?indid=1311

8. Militant Islam Monitor.org, *Abdulrahman Alamoudi – Head of American Muslim Council goes to jail for 23 years.* http://www.militantislammonitor.org/article/id/306

9. Newsmax.com, *Steve Emerson: Hillary Clinton and Hamas,* http://archive.newsmax.com/archives/ic/2006/1/29/230642.shtml

10. Fox News Insider, *Fast Facts: Huma Abedin, Anthony Weiner's Wife,* http://foxnewsinsider.com/2011/06/07/fast-facts-huma-abedin-weiner/

11. Video, *Bill Clinton speaks on Islamic society of North America (ISNA).* http://www.youtube.com/watch?v=zWp5cVhyCVs

12. Video in English with Turkish sub-titles, *Bill Clinton: Fethullah Gulen's Contribution to the World, Turkish Cultural.* http://www.youtube.com/watch?v=MPiPOL9-EQs

13. Newsmax.com, *Insider Report: Clinton Admired Hitler Too.* http://archive.newsmax.com/archives/articles/2003/10/5/184006.shtml

14. Video, *CNN Claims Gore is 'Bitter' Over 2000 Presidential Defeat.* http://www.youtube.com/watch?v=rLMD8OlcX38

15. Winston Churchill Leadership, *Winston Churchill on Politics…* http://www.winston-churchill-leadership.com/churchill-quote-politics.html

16. InvisionFree, *Chicago Tribune Editorial Slanders Gore,* http://s8.invisionfree.com/Al_Gore_Support/ar/t3938.htm

17. Newsmax.com, *Gore Laments U.S. 'Abuses' Against Arabs,* http://archive.newsmax.com/archives/ic/2006/2/12/220618.shtml

18. Front Page Mag.com, *Al Gore's Arab Pander,* by Lowell Ponte. http://archive.frontpagemag.com/readArticle.aspx?ARTID=5552

19. Front Page Mag.com, *Kerry's IRanian Connection Fights Democracy,* by Robert Spencer. http://archive.frontpagemag.com/Printable.aspx?ArtId=11492

20. Gateway Pundit, *Brrrr...Al Gore Braves Snow & Ice Storm to Testify to Congess on Global Warming...Update: Arctic Gulls Return to Northeast,* posted by Jim Hoft. http://www.thegatewaypundit.com/2009/01/brrrr-al-gore-braves-snow-ice-storms-to/

21. The New York Times, *Gore Wins Holl ywood in a Landslide,* by Adam Nagourney. http://thecaucus.blogs.nytimes.com/2007/02/25/gore-wins-hollywood-in-a-landslide/

22. http://www.conbio.org/workinggroups/religion/docs/Islam.pdf

23. Future Islam, *A Journal of Future Ideology that Shapes Today the World of Tomorrow.* http://www.futureislam.com/aboutus.asp

24. Future Islam, *Winning the Struggle Against Global Warming,* by Brendan Mackey & Song Li.http://www.futureislam.com/20070501/insight/Brendan_song/Winning_the_Struggle_against_Global_Warming.asp

25. Future Islam, *Contributors.* http://www.futureislam.com/authors/ourcontributors.asp

26. Future Islam, *A Journal of Future Ideology that Shapes Today the World of Tomorrow.* http://www.futureislam.com/aboutus.asp

27. Ibid

28. The Telegraph, *Barack Obama and Al Gore to discuss climate change.* http://www.telegraph.co.uk/news/worldnews/barackobama/3686593/Barack-Obama-and-Al-Gore-to-discuss-climate-change.html

29. The Bostom Globe, *Obama vows action on global warming,* posted by Foon Rhee. http://www.boston.com/news/politics/politicalintelligence/2008/12/obama_vows_acti.html

30. Ibid

31. The Telegraph, *Climategate: the final nail in the coffin of 'Anthropogenic Global Warming'?* by James Delingpole. http://blogs.telegraph.co.uk/news/jamesdelingpole/100017393/climategate-the-final-nail-in-the-coffin-of-anthropogenic-global-warming/

32. Watts Up With That?, *Climategate 2.0 emails – They're real and they're spectacular!* http://wattsupwiththat.com/2011/11/22/climategate-2-0/

33. The Examiner, *Al Gore sells out to Big Oil for estimated $10 mil, tries to dodge taxes on it.* http://washingtonexaminer.com/al-gore-sells-out-to-big-oil-for-estimated-100-mil-tries-to-dodge-taxes-on-it/article/2517451#.U0YzUqyThdh

34. The New York Times, *Al Jazeera Seeks a U.S. Voice Where Gore Failed,* by Brian Stelter. http://mediadecoder.blogs.nytimes.com/2013/01/02/al-jazeera-said-to-be-acquiring-current-tv/

35. The Examiner, *Al Gore sells out to Big Oil for estimated $10 mil, tries to dodge taxes on it.* http://washingtonexaminer.com/al-gore-sells-out-to-big-oil-for-estimated-100-mil-tries-to-dodge-taxes-on-it/article/2517451#.UOYzUqyThdh

36. Politico, *Glenn Beck tried to buy Current TV,* by Dylan Byers. http://www.politico.com/blogs/media/2013/01/glenn-beck-tried-to-buy-current-tv-153232.html

37. New York News & Features, *Al Jazeera's Edge.* http://nymag.com/nymetro/news/media/columns/medialife/n_8648/index1.html

38. http://thestar.com.my/news/story.asp?file=/2006/4/12/nation/200604121 52145&sec=nation

39. http://usasurvival.org/docs/Ltr2Chairman-McCaul_Al-Jazeera.pdf

40. http://www.shoebat.com/wp-content/uploads/2012/10/Obama_Wahhabist_Fundraising_Empire_101112.pdf

41. New York Times, *President Apostate?* by Edward N. Luttwak. http://www.nytimes.com/2008/05/12/opinion/12luttwak.html?_r=1&oref=slogin&pagewanted=print

42. Daniel Pipes, Middle East Forum, *Confirmed: Barack Obama Practiced Islam,* by Daniel Pipes. http://www.danielpipes.org/5354/confirmed-barack-obama-practiced-islam

43. The New York Times, *Obama: Man of the World,* by Nicholas D. Kristof. http://www.nytimes.com/2007/03/06/opinion/06kristof.html?_r=1

44. Daniel Pipes, Middle East Forum, *Was Barack Obama a Muslim?* by Daniel Pipes. http://www.danielpipes.org/5286/was-barack-obama-a-muslim

45. Daniel Pipes, Middle East Forum, *Confirmed: Barack Obama Practiced Islam,* by Daniel Pipes. http://www.danielpipes.org/5354/confirmed-barack-obama-practiced-islam

46. Breitbart TV, *Durbin, Baltimore Police Chief: 'Creepy' NRA members want to attack law enforcement.* http://www.breitbart.com/breitbart-tv

47. USA Survival News, *New Video: The Frank Marshall Davis Story You Haven't Heard – Until Now,* James Simpson. http://www.usasurvival.org/marshall.fbi.files.html

48. http://www.usasurvival.org/marshall.fbi.files.html

49. Newsmax, *Obama Espoused Radical Views in College,* by Ronald Kessler. http://www.newsmax.com/RonaldKessler/obama-college-marxism-occidental/2010/02/08/id/349329

50. Google Books, [SEARCH] *To avoid being mistaken for a sellout, I chose my friends carefully. The more politically active black students. The foreign students. The Chicanos. The Marxist professors and structural feminists and punk-rock performance poets.* http://books.google.com/books?id=HRCHJp-V0QUC&pg=PA100&lpg=PA100 &dq=To+avoid+being+mistaken+for+a+sellout,+I+chose+my+friends+carefully.+ The+more+politically+active+black+students.+The+foreign+students.+The+Chi canos.+The+Marxist+professors+and+structural+feminists+and+punk-rock+perfor mance+poets&source=bl&ots=PG7v537ISI&sig=M5t4LhWIZOEKWiHTkOBwCaDTjv E&hl=en&ei=sY_NTpexN6-nsAKQ37HNDg&sa=X&oi=book_result&ct=result& resnum=8&ved=0CEsQ6AEwBw#v=onepage&q=chicanos&f=false

51. The Seattle Times, *Old friends recall Obama's years in LA, NY*, by Adam Goldman and Robert Tanner. http://seattletimes.com/html/localnews/2004417706_ap youngobama2ndldwritethru.html

52. Ibid.

53. Harvard Law School, *Obama first made history at HLS*. http://www.law.harvard. edu/news/obama-at-hls.html

54. WND, *Did Radical Muslims Help Send Obama to Harvard?* by Jerome R. Corsi. http: //www.wnd.com/2009/07/104684/

55. Newsmax, *Obama Had Close Ties to Top Saudi Adviser at Early Age,* by Ken Timmerman. http://www.newsmax.com/KenTimmerman/obama-sutton-saudi/ 2008/09/03/id/339914

56. Ibid

57. http://islamicstudies.harvard.edu/overview/history.php

58. Daily Inter Lake.com, *Does 1979 newspaper column shed light on 2008 campaign story? 1979 article by Vernon Jarrett about Khalid al-Mansour,* Frank Miele. http:// www.dailyinterlake.com/opinion/columns/frank/article_7924e4f0-0468-11e 2-8da2-0019bb2963f4.html

59. Canada Free Press, *Obama's ineligibility: Muslim-leftist radical in the White House.* http://www.canadafreepress.com/index.php/article/40313

60. The Washington Times, *HYMAN: Obama's Kenya ghosts.* http://www.washington times.com/news/2008/oct/12/obamas-kenya-ghosts/

61. Newsmax, *Obama Had Close Ties to Top Saudi Adviser at Early Age,* by Ken Tim merman. http://www.newsmax.com/KenTimmerman/obama-sutton-saudi/2008/ 09/03/id/339914

62. The Wall Street Journal, *Obama and Ayers Pushed Radicalism on Schools,* by Stanley Kurtz. http://online.wsj.com/article/SB122212856075765367.html

63. Digital Journal, *Another Questionable Barack Obama Answer About His Association With Rashid Khalid,* by Susan Duclos. http://www.digitaljournal.com/article/255831/Another_Questionable_Barack_Obama_Answer_About_His_Association_With_Rashid_Khalidi

64. National Review Online, *The L.A. Times Suppresses Obama's Khalidi Bash Tape,* by Andrew C. McCarthy. http://www.nationalreview.com/articles/226104/i-l-times-i-suppresses-obamas-khalidi-bash-tape/andrew-c-mccarthy

65. WND, *Obama Worked with Terrorist, Senator helped fund organization that rejects 'racist' Israel's existence,* by Aaron Klein. http://www.wnd.com/2008/02/57231/

66. The New York Sun, *Mideast Parley Takes Ugly Turn At Columbia U.,* by Sol Stern and Fred Siegel. http://www.nysun.com/new-york/mideast-parley-takes-ugly-turn-at-columbia-u/8725/

67. USA Survival News, *Marxism in America,* remarks of Larry Grathwohl. http://www.usasurvival.org/grathwohl_remarks.html

68. The Electronic Intifada, *How Barack Obama learned to love Israel,* Ali Abunimah. http://electronicintifada.net/content/how-barack-obama-learned-love-israel/6786#.TtVhl3pcVdg

69. BizzyBlog, *TUCC's Church Bulletins from July 2007 Make Whether Obama Was Present on July 22 Irrelevant.* http://www.bizzyblog.com/2008/03/17/tuccs-church-bulletins-from-july-2007-probably-make-whether-obama-was-present-on-July-22-irrelevant/

70. The Electronic Entifada, *Engaging Hamas and Hizballah,* Ali Abunimah. http://electronicintifada.net/content/engaging-hamas-and-hizballah/7196#.TtVkB3pcVdg

71. IPT The Investigative Project on Terrorism, *Individual Terrorists – Mousa Abu Marzook.* http://www.investigativeproject.org/profile/106

72. Jewish Virtual Library, *Mousa Abu Marzook (1951–).* http://www.jewishvirtuallibrary.org/jsource/biography/marzook.html

73. Jihad Watch, *Platitudes and naivete: Obama's Cairo Speech* [PREPARED BY WHITE HOUSE]. http://www.jihadwatch.org/2009/06/platitudes-and-naivete-obamas-cairo-speech.html

74. Ibid

75. The White House, *Remarks by the President on a new beginning, Cairo University,, Cairo Egypt.* http://www.whitehouse.gov/the-press-office/remarks-president-cairo-university-6-04-09

76. Ibid

747. Daniel Pipes Middle East Forum, *Assessing Obama's Cairo Speech,* by Daniel Pipes. http://www.danielpipes.org/blog/2009/06/assessing-obamas-cairo-speech

78. Discover The Networks.org, *Arif Alikhan.* http://www.discoverthenetworks.org/individualProfile.asp?indid=2401

79. Times Union.com. *La Deputy Mayor Arif Alikhan,* by Hadeer Nagah. http://blog.timesunion.com/muslimwomen/la-deputy-mayor-arif-alikhan/382/

80. US 4 Arabs.com, *Arif Alikhan appointed to DHS Post, CAIR-LA Congratulates Calif. Muslim Appointed to DHS Post, Arif Alikhan will serve as Assistant Secretary for Policy Development.* http://www.us4arabs.com/content/view/1590/31/

81. Discover The Networks.org, *Kareem Shora.* http://www.discoverthenetworks.org/individualProfile.asp?indid=2402

82. Discover The Networks.org, *American-Arab Anti-Discrimination Committee (ADC).* http://www.discoverthenetworks.org/groupProfile.asp?grpid=6173

83. The Global Muslim Brotherhood Daily Report, *Esposito Protoge Appointed to Obama Advisory Council.* http://globalmbreport.org/?p=1414

84. Front Page Mag.com, *Appeasing the Muslim Brotherhood,* by Nonie Darwish. http://frontpagemag.com/2010/nonie-darwish/appeasing-the-muslim-brotherhood/

85. IPT The Investigative Project on Terrorism, *John Esposito: Reputation vs. Reality.* http://www.investigativeproject.org/1443/john-esposito-reputation-vs-reality

86. Georgetown University, *John L Esposito, Bio,* http://explore.georgetown.edu/people/jle2/

87. CAIR, *CAIR Congratulates Dalia Mogahed on Appointment to President's Advisory Council.* http://www.cair.com/ArticleDetails.aspx?ArticleID=25849&&name=n&&currPage=1

88. Newsmax, *Franklin Graham: World's Christians in Grave Danger,* by Chris Gonsalves and Kathleen Walter. http://www.newsmax.com/InsideCover/franklin-graham-christians-muslims/2011/03/18/id/389992?s=al&promo_code=BE61-1

89. Mother Jones – Politics, *Franklin Graham's New Obama-Muslim Conspiracy Theory,* by David Corn. http://www.motherjones.com/politics/2011/03/franklin-graham-obama-muslim-brotherhood-conspiracy-theory

90. American Thinker, *Soros, Obama, and the Millionaires Exception,* by Ed Lasky. http://www.americanthinker.com/2007/04/soros_obama_and_the_millionair.html

91. Human Events, Powerful Conservative Voices, *The Obama-Soros Connection,* by b patterson. http://www.humanevents.com/2010/09/09/the-obamasoros-connection/

92. WashingtonPost.com, *Why Obama has to get Egypt right,* by George Soros. http://www.washingtonpost.com/wp-dyn/content/article/2011/02/02/AR2011020 205041.html?hpid=opinionsbox1

93. American Thinker, *Barack Obama and Israel,* by Ed Lasky. http://www.american thinker.com/2008/01/barack_obama_and_israel.html

94. The Jerusalem Post, *E-mail reveals anti-Semitism at US think tank,* by Benjamin Weinthal. http://www.jpost.com/International/Article.aspx?id=252605

95. USA Survival News, *Whittaker Chambers, Alger Hiss, and Panettagate,* by Cliff Kincaid. http://usasurvival.org/ck07.08.2011.html

96. http://www.tameri.com/csw/exist/pascal.shtml

97. Ibid, p. 74

98. Ibid, p. 74

99. ReporterOnline, *Peter Singer: A More Sustainable World.* by Maximiliano Herrera. http://reportermag.com/article/10-10-2008/peter-singer-a-more-sustainable-world

100. *Dictionary of ethics, theology, and society*, Ecological Theology, by Paul A. B. Clarke and Andrew Linzey, Page 263, Singer 1987: 7

101. Heavy Petting, Peter Snger. http://www.utilitarian.net/singer/by/2001----.htm

102. Google Books, *A Companion to Ethics,* by Peter Singer. http://books.google.com/books?id=17i10ZZu8O4C&pg=PA103&lpg=PA103&dq=%22christian+ethics+is+intolerant+and+breeds+intolerance%22&source=bl&ots=q6Ys9rDdy9&sig=P6uGMlXDDeX8VNVF94FTAJfSQsk&hl=en&ei=jQjLTrDDNIyAsgLF75y3Dg&sa=X&oi=book_result&ct=result&resnum=1&ved=0CBsQ6AEwAA#v=onepage&q=%22christian%20ethics%20is%20intolerant%20and%20breeds%20intolerance%22&f=false

103. Chai Online, *Islam and Animals, Section Five,* by Al-Hafizz B.A. Masri

104. Saudi Aramco world, *The Academy of the Rain Forest,* by Tor Eigeland. http://www.saudiaramcoworld.com/issue/199206/the.academy.of.the.rain.forest.htm

105. http://www.harunyahya.com/theauthor.php

106. http://www.youtube.com/watch?v=gEjpA_f15L4

107. http://books.google.cm/books?id=zsoUAAAAIAAJ&pg=PA64&lpg=PA64&dq=Sami+A.+Hanna+Islamic+socialism&source=bl&ots=BjOriv86R-&sig=Iso4hwETk8fzyVfDBDLZmGQYSIo&hl=fr&ei=zi3YTq72C8n5sQLrg6zUDQ&sa=X&oi=book_result&ct=result&resnum=1&ved=0CBkQ6AEwAA#v=onepage&q=the%20common%20themes&f=false

108. Islam Social Sciences, *Shared Responsibility and Islamic Socialism,* by Sami A. Hanna. http://toyer-farrath.blogspot.com/2010_01_01_archive.html

109. *Exerpts from the Fundamental Law of Land Socialization (1918)*. http://personal.ashland.edu/~jmoser1/socialization.htm

110. CNS News.com, *Critics Protest Promotion of 'Seditious' Islamic Finance,* by Patrick Goodenough. http://cnsnews.com/node/38902

111. Bible Gateway.com, John 122:1-6, NKJV. http://www.biblegateway.com/passage/?search=john%2012:1-6&version=NKJV

112. Arabic website. http://islamstory.com/

113. New Islamic Directions, *Responding to the Fort Hood Tragedy,* by Imam Zaid. http://www.newislamicdirections.com/nid/articles/responding_to_the_fort_hood_tragedy/

114. A Common Word, [CLICK] Signatories. http://www.acommonword.com/?lang=en&page=new

115. ISNA, Islamic Society of North America, *Muslim American Organizations Denounce Shooting Incident at Foot Hood*. http://www.isna.net/articles/News/Muslim-American-Organizations-Denounce-Shooting-Incident-at-Fort-Hood.aspx

116. Gateway Pundit, *American Socialists Release Names of 70 Congressional Democrats in Their Ranks,* by Jim Hoft. http://www.thegatewaypundit.com/2010/08/american-socialists-release-names-of-70-congressional-democrats-in-their-caucus/

SECTION

8

Nexus Of Politics And Prophecy

CHAPTER
19

BIBLICAL HORIZONS

SCRIPTURE PREDICTS PERFECTLY

*I*n today's world, uttering the word, "Bible" will illicit accusations that one is unintelligent, uneducated, a fool, or an extremist. It is a way to dismiss anyone who engages in critical thinking. An examination of the holy-writ should help us determine if the alleged prophetic words were nothing more than the result of people guessing the future. If they were accurate, these prophets were lunatics, perfect guessers or custodians of superior knowledge that cannot be explained via earthly means.

However, saying the word "prophecy" instantly evokes images of Nostradamus or the Mayan Calendar among the secular world—those Mayans didn't fare so well when it came to predicting the world's end; if you're reading this, it's all the proof you need. Such prophecies lack the precise information that exists within the Bible, which includes geographic locations. Nostradamus never mentioned the Grassy Knoll in Dallas when he spoke of assassinations, yet many assume he was referring to Kennedy when he spoke of such things. Nostradamus reportedly spoke of a region in Germany called, "Hister."[1] Secularists with a penchant for granting credibility to Nostradamus gleefully point to *this* writing while scoffing at Scripture.

The Bible focuses on Israel and surrounding nations. Nostradamus is not France-centric while the Bible *is* Israel-centric, predicting its own revival and harassment at the hands of surrounding nations. Today, world peace is dependent upon Israel, not France. Neither is Mayan history significant, since it no longer exists and the world has out-lived its deadline.

The Y2K predictions and the Mayan Calendar's prediction came and went; the phony prognosticators failed. The prudent will shun the idea of a European Union emerging as the antichrist.

What is coming on the horizon is an Islamic Union led by Turkey. If this sounds too bold, perhaps reading the Word of God will help us see that He does not mince words either. In Zechariah, 9:13, the Lord, without apology, declares:

> I will rouse your sons, O Zion, against your sons, O Yavan. (Zechariah 9:13)

In this passage, Israel is seen fighting against Ionia, or Yavan, not the European Union.

In several Bible versions, the word "Yavan" is translated to mean "Greece" but Ionia/Yavan was simply a province that was located on the west coast of what is today, Turkey. This is crucial because the clear context of this battle is the return of Christ:

> Then Jehovah will appear over them. (Zechariah 9:14)

The war with Islam is not simply a prelude to another invasion by a European antichrist as is commonly taught; it is about the appearance of Christ Himself, in person, to fight Turkey. He will also fight Egypt (Isaiah 19) to rescue the remnants of the Copts who survive the impending massacre during Egypt's coming civil war.

Turkey (Iron) will take over the weakened clay nations of Egypt, Sudan/Somalia, Tunisia and Libya (Daniel 11:42-43), which recently opted for Sharia rule over western secularism or democracy. This is exactly what we stated long ago. We will also see the Azerbaijanis, Uzbeks and the Turkmens joining Turkey's Islamist model and pledging allegiance to the New Ottomans.[2]

A contest between the saber-rattling Iran (the Bear) and the fast-moving, calm, cool and collected Turkey (the Leopard) will ensue. Turkey will emerge as politically victorious in the region, with an accepted Islamist model; the West will accept it as the mini-superpower in the Mediterranean region.

Iraq will weaken as a result of America's exit and will be devoured by Iran. By this, Turkey will control the Suez Canal and the Bosporus Strait, while Iran will continue to control the Strait of Hormuz. This will undermine the US naval hegemony in the region, which will eventually use its military armada alongside other allied European nations including Greece, Spain and Italy in a show-down with Turkey.

Eventually, the West will enter an era like that of the late 1930s, when Neville Chamberlain famously declared there would be, "Peace in Our Time". Thus we will see the fulfillment of Scripture:

> While people are saying, "There is peace and security," destruction will come...(1 Thessalonians 5:3)

At this point, the West will finally awaken to the fact that secular (moderate Islam) and Fundamentalist (radical Islam), are two faces of the same coin. They will see that there is no real difference between the likes of CAIR and Hamas.

The good news—unlike that which modern prophecy buffs have taught—is the United States will continue to be the strongest military power that will stand against Turkey in the end. The US fits the profile of "the mightiest fortresses" (Daniel 11:39) which will eventually destroy this Islamic alliance:

> I am going to bring foreigners against you...They will bring you down to the pit, and you will die a violent death in the heart of the seas. (Ezekiel 28:7-8).

I believe the United States, alongside other allies, will wake up in the end, despite the rampant corruption and wickedness that has infected its head today. Christians must stop giving heed to fatalists who warn of the impending doom of America. America's citizens should fulfill their biblically-mandated duty to their nation and recognize that Satan's kingdom is the one that is doomed.

Neither America nor Europe is present in that prophetic model. I don't see Europeans directly threatening Israel but I *do* find Turkey parking its naval fleet on the Mediterranean as a direct threat to Israel. I saw Turkey's Recep Tayyip Erdoğan—hailed as a hero throughout the Muslim world—angrily walk out on Israel's President, Shimon Peres at Davos in 2009.[3] This incident helped turn the tide of Turkey-Israel relations sour since that time.[4]

Yet, it was Turkey's Prime Minister Erdoğan who brokered a deal ordering Hamas to release Gilad Shalit—something the US, the EU and the UN all failed to do.[5] As France's Sarkozy put it, Erdoğan emerged as the perfect peace broker. At some point, Erdoğan will even have Hamas recognize Israel during this Hudna (a tactical cease-fire in the Islamic world).

The Islamists are changing "set times and set laws" (Daniel 7:25) by introducing Sharia law. The Gog of Turkey, PM Erdoğan, succeeded for years in establishing himself permanently by concocting the Ergenekon Conspiracy, an alleged plot to overthrow the government through an elaborate network of retired military officers and other high ranking officials.[6] Erdoğan does "not honor the desire of women" (Daniel 11:37), prohibiting them entry into the government, and promotes the wearing of the Hijab.

No European leader is setting his eyes on Jerusalem; Erdoğan is the one who declared during his speech to Arab leaders at a summit in Libya that, "Jerusalem is the apple of the eye of each and every Muslim."[7] No French, Italian or German European Union leader has made any such proclamations. As we predicted in *God's War on Terror*, Turkey failed entry into the European Union. Remember, the beast is the body of a Leopard (Revelation 13:2). It is Greco-Roman, not European, with its feet being that of a Bear (Iran) and its mouth that of a Lion (Babylonia).

The Babylon of the End-Times is not Iraq, which quickly began the process of being annexed by Iran shortly after US troops were pulled out in December of 2011. Most modern prophecy buffs predicted the revival of Iraq's Babylon by Saddam Hussein. Such predictions are in the dustbin of history. They failed to examine Scripture closely and subsequently, they isolated verses, which invariably take those excerpts out of their original context. The Bible in End-Times prophecy never mentions any of the ancient cities of Babylon. In every Bible verse where a location within this predicted Babylon is mentioned, the location or city is in Arabia, not Iraq (Isaiah 21, Jeremiah 49). It is Kedar, Dumah, and Arabia; there is no mention of Babel, Sumer, Accad, Erech, and Calneh in any of these verses. Arabia's Islam is the mouthpiece (mouth of a lion) that rules and rides this beast. It is the harlot from the desert (Revelation 17:3) that sits on many waters and is the "desert of the sea" (Isaiah 21), which John saw. Christ proclaimed that Pergamum will be where the seat of the antichrist sits (Revelation 2:12-13), not Rome. The future seat of Satan, according to Revelation, is in modern day Turkey. Pergamum is on the sides of the northern lands (Asia Minor/Turkey).

Although there are not many popular prophecy buffs who have been sharing my interpretations over the last several decades, I am in good company. Not only are we already seeing it come to fruition but many scholars of the past—Hilaire

Belloc, Bishop Fulton Sheen, Gregory Palamus of Thessalonica, Vernon Richards, Sir Robert Anderson, Cyril of Jerusalem, Sophronius the Patriarch of Jerusalem (560-638), Maximus The Confessor (580-662), John of Damascus (676-749), Eulogius of Cordova, Paul Alvarus, the Martyrs of Cordova, John Calvin and Jonathan Edwards the great American Revivalist—also saw Islam playing a major, End-Times role. These and many others simply focused on the literal proclamations in the Bible. Those who focus on Europe have twisted themselves into allegorical knots so they could reach conclusions they wanted to reach.

UNDOING THE RUSSIAN MYTH

Consideration must be given to the possibility that the fall of the Soviet Union is what sparked the Islamic Revolution amongst Sunni nations. It's hard to argue that the rise of Islam didn't coincide with the fall of Soviet communism; it did. The West viewed this as a victory because it eliminated its arch enemy—the Soviet Union.

However, like medicinal treatments, military victories are rarely without side effects. The breakup of the Soviet Union allowed for Independent states but it also created an opportunity for Islamists within those states. The Commonwealth of Independent States (CIS) was created in 1991 and consisted of Russia and 10 other Republics that had been part of the Soviet Union. Georgia joined later, bringing the number to 12.[8] Yes, it's true that states formerly under the thumb of a repressive Communist regime were now free to govern themselves but what shouldn't be lost on anyone is the fact that large Muslim populations dominate several of these former Soviet satellite countries.

The United States helped the Taliban defeat the Soviets in Afghanistan in the 1980s. At the time, it was hailed as an enormous victory because Soviet-style communism had been viewed as the greatest threat to freedom in the world. The Soviet defeat in Afghanistan ultimately played a key role in the fall of the Soviet Union itself.

CIS member states that broke from the Soviets were granted sovereignty in the group's charter.[9] Many of those countries were located to the north of Afghanistan and to the south of Russia. Countries in this cluster are made up of significant Muslim majorities. They include Kazakstan, Kyrgystan, Tajikstan, Uzbekistan, and Turkmenistan. Interestingly, the CIS countries to the west of this cluster, with the exception of Azerbaijan, are mostly Christian. They include Belarus, Ukraine, Moldova, Georgia, and Armenia.

If one is inclined to believe that the End-Times are not that far off and that Russia is to be the home of the antichrist, would it not have made more sense for the Soviets to win in Afghanistan while maintaining control of these Muslim-dominated satellite countries? Conversely, if the antichrist is going to rise in an Islamic country, wouldn't Russia's loss of Muslim lands increase the odds?

YUGOSLAVIA AND KOSOVO

Although the country formerly known as Yugoslavia was not under the control of the Soviet Union in the years prior to 1991, it closely mirrored the communist super power's model, albeit in a more liberal fashion.[10] It was a socialist country made up of six socialist republics—Bosnia and Herzegovina, Croatia, Macedonia, Montenegro, Serbia (Kosovo and Vojvodina), and Slovenia.[11]

Coincidentally or not, Yugoslavia and the Soviet Union each began to dissolve into separate, independent states in the same year. Friction between Yugoslavia's republics had been gradually building since the death of Marshal Tito in 1980; he had been the country's leader for decades prior and was a one-time ally of Joseph Stalin. Like Russia, the country formerly known as Yugoslavia had significantly weakened since; its territories do not have the solidarity or the leadership that would form a powerful nation.

According to statistics provided by Ontario Consultants on Religious Tolerance, the Kosovo region within the borders of what was Yugoslavia has the highest Muslim population per capita at 81%.[12] The *BBC* puts that number at 90%.[13] This is also the very same region that made the international news headlines in 1999 when NATO and the United States, under the Clinton administration, launched attacks against the Serbs, who had invaded Kosovo in response to Kosovo's desire for independence.

Prior to the turn of the 21st Century, Yugoslavia was a place of great sectarian and religious strife. War had become almost commonplace. This strife seemed to culminate with the NATO action against Yugoslavia's communist leader Slobodan Milošević in 1999; he had done his part to exacerbate tensions and ultimately, the conditions for war. The United States and NATO ultimately prevailed; Kosovo was returned to its Muslim majority, the Kosovo-Albanians.[14]

While the Muslim population of Kosovo was significant in size, it wasn't regarded as being all that devout. Many of the region's Muslims were quite secular at the end of the twentieth century. In the ensuing years, however, concerns began growing that a radical Islamic element was incubating and putting down its roots.

A consequence of NATO's involvement in the region would come years later, in 2008, with Kosovo's independence. The *New York Times* reported then that Russia objected, but to no avail.[15] Three years later, *Russia Today* reported that Kosovo was becoming fertile ground for Islamic extremism. In particular, the concern was over a liberally practiced version of Islam being supplanted by a Wahhabist version.[16]

Regardless of the degree to which Kosovo's majority Muslim population practiced the religion *then*, Islamic fundamentalism's rise in Europe and the Middle East should be the primary concern *now*. Islamic fundamentalists who desire another Western outpost see an opportunity in Kosovo. For that matter, the other remaining republics—except for Croatia and Slovenia—have significant, if not majority, Muslim populations.

Muslim leaders in separate countries across the Middle East began to coalesce two decades after Yugoslavia began to fracture. Those Middle Eastern countries shared one common goal—a Caliphate. How can Russia, a country that has lost power and the control of several nations, give rise to the antichrist? Would it not make more sense for Islamic nations that are gaining power while unifying in furtherance of a common goal, to play such a role?

CHECHNYA

Another Islamic region that saw an opportunity upon which to capitalize at the end of the cold war was Chechnya, which sits just to the northeast of CIS member state, Georgia. Chechnya attempted to declare its independence from Russia in 1991 and though still a Republic of Russia, it was also home to a nearly unmatched level of Islamic extremism and barbarism that began to escalate with the fall of the Soviet Union.

Chechnya was one region that Russia simply was not willing to relinquish. In hindsight, the Chechen rebels' propensity for violent terrorism almost certainly played a role in that decision. Russia sent troops to Chechnya in 1994 to quash the revolution and war ensued.[17] The willingness of Chechen rebels to target civilians on several occasions revealed the face of evil to those who were willing to admit that's what they were seeing. The Chechen rebels even attempted to use JBTW to justify their own terrorist tactics.

Consider the despicable act of taking hostages inside a hospital. In 1995, that's exactly what the rebels, led by Shamil Basayev did in Budyonnovsk. On the way there, the rebels shot pedestrians in the streets and "round(ed) up hostages by the truckload," according to the *New York Times.*[18]

When confronted about engaging in the horrendous act of killing healthy civilians before setting up shop in a place where he could execute injured ones, Basayev actually attempted to justify his actions by blaming others:

> Mr. Basayev said at the news conference that he had not planned to attack the city. He and his comrades were on their way to Moscow, he said, but a greedy police officer demanded a bribe far larger than they could afford to let them pass. That started the shooting.[19]

In other words, the murder of innocent civilians who had absolutely no connection to Basayev's grievances was the fault of someone other than Basayev. That's assuming that the terrorist's account was correct, which elevates a despicable terrorist to a level much higher than he deserves. Murdering innocent civilians tends to harm credibility.

In 2002, between 40-50 Chechen, Muslim rebels raided a Moscow theater and took hundreds of hostages. The demands were basic but unrealistic. All Russian troops had to be withdrawn from Chechnya. Ironically, the tactics seemed to validate a Russian presence in Chechnya in the first place.

Once again, the actions of the militants did more to justify Russia's insistence that Chechnya not be handed over than to validate their cause. The terrorists used JBTW in an attempt to communicate that they were representing an oppressed people. In reality, they were terrorizing innocent people to push an Islamic agenda.

During the hostage crisis, a video message on behalf of the terrorists, which consisted of a burqa-clad woman speaker, was aired on *Al Jazeera.* Here is some of what she said:

> "Every nation has the right to their fate. Russia has taken away this right from the Chechens and today we want to reclaim these rights, which Allah has given us (in the same way he has given it to other nations). Allah has given us the right of freedom and the right to choose our destiny. And the Russian

occupiers have flooded our land with our children's blood. And we have longed for a just solution."[20]

The crisis ended in horror when Russian troops stormed the theater after a chemical substance was piped into the ventilation system. The majority of the terrorists were killed. Unfortunately, so were more than 100 hostages.

Basayev took credit for the terrorist attack.[21]

Perhaps the most despicably heinous operation that Shamil Basayev took credit for was in Beslan, Russia two years later. If a case were to be made that the antichrist would be a Muslim, it could begin with an account of the school massacre at Beslan.

As the school year in the meager town was being ushered in on September 1, 2004 several gunmen stormed an elementary school. The date was important because it represented the beginning of the new school year, a time of celebration, when parents would join their first grade children for their very first day of school. Children and adults were rounded up and taken hostage in the gymnasium by Basayev's thugs, who had stormed the building moments earlier after arriving in trucks. For three days, innocents were held captive and terrorized; explosives were connected to the gym's basketball hoop. Adults were murdered in front of young children.

The days were hot and the hostages were not permitted to use the restrooms or drink water. Captives were forced to drink urine; mothers were given the option of taking their younger children to safety while leaving older children behind—or staying.[22]

Ultimately, the siege ended after three days. With tensions high and parents eager to help storm the school, a loud explosion rocked the gymnasium; survivors insisted that at least one of the bombs tied to the basketball hoop had exploded.[23]

Along with about the same number of adults, more than 150 children were murdered at Beslan, many as they attempted to run for freedom. Innocent children were murdered in the name of liberty; it was the most twisted and grotesque form of JBTW that could be uttered.

One of the survivors had this to say about the Chechen terrorists:

"They are not human. And there is no place for them on this earth."[24]

Fortunately, the mastermind responsible for all of this carnage, Shamil Basayev, ultimately met his end in 2006. Nearly two years after the massacre at

Beslan, Basayev was in a truck carrying more than 200 pounds of dynamite when it exploded in Ingushetia, which borders Chechnya to the west. There wasn't much left of him and sane people cheered.[25]

Though Russian Prime Minister Vladimir Putin is considered an adversary of the West, he reportedly called Basayev's death, "deserved retribution." It was on this that Russia and the United States could agree.[26]

Three years later, Russia ended its war with Chechnya after securing an ally in the seat of power there. Ramzan Kadyrov, the president of Chechnya, was pro-Kremlin. He was also the son of a Chechen religious leader. The Kadyrovs pledged their allegiance to Russia after Putin's forces showed their superiority.[27] Though a Muslim, Kadyrov had the backing of a nation that had quashed Chechnya's rebellion. Chechnya's new president could either bask in the riches afforded him by Moscow and control his country or align with the Muslim rebels and be replaced. He chose self-preservation.

As the years go on, the narrative of Chechen rebels is likely to mirror that of Iranians who protested the Shah in the late 1970s, as well as the voices of the 'Arab Spring' who embraced the fall of tyrants. Yes, The Shah, Ali Mubarak, Gadhafi, etc. were oppressive but the vacuum left by their removal was filled by something far worse than what they wrought.

The facts are these. While Kadyrov admittedly does the bidding of the Russians, hospital patients, theater attendees, and school children are not being terrorized by the likes of Shamil Basayev. Once barbaric Chechen rebels begin winning the political argument that Kadyrov is the problem, Chechen barbarism is sure to resurface.

Nonetheless, the story of Russia's victory relative to Chechnya was not about imperialism; it was about stemming the tide of Islamism and it was defensive, not offensive, in nature.

During the cold war between the West and the Soviet Union, each side was despised by the other. Americans were taught that the Soviets wanted to conquer the world; they had so much more land under the U.S.S.R. banner than did the United States. School children were shown maps at the time that demonstrated as much. It was intimidating. No doubt, this premise is partially what led the Americans to support the Taliban's effort to defeat the Soviets in Afghanistan. To the West, Communism was the primary threat; Islam wasn't on the radar, save for random terrorist attacks.

In hindsight, at least to some degree, the Soviets were fighting Islamism, which was something westerners didn't really understand until September 11, 2001.

As corrupt as the Soviet government was (it's a point conceded), the fact remains that as the West was fighting the Soviets, the Soviets were fighting Islamists who knew exactly how to exploit America's ignorance to their advantage.

JBTW can take many, many forms.

WHAT ABOUT CHINA?

Other prophecy teachers say that China is the greatest threat. Yet, China is quite isolated by the Himalayas, Siberia, deserts, and the Pacific Ocean. Among its biggest challenges is keeping the country together; it depends solely on *exports*. Japan is stronger than what it gets credit for and has a very powerful air force. China's average income is $1000 annually; it's like Nigeria. Their citizens are hostages, economically. A withdrawal of money would cause China to starve.

Some argue that China is the King of the East, since it can seemingly provide the 200 million-man army predicted in the Bible. This conclusion is based on one verse:

> Then the sixth angel poured out his bowl on the great river Euphrates, and its water was dried up, so that the way of the kings from the east might be prepared. (Revelation 16:12)

This interpretation, of course, isolates the text without exploring the rest of Scripture regarding literal nations from the east. In all of Scripture, not a single passage connects "Kings from the East" with China. The real connection is rarely considered.

> Now after Jesus was born in Bethlehem of Judea in the days of Herod the king, behold, there came wise men from the east to Jerusalem," (Matthew 2:1)

We know that these wealthy kings of the east were from the regions of Babylonia and Persia. Why not consider this option? Westerners argue that the reason the Kings of the East in Revelation come from China is the staggering number of soldiers—a 200-million-man army. Cannot Islam easily muster this total when factoring in Iraq, Iran, Afghanistan and Indonesia, east of the Euphrates with several kings? Why do so many apply Revelation's prophecies to a future attack on Israel by Russia or China? The conquest of Christian nations by Islamic warriors over the past 1,400 years was recognized as a literal fulfillment of Bible prophecies by the great majority of Biblical commentators in previous centuries, including Martin Luther and Sir Isaac Newton.

Many correctly suggested that the 200-million warriors described in Revelation 9:16 were figurative and inclusive of all Islamic warriors and sympathizers throughout the centuries-long war against non-Islamic territories. Others surmise that "Sinim" refers to China because it refers to those people who live in the eastern most part of the known world.

> Surely these shall come from afar; Look! Those from the north and the west,
> And these from the land of Sinim. (Isaiah 49:12)

That passage does not refer to any wars, punishments, or tribulation against that country; it does seem to point to the return of the Jewish people from that location to Israel. This is not evidence that China is destroyed. If Sinim is indeed China, then the Chinese Jews will have a phenomenal homecoming party!

UYGHURS

While there has been a long and bloody history of wars between the Turks and the Russians, there has also been a Turkish influence in China. That influence is manifested in a Muslim people known as the Uyghurs, which have a presence in China's Xinjiang province in the northwestern part of the country. Interestingly, that region of China borders countries that were part of the CIS.

In particular, Kazakstan, Kyrgystan, and Tajikstan (each borders China) are all home to the Turkish-influenced Uyghurs. Ironically, there is a Uyghur presence in Afghanistan as well.[28] Muslim Uyghurs that were primarily known as being Muslim in name Only (MINO) had a greater opportunity to be exposed to radicalization as a direct result of former Soviet satellite countries that bordered China, declaring independence. In fact, the rise of Islamic terror attacks in China seemed to coincide with the fall of the Soviet Union.

In particular, the Council on Foreign Relations (CFR) reported that Uyghurs were responsible for 200 terrorist attacks between 1990 and 2001 in China. The Uyghurs, whose presence predominates in China's northwestern province of Xinjiang, refer to the region as "Eastern Turkestan" and have historical ties to Turkey. In the CFR report, Chien-peng Chung makes some very specific charges about the Uyghurs' ties to Islamic fundamentalism:

The (Chinese) government considers these activists part of a network of inter-national Islamic terror, with funding from the Middle East, training in Pakistan, and combat experience in Chechnya and Afghanistan.[29]

As for the motivation behind the Uyghurs' increase in Islamic-inspired attacks, Chung clearly ties it to the breakup of the Soviet Union:

The latest wave of Uighur separatism has been inspired not by Osama bin Laden but by the unraveling of the Soviet Union, as militants seek to emulate the independence gained by some Muslim communities in Central Asia.[30]

So, perhaps those who insist that Sinim represents China in the End-Times might be interested in finding common ground with us. Xinjiang is both part of China and predominantly Muslim. If we concede that a *portion* of China might be included in Sinim, might those who suggest *all* of China is Sinim concede that Islamic territories to China's west might be included as well?[31]

FOOTNOTES

1. The Expository Files, *What Nostradamus Said About Adolf Hister...that's right, Hister.* http://www.bible.ca/ef/topical-what-nostradamus-said-about-adolf-hister-...thats-right-hister.htm

2. Jewish Voice Today, Jewish Voice Ministries Int's, *2012 and the Turkey Connection,* by Walid Shoebat. http://content.yudu.com/Library/A1uzmn/JewishVoiceToday maga/resources/13.htm

3. Video with English translation, *Turkish PM Erdogan Slams Shimon Peres For Israeli Killings And Walks Off Stage.* http://www.youtube.com/watch?v=0rbQsHkVQ_4

4. BBC News, Video with English translation, *Turkish PM storms off in Gaza row.* http://news.bbc.co.uk/2/hi/business/davos/7859417.stm

5. Y net News.com, *Peres lauds Erdogan efforts on Shalit,* by Omri Efraim. http://www.ynetnews.com/articles/0,7340,L-4134596,00.html

6. BBC News, *'Deep state plot' grips Turkey,* by Orhan Pamuk. http://news.bbc.co.uk/2/hi/europe/7225889.stm

7. Haaretz, *Amr Moussa: Arabs must prepare alternatives to failing peace process,* by Avi Issacharoff and Reuters. http://www.haaretz.com/news/amr-moussa-arabs-must-prepare-alternatives-to-failing-peace-process-1.265380

8. Encyclopedia Britannica, *Commonwealth of Independent States (CIS)*. http://www.britannica.com/EBchecked/topic/128945/Commonwealth-of-Independent-States-CIS

9. http://untreaty.un.org/unts/120001_144071/6/8/00004863.pdf

10. BBC, *Yugoslavia: 1918–2003,* by Tim Judah. http://www.bbc.co.uk/history/worldwars/wwone/yugoslavia_01.shtml

11. About.com Geography, *New Countries of the World, The 34 New Countries Created Since 1990,* by Matt Rosenberg. http://geography.about.com/cs/countries/a/newcountries.htm

12. Religious Tolerance, Religious aspects of the Yugoslavia – Kosovo conflict, by B.A. Robinson. http://www.religioustolerance.org/war_koso.htm

13. BBC News, *Muslims in Europe: Country guide.* http://news.bbc.co.uk/2/hi/europe/4385768.stm

14. History of Kosovo and Metohija, *The history of Yugoslavia.* http://www.kosovo.net/serhist2.html

15. The New York Times, *Kosovo Declaares Its Independence From Serbia,* by Daniel Bilefsky. http://www.nytimes.com/2008/02/18/world/europe/18kosovo.html?pagewanted=all&_r=1&

16. RT.com, *Fears radical Islam may take hold in Kosovo.* http://rt.com/news/radical-islam-kosovo-poverty/

17. BBC News, *Timeline: Chechnya.* http://news.bbc.co.uk/2/hi/europe/country_profiles/2357267.stm

18. The New York Times, *Chechen Rebels Said to Kill Hostages at Russian Hospital,* by Michael Specter. http://www.nytimes.com/1995/06/16/world/chechen-rebels-said-to-kill-hostages-at-russian-hospital.html?pagewanted=print&src=pm

19. Ibid

20. CNN World, *Gunmen release chilling video.* http://articles.cnn.com/2002-10-24/world/moscow.siege.video_1_gunmen-release-chechens-russian-authorities?_s=PM:WORLD

21. BBC News, *Chechen warlord claims theatre attack.* http://news.bbc.co.uk/2/hi/europe/2388857.stm

22. CBS News, Video, *New Video of Beslan School Terror,* by Rebecca Leung. http://www.cbsnews.com/stories/2005/01/20/48hours/main668127.shtml

23. The Guardian, *When hell came calling at Beslan's School No. 1,* Nick Paton Walsh and Peter Beaumont. http://www.guardian.co.uk/world/2004/sep/05/russia.chechnya

24. CBS News, Video, *New Video of Beslan School Terror,* by Rebecca Leung. http://www.cbsnews.com/stories/2005/01/20/48hours/main668127.shtml

25. http://www.foxnews.com/story/0,2933,202753,00.html

26. Ibid

27. BBC News, *Russia 'ends Chechnya operation'.* http://news.bbc.co.uk/2/hi/europe/8001495.stm

28. Joshua Project, *People in Country Profile.* http://www.joshuaproject.net/people-profile.php?peo3=15755&rog3=TU

29. Foreign Affairs, *China's "War on Terror": September 11 and Uighur Separatism,* by Chien-peng Chung. http://www.foreignaffairs.com/articles/58030/chien-peng-chung/chinas-war-on-terror-september-11-and-uighur-separatism

30. Ibid

31. World Atlas, *Asia.* http://www.worldatlas.com/webimage/countrys/as.htm

CHAPTER
20

THEO-GEO POLITICS

PROJECTION ARTISTS

*I*n addition to being full of JBTW artists, the Muslim world certainly has its share of projection artists as well. *Projection* is a defense mechanism in which an individual attributes his own weaknesses, desires, etc. onto others. Much of what the Muslim world accuses infidels of doing falls into this category; it allows one to take his own guilt and place it onto others, which makes hate of others much easier. What makes such tactics effective is that the accuser is so intently familiar with his own characteristics that he can enunciate them with near perfection. When those characteristics are subsequently expressed, yet mis-applied, the lie about who possesses those characteristics takes hold. This principle is central to JBTW.

It's the perfect argument against adopting a 'words will never hurt me' mindset.

Of course, in the Middle East, the worst thing to be is either a Jew or a woman. These are evil since hell is filled with them (remember Rauf's quote). Every evil is sanctioned in the Muslim world. Adultery is cloaked in *Muta* and *Misyar*. Rape is cloaked in the right to own concubines. Murder is cloaked in Jihad against the collaborators and the Zionist enemy that corrupted God's Word, the Bible.

When I first read the words of Isaiah, I wept. The proclamations he and other Jewish prophets made simply boggled my mind and even busted all the myths that had consumed my mind and soul.

I remember the first time I visited the Shrine of the Book at the Israel Museum during my teenage years; I was fascinated to see the oldest manuscript of the Book of Isaiah.

Directly beneath the dome is an imposing showcase (shaped like a wooden Torah rod) containing a replica of the Great Isaiah Scroll (written circa 100 BC).

This find was extremely important, as it is 1,000 years older than the oldest biblical manuscript available before. From that moment on I was always fascinated with archeology and constantly asked questions about these finds but the most common answer from my Muslim family, friends and theologians was rooted in projection and lies. They would tell me, "The true Jewish book is lost and the current one has been corrupted."

In fact, Islam teaches that the Mahdi…

> "…will guide the people to a mountain in Syria from which he will bring out the volumes of the [true] Torah [Jewish Tannach] to refute the Jews."

This is classic *projection*. All throughout the Muslim world, it is accepted as fact that the Jewish holy books have been corrupted and that the originals have been lost. The first thing I get when I discuss the Good Book with Muslims is something like, "Hasn't the Bible been corrupted by the Jews?" Hundreds of thousands of websites in Arabic discuss how the Jews have corrupted the Bible.

There is a reason this technique has been so effective. It is the Muslims who have corrupted the Bible and because that is so, accusations of such a thing being levied at the Jews by Muslims takes hold because it comes with so much detail— mis-applied, projectionist detail.

CRITICAL THINKING

Having socialized with so many Jews over the years, I became obsessed with critical thinking. I learned how to answer questions with questions—the same questions that haunted my own soul. One such experience occurred as I began reading the prophets. It hit me. Of all the nations on earth, excluding Israel, I could not name one that had won two wars in only six days. Israel's first was when they established the Jewish state during the time of Joshua (1400 B.C.) and the second when they returned again and recaptured Judea during the Six Day War in June of 1967. My dhimmi mother had told me all about it. During the battle for Jericho in Joshua's time, as documented in the Good Book…

> …and the second day they marched around the city once, and returned into the camp. So they did six days. (Joshua 6:14)

It was on the dawn of the seventh day before the day began that…

...they rose early about the dawning of the day, and marched around the city in the same manner seven times. (Joshua 6:15)

Joshua had a Six Day War.

No one can name any literal references in the Bible, to a nation God destroys in the end-times, that is not currently Muslim. Why are all these nations—discussed by the ancient Jewish prophets—part of today's Muslim world?

Why is the Muslim world so confident that it can destroy Israel after having failed several times in the past? We were so confident during the War of Independence in1948, the Six ay War of 1967, and the Yom Kippur War of 1973. Each and every time we built such confidence, we simply got defeated in the end. While winning or losing battles does not prove the existence of any god, the question that no one can answer is:

Why is it that a Jewish prophet named Amos predicted that it would be impossible to uproot Israel even though the Arab world tried several times already?

Amos stated:

And I will plant them upon their land, and they shall no more be pulled up out of their land which I have given them, says the LORD thy G-d. (Amos 9:15)

Western documentaries consistently portray the Bible as simply a record of historic events that pertain to the Jewish people and nothing more. That prompts a line of questioning for those willing to pursue it. If, as Amos says, "they shall no more be pulled up," how can this be explained in an historical context, especially since Israel *has* been "pulled up" by the Romans and the Babylonians? How is it that this proclamation says this is impossible unless it pertains to our time?

This Jewish Good Book was creating headaches for me. My wife's Catholic sisters thought I was going crazy. They warned me not to read from the book, that it was the job of a priest to interpret Scriptures. Maricela, Maria's sister, thought I should not be asking these questions but I was not dissuaded; the burn was too intense.

The Good Book predicted another war, which includes the very nations Islam is taking over today. This battle will involve...

...Cush (Sudan/Ethiopia/Somalia) and Put (Libya), Lydia (Turkey) and all Arabia...along with Egypt. (Ezekiel 30:5-6)

How did the Jewish Good Book predict the areas where the 'Arab Spring' of 2011 would be home to a Muslim Winter?

During an appearance on *Fox News* with David Asman, I maintained that the Egyptian Revolution was an Islamic revolution more than it was a Democratic one. Asman stood with the Egyptian fellow who was being interviewed opposite me; I was written off as a person who knows little about the Muslim world. While the Muslim world can proudly quote their Qur'an on any television network without consequence, especially from the left, the Jews and the West are looked upon as fools if they dare give a verse from their holy writ on secular television.

CHRISTIAN CHURCH INDUSTRY

Jesus was not a moderate and JBTW is not reserved exclusively for Muslims. There is a Christian church industry in which the agenda has more to do with church growth than preaching the controversial truths demanded of Scripture. In many cases, this affliction known as *truth avoidance* involves the demonization and marginalization of Israel; it is a corruption of Scripture.

While the Bible makes proclamations about Babylon, in every biblical End-Time prediction regarding the destruction of Babylon, the Jewish Good Book never mentions any of the cities of ancient Babylon.

I entered the clueless Church industry and asked thousands to respond to the following fact:

> Every verse in the Bible where a location within this "predicted" Babylon is mentioned, is found in Arabia (Kedar, Dumah, Dedan), not in Iraq (ancient Babylon). In all these proclamations, we have no mention of any Babylonian city like Babel, Sumer, Accad, Erech, and Calneh.

Amazingly, in Isaiah 21, Jeremiah 49, and Isaiah 13 cities within Arabia are destroyed, not cities in Bablyon. It is this "desert of the sea" (Isaiah 21:1) that will be destroyed by Elam (Iran) in verse 2. Today, the enmity that Iran has for Saudi Arabia is greater than the enmity it has for Israel. The saber-rattling Iran, coupled with the calm, cool, collected and fast moving Turkey (Ezekiel 38, Zechariah 9) will meet their end when they invade Jerusalem (Zechariah 12, 14).

It was from the Good Book that I predicted years ago that Turkey would emerge as politically victorious in the region, with an accepted Islamist model, and this will infect the Mediterranean region. It is from the same Good Book that we know that Iraq will weaken as a result of America's exit to simply be devoured by Iran. By this, Turkey will control the Suez Canal and the Bosporus Strait, while Iran controls the Strait of Hormuz. This will undermine the US naval hegemony in the region, which will eventually use its military armada alongside other allied European nations including Greece, Spain and Italy in a showdown with Turkey.

Even Lebanon—where Hezbollah lobs rockets at Israel—will be doomed:

Lebanon will fall before the Mighty One. (Isaiah 10:34)

In Egypt, we will have a civil war. (Isaiah 19)

I even began to see that the Psalms of David are not simply poetic recitations. Poetic style was the focus of the Qur'an but the Bible had details—tons of it. In Psalm 83:5-8 we have an alliance of nations coming against Israel:

They form an alliance against you—the tents of Edom and the Ishmaelites, of Moab and the Hagrites, Gebal, Ammon and Amalek, Philistia, with the people of Tyre. Even Assyria has joined them to lend strength to the descendants of Lot. (Psalm 83:5-8)

When I looked at the multiple battles Israel fought against Muslim countries from 1948 until today—some of which I witnessed first-hand—Israel always came out on top but what source other than the Bible can name such an alliance coming against Israel?

These nations will be judged specifically based on their treatment of the Jewish people:

I will enter into judgment against them concerning my inheritance, my people Israel. For they scattered my people among the nations and divided up my land. (Joel 3:2)

How could the Jewish prophets perfectly guess that Israel would be sliced into two states? Even now, "Palestine" is divided between the West Bank, run by the P.A. (Palestinian Authority) and the Hamastan of Gaza.

In fact, Palestine refers to a coastal section of land in the area of today's Gaza Strip that was inhabited by the ancient Philistines who were not native to Israel or the region. How could the Bible state "Philistia" (Gaza) in its prophecies unless the prophets were either perfect guessers or vessels for G-d's word?

How did the Jewish Good Book perfectly predict all of these plans to destroy Israel thousands of years in advance? Why was it that whatever Allah loved, the G-d of Israel hated, and whatever the G-d of Israel loved, Allah hated? Why are the Jewish people at the top of both lists?

I began to ask a series of questions: Was the Jewish Good Book corrupted? If so, who really corrupted it?

This one is easily answered when factoring in the projection defense mechanism we discussed earlier. Those who corrupted the Jewish Good Book were the very ones who accuse it of having been corrupted by others. If one thinks wisely, it's obvious that Islam took selected portions of the Jewish Good Book and after twsting it, laced it with deadly cyanide. The result was a concoction called the Qur'an, which is the corruption of the Jewish Good Book.

I finally began to see. It is the corruptors who accuse the virtuous of corruption, the murderers who accuse the innocent of murder, the haters who accuse the righteous of hate, the warmongers who accuse the peaceful of war, and the lovers of death who accuse those who love life of human right violations. It is the cowards who promote instant death that are given the title of the brave. Murderers are martyrs, their funerals are weddings, and their victims are criminals unworthy of a funeral. It's a fool's circle. Their heaven is debauchery and their earth is a hell devoid of even the most innocent of music or wedding dances. Everything is turned upside down. They can't see any of this until they are permitted to think— deeply—and exchange their holy cloak, these phony religious cellophane wrappings, with the fruit of love and longsuffering, in order to offer life as a living sacrifies, not a dead one. Isaiah opened my eyes:

> "Woe to those who call evil good and good evil; who put darkness for light, and light for darkness; who put bitter for sweet, and sweet for bitter!" (Isaiah 5:20)

I recall years ago when I ran into one Shalom Eliahu, a frail old Jewish man; we crossed paths when I went to watch the giant menorah erected on mainstreet in downtown Walnut Creek, California. As we talked, Shalom thought I was meshuganeh (crazy) to think that Turkey would one day invade Israel. He laughed out loud at the notion. While at a gathering years later, Shalom excitedly approached me. The now infamous flotilla had just come to Gaza from Turkey in 2010 and the Turks looked like the new, emergent enemy of the Jews (after Iran).[1]

Years after that first meeting, Shalom was a total believer. He asked me, "How in the world did you know about Turkey becoming an enemy of Israel? I remember when I laughed you off years ago." I instantly said, "I stole the information from your ancestors; they had no copyright to the old manuscript we call the Bible."

If there is a difference between JBTW in the Islamic world and JBTW in the Christian world, it may just be that the former does so with the intent of deceiving others while the latter does so with the intent of deceiving itself.

FOOTNOTES

1. The Guardian, *Israel attacks Gaza flotilla – live coverage,* posted by Adam Gabbatt

CHAPTER
21

ANTICHRIST:
ISLAMIC OR EUROPEAN?

DECEIT AS A KEY COMPONENT

Prophecy students in the West have forgotten that Muslim nations play the key role in End-Times. In Daniel 8:25, The Bible states that the Antichrist uses false peace and "deceit" to "destroy many".

The element of deception is critical; western media continues to repeat the mantra that "Islam is a peaceful religion." Islamists are ahead of the game. Egypt's Ikhwan knows that if they appear as the fundamentalists they are, the jig will be up and the American tiger will be roused. They learned from Iran's saber-rattling and al-Qaeda's explosive tactics. They saw the bombing at Tora Bora. They discovered that the secret to incapacitating the West, to get it to lower its defenses, is to portray a moderate Muslim Brotherhood. By peace, they are deceiving many. The Turks watch the Brotherhood very closely and follow suit. The West, almost hypnotically, seems to respond with willful ignorance.

Westerners' lack of understanding relative to the Middle East is also reflected in its lack of understanding when it comes to Biblical prophecy. The Bible is a Middle Eastern book, centered on the Middle East, and written from a Middle Eastern perspective—not a Western one—and guided by the hand of God. Consequently, many ignored that the spirit of the antichrist denies the Father and Son (1 John 2:22) and is anti-Trinity. This would hardly fit the profile of the Catholic nations that praise the Father, the Son and the Holy Ghost. They forgot, it's an Arian Heresy; Muhammad was the greatest heretic in history who denied the Trinity.

The debate within prophecy circles about whether the beast of Revelation is Middle Eastern— involving Islamic nations—or European has become more spirited of late. A typical example of criticisms against the former interpretation by modern western prophecy teachers is the notion that an Islamic Antichrist is "impossible," "unbiblical," "unorthodox," "untraditional" and even "revisionist." One such proponent—David Reagan—said: "beware of Lone Ranger interpretations of prophecy that are not widely shared."[1]

Western prophecy teachers typically admonish anyone who disagrees with this view. "The traditional viewpoint has been that the Antichrist will be a European of Roman descent," they say. Implicit in this adamant insistence is a claim to the gift of interpretation that includes being able to specifically assert, with pinpoint accuracy, that Antichrist is Italian and that this is the Biblical-traditional-orthodox view. Are these modern western prophecy teachers correct? Is the Middle Eastern model an interpretation of "lone rangers" and Bible revisionists or are those who believe Antichrist will be Italian, the "lone rangers" and Biblical revisionists?

A FEW CHALLENGES

To shed some light on the magnitude of detailed evidence, challenges, and questions presented in my book, God's War on Terror, I decided to choose only three out of hundreds of challenges to many modern western prophecy teachers:

CHALLENGE NUMBER ONE

> *Identify which of the following are "lone rangers," "unorthodox," "revisionist," and "untraditional"? Martin Luther, John Calvin, John of Damascus, John Wesley, Jonathan Edwards, Hilaire Belloc, Gregory Palamus, Josiah Litch, Cyril of Jerusalem, Sophronius, Maximus the Confessor, Eulogius, Paul Alvarus, Sir Robert Anderson, Selnecker, Nigrinus, Chytraeus, Bullinger, Foxe, Napier, Pareus, John Cotton, Thomas Parker, Increase Mather, Cotton Mather, or George Stanley Faber?*

All of these high-caliber commentators believed that Islam will play a huge role in the coming Antichrist threat and while the church looks to the west, he will creep in unnoticed from the east.

I am not saying that these views are inspired or absolute but my challenge here is modeled after a style of questioning that Jesus used when He encountered the Pharisees who challenged His authority. Jesus brilliantly used John the Baptist as a reference. To use a chess allegory, it was checkmate. If they had said that John was no authority, either they would have been stoned or rejected; had they accepted John's authority, they would have to accept the truth (in the flesh).

Here are a few of the old school, Bible-affirming, Christian commentators who taught that Islam was one of the two legs in the Book of Daniel. They believed that both Islam and the Papacy were the prediction in Daniel, the Book of Revelation or both. (Calvin on Islam and Revelation by Francis Nigel Lee), They even believed that Islam was the forerunner to Antichrist. Were they all revisionists and Lone Rangers?

I might add to the list, Rev. Professor Dr. Francis Nigel Lee who sums up the traditional view in his excellent work, Islam in the Bible:

> "Then, those two legs in turn—from the seventh century onward—would degenerate respectively into the Papacy (which progressively took over the West) and Islam (which progressively took over the East." (p. 5)[2]

Seeing Islam predicted in the Bible is neither revisionism nor a private interpretation. The evidence supporting this view is more than substantial:

John Wesley (1841)—In his great work, Doctrine of Original Sin, Wesley commented on Daniel 2 that the iron teeth closely match Islam. (Works, 1841)

Hilaire Belloc (1938)—Amazingly, Belloc foresaw Islam's rise to threaten Christianity:

> "Will not perhaps the temporal power of Islam return... I cannot but believe that a main unexpected thing of the future is the return of Islam." 2 (Helaire Belloc, The Great Heresies, chapter 4, pg. 127-128)

Gregory Palamus of Thessalonica (1354)—Many modern, western prophecy teachers have rejected Islam as the one to behead the believers in Revelation 20:4, yet this interpretation is historically common. Gregory interpreted Jesus' declaration that...

> "The time will come, that whosoever kills you will think that he does God a service" (John 16:2) to be the Islamic persecution.

Josiah Litch (1840)—In his work, Fall of the Ottoman Roman Empire, Litch interpreted Revelation as the ushering in of Islam:

> "There is so general an agreement among Christians, especially protestant commentators, that the subject of this prediction is Mahommedism [Islam]."

He even described the magnitude of Islam's role as Antichrist to the extent of calling it the "general agreement among Christians, especially protestant commentators."

Cyril of Jerusalem (315-368 A.D.)—Western prophecy teachers who disregard Philip Goodman's excellent work, The Assyrian Connection, which asserts that Syria could produce Antichrist, or my explanation of Turkey's role, ignored many distinguished theologians and early Church fathers like Cyril of Jerusalem. In his Divine Institutes, and before the advent of Islam, Cyril believed that Antichrist would proceed forth from the region of ancient Syria, which today extends from Syria well into portions of Asia Minor (Turkey) 3 (Saint Cyril of Jerusalem, Divine Institutes 7:17 A.D. 307)

Sophronius, Patriarch of Jerusalem (560-638) and **Maximus the Confessor** (580-662)—Sophronius identified Islam with Antichrist and lived through Islam's invasion of Jerusalem. Maximus was also an important theologian and scholar of the early Church who helped defeat the Monothelite heresy and referred to the Muslim invasions as "announcing the advent of the Antichrist."

John of Damascus (676-749)—Another very important figure in the early church. In his famous book, Against Heresies, he likened Islam to the forerunner of Antichrist.

Eulogius, Paul Alvarus and the Martyrs of Cordova (9th century)—Believed Muhammad to be a false prophet and the precursor to the Antichrist

Martin Luther (1483–1546)—While many are aware that Luther (father of the Protestant Reformation) came to view the Roman Catholic Papacy as the spiritual seat of the Antichrist, few are aware that Luther believed that the Turks were the Kingdom of Antichrist:

> "The Pope is the spirit of antichrist, and the Turk (Muslim) is the flesh of Antichrist." (Martin Luther, Tischreden, Weimer ed., 1 No. 330)

In his 1520 Open Letter to the Christian Nobility, Luther declared:

> "There is no doubt that the true Roman Empire, which the writings of the prophets foretold in Numbers 24[:24] and in Daniel [11:30], has long since been overthrown...That was brought to pass...especially when the 'Turkish' [Mohammadan] Empire arose almost a thousand years ago."6 (Works, Holman, Philadelphia, 1915, II, pg. 149 & 154.)

John Calvin (1509-1564)—Elaborating on the fourth kingdom, Calvin wrote:

"It does seem that the fourth iron kingdom was in fact both the pre-Papal and the pre-Islamic, undivided Pagan Roman Empire, as well as the later Western-Roman Papal and the contemporaneous Eastern-Roman Islamic Empire into which it then subdivided... Thus they correspond to the two legs of the later Roman Empire—Islam and the Papacy."

Even more amazing, Calvin went as far as connecting Daniel 11's Antichrist to being Muslim.

"In Daniel 11:37, that Prophet predicted the coming of a terrible tyrant. This is how he described that tyrant: 'Neither shall he pay regard to the God of his fathers, nor to the desire of women.' Applied to the Unitarian Muslims, this might well mean that they would ignore the Trinitarian God of their forefathers—and with their licentiousness and polygamy also disregard the desire of women..." (Calvin On Islam Revelation Prof. Dr. Francis Nigel Lee, Lamp Trimmers El Paso, 2000)

Jonathan Edwards (1703-1758)—Edwards was the great American congregational preacher, revivalist, and president of Princeton University. Like Luther and Calvin, he saw Islam as one of the premiere—though not exclusive—elements of the Antichrist Kingdom. Referring to the three unclean spirits that proceed forth from the mouth of the dragon in Revelation 16:14, Edwards commented that, "there shall be the spirit of popery, the spirit of Mahometanism (Islam), and the spirit of heathenism all united." Referring to the False Prophet of Revelation 13, Edwards says that, "here an eye seems to be had to Mahomet (Muhammad), whom his followers call the prophet of God." 8 (Jonathan Edwards, The Fall of Antichrist, Part VII, page 395, New York, Published by S. Converse 1829)

In looking at the demonic locusts and horsemen in Revelation 9, Edwards saw a clear allusion to the Muslim armies: "Satan's Mahometan (Muslim) Kingdom shall be utterly overthrown. The locusts and the horsemen in the 9th chapter of Revelation have their appointed time set there, and the false prophet shall be taken and destroyed. And then—though Mahometanism [Islam] has been so vastly propagated in the world, and is upheld by such a great empire—this smoke, which has ascended out of the bottomless pit, shall be utterly scattered before the light of that glorious day, and the Mahometan Empire shall fall at the sound of the great trumpet which shall then be blown." 9 (Jonathan Edwards, The Fall of Antichrist, Part VII, page 399, New York, Published by S. Converse 1829)

Islam falling at the sound of the great trumpet definitely carries her into the Great Tribulation. This view contradicts that of many modern, western prophecy teachers who allege that Islam is removed prior to Christ's coming. Many modern western prophecy teachers who attempt to debate the issues through their newsletters often corner themselves further when they say things like, "The Middle Eastern Muslim nations will suffer overwhelming defeats…before the Tribulation begins and before the Antichrist arrives on the scene." Islam as he contends must be "removed" to set the stage for the European Antichrist and the Battle of Armageddon. Please review our third challenge to see why this cannot be so.

Sir Robert Anderson (1841-1918)—perhaps one of the best prophecy experts who unlocked the seventy weeks of Daniel in his remarkable book The Coming Prince. Anderson commented: "Now, Daniel 2 expressly names the Mediterranean ("the Great Sea") as the scene of the conflict between the four beasts. But there is no doubt that Egypt, Turkey, and Greece will be numbered among the ten kingdoms." Anderson would tend to agree with Goodman's view supporting a Seleucid-Grecian model. A revival of a Roman Empire does not mean a revival of a European Union. Anderson, in fact, does not agree with the European model: "Is it possible that the most powerful nations of the world, England, Germany, and Russia, are to have no part in the great drama of the Last-Days?" In fact, he even argues for a Middle Eastern dominance:

> "It has been confidently urged by some that as the ten toes of Nebuchadnezzar's image symbolized the ten kingdoms—five on either foot—five of these kingdoms must be developed in the East, and five in the West. The argument is plausible, and possibly just; but its chief force depends upon forgetting that in the prophet's view the Levant and not the Adriatic, Jerusalem and not Rome is the center of the world"[3] (Page 273)

WHY THE EUROPEAN UNION MODEL IS FLAWED

Anderson was adamant about focusing on the Levant (Eastern) parts rather than on the Adriatic (West). Even if we insist on western involvement, North Africa (Phut) is a literal reference mentioned in judgment on The Day of the Lord when

Christ is present. It is a location that historians unanimously agree was part of the Western Roman Empire. Should anyone dare to exclude this from their model?

The European model is not the orthodox or even the traditional view, nor is Roman strictly Italian. Alexander the Great was Macedonian, not Athenian. Antiochus Epiphanies, another biblical prediction, was Syrian, not Athenian or Cypriot. Why then, when it comes to Antichrist, do so many insist on an Italian origin while ignoring the entire empire? Those who listen to Jesus in Revelation 2:12-13 hear him say that Pergamum (Turkey) is where the seat of the Antichrist sits. The notion that it sits in Berlin is the result of gymnastically altered interpretations.

Another example of such flawed methodologies are claims of smoking gun-like conclusions—that Antichrist must be Italian since the Bible says, "the prince who is to come," in Daniel 9:26, will be from "the people who destroy the Temple." Proponents of the European model have adopted the premise that says it was the Romans who destroyed the Temple in A.D. 70. At first blush, that is an obvious conclusion that should close the book on the subject.

However, if we look deeper, we quickly find that while the people who made up the Roman legions that destroyed Jerusalem were mostly Eastern Roman Citizens, not Europeans. In fact, they were primarily from the Middle East—Arabs, Syrians, and Turks. This is discussed in much greater detail in my book, *God's War on Terror* but what is important here is that while the Jewish Temple sat on land ruled by Romans, it was destroyed by Arabs who were under Roman rule.

Perhaps a smoking gun can be found in the words of many modern western prophecy teachers who say things like, "the five kings 'fallen' [in Revelation 17] would be the following empires: [1]Egyptian, [2]Assyrian, [3]Babylonian, [4]Medo-Persian, and [5]Grecian. The 'one' empire—the one existing at the time Revelation was written—would be the [6]Roman." Modern prophecy teachers like John Walvoord and David Reagan seem to support this view.

Yet, the woman riding this beast in Revelation 17, riding these seven heads and seven mountains (empires) rides a resurrection of all these—they all exist in the end, together.

How do so many modern western prophecy teachers say that the woman rides a single mountain—only the seventh? How many of these resurrected mountains are today Muslim? Many modern western prophecy teachers attempt to please two opposing interpretations that say the seven mountains are both Rome and the seven empires. If so, then Rome must rule all the previous six mountains (all

Muslim), both spiritually and dictatorially. This is an absurd assumption that has not been made by any credible analyst, historian, politician, or theologian.

The combining of the previous seven kingdoms is confirmed in Daniel 2. The whole statue (gold, silver, bronze, iron and clay) are destroyed at the "same time." (Daniel 2:34-35) These composites must then include Babylon (Muslim), Persian (Muslim) Grecian (Muslim) with whatever position you like on who the iron was.

To identify European nations as the only composite will not only minimize the extent of this prophecy but the volume of literal references to Muslim nations destroyed on the Day of the Lord, all of which correspond to Revelation 17 and Daniel 2.

Let's not forget North Africa (Phut), which encompasses five Muslim nations that have historically been part of the western wing of the Roman Empire; they are mentioned literally in several End-Times references. In order for the pieces of these modern western prophecy teachers' puzzles to fit, this entire Muslim region must be irrelevant; it's like being told that a jigsaw puzzle has been completed while its pieces are still in the box.

The methodology of these teachers forces so many Biblically prophetic verses to be eliminated, tossed aside, or rearranged and placed into a different time. Who is then the revisionist? In this case, such prototypical modern western prophecy teachers must look in the mirror and determine if they are engaging in projection when they accuse others of what they themselves are guilty of doing.

One modern prophecy teacher argues that viewing Islam in the context of current events requires heeding the advice of Ray Stedman who warned, "Don't look horizontally at current events."

Before a man rebukes others, he should first determine if such a rebuke applies to him.

In 1981, when Greece joined as the tenth nation of the European Union, it was the modern prophecy teachers who announced they had unlocked the mystery and validated the fulfillment of Revelation 17 and its ten horns. Embarrassingly, the European Union later mushroomed into more than twenty nations.[4] Did Daniel make an error? Were we supposed to have over twenty toes in the statue of Daniel 2, all protruding out of the western leg, with no toes in the eastern? That's quite a birth defect. Who ignored Stedman's warning?

If anything, many modern western prophecy teachers should heed the rebuke of Jamieson Fausset & Brown:

> The ten toes are not upon the one foot (the west), as these interpretations require, but on the two (east and west) together, so that any theory which makes the ten kingdoms belong to the west alone must err.[5]

Today's modern prophecy analysts know this and are running back to the drawing board, not to confess their error but to use linguistic gymnastics to claim that their model must now shrink to ten. They still chose to tweak the theory.

Dr. Arnold Fruchtenbaum—a favorite of many modern western prophecy teachers—disagrees and even discounts Europe's significance altogether:

> It has become common today to refer to the ten kingdoms as being in Europe only, especially the Former Common Market, now the European Union. But the text does not allow for this kind of interpretation. At the very best, the European Union might become one of the ten, but it could hardly become all of the ten."[6] (Page 36)

According to Fruchtenbaum, as those modern western prophecy teachers argue about when the European Union expands and shrinks to the right size, it doesn't really matter. The best they can hope for is that the European Union itself—regardless of size—will be lucky if it achieves ten percent of what those teachers boldly predict it will become.

IS THE FOURTH KINGDOM ROMAN?

When it comes to reconciling the "little horn" in Daniel 7:20 with Daniel 2, modern western teachers insist that Antiochus Epiphanies is the whole interpretation, yet perhaps the best advice on this whole controversy is to heed the words of Rev. Dr. Matthew Henry:

> "Who is this enemy whose rise, reign and ruin are here foretold? Interpreters are not agreed. Some will have the Fourth Kingdom to be that of the Seleucidae and the 'little horn' to be Antiochus...Others will have the Fourth Kingdom to be that of the Romans, and the 'little horn' to be Julius Caesar and the succeeding emperors, as Calvin says. The Antichrist, the Papal Kingdom, says Mr. Joseph Mede...Others make the 'little horn' to be the Turkish Empire; so Luther, Vatablus, and others. Now I cannot prove either side to be in the wrong. And therefore, since prophecies sometimes have

many fulfilling and we ought to give Scripture its full latitude (in this as in many other controversies)—I am willing to allow that they are both in the right." 12 (M. Henry: A Commentary on the Holy Bible, with Practical Remarks and Observations, London: Marshall Bros. Ltd., n.d., IV:1270f.)

In short, the Bible does not support the notion that the Antichrist arises from Europe. Don't blame me, though. I'm just relaying what is clearly written about that not being true.

CHALLENGE NUMBER TWO

Cite any literal reference to a nation that God destroys in the End-Times that is not Muslim?

One needs to slowly ponder this question in order to fully grasp its magnitude—no one can escape the fact that in the Bible, God destroys many nations in the End-Times and all of them are Islamic today. The evidence mounts when one finds out that all the verses in which Christ fights nations referred to literally, without exception, are Muslim.

During a lecture in front of a private audience that included prominent prophecy authors exclusively, at the Pre-Trib Prophecy Conference in Dallas Texas, I asked the same question and no hands were raised in response. Mildly frustrated, I finally decided to choose someone out of this elite, albeit silent, audience. I pointed to Dr. Randall Price, a prominent Bible Prophecy teacher and asked him to respond, which he did thusly:

"When you ask about literal references, there aren't any."

Grant Jeffrey, another well known author, attempted once to respond with Cush, not realizing that the biblical reference to Cush sometimes translated to Ethiopia as defined in the Unger Bible Dictionary as a landmass south of Egypt. Today, this would be Sudan and Somalia. Jeffrey chose one of the most fundamentalist Muslim nations as a response to find non-Muslim nations in end-times.

In fact, Arnold Fruchtenbaum points to Cush as Somaliland. One of these modern teachers, in attempting to take on my second challenge, inadvertently ended up supporting my view:

"Yes, I can. It is Babylon, whose destruction is described in detail in Revelation."[7]

He ignored the crucial word in that question; that word is "literal". If Babylon is his response to a question about a literal reference to a non-Muslim nation that God destroys, this would still support my view—Mystery Babylon is an allegoric reference and all the references to Babylon in prophecy point to Arab cities, not European ones.

CHALLENGE NUMBER THREE

In every portrayal of Christ's return to the earth, is He not fighting a nation that today is Muslim?

The significance of this question is simple; scholars are unanimous in their sentiment that Christ's second coming must happen after Antichrist appears. Christ's mission will be to destroy Antichrist and establish His Millennium kingdom. This is why supporters of the European Union model insist that Islam must be destroyed before the Tribulation, since Islam's involvement destroys their whole model. Yet, the Bible leaves no room for debate since in the context of all of them, Christ fights Muslim nations. Christians attending prophecy conferences need to ask:

"Is Jesus on earth on the Day of the Lord?"

The Day of the Lord or the Day of Wrath is an aspect of prophecy about which one prophecy teacher says:

"God has appointed a day when He will deal with all the kingdoms of the earth and their political leaders by pouring out His wrath through the return of His Son, Jesus the Messiah. (Lamplighter by David Reagan, the message of Psalm 2)

In Ezekiel 30, we are told of that day:

For the day is near, even the Day of the Lord is near (Ezekiel 30:3)

What nations are dealt with on that day? Not all scholars agree on the context, yet this is the Day of the Lord in which Cush and Phut, Lydia [Turkey], all of Arabia, Libya and the people of the covenant land will fall by the sword along with Egypt (Ezekiel 30:5). Other prophecies show these nations as being cast into Hell, including Asshur (Iraq and Syria—Ezekiel 32:22-23), Elam (Iran—Ezekiel 32:24-25), Meshech & Tubal (Asia Minor / Turkey—Ezekiel 32:26), Edom

(Arabia—Ezekiel 32:29). These are punished for terrorizing Israel and the believers (Ezekiel 32:22-24 & 27).

Perhaps sharing a few excerpts from the volume of hundreds of prophecies about Jesus' wars during the Great Tribulation can shed more light on what to expect:

> See, Jehovah is riding on a swift cloud and is coming to Egypt. The idols of Egypt tremble before him, and the hearts of the Egyptians melt within them. (Isaiah 19:1)

This would remind us of the song, "behold He comes." Yet, rarely do they tell you which verse the song applies to or whom Jesus fights; He fights Egypt:

Take a look at Christ's judgment of the nations:

> I will gather all nations and bring them down to the Valley of Jehoshaphat (Joel 3:2)

Then the Lord continues:

> Now what have you against me, O Tyre and Sidon [Lebanon] and all you regions of Philistia? [Gaza] (Joel 3:4)

It couldn't be clearer! It was as if Jesus himself was speaking directly to Hezbollah (Tyre and Sidon) and Hamas (Philistia), challenging them over the bloodlust they had for the Jewish people. Their fight against Israel is, in reality, a declaration of war on the King Himself.

In Isaiah 25:9-10 at the time of the Lord's return, we have Christ fighting Moab:

> And it shall be said in that day, Lo, this is our God; we have waited for Him, and He will save us: this is the LORD; we have waited for Him, we will be glad and rejoice in His salvation. For in this mountain shall the hand of the LORD rest, and Moab shall be trodden down under Him, even as straw is trodden down for the dunghill." (Isaiah 25:9-10)

In Isaiah 63, scholars unanimously agree that He fights Edom (Arabia). Even many modern prophecy teachers admit that Edom is a land of Arabs (God's Plan for the Ages, page 76)

Are the Arabs destroyed prior to the coming of Christ as these teachers claim? Is it then that Antichrist establishes his European rule? The Bible contains an abundant number of verses in which Christ fights nations that are Islamic. Your challenge is to find a verse in the Bible that describes nations that Christ fights which are NOT Islamic.

FISH AND SHEEP

If you've ever found yourself wondering why fish never learn their lesson after biting a barbed hook, we have a better question: Why do so many never learn the lesson of Islamic JBTW? Islam has been using peace as a tool of deceit for centuries. Is not a man smarter than a fish? Yes, but man is also susceptible to deceit. The key is to see the hook.

Deception is at the core of Islam; it is a central tenet in Islamic text. Terms and tactics like Muruna, Taqiyya, Kitman, Hudna, and others include deception as foundational principles. Deception in earthly warfare may be a legitimate stratagem of war but deception in spiritual warfare belongs only to one side.

Westerners have been taking the bait for centuries. In fact, there is so much empirical evidence they are being deceived that collectively, their ability to learn is on par with fish that continue to end up with barbed hooks piercing their mouths.

Jesus told his disciples he wanted to make them "fishers of men" but he didn't want them to do it with the hook of deceit. He wanted them to do so with the sword of truth, which would leave such men healed, not scarred.

Another metaphor that has endured within Christianity involves lost sheep. Such sheep are led astray by deceivers. The Muslim JBTW artist is a wolf in sheep's clothing. He does so for the sole purpose of deception and ultimately, the destruction of unsuspecting victims. Deceit's strength is found in numbers. The more sheep the wolf deceives, the more powerless the flock becomes.

Jesus Himself said:

> "Suppose one of you has a hundred sheep and loses one of them. Doesn't he leave the ninety-nine in the open country and go after the lost sheep until he finds it? 5 And when he finds it, he joyfully puts it on his shoulders and goes home. Then he calls his friends and neighbors together and says, 'Rejoice with me; I have found my lost sheep.'"[8]

When multiple wolves on multiple fronts sport multiple disguises—as is done with multiple forms of Jihad—the flock can break apart; few are left. This all happens through deceit, under the guise of peace.

Again, Daniel 8:25 talks about the Antichrist:

"Through his cunning
He shall cause deceit to prosper under his rule;
And he shall exalt himself in his heart.
He shall destroy many in their prosperity.
He shall even rise against the Prince of princes;
But he shall be broken without human means.

In the name of peace, he will "destroy many".[9]

In Mark 13: 5-6, Jesus says:

"Take heed that no one deceives you. For many will come in My name, saying,
'I am He,' and will deceive many.[10]

This we know. The antichrist will deceive in order to convey peace and declare he is the Prince of Peace in an attempt to destroy. He will use peace to "deceive many". Is that not what the wolf does? Is it not what the fisherman who uses a barbed hook does? After all, Islam views non-Muslims as less than human, even lower than bottom-feeding fish.

If the Antichrist is prophesied to use deception to convey peace before unmasking himself, wouldn't an Islamic Antichrist fit the bill perfectly?

Wouldn't it be a worthwhile pursuit to quicken that unmasking?

FOOTNOTES

1. Lamb & Lion Ministries, *The Antichrist, Will he be a Muslim?* by Dr. David R. Reagan. http://lamblion.com/articles/articles_islam4.php

2. *Islam in the Bible*, by Rev. Prof. Dr. Francis Nigel Lee, Queensland Presyterian Theological College. http://www.dr-fnlee.org/docs/iitb/iitb.pdf

3. Google Books, *The Coming Prince, The Marvelous Prophecy of Daniel's Seventy Weeks Concerning the Antichrist,* Sir Robert Anderson (1841–1918). http://books.google.com/books?id=GPI88qWxWP4C&printsec=frontcover&dq=%22The+coming+prince%22&hl=en&sa=X&ei=S8r0UOLOMITc8ATmpoGoAQ&ved=0CCOQ6AEwAA

4. European Union, *List of Countries.* http://europa.eu/about-eu/countries/index_en.htm

5. Christian Classics Ethereal Library, *The Revelation, Chapter 13.* http://www.ccel.org/ccel/jamieson/jfb.xi.xxvii.xiv.html?bcb=right

6. Google Books, *The Footsteps of the Messiah (p. 36),* by Arnold G. Fruchtenbaum. http://books.google.com/books?id=wx81NgAACAAJ&dq=%22footsteps+of+the+messiah%22&hl=en&sa=X&ei=QszOUMPwL4b28gTK9IC4AQ&ved=0CDoQ6AEwAQ

7. Lamb & Lion Ministries, *The Antichrist, Will he be a Muslim?* by Dr. David R. Reagan. http://lamblion.com/articles/articles_islam4.php

8. Bible Gateway.com, *Luke 15:4-6, NIV.* http://www.biblegateway.com/passage/?search=Luke%2015:%204-6&version=NIV

9. Bible Gateway.com, *Daniel 8:25, NKJV.* http://www.biblegateway.com/passage/?search=daniel%208:23-26&version=NKJV

10. Bible Gateway.com, *Mark , NKJV.* http://www.biblegateway.com/passage/?search=Mark%2013:5-6&version=NKJV

EPILOGUE AS PROLOGUE
The Harlot and Three Saudi Appendices

John the Apostle, while blessed, pure, adorned with clean white garments, and imbued with the Holy Spirit, wrote of a harlot:

> 1Then one of the seven angels who had the seven bowls came and talked with me, saying to me, "Come, I will show you the judgment of the great harlot who sits on many waters, 2with whom the kings of the earth committed fornication, and the inhabitants of the earth were made drunk with the wine of her fornication." **Revelation 17: 1-2**

In a literal sense, fornication is sexual activity between two people who are not married to each other. Applied to Saudi Arabia and western leaders, it is also about secret business conducted between two parties whose allegiances are professed to others.

In the case of American leaders, an oath was taken by each and every one of them to defend the US Constitution. This simply cannot be done while simultaneously dealing so closely with the Saudis. In the case of the Saudi Royal family, an oath was taken to defend Islam. That simply cannot be done while simultaneously dealing so closely with Americans.

Western leaders know the truth about what they're doing but choose to believe the lies of a harlot who is committed to another:

> Lie to me and tell me everything is alright
> Lie to me and tell me that you'll stay here tonight
> Tell me that you'll never leave,
> oh and I'll just try to make believe
> that everything, everything you're telling me is true
> —*Johnny Lang, "Lie to Me"*

The United States is incredibly dependent on Saudi oil. Like the harlot who seeks to lie, cheat, and steal without consequence, the Saudi Royal family will continue to be the beneficiary of both western wealth and blind western eyes as long as it keeps putting out…oil. If the powerful few in the west can be taken care of personally while confident that their transgressions will not be brought to light, they will sell out their own nation—and many have. In fact, the threat of transgressions being revealed holds tremendous earthly power, which is one reason why dancing with the devil is so dangerous.

In the film, "The Dead Zone" an aspiring, yet wicked politician named Greg Stillson (played by Martin Sheen) is running for a seat in the US Senate when he learns of an editorial that is going to appear in the local paper and will do great damage to his chances of winning. Stillson's goons enlist the help of a harlot to seduce the married writer, which she does successfully when photographs are taken of their encounter and shown to the editorial's author. After Stillson tells the writer to "stay out of the campaign business" in return for him staying "out of the publishing business", the writer wrestles with his conscience and asks, "What if I don't make a deal, Stillson?" As Sheen's character prepares to leave the writer's office, he says, "Oh, you'll make a deal. Otherwise, I'll have Sonny here take your (expletive) head off."

When the Saudi Royal family tells its American customers that the peninsula is held hostage by terrorists, westerners willfully believe it because it's more convenient and profitable to believe *half* truths than it is to confront uncomfortable *whole* truths. It's also believable because it is a half truth. The Royal family does indeed combat terrorists but it was they who opened the Pandora's box in the first place. The whole truth is that western power brokers and politicians *want* to be lied to; they'll pay a premium for it—and they do. They'll even throw in an extra fur coat and a tip for the pimp if it means silencing the cries of their own consciences with louder and more frequent adulterous praise.

The world of a harlot is full of love/hate relationships. The Saudi Royal family loves the West's money but knows it's supposed to secretly hate doing business with non-Muslims. Conversely, that same family hates having to deal with Islamic fundamentalists who violently remind them of their betrayal while sharing the same beliefs about spreading Islam all over the world.

The harlot tells her *western* John that she is a brutalized victim in another relationship and is doing all she can to defuse that situation. While garnering sympathy for problems largely of her own making, she assures her western John that many of the profits gained from their business dealings go toward *combating* the problem and dealing forcefully with her terrorist abusers. The money is directed toward institutions that employ JBTW and publicly denounce extremism. This is another lie the harlot's Western John has no problem believing.

The truth is the harlot loves the *money* of the John it secretly hates while financing entities and movements that more effectively act on that hatred and simultaneously further the movement—Islam. How some of the money is spent eases some of the pain caused by how it was earned—by dealing with infidels. While seeking victim-hood status with the West, the harlot finances movements and groups that ultimately seek to subjugate *all* non-Muslims—globally— including the customer whose money the harlot earns.

While the Saudi Royal family funds terrorists, it tells westerners it's either just paying protection money or sending money to non-violent charities; the Saudi Royals want westerners to believe that they're innocent and are held hostage by the likes of Al-Qaeda while knowingly funding such groups (the harlot wants her John to believe she's not cheating on him too much).

A very real danger to western civilization is the harlot's other (Arabic) "John". The harlot and he are quite like-minded when it comes to the goals of Islam. On that, both the harlot and he agree. When the Western John pays the harlot, he cares not what she does with the money, even if it's spent on his own destruction.

That is what the Saudi harlot is doing and hopefully, the following three appendices will illustrate this reality.

In **Appendix A**, you will learn who is really behind the efforts of Huma Abedin's IMMA. That Abedin was able to obtain a US State Department security clearance with her background is astounding. Once you see her connection to the Saudi Royal family, the dots should be easy to connect relative to the disinterest of western leadership when it comes to investigating her background. Their pleas of ignorance are like those of a man who walks through his front door at 3am with lipstick on his collar and finds his wife awake, waiting for him.

"What lipstick?"

In **Appendix B**, it will be obvious that the Republican George W. Bush administration went out of its way to protect the Saudis despite the latter's direct culpability in the worst attack on US soil. The affection showed toward the Saudis during the Bush years—*post* 9/11/01—involved giving them a pass *on* 9/11.

It is beyond dispute.

In **Appendix C**, it's the Democrats' turn. Barack Obama's cousin—Musa Ismail—divulged to Arabic audiences that western contributions to his grand-mother's foundation were actually being re-directed toward the wahhabist educa-tion of Kenyan students…in Saudi Arabia.

Yet, western media remains as silent as a complicit participant.

In **Revelation 18:12-24,** John the Apostle wrote:

> 23 The light of a lamp shall not shine in you anymore, and the voice of bride-
> groom and bride shall not be heard in you anymore. For your merchants were
> the great men of the earth, for by your sorcery all the nations were deceived.
> 24And in her was found the blood of prophets and saints, and of all who were
> slain on the earth."

Bear in mind, as you read the following three appendices, that each involves the role of the Saudi Royal family in high level American politics. It is also impor-tant to remember that none of what follows is based on conjecture or speculation; it is rooted in fact.

America, you've been warned.

APPENDIX A
The Abedin "Affairs" with Al Saud

Walid Shoebat

I thought I had it all figured out[1], that Huma Abedin and her family, for years, were only working for Muslim Brotherhood interests. After all, I spent a week re-sifting through scores of Arabic sources, which confirmed that Huma's mother Saleha was not simply a *member*, but a *leader* in Egypt's Muslim Brotherhood's Sisterhood branch. The Abedins were for decades affiliated with an al-Qaeda financier named Abdullah Omar Naseef, who had appointed the Abedins to start the Institute of Muslim Minority Affairs (IMMA), not that working with this man was not problematic enough, but still, who was behind Naseef and what were the goals of this IMMA establishment?

Other issues just weren't adding up; these fish were looking larger by the day—much larger than I had previously thought. I watched politicians who sided with Huma, none of whom spent a nickel trying to refute McCarthy's court-style presentation;[2] they responded with familiar one-line rebuttals that lacked the acknowledgment of facts. There is also something terribly wrong when five members of congress are being muzzled as ordained by the highest powers in both that establishment and in the State Department. Newt Gingrich and a few other patriots had the common sense to finally come out of the closet, but not without ridicule.

Was Huma a big fish to have the might of some American politicians come to her defense or is there some other player in the mix that the American people are not aware of? Even President Barack Obama felt it necessary to pay tribute and voice strong support for Huma Abedin during a Muslim Iftar dinner on August 10th, saying that the top aide to Secretary of State Hillary Clinton has been "nothing less than extraordinary in representing our country and the democratic values that we hold dear."

Just who are all of these elite and powerful bowing to? The only powerful man that a United States president would bow to was when Obama bowed to the King of Saudi Arabia treating him as if he was the King of Kings. Could it be possible that this far-away place holds the power to make the kings of the earth bow?

I began to research further. My findings all started as I was researching Huma's father, "Sayed Zaynul Abedin" in Arabic, looking for further clues, hoping that I could find something. Then suddenly there it was, an unbelievable document commissioned by the late King Fahd bin Abdul Aziz,[3] detailing the years of accomplishments by the kings of Al-Saud.

I couldn't believe my eyes! As I read, the king's book gave me all the answers to all the clues I have been looking for. The more I read the Arabic squiggles, the more quickly I realized that my older discoveries were perhaps the *lesser* of the two evils—an appetizer—in comparison to what is in this manuscript. It began to connect the dots between the Abedins' *Institute for Muslim Minority Affairs*—on whose Board Huma Abedin served for years—and the Wahhabist plans of Saudi Arabia, commissioned by the House of Saud.

This book had the king's blessings and approval on literally every page. I perused, beginning with the long, grandiose and fanciful title: *"The Efforts of the Servant of the Two Holy Places, King Fahd bin Abdul Aziz to Support The Muslim Minorities".* The king presents himself as the "Servant of the Two Holy Places" (Mecca and Medina) where multitudes flock, great and small, rich and poor, to pay tribute while they circumambulate, giving their allegiance to the call of Allah.

The House of Saud had another holy "affair" besides multitudes circumambulating around the Ka'ba; everything in this holy writ was revolving around "The Muslim Minority Affairs" as it was the key to another kingdom, in which the Abedins played a central role. The House of Saud had used Huma's father Sayed Zaynul Abedin's work *Muslim Minorities in the West* published in 1998 as part of 29 works[4] to construct a plan to conquer the world with Islam (#11. P. 134) and "The Muslim Minority Affairs" in the west was a major discussion with the United States mentioned throughout. The king of his pride had let out state secrets like others did with Wikileaks. I realized quickly that I was on a mission and thanks to American technology (the Internet), I was reaching all the way into the dirty plans of the servants of Mecca and Medina, to reveal even more unknowns about the mysterious Abedins.

I grabbed my miniature camera and quickly took snapshots so I could later translate this grand plan entitled, *Shu-un al-Aqaliyyat al-Muslima*. In English, *"The Muslim Minority Affairs"*. Page after page explained the "Affairs", not simply as a title, or as a religious or even a social entity, but as a Saudi foreign policy, a jurisprudence and commandment from the highest of authorities commissioned to the Saudi Ministry of Religious Affairs. It was an entire management system using "The Muslim Minority Affairs" as the main vehicle to bringing victory against an infidel world.

It spoke of recruiting Muslims that live in non-Muslim lands and transforming them as a collective unit. It spoke of already established centers, educational programs, mosques and organizations in the United States like ISNA and MSA, all geared towards hindering any western plan for Muslim assimilation in a non-Muslim host nation. It mentioned "The Muslim Society of North America (ISNA) and the Muslim Students Association (MSA) established in the United States in 1962" (p. 65), as key agents to protect Muslims from assimilation.

It named the mosques and centers in major United States cities established to carry out the mission. Five decades of efforts were spent with billions to ensure that Muslims will be an unassimilated group which then can influence the non-Muslim host nation and other nations, regardless of how small the numbers of Muslims, by shifting the demographic scale due to their population growth in favor of this Saudi agenda.

It explained how a gradual change would ensue by becoming a major revolutionary powerhouse that will tilt the host nation in favor of Muslims due to their increase as a population. It was a conundrum to transform a nation from within, where a Minority population can act as a fifth column, incubating in the host nation with the intent of gradually implementing the Wahhabist plans.

It was as if I was watching a science program on how a cell is invaded by a virus, where it gradually does its thing until the host cell finally succumbs to the disease.

(Title: The Efforts of the Servant of the Two Holy Places King Fahd
bin Abdul Aziz in Support of Muslim Minorities)

My gift is that I can provide, from the Arabic sources, things that my ex-enemy (the average American) is not expected to review, regarding things considered taboo, not to be discussed or translated. This taboo now seems to have migrated from Mecca where, if exposed, would force the American media to ridicule such a mission.

I felt as if destined to provide the insight of a defector who switched sides. That is what I do; I am, after all, a surfing watchman on the wall. But sounding the horn with my discoveries would put me under the lens of many unmerciful western critics who dismiss detailed facts with a strike of a comment—dismissal that is void of any detail.

I knew that I needed to quickly take more snapshots and translate some of this toxin to show this is no bluff. We are unequivocally talking about a grand conspiracy that is no manufactured theory.

Yet, I realized people still needed to know now, not that I expect them to believe (I predict many won't) but so that history some day records it; the watchman sounded the horn and the blood of the saints is not on his hands.

There was another document I had discovered which I included in my previous report (see Exhibit below), an official detailed testimony which I translated. It discusses how in 1965, during the Hajj (Pilgrimage), that the parent organization for the Abedins' IMMA—WAMY—was born. WAMY stands for *World Association of Muslim Youth*, which came about when Muslim leaders, scholars, movers and shakers from the farthest corners of the globe flocked to Mecca to create it and launch it worldwide.

Dr. Salih Mahdi al-Samarrai (literally Samurai) came all the way from the orient to answer the call representing the Islamic Center of Japan. He explained how WAMY was envisioned.[5] It was created through the collaboration of the Wahhabist and Muslim Brotherhood lead by Said Ramadan who was the son-in-law of Hassan al-Banna, the founder of the Muslim Brotherhood including Ahmad Bahefzallah, the Abedin's immediate boss, and financiers like the wealthy Abdullah Omar Naseef.

IMMA's founders were the same as WAMY's. IMMA, which the Abedins ran in the West, and while being commissioned by the evil kingdom of Al Saud, was also conceived in the same place in the early seventies. Sayed Zaynul Abedin would nurture it under the designed hierarchy and watchful eye of the Saudi government as they appointed Ahmad Bahafzallah of WAMY with Naseef as the godfather of the operation.

To ensure that my critics cannot find any gap to insert their sharp edged critical pen, I decided to research the history of IMMA to show how it connects to the House of Saud's evil plan with evidence as clear as the sun. The critics would argue that "the glove did not fit, you must acquit". Yet, the Saudi Manifesto had all the fingerprints I needed:

> "Tt [*Muslim Minority Affairs*] will work *under the umbrella* of the *Muslim World League (MWL)* and the International Islamic Relief Organization (IIRO) and *World Association of Muslim Youth (WAMY)* and others" (p. 6, also see p. 23)

"The Muslim Minority Affairs" was designed as a global plan. The Abedins' Institute of Muslim Minority Affairs (IMMA) is its western branch and a perfect fit. The Arabic Dictionary on Media Icons[6] by Zarkali shows IMMA's exact hierarchy, supervisors and parent organizations being exactly what was in the Saudi manifesto:

> "Sayed Z. Abedin is a *specialist* on *Muslim Minority Affairs* issues...In the early 1970s, Sayed Z. Abedin went to Saudi Arabia for one year as a visiting professor. He was welcomed by *King Abdulaziz University*, which *provided him the means to create a scholarly program regarding Muslim Minorities*. Dr. *Abdullah Omar Naseef*, the Dean of King Abdulaziz University then *envisioned the creation of an academic entity called the Institute of Muslim Minority Affairs (IMMA), under the management of Ahmad Bahafzallah, who was the General Trustee for the World Assembly of Muslim Youth (WAMY)*. Professor Sayed Z. Abedin was *encouraged to supervise the Muslim Minority Affairs* and

served as IMMA's chief editor." (Al-I'lam by Zarkali, is an encyclopedia on major figures in the Arabic-Muslim Media, p. 218)

Everything fit, like a glove. Abdullah Ghazi,[7] a graduate of Harvard University in Comparative Religion, provides additional testimony as he reminisces about how he met the Abedins:

"Later we shifted to Gary in Indiana State, 40 kms from Chicago. In 1976, I met *Rabita (MWL) chief Dr. Abdullah Omar Naseef* and *Dr. Zainul Abedin* of *Institute for Muslim Minority Affairs*. They encouraged me to take up this venture. The first book to come out was Our Prophet, an assignment from *King Abdul Aziz University*, Jeddah at *Dr. Naseef's behest...*"

So let's delve into the idea of "The Muslim Minority Affairs" and hear it right from the horse's mouth. Weeding through the first chapter, replete with hyperbole about the king's self-glorification, I skipped the hogwash to chapter II. King Fahd bin Abdul Aziz wrote as he began to jot the first statements. Here the Saudi manifesto introduces the whole of mankind's destiny, including the demonic world all of which will some day become Muslim:

"The religion [Islam] was destined to rule both races of the globe, mankind and demons."

First, some Arabic, then some translation...

الفصل الثاني

الأقليات المسلمة في العالم

المبحث الأول: مفهوم الأقليات المسلمة وتاريخ ظهورها

الإسلام دين عالمي بعث الله به نبيه محمدا ﷺ للثقلين: الإنس والجن، فهو دين للبشرية جمعاء، كما جاءت بذلك النصوص من القرآن الكريم والسنة النبوية الصحيحة، وكما تأكد ذلك من انتشار الإسلام في بقاع الأرض، ودخول الناس فيه أفواجا.

CHAPTER II
THE MUSLIM MINORITIES IN THE WORLD
Study Number One
The Concept of Muslim Minority and its History

Islam is *the religion of the whole world*; sent by Allah through Muhammad to *both races*, the Jinn (demons) and Ins (mankind). It is a reliqion for all humanity as commanded by the Holy Quran and the Prophet's correct path. This promise was confirmed since Islam did spread throughout the earth and multitudes streamed to it.

(Chapter II, *"The Muslim Minority in the World: Understanding The Purpose of Muslim Minority"* p. 27)

It details how the Kingdom through the Muslim Minority Affairs will catapult Islam's destiny by shifting the demographic scale to favor Muslims.

فــالتجمع الإسلامي الموجود في قارات العالم إما أن يكون في صورة " دول إسلامية "، وإما أن يكون في صورة " أقليات مسلمة ".

والحكم على هذه بأنهـا دولة، أو تلك بأنهـا أقليـــة، يتم وفق عـــدد من المعايير،

29

أولها المعيار العددي، بمعنى أن الدولة التي يزيد عدد المسلمين فيها عن نصف مــجموع السكان، ويقول دستورها إن دين هذه الدولة الرسمي هو الإسلام، أو أن الشريعــة

المبحث الثاني: الأقليات المسلمة على خريطة العالم

سجل تعداد المسلمين في السنوات الأخيرة صعودا كبيرا؛ حيث بلغ عددهم مليارا وثلاثمائة مليون نسمة، منهم (900) مليون نسمة في الدول الإسلامية، و (400) مليون نسمة يعيشون في تجمعات وأقليات مسلمة.

إفريقيا (250) مليون مسلم، ويعيش في قارة أوروبا (60) مليون مسلم، وفي قــارة أمريكا الشمالية والجنوبية عشرة مــلايين مــسلم. ووفق هذه الإحــصــائيــات فــإنه من المنتظر أن يصل تعــداد المسلمين إلى مليارين وستمـائة ألف خــلال وقــت قــصــير، بحــيــث يتــحــول المسلمون إلى قــوة عظمى ومؤثرة في العالم، بعد أن يكونوا قــد غيروا - وفق هذا التــصــاعــد السـريع في عددهم - التــوازن الديموغرافـــي في العــالم لصالحهم. ويلاحظ فـــي الإحصاءات المعلنة عن الأقليات

"The Muslim societies in all continents of the world exist in either 'Muslim nation' or 'Muslim Minorities'. The assessment to determine what constitutes 'state' from a 'minority state' is done based on a number of measures. First, the numbers scale, which is, if a nation has Muslims who exceed half the population and its Constitution states that Islam is its official religion or that Islamic Sharia is its source of law, this state is then considered an Islamic state." (p.29) "Since the number of Muslims has risen greatly in the last years where they became 1.3 billion Muslims. From these we have (900) million already in Muslim nations. The *400 million live as communities and as Muslim Minority*" (p. 31) "... In Africa resides (250) million Muslims and in Europe resides (60) million Muslims and in North America and South America resides (10) million Muslims. So, according to these statistics it is expected that the number of Muslims will reach 2.6 billion six hundred thousand within a short span of time. The Muslims then will become a mighty and effective power in the world, of course, due to the increase in their numbers—then shift the demographic balance in their favor." (p.32).

The manifesto maps out, with statistics and demographic analysis, every nation on the face of the globe where Muslim minorities exist. Regardless how small the numbers, these are expected to advance the Wahhabist plans set by the popular revivalist movement[8] instigated by an eighteenth century theologian[9] Muhammad ibn Abd al-Wahhab (1703–1792)[10] from Najd[11], Saudi Arabia.[12]

ولأن الله كــتب لهذه البــقــاع دورا تاريخــيا تؤديه نحــو المسلمين، فقد قــيض
لها إمامين جليلين هما الإمام محمد بن سعود، والإمام محمد بن عبد الوهاب -رحمهما الله
- وقد تزامنت ولاية الإمام محمد بن سعود مــع ظهور الدعوة الإصلاحــية على يد
الشيخ المجدد محمد بن عبد الوهاب، فتعاون الإمامان على الحكم بما أنزل الله، ومقاومة
البدع والأضــاليل، ورد الناس إلى دين الله وعقيـــدة الإسلام الصافية.

"Allah destined this region [Saudi Arabia] for an historic roll. So He commissioned the two Imams—Muhammad bin Saud and Muhammad bin Abdul Wahhab, may Allah have mercy upon them. But the times have passed on Imam Muhammad bin Saud by the emergence of the reformer—Muhammad bin Abdul Wahhab. So the two Imams cooperated together to judge by what Allah brought forth, to fight against heresy and to bring Muslims back to puritan Islam." (p. 8)

"The Muslim Minority Affairs" program – according to the manifesto – can arrange "Muslim Minority activism" to advance the goal through the building of mosques, schools and Islamic centers where minorities exist (pg. 8-13, 17) in order to "establish a global Sharia in our modern times." (pg. 9-10) The measure also aims to "prevent the 'hurdle' Muslims encounter from 'assimilation and melting' in non-Muslim societies". (p. 24)

The horror began as I reviewed the United States and Canada, where it shifts sounding more like an Arab version of Mein Kampf to describe the major hurdle not mentioned under any other continent—The Jews.

التحدي الصهيوني:

وهو من التــحــديات الكبيـــرة التي تواجـــه المسلمين خـــاصة في الولايات المتحدة الأمريكية وكندا؛ حيث يستغل اليهود إمكاناتهم المادية والإعلامية في تشــويه صـــورة الإسلام والمسلمين هناك، وترسيـــخ الكثـــيــر من الأكـــاذيب والأضـــاليل

79

جهود خادم الحرمين الشريفين الملك فهد

في أذهان شعـــوب هذه الدول، كـــمــا يوظف اليهود جهودهم، ويوجهون أموالهم، ويستغلون مناصبهم ومواقعهم القيادية في خدمة أهداف دولتهم الصهيونية في المنطقة العربية، ويستغلون المواقف والأحداث في مزيد من تشويه صورة العرب والمسلمين هناك. كما تبذل المنظمات الصهيونية جهودا مستميتة لوقف انتشار الإسلام في تلك المناطق.

احتياجات ثقافية وتعليمية:

"The greatest challenge that faces Muslims in the United States and Canada *are the Jews* who take advantage of their material ability and their media to distort the image of Islam and Muslims there by spreading their lies and distortions in the minds of the people in these countries. The Jews employ their efforts and direct their material wealth and their high positions to serve Zionist interests in the Arab region. They [the Jews] take advantage of situations to distort the image of Arabs and Muslims. The Zionist organizations spend enormous efforts to obstruct the spread of Islam in these areas." (pg. 79-80)

Yet I wonder, what will my critics say? Will my critics doubt Mein Kampf or that six million Jews were incinerated as a result? Will they deny that 19 Saudis instantly converted the World Trade Center into two furnaces, incinerating 3000 Americans, alive?

That wasn't enough to bring the wealthy influential perpetrators to justice. They are still on the loose while politicians who seek buckets of oil remain plagued with collective silence.

The Muslim Minority Affairs idea is not isolated to the Abedins or even to the Saudis; Salafists and Muslim Brotherhood support the same concept, even link to each other using what they term: "the Jurisprudence of Muslim Minority Affairs."

In other words, IMMA is not simply a name of an establishment; it represents a definition, a jurisprudence rooted in a sinister doctrine with short and long-term goals.

Qaradawi has a similar manifesto[13] for the Brotherhood. Muslim Minority Affairs scholars across the board have an obsession using this jurisprudence steering Muslims into this theocratic collective revolution.

Even Europe's Abdul-Majid al-Najjar, Assistant Secretary-General of the European Council for Fatwa and Research who works on bettering Muslim relations with the West, in Arabic, he adheres to the same concept:[14]

> "It was ordained that Islam was assigned the mission to inherit the globe. It is a mission possible through only the collective religious performance and mission impossible through individual religiosity."

An IMMA favorite, Taha Jaber al-Alwani, whom the Abedins say is the source for their doctrine is an ardent anti-Semite[15] who by the way runs the United States Department of Defense program[16] for training Muslim military chaplains in the U.S. military. This is the *first* time we translated some of his quotes on the issue of The Muslim Minority Affairs:

> "... it [MMA] is a Jurisprudence for a group confined to its special circumstances which is *allowed what others are not*. Its exercise needs an understanding of social sciences, especially sociology, economics, political science and international relations... for the fundamentals of success for the Muslim Minority Jurisprudence *it must adhere to the collective earth concept*."[17]

Alwani, a man commissioned by our government, even calls for a soon-to-be military conquest and provides an official *fatwa*[18] preparation for the use of force:

> "Commitment to the Quranic concept of Geography: The land belongs to Allah, his religion is Islam, and every country is already in the House of Islam—now in the present time—since *they will be in the House of Islam by force in the near future.* The whole of humanity is a Muslim Nation: it is either 'the religion of the nation' which has embraced this religion [Islam], or a 'proselyte nation' we are obliged to conquer." (*Alwani, The Jurisprudence of Muslim Minority Affairs. No. 7*)[19]

Alwani speaks of a future, literal war and is perhaps himself a reason why we see people like Nidal Malik Hassan attacking military personnel. He probably snapped and just couldn't wait for Alwani's grand finale.

It's on all levels, military and civil. In America, even the Director of the Islamic Center of Lubbock Texas Mohammed bin Mukhtar Shanqeeti agrees:

> "The Muslim Minority Jurisprudence is not a heresy or a novel, it's an ancient doctrine *filled with the provisions for Muslims living in Dar al-Kufr* (House of the Heathen) or Dar Al-Harb (House of War)."[20]

Even the Abedins' Journal for Muslim Minority Affairs (JMMA) confirms that their program stems from these same extremist sources:[21]

> "The theory of the Jurisprudence of Muslim Minorities is most easily clarified by *shedding light on its founders*" which the notes state are *none other than Muslim Brotherhood "Yusuf al-Qaradawi" and "Taha Jabir al-Alwani".*[22]

In a nutshell, The Muslim Minority Affairs program is part of a grand plan to destroy America from within, exactly as what the Muslim Brotherhood planned, which was exposed in the HLF trial.

It will probably take years before Americans completely understand why, when it comes to The Muslim Minority Affairs, these are "allowed what others are not" as the Abedin's favorite al-Alwani says. Shanqeeti says that The Muslim Minority Affairs "has provisions for Muslims living in Dar al-Kufr…" What allowances and what provisions?

The Muslim Minority Affairs plan actually combines two Islamic Jurisprudences: *The Minority Affairs Jurisprudence and the Jurisprudence of Muruna* (Flexibility).

Muruna is the "process of permitting evils", specifically for Muslim Minorities by "sanctioning prohibitions for the sake of an interest".[23, 24] This jurisprudence, as mad as it sounds, permits "reversing Sharia rulings" in order to "gain interests". Imagine what "sanctioning prohibitions" means. If it says, "thou shall not kill" now it's "thou can kill" for an "interest".

Qaradawi even permits the "killing of Muslims whom the unbelievers use as shields" in times of war, since "leaving these unbelievers is a danger to the Muslims, so it is permissible to kill these unbelievers even if they killed Muslims with them in the process."[25] He adds:

> "Sharia's ability to be flexible and inclusive is that it cares for their needs while excusing the burdens Muslims have to endure. For the sake of their destiny, it was *made lawful* for them to have *exceptions from the law* that are appropriate for them since these exceptions match their general goals to make it easy for humanity by removing the chains of [Sharia] rules they were made to adhere to in previous Sharia rulings."

By reversing Islamic law, *Muruna* concludes an amazing doctrine that sanctions all prohibitions:[26]

"When evil and harm conflict as necessities demand, we must then choose the least of the two evils or harms. This is what the experts in jurisprudence decided…if interests and harms/evils conflict, or benefits conflict with evils, what is then to be decided is to review each benefit and each harm and its consequences, so the minor evils are forgiven for the sake of the greater long-term benefit. The evil is also accepted even if that evil is extreme and normally considered deplorable."

So the ruling on marriage with non-Muslims as we have with Huma and Anthony Weiner is a minor evil, which now becomes sanctioned even if Sharia prohibits it. While the media argues that Huma marrying a Jew is evidence of her assimilation, in actuality it is more the reason for suspicion, especially since her mother is a Muslim Brotherhood leader who never denounced the marriage. That with Huma's years of service as part of a Wahhabi scheme provides more concerns.

Besides much evidence reported on the Abedin's boss Abdullah Omar Naseef contributions for al-Qaeda, we have the WTC vs. Al Baraka, et. al.[27] It mentions Naseef, who arranged to meet Osama bin Laden and launch what seems like a major attack, right from one of Naseef's Muslim World League (MWL) offices:

"...a Memo on IIRO [International Islamic Relief Organization]/MWL letter-head detailed a meeting between Abu Abdallah (Osama bin Laden), Dr. Abdullah Omar Naseef, Sheik Abdel Majeed Zindani, and Dhiaul Haq, in which it is stated that, 'the attacks will be launched from them (these offices)...You must pursue finding an umbrella which you can stay under...and I prefer the name of the League (most likely, Muslim World League) because Dr. Naseef is one of the brothers...'"

While these statements were only in the preliminary documents that were removed in later documents, possibly since they are regarding older operations prior to 9/11, Naseef, according to this, was in *direct* communication with Osama bin Laden; this might shed a different light on the matter of Huma Abedin. For years, she had close ties with Naseef.[28] Naseef was proven to have been an al-Qaeda financier. The Naseef / Huma connection has no degrees of separation as many claimed. These statements made by the media were simply false.

Andrew McCarthy wrote that Naseef could have escaped the civil lawsuits on a technicality:[29]

"...he was named as a defendant in the civil case brought by victims of the 9/11 atrocities. (In 2010, a federal court dropped him from the suit—not because he was found to be uninvolved, but because a judge reasoned the American court lacked personal jurisdiction over him.)"

The Abedins went back and forth from east to west, even working during 1978 with Maulana Muhammad Yousuf of Jamaat-e-Islami in India.[30] Yusuf came after[31] Abu Al-Ala Maududi, who was key[32] in the Tabligh[33] in the Indian subcontinent's equivalent of the Muslim Brotherhood. It has extensive ties to Wahhabists, including Al-Qaeda and other terrorist groups. They represent an extremist Salafist brand. Then they travel to Saudi Arabia working with Naseef who spearheaded IMMA and commissioned the Abedins from Saudi Arabia to launch the program in the U.S. and the United Kingdom.

Do Americans think they circulated the earth, promoting this program solely by themselves? Were the Abedins fulfilling an "American dream", "representing our country and the democratic values that we hold dear" as President Obama says? Or is it that they are fulfilling a Saudi fantasy that our silence is making a reality?

What is ISNA's Mohamed Magid, an entity in the Saudi manifesto, doing in the White House, sitting across the table from Huma Abedin who was an IMMA assistant editor, another entity created by the House of Saud?[34]

The Abedins' boss, Abdullah Omar Naseef, never faced American justice. Is oil more powerful than justice? Why does the State Department keep the masses in the dark, not wanting them to connect the dots between the Saudi Wahhabist plans and the Abedins' IMMA?

Only then, when they connect the dots, can they begin to unravel why the Abedin family works with nefarious characters like Naseef and Qaradawi.[35] Only then can they understand how inter-linked these organizations are, their layers and sub-layers. IMMA was and is a family affair under Saudi management, a foreign entity that intends to do harm to United States interests.

Only when Americans finally wake up and ask politicians why it is taboo to discuss Huma Abedin, and demand the refutation of facts coupled with answers that are devoid of rhetoric. Only then will they support courageous congressmen before those congressmen are long gone. These are heroes, not slanderers as McCain implies. They represent the interests of the people and not the policy of silence. House Speaker John Boehner said to question Huma Abedin's loyalty is "dangerous"; silence is more deadly. When Bin Laden was finally given justice, no one was looking for jurisdictions. Yet, Al Saud and their henchmen still roam free, making sure America remains addicted to oil and constantly silent.

EXHIBIT A.1

The establishment of the World Assembly of Muslim Youth
By Dr. Salih Mahdi al-Samarrai
President of the Islamic Center of Japan

I was in an interview with Dr. Omar Hafez about the beginning of the establishment of the World Assembly of Muslim Youth; he said to me: 'Why don't you write it down as a good deed of what the vision of the Islamic banks contributed? Dr. Ahmed Najjar (Allah's mercy be upon him), and this is something that encouraged me to write. The hobby is to search for the roots: the first Muslim Japanese, the first Muslim English, the first Muslim American. The first stand for the Islamic Call (Da'wa) was established in the Hijaz before the one hundred and twenty years needed to spread Islam in America, with Muslims in North America benefiting from the roots of the Muslims in Latin America and other regions whose history I have neglected to document in this regard.

Since the beginning of the Kingdom of Saudi Arabia and when Allah took care of its founder, the late King Abdul Aziz, he has been calling the men of thought in the Muslim world for conferences and seminars and to the delegations visiting Mecca, to attend seminars and do Hajj (pilgrimage) and return. This responsibility began in 1965, when I came from Japan. I was a student at that time and was responsible for the Muslim Student Association in Japan. I came at the invitation of the Muslim World League and joined the delegations of young students from America and Europe, and was coordinating with the Association of the late Dr. Said Ramadan, head of the Islamic Center in Geneva where he had at the time, a strong relationship with the youth and student organizations globally.

We attended the second conference of the Muslim World League, sponsored by King Faisal bin Abdul Aziz (may Allah have mercy on him). It was attended by delegations from the Islamic world including the Chief Ministers of northern Nigeria, the martyr Ahmed Bello, and was attended by known leader Sheikh Abdullah Kashmiri, along with colleague Aslam Bek. Mr. Saleh Ozjan from Turkey, was in attendance, whom I saw for the first time after ten years of correspondence; it was attended by Sheikh Amjad Zahawi Chief Scientist in Iraq and Sheikh Mohammed Mahmoud Al Sawaf (may Allah have mercy on them) from Iraq, and Kamel-Sharif and the now deceased Moroccan leader Allal El Fassi and deceased Musa al-Sadr of Lebanon and the now deceased Omar Baha Al Amiri of Syria, Abdul Rahman Al Khalifa, Jordan and the now deceased Dr. Said Ramadan from Egypt and Khaled Kepa from Japan and then came Dr. Tawfiq Al-Shawi with a delegation from Germany as well as attendees from Sudan, Britain, France and others.

These are the names I remember. The conference started at a time when the Islamic nation was undergoing turmoil from Palestine to Kashmir to Yemen and other places.

At the head of the delegation was the Kingdom's late Sheikh Abdul Aziz bin Baz. Heading the delegation was Sheikh Mohammed Bin Srour and the late Saleh Qazzaz.

After attending the conference, we were convicted by the Hajj and all returned to the country they came from.

In 1972 I was a professor at the University of Riyadh (King Saud), prepared by the late Sheikh Hassan Al-Sheikh, Minister of Education at the time. A program to invite the leaders of young people from all over the world was coordinated with Dr. Tawfiq Al-Shawi and entrusted to Mr. Hamad Alsalifaih, official of Islamic Awareness at the Ministry of Ma'aref, in order to draw the calls and create a conference for young people.

I learned this when I went to Sheikh Hassan Al-Sheikh and I said: 'With all due respect to your staff in your esteemed ministry, it would be better if you seek the assistance of the elite professors and residents at the University of Riyadh who have the experience and knowledge on youth issues and the next phase will be more useful.' He said to me, 'Give me names.' I decided to sit down with Dr Abdul Rahman Al-Sheikh, then Dean of the Faculty of Agriculture, where I work, and later became minister of agriculture. Together, we created a list of the names he agreed to.

I sat down with His Excellency Dr. Abdul Rahman Al-Sheikh; we identified the following names of teachers for the cause:
    1 - Dr. Abdul Rahman Al-Sheikh
    2 - Dr. Abdullah Omar Nassif (Naseef)
    3 - Dr. Mahmoud Sifr
    4 –Dr. Abdulwahab Al Mansouri
    5 - Dr Ahmad Farid Mustafa
    6 - Dr Mohammed Obaid
    7 - Dr. Bakri
    8 - Dr. Saleh Al-Samarrai

The names were approved by His Excellency (H.E.), Sheikh Hassan and entrusted to His Excellency, Dr. Ahmad Mohamed Ali, an agent of the Ministry. We initiated a number of meetings to receive the youth and students from all over the world.

There was a row from the staff of the Ministry of Education facing a row of professors. At the top of the session chaired by H.E. Dr. Ahmad Mohamed Ali, who was developing the program for the symposium and arranged for lecturers and editors at the meetings and create the name of the seminar; it was decided to operate a secretariat.

Delegations came; preparers arranged the program, gave lectures and had discussions. After the completion of the program, they began another preparatory session with the delegations to do during the Hajj, which was accomplished as well, after their visit to the city of Medina. All then returned to the country where they came from.

This was followed by the establishment of the secretariat, headed by H.E. Dr. Abdul Rahman Al-Sheikh, with the help of Mr. Hamad Alsalifaih. After them followed Dr. Abdul Hamid Abu Sulayman, and Dr. Ahmed Tutunge, who gave the seminar a boost before being followed by the qualified men: Dr. Ahmed Bahafezallah, and Dr. Tawfiq al-Qaseer and then Dr. Mani' al-Juhani then, Dr. Saleh Al Wahaibi. Assisting these men were loyalists from various parts of the Kingdom and outside like Dr. Basahel Suliman, Dr. Auich bin Harbi Al-Ghamdi, Dr. Abdul Wahab Noreli, Dr. Saleh Bab'eer and many puritans which Allah knows. It would be better if I wrote a book, a thesis for all the men who contributed to the support of the symposium from home and abroad. Our predecessors always wrote to benefit the generations after them.

This certificate is attributed to all those involved who assumed a role, receiving the full reward and the reward is to the most loyal, "and ordered not to worship Allah, keeping religion pure for Him... It is the best word to those who called on God and work righteousness, and said I am a Muslim."

Note: I was working on the draft article and had spoken with H.E. Dr. Abdullah Omar Nassif on the subject in which he said: "During my studies in the West and then during a visit to the Kingdom, I spoke with the Rabita to establish a seminar for the World Association for [Muslim] Youth, which they were so willing to adopt." Thus, each view, that history starts from when the person begins it; if their accounts are included, we will get the complete history.

FOOTNOTES

1. Proof: Huma has Ties to Muslim Brotherhood – Countless Documents Surface. http://www.shoebat.com/documents/Huma_Brotherhood_Connections_072412.pdf

2. PJ Media, *Our government and the Muslim Brotherhoodd – My Speech in Washington,* by Andrew C. McCarthy. http://pjmedia.com/andrewmccarthy/2012/08/09/our-government-and-the-muslim-brotherhood-my-speech-in-washington/?singlepage=true

3. Arabic document. http://d1.islamhouse.com/data/ar/ih_books/single/ar_ghod_king_fahd.pdf

4. Arabic website. http://www.kl28.net/knol7/?p=view&post=1096052&page=30

5. Arabic website. http://dr-samarrai.com/?articles=topic&topic=21

6. Google Books, Arabic document. http://books.google.com/books?id=fMMf8wd1VeYC&pg=PT217&lpg=PT217&dq=#v=onepage&q&f=false

7. Aligarh Movement, *Teaching Should be Centered Around the Child, his Needs and Temperament,* Dr. Abidullah Ghazi. http://aligarhmovement.com/aligarians/abidullah_ghazi/a_ghazi_interview_iv

8. Wikipedia, *Mujaddid.* http://en.wikipedia.org/wiki/Mujaddid

9. Wikipedia, *Theology.* http://en.wikipedia.org/wiki/Theologian

10. Wikipedia, *Muhammad ibn Abd al-Wahhab.* http://en.wikipedia.org/wiki/Muhammad_ibn_Abd_al-Wahhab

11. Wikipedia, *Najd.* http://en.wikipedia.org/wiki/Najd

12. Wikipedia, *Saudi Arabia.* http://en.wikipedia.org/wiki/Saudi_Arabia

13. 4shared. http://www.4shared.com/office/R9BP9HpB/__-____.html

14. Arabic website. http://www.feqhweb.com/vb/t43.html

15. WND, *U.S. Chaplains Vetted by Muslim Who Condemns Jewish "Trickery",* by Bob Unruh. http://www.wnd.com/2011/07/320161/

16. Ibid

17. Arabic website. http://taghrib.org/pages/content.php?tid=6

18. http://www.kantakji.com/fiqh/Files/Fatawa/207.txt

19. Majlisul Ilm – The Scholarly Session of The Indian Islamic Association. http://majlisulilm.weebly.com/other-religions-festivlas.html

20. Arabic website. http://www.onislam.net/arabic/ask-the-scholar/8437/8381/53694-2004-08-01%2017-37-04.html

21. Andrew Bostom, *The Abedin Family's Pro-Jihadist Journal,* by Andrew Bostom. http://www.andrewbostom.org/blog/2012/08/06/the-abedin-familys-pro-jihadist-journal/

22. Taylor & Francis Online, *The Legal Methodology of "Fiqh al-Aqalliyyat" and its Critics: An Analytical Study,* Tauseef Ahmad Parray. http://www.tandfonline.com/doi/abs/10.1080/13602004.2012.665624

23. PJ Media, *Muruna: Violating Sharia to Fool the West,* by Walid Shoebat and Ben Barrack. http://pjmedia.com/blog/muruna-violating-sharia-to-fool-the-west/

24. Arabic website. http://www.qaradawi.net/library/66/3269.html

25. Arabic pdf download. http://www.hdhod.com/file/74481/

26. Arabic website. http://www.qaradawi.net/library/66/3269.html

27. http://www.netafoundation.org/file/FeaturedDocs/WTC_v_Al_Baraka_etal.pdf

28. Proof: Huma has Ties to Muslim Brotherhood – Countless Documents Surface. http://www.shoebat.com/documents/Huma_Brotherhood_Connections_072412.pdf

29. Ruthfully Yours, *Andrew McCarthy: Huma Abedin's Ties Are Not Just a Family Affair***,* by Ruth King. http://www.ruthfullyyours.com/2012/07/27/andrew-mccarthy-huma-abedins-ties-are-not-just-a-family-affair/

30. Arabic website with English available. http://www.al-islam.com/Content.aspx?pageid=1361&ContentID=2414

31. Arabic website. http://www.saaid.net/monawein/k/11.htm

32. Arabic website. http://www.dawalh.com/vb/showthread.php?t=3614&page=1

33. Middle East Forum, *Tablighi Jamaat: Jihad's Stealthy Legions,* by Alex Alexiev. http://www.meforum.org/686/tablighi-jamaat-jihads-stealthy-legions

34. Walid Shoebat, *Huma sits with ISNA President at White House Iftar dinner.* http://shoebat.com/2012/08/12/huma-sits-with-isna-president-at-white-house-iftar-dinner/

35. Proof: Huma has Ties to Muslim Brotherhood – Countless Documents Surface. http://www.shoebat.com/documents/Huma_Brotherhood_Connections_072412.pdf

APPENDIX B
9/11: 3000 Americans for Three Saudi Princes
New details about the Trouble Omissions of Saudi Arabia's wealthy from 9/11 Commission Report

Walid Shoebat and Ben Barrack

What is a Saudi prince worth? The answer is one Saudi prince is worth 1000 Americans. Evidence suggests it's a simple mathematical equation involving a deal being struck between the U.S. and Saudi Arabia that included the deaths of three Saudi princes who met very suspicious ends in July of 2002, within days of each other.

In a *Vanity Fair* article,[1] a former C.I.A. operative was cited as the source that identified those three princes as having been named by captured #3 man in al-Qaeda, Abu Zubaydah during interrogation sessions. Each of these three princes were said to have been financiers of 9/11. Many believe that the 9/11 Commission Report omitted the princes' involvement and that a 28-page, redacted chapter in a Joint Inquiry report—which remains classified—confirms foul play by Saudi Arabia regarding these deaths.

With that as a backdrop, what we provide in this report are more details about the deaths of those Saudi princes, courtesy of Arabic sources, believed to have never been released in English until now.

We include the only eyewitness account and translated reports that could help provide more pieces to this complex puzzle.

To date, in English, we cannot find any testimonies, eyewitness accounts, details, or any official investigation that provides any evidence which brings closure to these mysterious deaths, aside from the typical few lines and obituary notices.

The first was the story of Prince Ahmed bin Salman bin Abdulaziz, the well-known horse racing enthusiast and owner of Kentucky Derby winner War Emblem.[2] Less than one year earlier, bin Salman was allowed to fly out of the United States on 9/16/01. His cause of death was ruled a heart attack during routine abdominal surgery on July 22, 2002.[3]

The United States still refuses to release the names of over 140 Saudis who were permitted to leave the country on several planes in the days after 9/11. Prince bin Salman was one of the few who was identified as such, in a 9/11 Staff Report published about one month after the Commission Report was released; the Staff Report focused on the issue of terrorist travel.[4]

The second curious death is that of Prince Sultan bin Faisal bin Turki bin Abdullah al-Saud who mysteriously died on his way to bin Salman's funeral in a car accident one day later, on July 23, 2002.

The third is Fahd bin Turki bin Saud al-Kabir, who mysteriously got lost in the desert and died of thirst on July 30th, 2002.

Before we discuss the Arabic sources we examined, a crucial link is necessary between these three deaths and Abu Zubaydah, when he was captured in March of 2002.

In 2003, *TIME Magazine* published an article by Johanna McGeary[5] that focused on Zubaydah, considered to be "the Rosetta stone of 9/11" who provided a wealth of information about the internal dealings between al-Qaeda and Saudi Arabia. According to McGeary, Zubaydah was a:

"...leading member of Osama bin Laden's brain trust and the operational control of al-Qaeda's millennium bomb plots as well as the attack on the USS Cole in October 2000."

Subsequently, the U.S. depended largely on its allies to do some of the dirty work. Jordan—after an al-Qaeda attack on a hotel there—was asked to help get some of Abu Zubaydah's henchmen as they were rounded up in a Jordanian prison. It was my cousin—

Jawad Younis—who took the case, defending Abu Zubaydah's terrorists[6] to save some of the al-Qaeda operatives[7] from facing the hangman. Abu Hushar (named in the 9/11 Commission Report on Page 175)[8] and Abu Sammar weren't so lucky; both got sentenced to death by hanging.

As an aside, Jawad's brother—Kamal Younis—helped to plant seeds of doubt about my terrorist past to one gullible American named Eileen Fleming[9] while his brother Jawad, the prominent lawyer,[10] works with other Muslim Brotherhood activists to topple the Kingdom of Jordan and convert it to a Muslim Brotherhood state. Yet, people like Fleming give *them* credibility and attempt to impugn mine.

McGeary wrote that after Zubaydah was captured in Pakistan, he was transferred to Afghanistan.[11] While in captivity, he was sedated with truth serum (sodium pentothal), then the two Arab American agents told him that he was in a Saudi prison facility, to induce fear and make him empty his memory bank.

Zubaydah's reaction "was not fear, but utter relief." Happy to see 'Saudi agents', he:

> "...reeled off telephone numbers for a senior member of the royal family who would, said Zubaydah, 'tell you what to do'. The man at the other end would be Prince Ahmed bin Salman bin Abdul Aziz, a Westernized nephew of the late King Fahd and a publisher better known as a racehorse owner."

It cannot be understated that this was the same Prince bin Salman who was allowed to fly out of the United States on 9/16/01 without being questioned or interviewed. This is a glaring indictment of Bush administration policy relative to unfettered Saudis on American soil in the days after 9/11/01.

Abu Zubaydah mentioned all three royal-princes as intermediaries.

Yet, an examination of Arabic sources provides more reasons to suspect foul play. Take Prince Sultan bin Faisal bin Turki bin Abdullah al-Saud. There were four media reports that gave scant information about the circumstances of his death.

The official statements were provided to Al-Jazeera[12], to Okaz[13], to Al-Iktisadiyeh[14], and Asharq Al-Awsat[15], based in London. Only Asharq Al-Awsat preserved their version of the story in its archives; all the others purged their articles, which we had to obtain from other sources.

Okaz was a call-in by Faisal's half-brother Abdullah[16], who called the paper to issue a summary of the death.

There was only one eyewitness account, provided secondhand from Sultan's other brother. Prince Khalid relayed the testimony of an Ethiopian "Akhwiya"[17] by the name of Muhammad Hassan. "Akhwiya" is a term used only in Saudi Arabia, for what they consider lower class, handpicked non-Saudi helpers who usually tag along and hang around Saudi royals in hopes of gaining special favors.

Al-Jazeera's exclusive interview by Abdullah al-Kathiri with Prince Khalid seems more like an attempt to portray Hassan as an alibi in an oddly created section subtitled, "Eye Witness Account" to answer the question about how the prince was the only one killed in the alleged accident, despite having several helpers with him.

The story goes—as told by Hassan—that Prince Sultan took off at 2:00 AM en route from Jeddah to Riyadh after he paid sums of money to the usual beggars who surrounded his castle. While it's unusual to have beggars two hours past midnight, more troubling were the number of conflicting reports about how many cars were trailing the prince during his trip to attend Prince bin Salman's funeral—after the latter had died of a heart attack a day before.

Al-Jazeera reported that "several cars" trailed the prince while Asharq Al-Awsat cited the prince's business manager Hamdan Khalil Hamdan as saying that "two cars" trailed behind. Okaz reported there was only "one car" trailing the prince and then finally produced merely one lone man—an Ethiopian named Muhammad Hassan—who was trailing the prince.

The story continues that when Prince Sultan stopped in Ta'if to lead the group in morning prayers, one of the helpers (no name) offered to accompany the prince in his car and was shunned away by Prince Sultan, who loved to speed. As a gesture of self-sacrifice, the prince allegedly told him, "you are the only son of your mother".

After the prayers were finished, which would still be pitch dark (4-5 AM), they continued on the journey while the entourage followed the prince, who was speeding recklessly. Then all hell broke loose 70 miles before reaching Riyadh, in an area called Alhawmiyat. Hassan allegedly witnessed the tire explode while he was trailing directly behind prince Sultan. The vehicle (an Audi) then rolled several times in the air, crashing to the side of a mountain. As to the debris and how car pieces were strewn all over the place (an unexplained piece of the puzzle that had no source), Hassan assumed it was the result of the high rate of speed at which the prince was traveling. No reference was provided to the shattering of the vehicle or how this piece of information came about. But for Hassan to see a tire blowout, we must assume that he was traveling at the same high rate of speed as well. Why would the prince refuse passengers because he was a speeding fanatic while also expecting one of those would-be passengers—Muhammad Hassan (a name akin to Bob Smith)—to speed in order to keep up with him?

Hassan even relayed a miraculous ending to the prince's demise, saying that after his high-speed crash, Sultan died with his body hanging halfway out of the car while facing Mecca, and miraculously pointing his right index finger (a typical gesture Muslims make) to proclaim that Allah is the indivisible One God.

There was not a single firsthand account—no photos of the scene of the accident nor of the wreckage, no statements from police, nothing.

If foul play was involved, Alhawmiyat (where the death allegedly occurred) is an excellent place to claim an accident. A search of Alhawmiyat in Arabic shows the notoriety of this place for car accidents. Yet, how is it possible to find countless reports that include many photos of vehicles crashed by lay persons, as well as by several VIP's but nothing on prince Sultan? For example, Prince Muhammad bin Nay, while accompanying a Malaysian diplomat, had an accident and didn't even die. Nonetheless, several photos of the accident scene can be found, as can hospital photos, wreckage photos, etc.[18] An ambassador from Bosnia even had a simple accident and a report with a photo can be found.[19] Yet, a Saudi prince dies on his way to the funeral of another Saudi prince who died mysteriously one day earlier and there is nothing of the sort?

Prince Fahd bin Turki bin Saud al-Kabir's story about being lost in the desert is another unsolved mystery. What little detail of the story we found came from only a couple of purged media sources, which we got elsewhere.[20] They relayed the testimony of "Brigadier Abdul Qadir Altalha" who can be verified and *does* exist as someone working for the kingdom's authority. The prince's death was issued in the form of a statement from Altalha that was more about being an official warning that communicated, "beware of wandering in the desert" than it was an announcement of the death of a royal Saudi. It was definitely a great idea for minimum circulation and the report only existed on a handful of sites. We translated the report verbatim:

> "An accident forced the death of three Saudis, including a Prince who died of thirst in the desert. Saudi authorities had issued a warning urging citizens not to hike in the desert during the hot summer days in order to preserve their lives. The Royal Court issued a statement in Riyadh yesterday which mourned Prince Fahd bin Turki bin Saud Al-Kabeer, aged twenty-five years,

who died Monday afternoon as a result of thirst during a trip that was carried out in the desert of the southern province of Rumah near the Omani Centre, 90 kilometers east of the capital. The details of the incident as relayed by Brigadier Abdul Qadir Altalha were that three victims were on a picnic with two other colleagues in the Rumah area. While they were returning, the car fell into a ditch, which rendered it unusable, prompting three of them to move in an attempt to get rescued from the desert. The three lost the road and decided to return to the car and died beside it as a result of thirst. The other two were lucky and were able to guide a colleague to their place by using their mobile phone."

None of those stories add up. A man with a royal pedigree is stranded in the desert without fancy, sparkling water and leaves his vehicle on foot to get help while his other 'helpers' have a cell phone and were able to use it? The two who stayed behind got rescued while the royal prince lay dead by his car? Why are there no names of the eyewitnesses attached to the story except Prince Fahd and an official named Altalha? The story seems like an alibi to answer how a body was found. How could the other two who died with the prince have no names or any mention of an obituary showing they died with a royal?

When it comes to any 'Al Saud' stranded somewhere, the Kingdom sends its best. The story of Princess Lawlawa bint Mashhur is a case in point. When the Jeddah flood of 2011 left an entire city stranded,[21] a private chopper was sent at night not to rescue all or even some of the girls who were drowning at Dar al-Hekma College, but to pick up only one—Princess Lawlawa[22]—while leaving the rest of the women stranded; those left behind can be seen getting rescued a day later by courageous civilians.[23]

Countless people died in Jeddah and were buried under the mud and debris. This is a government that left girls to die in a fire, fearing that their rescue could lead to the possibility that some female flesh might be revealed while government officials sin in secret.

And why would a simple abdominal surgery cause a healthy young athlete like prince bin Salman a heart attack? These are accounts that remain highly suspect. While coverage by cameramen who visited the funerals was in abundance, none asked serious questions or took photos of the sites of these deaths; none provided any details apart from the fantastic, princely piety and self-sacrifice.

Consider the mathematical probabilities of the following events actually taking place:

- Three princes named by Abu Zubaydah as having helped plan 9/11 all die mysteriously within four months of Zubaydah's capture and within one week of each other.

- The stories of these three princes are not included in the 9/11 Commission Report or available in the original Arabic media sources.

- There are no photos or verifiable names of individuals present during these deaths.

- One prince dies in a car accident with his finger pointing toward Mecca, after his vehicle had flipped several times in the air.

- One prince dies after leaving behind a functioning mobile phone and walking through the desert without water, before dying next to the car he left to find help.

Perhaps a Washington Post article written by Douglas Farah in 2002 can provide some insight into what happened.[24] In that article, Farah references a National Security Council task force that was making recommendations to President Bush about how best to hold the Saudi government accountable for cracking down on al-Qaeda's financiers.

Farah relayed what officials told him might happen if the Saudis didn't play ball:

> ...they said the United States would first present the Saudis with intelligence and evidence against individuals and businesses suspected of financing al Qaeda and other terrorist groups, coupled with a demand that they be put out of business. In return, one senior official said, the administration will say, "We don't care how you deal with the problem; just do it or we will" after 90 days.

This article was written four months after the mysterious deaths of three Saudi princes who had been outed by a captured Abu Zubaydah four months earlier than those deaths.

Farah reported another interesting assertion by these officials, who allegedly...

"...said they would press the Saudis to act even if there was not enough information to convict someone in a court of law."

Three. Saudi. Princes.

Besides the mathematical impossibilities, mysterious deaths are not unusual when it comes to the Saudi Royal clan, though not without reason.[25] A French-Jewish mother named Candice Cohen-Ahnine—in a high-profile custody battle with a Saudi prince—died after falling from a fourth-story apartment, amid suspicions of foul play.

The United States knows full well that Saudi Arabia is the main apparatus that brings the fundamentalists out of Pandora's box when needed. Yet, it relies on the same royal family to put those fundamentalists back in because it knows that its survival depends on keeping this beast locked up. George W. Bush himself, in an op-ed that appeared in the Wall Street Journal,[26] encouraged westerners to embrace the Arab Spring, even suggesting that the fall of Middle Eastern dictators is somehow equivalent to the collapse of the Soviet Union.

The United States seems to support the Arab Spring no matter where it springs up, except of course and God forbid, if it erupts in Saudi Arabia. That's when the U.S. will be deathly silent because it likely will have meant that 3000 Americans were sold for three princes and countless barrels of oil; the dealings continue.

Caveat emptor.

SAUDI NATIONALS FLOWN OUT OF US SHORTLY AFTER 9/11

While the three Saudi Princes who met bizarre ends, almost certainly as a result of the capture and subsequent interrogation sessions with Abu Zubaydah, other members of the Royal family have escaped justice altogether. Indications are that had Zubaydah not been captured, Prince Ahmed bin Salman bin Abdulaziz, Prince Sulatan bin Faisal bin Turki bin Abdullah al-Saud, and Fahd bin Turki bin Saud al-Kabir would have as well.

Are we to believe that these men of royalty were the only ones who were involved in 9/11 and that justice was done through clandestine foul play? All is now well, right? If they were the only three, why weren't they arrested and tried publicly? Why weren't they handed over to U.S. authorities? Could it be that they knew far more than Zubaydah did?

Overwhelming evidence indicates that both the Bush administration and the 9/11 Commission decided not to target the source of al-Qaeda's funding and in instances when they appeared to be on the right track, they turned back. The Rabita Trust is a case in point. While it was designated a "Global Terrorist Entity" and had its assets frozen one month after 9/11, founder Abdullah Omar Naseef has escaped accountability; most American people don't even know who he is.

The story of Naseef's freedom today is anecdotal when one looks at how Saudi nationals were handled by the US Government in the days and weeks after 9/11.

After 9/11, flights were grounded until no earlier than 9/13. However, this wasn't like flipping a switch; restrictions on certain flights were still in place. A simmering controversy that involved the flights of several Saudi nationals out of the United States in the days after 9/11 surfaced in the weeks leading up to the release of the 9/11 Commission Report.

In fact, in the 9/11 Commission Staff Report on Terrorist Travel after 9/11,[27] it was conceded that the son of Prince bin Salman (the same bin Salman who would die from that mysterious heart attack) boarded a flight from Tampa, FL to Lexington, KY on 9/13/01, to rendezvous with his father. Both men were on a chartered flight from Lexington to London, England on 9/16/01.

In an article entitled, "The Great Escape," that appeared in the New York Times[28] prior to the release of the 9/11 Commission Report, Craig Unger wrote:

> ...there were still some restrictions on American airspace when the Saudi flights began.

According to Unger:

> We knew that 15 out of 19 hijackers were Saudis. We knew that Osama bin Laden, a Saudi, was behind 9/11. Yet we did not conduct a **police-style investigation** of the departing Saudis, of whom two dozen were members of the bin Laden family.

Judicial Watch, a legal government watchdog, obtained a list of passengers[29] on various flights between 9/11/01 and 9/15/01 courtesy of a Freedom of Information Act (FOIA) request of the Department of Homeland Security (DHS). Again, according to Unger:[30]

> According to newly released documents, 160 Saudis left the United States on 55 flights immediately after 9/11—making a total of about 300 people

who left with the apparent approval of the Bush administration, far more than has been reported before.

If, as was ultimately learned through obvious omissions in the 9/11 Commission Report, the Bush administration was reticent to go after entities with ties to the Saudi Royal family in the months and years after 9/11, shouldn't the American people know about decisions that were made which benefited the Saudi Royal family *immediately* after 9/11?

Moreover, as Unger rightly pointed out, despite the 9/11 Commission's conclusion that Saudi nationals were on chartered flights out of the country, a significant number of those nationals left the U.S. while restrictions on air space were still in place.[31] Had they not been Saudis, perhaps this could be explained away. The fact that so many Saudis were allowed to leave the country so soon after the attacks raises flags, especially relative to what we now know—and the Bush administration must have known at the time—about the involvement of the Saudi Royal family, in 9/11.

SAUDI PRINCE TURKI AL-FAISAL

According to documented 9/11 Commission staff statements,[32] 34 members of the Saudi Prince Turki al-Faisal's party departed from Las Vegas for Paris, France on September 24, 2001. The document further stated:

"...it appears that none of the 34 people on this flight was interviewed."

In 2004, as the 9/11 Commission was wrapping up its report, a post at the *Anger Management Course* blog included an excerpt from an article written by Margie Burns[33] that appeared at the *Baltimore Chronicle.* According to the author of that post, the article reported:

> All together, the hijackers made at least six trips to Vegas. Yet, a few days after 9-11, 31 passengers were allowed to fly out of Vegas, including one passenger named Al-Hazmi. **One Saudi royal aboard was Prince Turki bin Faisal, famous as the head of Saudi Arabia's bloodstained and much feared intelligence service from 1977 until he was abruptly fired in August 2001.**
>
> Whoa; time out. What, exactly, was the longtime head of Saudi Arabia's secret police doing in the United States, while 15 young Saudis were carrying out

their attacks? Prince Turki's brother was also on board the Vegas flight; another of their brothers is Saudi Arabia's foreign minister.

Why, exactly, did the fired head of Saudi intelligence hotfoot it over to this country, right after getting the boot? Or was he in the US when he was fired? His replacement was officially announced on August 31, 2001. Did National Security Adviser Condoleezza Rice, or anyone in the White House national security office, even know that these persons were in the United States? Given Prince Turki's documented contacts with Osama bin Laden and Pakistan's Inter Service Intelligence, which propped up the Taliban, why did the White House let these persons leave?

Some time thereafter, the *Chronicle* scrubbed any mention of Turki in a revised report.[34] The portion in bold above (as well as the two paragraphs beneath it) was replaced some time before May 30, 2004 with the following:

The Saudi royals aboard were mostly adults, with only a handful of young people born in the 1980s and 1990s. **At least one of these passengers, Ahmed bin Salman, the notable horse race fan and owner of a Kentucky Derby winner, died in somewhat suspicious circumstances a few months after his return home.** Another passenger, a British citizen, was his long-time chauffeur and major domo, to whom Ahmed Salman gave a prize horse race in return for his services.

Based on confirmed reports, one of them from the 9/11 Commission Staff Report itself,[35] we now know that Prince Turki flew from Las Vegas to Paris, France on 9/24/01. That squares with the first report from the *Baltimore Chronicle* but not with the second. The revised version (see the bolded portion) has Prince bin Salman flying out of Las Vegas too. How can this be? Bin Salman flew from Lexington to London on 9/16/01. Note that the revised report also says bin Salman flew with a British citizen. The Las Vegas flight went to Paris. This would seem to be another indicator that the *Chronicle's* first report was more accurate.

Naming bin Salman in 2004—two years after his death—may have seemed a safer bet than naming Prince Turki, who would become the Saudi Ambassador to the U.S. one year later (more on this later).

The newer version continued...

What were the Saudi royals and the others doing in Las Vegas? When did these officials and those connected with them go to Las Vegas, and how long did they stay there? What reason could the hijackers have had for trips to Vegas in the first place, other than to rendezvous with authorities, given that any extra movement increased their chances of getting caught? Is the White House really going to pretend that five skyjackers including the fervently devout Atta went to Vegas, separately and together at different times, only to fit in a little gambling? Was Las Vegas really just a convenient hub for the travelers? What other passengers on several other flights out were connected to these?

The removal of Turki's name from the *Chronicle's* article makes his presence in the U.S. immediately before and after 9/11 – which has since been confirmed – even more suspicious. *The Global Security* website made reference to Turki's flight out of the United States shortly after 9/11 as well.[36]

Considering what was known about Turki at the time—he had recently ended his tenure as Director of the General Intelligence Directorate,[37] Saudi Arabia's foreign intelligence service, after 24 years—it is at a minimum, curious that he was not interviewed. Later, Turki would become the Saudi ambassador to the United States[38] and was welcomed to the Oval Office during the Bush administration in 2006. Turki would serve in that capacity from 2005—2007.

In January of 2012, Turki was given a platform by Amy Kellogg of *Fox News*,[39] to express his views on Saudi Arabia's problems with Iran. This is noteworthy in light of Prince Alwaleed bin Talal's ever increasing influence over the "Fair and Balanced" network through his ownership in *Newscorp.*[40]

The 9/11 Commission report itself spoke of dealings Turki had with Taliban leader Mullah Omar during the Clinton administration in 1998. Apparently, it was not deemed appropriate to revisit the former Saudi intelligence chief's dealings with the Taliban before allowing him to fly out of the country after 9/11 without being questioned. As was the case with various organizations found to have financed al-Qaeda, the portrayal of Turki in the report is one in which no complicity in 9/11 was found. Groups known to have financed al-Qaeda were painted as practically innocent victims of infiltration; Turki comes across in the report as an ally, not a foe, of the United States.

That portrayal is seemingly belied by facts and testimony.

In a 2009 *New York Times* article penned by Eric Lichtblau,[41] it was reported that lawyers for the plaintiffs in a lawsuit that sought justice for the 9/11 victims, had come into possession of documents that implicated members of the Saudi Royal family, to include Prince Turki Al-Faisal. In fact, a link to many of those documents was posted in Lichtblau's piece.

In particular, one document that stands out is the transcript[42] of a sworn deposition conducted by the plaintiffs of the 9/11 families in a civil lawsuit. The Muslim man who was deposed (name redacted) allegedly fought against the Taliban (presumably for the Northern Alliance); his testimony implicated none other than Prince Turki Al Faisal.

We begin with the account of the deposed subject in which he discusses the details of a prisoner exchange in 1998 that involved a man named Said Jalal as the negotiator:

Q: Did—was Said Jalal working for anyone from Saudi Arabia?

A: When I—when I had gone with him to Kabul during this mission that he starts about exchange of prisoners, I went with him in Kabul. There was a guest house concerned Mullah Kabir, he was the deputy—the Deputy Prime Minister for Taliban and when I was there and I saw with him a cheque, money cheque, and the cheque was about a billion riyals, Saudi Riyals.

And at that time I guessed that he is not a simple person, he is not at the low level. Maybe he is—he is working with the—**I believed at that time he was working with the intelligent service of Saudi.**

Q: And who was the head of the intelligence service of Saudi?

A: At that time he was Turki Al Faisal.

A short time later, the deposed subject confirmed that the riyal is indeed Saudi currency. That, coupled with the fact that the cheque was for one billion riyals, indicated a very powerful person with access to Saudi money.

This is significant because of who this individual—according to the deposition—was meeting with:

Q: And—did Said Jalal at any time ever talk to you about Mullah Omar?

A: Yes. Every time he—he had came from—from Mullah Omar directly.

The subject proceeded to talk about several prisoner exchanges coordinated by Jalal on Mullah Omar's behalf.

In perhaps the most revealing exchange, the deposed individual talked about the purchase of hundreds of trucks by Mullah Omar, courtesy of Saudi money:

Q: Did people from Saudi Arabia come openly and give money to Mullah Omar and the Taliban?

A: Yes.

Q: When Said Jalal said that he gave 500 pick-up trucks to the Taliban and that he said that he personally made sure that Mullah Omar came to power, was—did Said Jalal buy these trucks with his own money?

A: No, because 500 pick-ups is not so little.

Q: It is not, right, it's not cheap?

A: Not cheap.

Q: Who was he buying—who do you—who was he buying these—who gave him the money to buy these trucks?

A: When **I believe that Said Jalal may be working with Turki Al Faisal**, that the money, I believe that **the money is from that intelligence service**.

Q: And do you personally know that Said Jalal was working with Turki?

A: I guessed yes.

If this is accurate testimony, it means that another Saudi Royal prince was actively working—through an emissary—to aid the Taliban at a time when Osama bin Laden and the Taliban were working very closely together. Turki's dealings with Mullah Omar were known during the Clinton administration so again, why would this particular Saudi prince be permitted to leave the United States less than two weeks after 9/11/01 without being questioned?

THIS IS NOT SECOND GUESSING

Those who make the claim that dredging these things up today is just second guessing run into a bit of a problem courtesy of William Murray, head of the Religious Freedom Coalition. One month after the 9/11 attacks, Murray, who had access to U.S. Congressmen, Senators, and powerful operatives within the Bush administration, published his post-9/11 diary.[43]

Here is an excerpt from what Murray wrote about what happened on 9/12/01:

> By mid afternoon on Wednesday I was convinced that not only was the United States a victim of Islamic Jihad, but that the attack had been perpetrated by an organization controlled by a Saudi citizen and that most of those involved were Saudi, and that furthermore **the attack was financed for the most part by Saudi businessmen and members of the Saudi royal family.**

Murray then relayed what he said to his wife that evening:

> "**These attacks were planned, financed and carried out by Saudi nationals and as a result the real culprits will never come to justice. We will bomb some third world nation like Afghanistan and our government will say our moderate Islamic friends with all the oil were not involved.** Worse, we will put a handful of people in jail like we did the last time the World Trade Center was bombed. The Islamic fanatics will think a trade off of four or five in jail getting three meals a day, versus thousands of Americans dead, is a great deal."

Perhaps one of Murray's most salient points came one day later—on 9/13/01—in response to a Senator who defended the Saudi Royal family's financing of Osama bin Laden by saying they were "coerced" into doing so.

Said Murray in response to the Senator:

> "**Maybe those millionaire Saudi businessmen should be more fearful of us than they are of Bin Laden.**"

Sadly, defending the Saudis against those who believed the truth should win out, would become a central theme of the 9/11 Commission Report—and ultimately, the U.S. Government.

ABLE DANGER

While stationed at Bagram Air Base in October of 2003, Lt. Col. Anthony Shaffer was informed that members of the 9/11 Commission were on base. Shaffer, who was a key member of a program known as Able Danger, which he—along with other team members—says identified lead hijacker Mohamed Atta one year before the attacks and well before the program was shut down in October of 2000. Shaffer met with the Commission's Executive Director Philip Zelikow at Bagram and briefed him on Able Danger's findings.

In his book *Operation Dark Heart,* Shaffer explains how after briefing Zelikow and other Commission members, the Executive Director was noticeably shocked and handed Shaffer his business card while telling him to contact his office upon returning to the United States, saying, "What you said today is very important." [1] The treatment Shaffer received subsequent to that briefing was contemptible on the part of his own government.

Upon Shaffer's return to the U.S. in January of 2004, Zelikow's interest in Able Danger seemed to do a 180; Shaffer faced significant consequences for bringing it to the 9/11 Commission's attention. Those consequences included the revocation of his security clearance. Shaffer learned upon his return to the states that the Inspector General of the Defense Intelligence Agency (DIA) was investigating him. The reasons given stemmed from three claims against him[44] that involved misuse of a government phone ($67); filing a false voucher ($180); and undue award of the Defense Meritorious Service Medal. Shaffer later learned that DIA was searching for a way to rescind his Bronze Star as well.

Shaffer had the following to say about treatment he received from DIA, in sworn testimony before the House Armed Services Committee just a few short years later:[45]

In my specific instance, DIA has been allowed by DoD to make an "example" of me to try and intimidate the others from coming forward by spending what we now estimate $2 million in an effort to discredit and malign me by creating false allegations, and using these false allegations to justify revocation of my Top Secret security clearance.

Incidentally, in the weeks after the 9/11 attacks, one of Shaffer's Able Danger teammates—Dr. Eileen Preisser—informed him in real time that she was meeting with Scooter Libby, Vice President Dick Cheney's assistant about the details of Able Danger. [2] This account confirms that Cheney's office was briefed on the program.

Able Danger received not one mention in the 9/11 Commission Report, which was released on July 22, 2004.

RABITA TRUST

One month after the September 11th attacks, the Treasury Department froze the assets of an entity known as the Rabita Trust (RT), identifying it as a Specially

Designated Global Terrorist Entity. RT was suddenly on a list of notorious actors and entities, along with 38 others. In an article published by the *Washington Post* at the time,[46] it became obvious that political considerations were a priority:

> The list was the product of tense debate within the U.S. government, which is torn by potentially conflicting priorities: stopping the flow of money, protecting intelligence sources and methods, and *avoiding affronts to key allies such as Saudi Arabia.*

Perhaps the premise that Saudi Arabia is an ally of the United States should have been subjected to more critical analysis after the 9/11 attacks. Abdullah Omar Naseef, who founded Rabita Trust in 1988 escaped the 9/11 civil trials.[47] As Andrew McCarthy points out,[48] none other than Wael Hamza Julaidan—an al-Qaeda founder—was put in charge of Rabita.

The *Washington Post* article expounded on the stickling political battle over identifying Rabita as a terrorist entity:[49]

> Government officials said federal agencies have argued for weeks about whether to publicly describe the Rabita Trust, a Muslim charity closely tied to the Saudi and Pakistani governments, as being affiliated with bin Laden. Ultimately, the Treasury Department listed the Rabita Trust, which top Pakistani officials helped establish to resettle refugees from Bangladesh. Pakistan's president, Gen. Pervez Musharraf, has had an official affiliation with the trust.

The *Washington Post* identified Julaidan as Rabita's "secretary-general" while also identifying the charity as an arm of the Muslim World League, an entity sanctioned by the Saudi Royal family.[50] None other than Abdullah Omar Naseef—Rabita Trust's founder—served as MWL's Secretary-General.[51] This would place him above an al-Qaeda founder[52] in charge of the organization Naseef founded.

Moreover, in a 2003 *Washington Post* article by Douglas Farah,[53] it was reported that radical Islamic charities which were allegedly shut down, remained open and that none other than al-Qaeda founder Julaidan, who had been designated a terrorist financier one year after 9/11, was not being held to account by the Saudis, as they promised.[54]

Wrote Farah:

A source with direct knowledge of U.S. actions said the "highest priority of the U.S. government is to get the Saudis to do what they said [they] would do and close down what they were supposed to close down." The source noted that, after agreeing to put him on the U.N. list, **senior Saudi officials publicly denounced Julaidan's designation**.

In another article by Farah,[55] he quoted one of the officials who was angry about the situation:

"We were livid at the disavowal of the Jalaidan designation," a senior U.S. official said. "The Saudi public statements in that case were nothing short of schizophrenic. Saudi Arabia is one of the epicenters of terrorist financing."

You read that right; the Saudi government openly protected an al-Qaeda founder. Perhaps more egregiously, however, are the subsequent omissions by the 9/11 Commission.

The 9/11 Commission Report identified Julaidan only in footnote #58 of Chapter 7 as having been in Tucson in the "1980s and early 1990s", hinting that his presence there may have had something to do with 9/11 hijacker Hani Hanjour spending so much time there in the mid-1990s. Despite this connection, neither Julaidan's Rabita Trust nor that entity's founder, Abdullah Omar Naseef, were mentioned in the 9/11 Commission Report.

MUSLIM WORLD LEAGUE (MWL)

As the Secretary-General of the Muslim World League (MWL) from approximately 1983—1993, Naseef headed an organization based in Saudi Arabia. The MWL is not just based there; it is funded and controlled by the Saudi Royal family. Additionally, the name Muslim World League is virtually synonymous with the term "Rabita".[56] In essence, Naseef's Rabita Trust could have been named the Muslim World League Trust. Once one makes that leap, it becomes obvious how close the Bush administration came to identifying the Saudi Royal family as a Specially Designated Terrorist entity in 2001.

A little more than six months after the 9/11 attacks, the Financial Times reported on the operations of a task force that included the IRS, the FBI, and the Secret Service. Named Operation Green Quest (OGQ), the objective was to disrupt the sources of terrorist fundraising. In this case, the Bush administration seemed to be on the right track as the MWL was identified as a target. Here is an excerpt from the article:[57]

> In northern Virginia they (OGQ) targeted, among others, the International Institute of Islamic Thought, the Graduate School of Islamic Social Sciences, the **Muslim World League** and the Fiqh Council of North America. These bodies were described by the Council on American-Islamic Relations (Cair) as "respected Islamic institutions" whose targeting "sends a hostile and chilling message to the American Muslim community and contradicts President Bush's repeated assertions that the war against terrorism is not a conflict with Islam".

In addition to the MWL, each one of the entities identified by the Financial Times had ties to the Muslim Brotherhood. Yet, political pressure applied by groups like CAIR—which has extensive Brotherhood ties of its own—seemed to be effective when it came to neutralizing any inclinations to pursue these avenues that the Bush administration may have had. In 2006, this dynamic was revealed when Bush referred to America's enemies as "Islamic fascists". After pressure was applied by CAIR, such words were never again uttered by the president.[58]

The MWL was not named in the 9/11 Commission Report.

INTERNATIONAL ISLAMIC RELIEF ORGANIZATION (IIRO)

The IIRO was spawned by the MWL and is not only funded by the Saudi Royal family but in 2003 it was led by Osama bin Laden's brother-in-law.[59] The Anti-Defamation League (ADL)[60] wrote the following:

> In July 2003, **during the 9/11 Commission hearings, numerous analysts identified IIRO as a major radical Islamic institution in part responsible for fueling Islamic militancy around the world**. Testimony delivered at the commission attested to the fact that **Mohammad Jamal Khalifa, the brother-in-law of Osama bin Laden**, arrived in the Philippines in 1988 and became the founding director of the IIRO. He used the IIRO to funnel Al Qaeda funds to the Abu Sayyaf group and the Moro Islamic Liberation Front.

Front Page Magazine (FPM) reported on a 2002 $100 trillion lawsuit which "named defendants (that) gave contributions to charities directly linked to the Al Qaeda terrorist organization." Prince Sultan bin Abdulaziz al Saud of Saudi Arabia was one of those defendants.[61] This lawsuit pointed to IIRO's Canadian branch director as having claimed that his organization was a "direct arm of the Saudi Royal family."[62]

FPM had the following to say about Sultan's dealings:[63]

> Sultan also has donated personal money to the al-Haramain Islamic Foundation, Muslim World League, and the World Assembly of Muslim Youth. All of these groups have been exposed by the brief of having sponsored, aided, abetted or materially financed al Qaeda.

Jonathan Schanzer cited a former FBI analyst as saying IIRO donated at least $280,000 to Hamas charities[64] while also reporting that Israeli officials identified IIRO as an organization that implemented a program to compensate the families of Hamas suicide bombers.[65]

The United Nations identified two IIRO branch offices[66]—in the Philippines and Indonesia—as terrorist entities from as early as 2007 through 2011.

According to an article in *Front Page Magazine* by Paul Sperry,[67] the President of the IIRO in the United States (IRO) shortly before 9/11 was a man by the name of Mohamed S. Omeish, who also shared an office with Abdurahman Alamoudi, a man eventually convicted on charges related to terrorism. Incidentally, Omeish served alongside Anwar al-Awlaki from late 2001 through early 2002;[68] they were the only two Muslim chaplains on the board of George Washington University's Muslim Students Association, a Muslim Brotherhood front.

Omeish's brother—Esam Omeish—is credited by Sperry with hiring al-Awlaki as an Imam at the Dar al-Hijrah mosque that aided the 9/11 hijackers.[69] That mosque allegedly received large donations from the IIRO.

In an article by Judith Miller for the *New York Times*, IIRO was identified as having been raided by the FBI in 2002.[70] Miller also reported that MWL was a parental entity, saying further that MWL and IIRO were housed in the same office. This places the MWL—a group that Naseef once led—above the IIRO.

In a separate *New York Times* article written by Eric Lichtblau in 2009,[71] it was reported that Treasury Department documents—obtained by plaintiffs in a case against alleged 9/11 perpetrators—identified the IIRO as a group that showed "'support for terrorist organizations' at least through 2006."

In 2009, the IIRO reopened in the United States.[72] According to the *Global Muslim Brotherhood Daily Report (GMBDR)*, the office is in Hialeah, FL and the president is Adnan Khalil Basha, who has also served as the Secretary-General for the IIRO in Saudi Arabia. According to the same report, another entity – Sana-Bell – which had originally been created to generate funds for IRO, shared an address with SAAR (mentioned later).

GMBDR reported in 2010 that the reopening of the IRO in the U.S. "seems designed to preserve the organization's ties to the Muslim World League (MWL), the IIRO's parent organization."

Moreover, the face of the then newly reopened IRO was Malik Sardar Khan, who shared an address with a Muslim World Congress front. According to the GMBDR report, none other than Abdullah Omar Naseef was listed as the President of both the MWC internationally as well as for its U.S. branch.

> The IIRO was not named in the 9/11 Commission Report, despite "numerous analysts" (according to the ADL) who, during the 9/11 Commission hearings, identified IIRO as an entity that funded al-Qaeda. Also receiving no mention were Mohamed S. Omeish, Esam Omeish, Sana-Bell, or Abdurahman Alamoudi, who had been arrested on charges related to terrorism nearly one year before the release of the report.

SAAR FOUNDATION

After 9/11, the FBI also raided the offices of the Sulaiman Abdul Aziz Rajihi (SAAR) Foundation.[73] Interestingly, SAAR's offices were located across the street from a Muslim Brotherhood front group known as the International Institute for Islamic Thought (IIIT). It also shared an office with the aforementioned Sana-Bell.[74] Abdurahman Alamoudi, who once served as executive assistant to the president of the SAAR Foundation,[75] was convicted of charges relating to terrorism and given a 23-year prison sentence in 2004. At the *New York Times*, Judith Miller had the following to say about Rajihi after the 2002 raid:[76]

> Officials said SAAR had been financed in large part by Suleiman Abdel Aziz al-Rajhi, a Saudi banker and financier who is said to be close to the Saudi ruling family.

SAAR was also implicated in the funding of another individual convicted of financing terrorism[77]—Sami Al-Arian, who pleaded guilty to doing business with the Palestinian Islamic Jihad (PIJ).[78]

> SAAR was not named in the 9/11 Commission Report.

WAMY AND AL-HARAMAIN

The World Association of Muslim Youth (WAMY) was the parent of the Muslim Minority Affairs program which was set up in the West by the Abedin family. WAMY is an organization that has worked extremely closely with the MWL and the IIRO. *Discover the Networks* reports that Osama bin Laden's nephew—Abdullah bin Laden—founded the organization.[79] One of WAMY's aims that is similar to IMMA is to:[80]

> Preserve the identity of Muslim youth and help overcome the problems they face in modern society.

It is important to understand this concept in the context of the goals of the Institute of Muslim Minority Affairs (IMMA), which seeks to turn Muslim minority lands into Muslim *majority* lands world wide as described in the Saudi Manifesto.[81]

WAMY, like the al-Haramain Islamic Foundation, was mentioned in the 9/11 Commission Report (WAMY was identified by name once, al-Haramain twice) but in both instances, the two organizations seemed to be painted as victims of exploitation instead of as what they are—terrorist-funding entities.

In talking about al-Haramain, the Report seemed to blame al-Qaeda's reliance on:

> ...al Qaeda sympathizers in specific foreign branch offices of large, international charities—particularly those with lax external oversight and ineffective internal controls, such as the Saudi-based al Haramain Islamic Foundation. Smaller charities...had employees who would siphon the money to al Qaeda. [3]

Note the implication. Al-Haramain was not responsible for controlling its own finances; it had been taken advantage of by al-Qaeda operatives:

> Al Qaeda and its friends **took advantage of Islam's strong calls for charitable giving, zakat.** These financial facilitators also appeared to rely heavily on certain imams at mosques who were willing to divert zakat donations to al Qaeda's cause. [4]

When making its lone reference to WAMY, the 9/11 Commission report also painted that organization as being victimized by sneaky al-Qaeda operatives:

While Saudi domestic charities are regulated by the Ministry of Labor and Social Welfare, charities and international relief agencies, such as the **World Assembly of Muslim Youth (WAMY)**, are currently regulated by the Ministry of Islamic Affairs. This ministry uses zakat and government funds to spread Wahhabi beliefs throughout the world, including in mosques and schools... **Some Wahhabi-funded organizations have been exploited by extremists** to further their goal of violent jihad against non-Muslims. One such organization has been the **al Haramain Islamic Foundation**...[5]

Americans were being told that groups like WAMY and al Haramain had essentially been infiltrated and deserved little more than wrist slaps. The notion that Wahhabists were being exploited by extremists was like saying Al Capone was exploited by his mobsters.

WAMY Founder, Abdullah bin Laden, was not named in the 9/11 Commission Report. WAMY and al Haramain were mentioned once and twice, respectively but only as innocent bystanders who had been unwittingly duped and infiltrated by al-Qaeda operatives.

INSTITUTE OF MUSLIM MINORITY AFFAIRS (IMMA)

Abdullah Omar Naseef founded the Institute for Muslim Minority Affairs (IMMA) in the late 1970s with the full backing of the Saudi Royal family. As our writings on the Saudi Manifesto demonstrate, the IMMA was commissioned, in part, after a meeting between Syed Z. Abedin and Naseef in Gary Indiana.[82] Abdullah Ghazi relays his experience thusly:

"Later we shifted to Gary in Indiana State, 40 kms from Chicago. In 1976, I met Rabita (MWL) chief Dr. Abdullah Omar Naseef and Dr. Zainul Abedin of Institute for Muslim Minority Affairs. They encouraged me to take up this venture. The first book to come out was Our Prophet, an assignment from King Abdul Aziz University, Jeddah at Dr. Naseef's behest..."

One of the people whom Naseef served with at the IMMA is Huma Abedin, the Deputy Chief of Staff for Secretary of State, Hillary Clinton. Abedin also served on the board of the Muslim Students Association's (MSA) George Washington University chapter in 1997 (a few short years later, both IRO President Mohamed S. Omeish and al-Qaeda terrorist Anwar al-Awlaki would serve on that same board as chaplains). The goal of the IMMA is to transform all Muslim minority lands into Muslim majority lands, including the United States of America.

Neither IMMA nor Abdullah Omar Naseef were mentioned in the 9/11 Commission Report.

NO JUSTICE FOR 9/11 FAMILIES

If one subscribes to the notion that the 9/11 attacks were an act of war comparable to Pearl Harbor with the Saudi Royal family assuming the role of the Japanese Empire by comparison, the attacks were not met with a warranted response. To take the analogy further, it would have been as if the United States decided to demand and expect that the Japanese emperor punish his fighter pilots for the attacks.

The only recourse left to the families of the fallen would be to file a civil lawsuit against the Japanese government.

The equivalent of just that happened when the families of 9/11 victims filed a lawsuit against Saudi Arabia and members of the Royal family for their alleged complicity in the attacks. After years of legal battles, the families were spurned by those who should have doggedly pursued justice on their behalf.

At one point, a district court cited the Foreign Sovereign Immunity Act (FSIA) and ruled that it protected Saudi Arabia, that the court had no jurisdiction over a foreign nation.[83] Isn't that what made the attacks an act of war? Using this logic, the families would be denied justice when the Bush administration failed to identify the enemy that attacked the nation he was charged with leading. Then, after deciding to pursue justice for themselves, those families would be told they had no right to do so.

In 2009, the *New York Times'* Eric Lichtblau reported, after the families had been through years of legal battles, that then Solicitor General Elena Kagan filed a brief with the U.S. Supreme Court in which she agreed with the district court ruling and sided with the Saudis.[84] The 9/11 families were justifiably livid and said, in part, the following in a statement:[85]

> The Administration's filing mocks our system of justice and strikes a blow against the public's right to know the facts about who financed and supported the murder of 3,000 innocent people. It undermines our fight against terrorism and suggests a green light to terrorist sympathizers the world over

that they can send money to al Qaeda without having to worry that they will be held accountable in the U.S. Courts for the atrocities that result.

Ultimately, the Supreme Court sided with the district court and the Obama administration; it refused to hear the case.[86]

A little more than one year later, Kagan was confirmed by the U.S. Senate as a Supreme Court Justice after having been nominated by President Barack Obama.

POSTSCRIPT

In late 2005, it was reported by *Government Executive* that the data mined by Able Danger was destroyed by Army major Erik Kleinsmith.[87] One of the reasons for doing so was that the program, identified as "intelligence on steroids" by Kleinsmith, gathered information on U.S. citizens:

> People's names and personal information litter the Internet. Data harvesting, by its very nature, is indiscriminate and sweeping. **Unavoidably, along with "Osama Bin Laden," an often-mentioned name like "Bill Clinton" will be harvested. That says a lot about the power, and the limits, of data mining**, and why Kleinsmith destroyed what he had; the military is not supposed to be gathering information on U.S. citizens.

The technology that was ultimately used in Able Danger was first used in an experiment with the Information Dominance Center (IDC) in early 1999 to look into any potential leaks of U.S. military technology to the Chinese. In the same article, *Government Executive* reported:[88]

> During construction of those link diagrams, **the names of a number of U.S. citizens popped up, including some very prominent figures. Condoleezza Rice**, then the provost at Stanford University, appeared in one of the harvests, the by-product of a presumably innocuous connection between other subjects and the university, which hosts notable Chinese scholars.
>
> **William Cohen, then the secretary of Defense, also appeared.** As one former senior Defense official explained, the IDC's results "raised eyebrows," and **leaders in the Pentagon grew nervous** about the political implications of turning up such high-profile names, or those of any American citizens who were not the subject of a legally authorized intelligence investigation. Rumors still abound about other notable figures caught up in the IDC's

harvest. **"I heard they turned up Hillary Clinton," the official said. The experiment was not continued.**

Ok, so based on this report, the China experiment was suspended. Yet, the technology was resurrected later that year to take the fight directly to al-Qaeda.

In late 1999 / early 2000, Able Danger was in full gear but Kleinsmith was told that because the harvesting had turned up the names of so many American citizens, he had 90 days to destroy them, which he did:

> By the spring of 2000, Kleinsmith said, the IDC had the list of 20 individuals whom Special Operations wanted investigated further under Able Danger. But in March, Kleinsmith was ordered to cease all work on the project. He believes the order came from outside the IDC's command. From May to June, Kleinsmith and his team destroyed the information, and possibly the linkages between Mohamed Atta, Al Qaeda, and convicted terrorists already sitting in U.S. prisons.

It's worth noting that *Government Executive* reported as a matter of fact that the names of Rice and Cohen came up during the China harvest; that Hillary Clinton's name came up is allegedly a matter of speculation and rumor.

However, what about the al-Qaeda harvest? If this technology was so sweeping that it uncovered tangential and innocuous relationships between the future National Security Advisor and the Secretary of Defense under Bill Clinton, why wouldn't it uncover a very tangible relationship between Hillary Clinton and Huma Abedin, a woman with distinct ties to both al-Qaeda and the Saudi Royal family through her boss, Abdullah Omar Naseef?

It's worth noting that Huma Abedin began working for Hillary Clinton in 1996, four years before the Able Danger harvest of al-Qaeda commenced. An important question remains:

> Did that harvest reveal the Hillary Clinton—Huma Abedin—Abdullah Omar Naseef connection?

Unlike the innocuous connections that might have come up elsewhere (between Bill Clinton and bin Laden, for example), Abedin's connection to both Hillary Clinton—as the first lady's employee—as well as to Naseef, the former Secretary-General of the MWL, founder of RT and IMMA, would not have been nearly as innocuous.

Based on the omissions of the 9/11 Commission Report, we are left to conclude that the Commission didn't just want to prevent the truth about Able Danger from coming out; it also wanted to avoid revealing the truth about those who were ultimately responsible for the attacks.

[1] Shaffer, Anthony, Operation Dark Heart, p. 178, St. Martin's Press, 2010

[2] Operation Dark Heart, p. 176

[3] The 9/11 Commission Report, p. 170; link is http://www.9-11commis-sion.gov/report/911Report.pdf

[4] Ibid

[5] Ibid, p. 372

FOOTNOTES

1. Vanity Fair, *The Kingdom and The Towers*. http://www.vanityfair.com/politics/features/2011/08/9-11-2011-201108

2. The New York Times, *Prince Ahmed bin Salman, Top Horse Owner, Dies at 43,* by Joe Drape. http://www.nytimes.com/2002/07/23/sports/prince-ahmed-bin-salman-top-horse-owner-dies-at-43.html?pagewanted=all&src=pm

3. The Vancouver Sun, *Saudi Arabia: The Teflon Kingdom,* Jonathan Manthorpe. http://www2.canada.com/vancouversun/columnists/story.html?id=7be93472-773b-4fe4-b105-03cea80616d0&p=2

4. Staff Report of the National Commission on Terrorist Attacks Upon the United States, *9/11 And Terrorist Travel*. http://www.statewatch.org/news/2004/aug/911-terr-trav.pdf

5. Time Magazine, *Confessions of a Terrorist,* by Johanna McGeary. http://www.time.com/time/magazine/article/0,9171,480226,00.html

6. CNN.com, *Jordan court sentences six bin Laden men to hang.* http://archives.cnn.com/2000/WORLD/meast/09/18/jordan.binladen.reut/

7. ITN Source, *Jordan/Lebanon: Six Muslim Militants Sentenced to Death for Plotting Attacks Against U.S. and Israeli Targets in Jordan.* http://www.itnsource.com/shotlist//RTV/2000/09/18/009180007/?s=*

8. 911comm-sec6.pdf, *From Threat to Threat*. http://www.fas.org/irp/offdocs/911comm-sec6.pdf

9. Veterans Today, *Phony Terrorist Sideshow: Walid Shoebat, Bin Laden Wannabee,* by Eileen Fleming. http://www.veteranstoday.com/2011/07/17/cnn-catches-up-to-the-new-fourth-estate-regarding-walid-shoebat/

10. Arabic website. http://www.albalqanews.net/NewsDetails.aspx?NewsID=12351

11. Time Magazine, *Confessions of a Terrorist,* by Johanna McGeary. http://www.albalqanews.net/NewsDetails.aspx?NewsID=12351

12. Arabic website. http://www.hafaralbaten.net/vb/showthread.php?t=2587

13. Arabic website. http://ahsaweb.net/vb/showthread.php?t=19114

14. Arabic website. http://www.alnadawi.com/vb/archive/index.php/t-10593.html

15. Arabic website. http://www.aawsat.com/details.asp?issueno=8435&article=114838

16. Arabic website. http://www.aawsat.com/details.asp?issueno=8435&article=114838

17. Arabic website. http://www.otaibah.net/m/showthread.php?p=993914

18. Arabic website. http://www.otaibah.net/m/showthread.php?p=993914

19. Arabic website. http://www.gunfdh.com/vb/showthread.php?t=110611

20. Arabic website. http://www.buraydahcity.net/vb/showthread.php?t=64682

21. Video in Arabic. http://www.youtube.com/watch?v=ToeV-YKeBo8&feature=related

22. Video in Arabic. http://www.youtube.com/watch?v=ztitcqgxAjA

23. Video in Arabic. http://www.youtube.com/watch?v=jqjhshv9_VY

24. The Washington Post, *Mexico's drug war quieter, but no less deadly,* by Nick Miroff. http://www.washingtonpost.com/

25. Atlas Shurgs, Saudi Islamic Police Detain Dozens for "Plotting to Celebrate Christmas", Pamela Geller. http://atlasshrugs2000.typepad.com/atlas_shrugs/sinister_saudi_arabia_home_of_wahhabism/

26. The Wall Street Journal, *George W. Bush: The Arab Spring and American Ideals,* by George W. Bush. http://online.wsj.com/article/SB10001424052702304192704577406612351805018.html

27. Staff Report of the National Commission on Terrorist Attacks Upon the United States, *9/11 And Terrorist Travel.* http://www.statewatch.org/news/2004/aug/911-terr-trav.pdf

28. The New York Times, *The Great Escape,* by Craig Unger. http://www.nytimes.com/2004/06/01/opinion/the-great-escape.html

29. U.S. Department of Justice. http://www.911myths.com/images/1/1f/DanMarcus_Box6_Saudis_Post9-11SaudiFlights.pdf

30. The New York Times, *The Great Escape,* by Craig Unger. http://www.nytimes.com/2004/06/01/opinion/the-great-escape.html

31. Ibid

32. Documents. http://govinfo.library.unt.edu/911/staff_statements/911_TerrTrav_App.pdf

33. Chronicle & Sentinel, *Anger Management Course*. http://web.archive.org/web/20040701104117/http://www.weblog.nohair.net/archives/000502.html

34. Chronicle & Sentinel, *Why Were Saudi Passengers Flown Out of the Country After 9/11?* by Margie Burns. http://web.archive.org/web/20040426080112/http://baltimorechronicle.com/040904SaudiCIA.shtml

35. Staff Report of the National Commission on Terrorist Attacks Upon the United States, *9/11 And Terrorist Travel*. http://www.statewatch.org/news/2004/aug/911-terr-trav.pdf

36. Global Security, Princee Turki bin Faisal ibn Abdul Aziz Al Saud. http://www.globalsecurity.org/military/world/gulf/turki-bin-faisal.htm

37. CNN.com, *Face Time with Prince Turki bin Faisal al Saud*. http://edition.cnn.com/2008/BUSINESS/02/26/prince.faisal/index.html

38. CNN.com, *Embassy official: Saudi ambassador to U.S. resigns*. http://web.archive.org/web/20061220160306/http://www.cnn.com/2006/WORLD/meast/12/12/usa.saudi.reut/index.html

39. Fox News.com, *Saudi prince discusses kingdom's Iran problem,* by Amy Kellogg. http://www.foxnews.com/world/2012/01/27/conversation-at-davos-with-prince-turki-al-faisal/

40. Huff Post News, *Saudi Prince Alwaleed bin Talal Seeks Deeper Ties To News Corp,* Tarek El-Tablawy. http://www.huffingtonpost.com/2010/01/18/saudi-prince-alwaleed-bin_1_n_426891.html

41. The New York Times, *Documents Back Saudi Link to Extremists,* by Erik Lichtblau. http://www.nytimes.com/2009/06/24/world/middleeast/24saudi.html?_r=4&

42. The New York Times, Documents, *Evidence of Financial Links Between Saudi Royal Family and Al Qaeda*. http://documents.nytimes.com/evidence-of-financial-links-between-saudi-royal-family-and-al-qaeda

43. Religious Freedom Coalition, *Journal of 911 events posted in October, 2001,* by W.J. Murray. http://www.religiousfreedomcoalition.org/2012/08/12/journal-of-911-events-posted-in-october-2001/

44. Able Danger Blog, *LT. Col. Shaffer's written testimony,* prepared by Anthony A. Shaffer, Lt. Col., U.S. Army Reserve, Senior Intelligence Officer. http://www.abledangerblog.com/2006/02/lt-col-shaffers-written-testimony.html

45. Ibid

46. IPT The Invetsigative Project on Terrorism, *More Assets Frozen in Terrorism Fight; Treasury Adds 39 Organiza,* by David S. Hilzenrath and John Mintz. http://www.investigativeproject.org/159/more-assets-frozen-in-terrorism-fight-treasury-adds-39

47. Discover The Network.org, *Rabita Trust (RT).* http://www.discoverthenetworks.org/printgroupProfile.asp?grpid=6411

48. National Review Online, *Questions about Huma Abedin,* by Andrew C. McCarthy. http://www.nationalreview.com/blogs/print/310198

49. IPT The Investigative Project on Terrorism, *More Assets Frozen in Terrorism Fight; Treasury Adds 39 Organiza,* by David S. Hilzenrath and John Mintz. http://www.investigativeproject.org/159/more-assets-frozen-in-terrorism-fight-treasury-adds-39

50. Klein Online, *Huma Directly Tied to Al-Aqida Charity Front-Man: Radical Islamic web grows for Hillary's Chief of Staff.* http://kleinonline.wnd.com/2012/07/26/huma-directly-tied-to-al-qaida-charity-front-man-radical-islamic-web-grows-for-hillarys-chief-of-staff/

51. History Commons, *Profile: Abdullah Omar Naseef.* http://www.historycommons.org/entity.jsp?entity=abdullah_omar_naseef_1

52. History Commons, *Profile: Wael Hamza Julaidan.* http://www.historycommons.org/entity.jsp?entity=wa_el_hamza_julaidan

53. Liberation News Service, *Al Qaeda's Finances Ample, Say Probers Worldwide Failure to Enforce Sanctions Cited.* http://www.mindspace.org/liberation-news-service/archives/000365.html

54. Press Room, U.S. Department of the Treasury, *Treasure Department Statement on the Designation of Wa'el Hamza Julidan.* http://web.archive.org/web/20100830162327/http://www.treasury.gov/press/releases/po3397.htm

55. The Washington Post, *Mexico's drug war quieter, but no less deadly,* by Nick Miroff. http://www.washingtonpost.com/

56. Wayback Machine, *Muslim World League.* http://web.archive.org/web/20080913161751/http://www.mosque.ch/view.asp?pageID=110

57. Financial Times.com, *US Muslims see their American dreams die,* by Nancy Dunne. http://specials.ft.com/attackonterrorism/FT3P6NEVBZC.html

58. Daniel Pipes, Middle East Forum, *CAIR upset over Bush's remark.* http://www.danielpipes.org/comments/52418

59. Front Page Mag.com, *Where is the Money From?* by Berkeley Jewish Journal. http://archive.frontpagemag.com/readArticle.aspx?ARTID=17801

60. Anti-Defamation League, *Backgrounder: Muslim World League Links to Terrorism.* http://archive.adl.org/main_Terrorism/Muslim_World_League_Backgrounder.htm?Multi_page_sections=sHeading_4

61. Front Page Mag.com, *Where is the Money From?* by Berkeley Jewish Journal. http://archive.frontpagemag.com/readArticle.aspx?ARTID=17801

62. Ibid

63. Ibid

64. Pundicity, *The Prospects of al-Qaeda in Hamas-Controlled Gaza,* by Jonathan Schanzer. http://schanzer.pundicity.com/460/the-prospects-of-al-qaeda-in-hamas-controlled-gaza

65. Ibid

66. Wayback Machine, *The List of individuals belonging to or associated with the Taliban.* http://web.archive.org/web/20110514132711/http://www.un.org/sc/committees/1267/consoltablelist.shtml

67. Front Page Mag.com, *The Great Al-Qaeda "Patriot",* by Paul Sperry. http://archive.frontpagemag.com/readArticle.aspx?ARTID=26058

68. Wayback Machine, *Our MSA Board.* http://web.archive.org/web/20020411101755/http://www.gwu.edu/~msa/board.htm

69. Front Page Mag.com, *The Great Al-Qaeda "Patriot",* by Paul Sperry. http://archive.frontpagemag.com/readArticle.aspx?ARTID=26058

70. The New York Times, *A Nation Challenged: The Money Trail; Raids Seek Evidence of Money-Laundering,* by Judity Miller. http://www.nytimes.com/2002/03/21/us/a-nation-challenged-the-money-trail-raids-seek-evidence-of-money-laundering.html?pagewanted=all&src=pm

71. The New York Times, *Documents Back Saudi Link to Extremists,* by Erik Lichtblau. http://www.nytimes.com/2009/06/24/world/middleeast/24saudi.html?_r=4&

72. The Global Muslim Brotherhood Daily Report, *Exclusive: Saudi Charity Designated as Terrorist Reopens Office in U.S.* http://globalmbreport.org/?p=2617

73. The New York Times, *A Nation Challenged: The Money Trail; Raids Seek Evidence of Money-Laundering,* by Judity Miller. http://www.nytimes.com/2002/03/21/us/a-nation-challenged-the-money-trail-raids-seek-evidence-of-money-laundering.html?pagewanted=all&src=pm

74. The Global Muslim Brotherhood Daily Report, *Exclusive: Saudi Charity Designated as Terrorist Reopens Office in U.S.* http://globalmbreport.org/?p=2617

75. Discover The Networks.org, *Abdurahman Alamoudi.* http://www.discoverthenetworks.org/individualProfile.asp?indid=1311

76. The New York Times, *A Nation Challenged: The Money Trail; Raids Seek Evidence of Money-Laundering,* by Judity Miller. http://www.nytimes.com/2002/03/21/us/a-nation-challenged-the-money-trail-raids-seek-evidence-of-money-laundering.html?pagewanted=all&src=pm

77. Discover The Networks.org, *SAAR Foundation (Safa Trust Group).* http://www.discoverthenetworks.org/groupProfile.asp?grpid=6397

78. Discover The Networks.org, *Sami Al-Arian.* http://www.discoverthenetworks.org/individualProfile.asp?indid=671

79. Discover The Network.org, *World Assembly of Muslim Youth (WAMY).* http://www.discoverthenetworks.org/printgroupProfile.asp?grpid=6425

80. World Assembly of Muslim Youth (WAMY). http://www.wamy.co.za/profile.htm

81. The Abedin "Affairs" With Al-Saud, by Walid Shoebat. http://www.shoebat.com/wp-content/uploads/2012/08/Abedin_Affairs_with_Al_Saud_0813122.pdf

82. Ibid

83. The New York Times, *Justice Dept. Backs Saudi Royal Family on 9/11 Lawsuit,* http://www.nytimes.com/2009/05/30/us/politics/30families.html?_r=1

84. Ibid

85. IPT, *On Behalf of the 9/11 Families United to Bankrupt Terrorism.* http://www.investigativeproject.org/documents/case_docs/992.pdf

86. Huff Post, *Supreme Court Will Not Hear 9/11 Victims Claims Vs. Saudi Arrabia.* http://www.huffingtonpost.com/2009/06/29/supreme-court-will-not-he_n_222256.html

87. Government Executive, *Army project illustrates promise, shortcomings of data mining,* by Shane Harris. http://www.govexec.com/defense/2005/12/army-project-illustrates-promise-shortcomings-of-data-mining/20758/

88. Ibid

APPENDIX C
The Obamas' Wahhabist Fundraising Empire

Walid and Theodore Shoebat

While Obama's connection to his Muslim family in Kenya is an acceptable topic for discussion in the Arab world, it is viewed as a 'great taboo' in the United States.

But why is that so? This 'taboo' should be considered unfair at best, purely prejudiced at worst. Is it fair that we censor such discussions just because Obama's relatives are 'Muslim'?

The Council on American Islamic Relations (CAIR) should condemn the media for keeping a tight lid on the subject. Isn't it time to go beyond what is disclosed by President Obama in his *Dreams from My Father* or *Wikipedia's* limited information, which includes the only photo[1] released by the Obama family?

We will cover only three of the closest Kenyan relatives to president Obama:
1. Sarah, Barack's beloved and benevolent grandmother
2. Sayid Obama, his closest favorite uncle
3. Musa Ismail Obama, his first cousin and Sayid's main sidekick.

After President Obama was inaugurated, the Muslim side of the Obama family in Kenya boomed; it went from rags to riches overnight. They became one of the most influential families in western Kenya and even extended their sphere of influence to Saudi Arabia. When Sarah, president Obama's grandmother (step-grandmother), decided to go to the *Hajj*, an obligatory pilgrimage to Mecca with Musa, president Obama's first cousin, they were welcomed with open arms and were provided a special escort with full security detail and first-class treatment at the Saudi royal court:[2]

> "His Royal Highness Prince Mamdouh bin Abdul Aziz accompanied the family of U.S. President Barack Obama in his palace in Jeddah after the performance of the Hajj this year. The event was attended by His Royal Highness Prince Faisal bin Thamer bin Abdul Aziz, and His Royal Highness Prince Abdul Aziz Bin Mamdouh Bin Abdul Aziz, and his HRH Prince Abdullah bin Nayef bin Abdul Aziz, and a number of other princes and officials."

The reason for such treatment—as explained in an exclusive interview with Musa Ismail Obama on Al-Jazeera[3]—is that a close relationship was built with Saudi royals. Like president Obama's call for education in the United States, the Kenyan Obamas embarked on a similar project.

President Obama's grandmother Sarah started the *Sarah Obama Benevolent Fund Institute*, otherwise known as the *Mama Sarah Obama Children Foundation*,[4] which raises 90% of its monies primarily from donors in the United States and some from Europe. Those monies are solicited as humanitarian aid[5] and according to the website, "to make a lasting impact on the lives of the orphans and underprivileged children by improving their housing, their education, their upbringing," which "continued to weigh heavily on Mama Sarah." All this and "to help the neglected HIV/AIDS infected and affected in Kogelo village by linking them to care-givers and professional health services providers."

(Barack Obama with step-grandmother Sarah)

That's what we're told, but when one peruses the foundation's real activities in Arabic, it reveals a very dark side to the family's efforts.

Musa Ismail Obama, the president's cousin—in an exclusive interview with Al-Jazeera TV—explained all the troublesome detail, which does not bode well when translated into English: *the bulk of the Sarah Fund as it turns out sends little to widows and orphans while the rest goes towards giving free scholarships to studying Sharia at the most influential Wahhabist centers in Saudi Arabia.*

(Mama Sarah begins her trip to see Barack inaugurated)

In the shocking interview, Musa was asked about his communications with cousin Barack, the president of the United States. The soft-spoken Musa explained that the President's preferred method of communications was through one chosen conduit that relays messages back and forth with the family in Kenya by going through Uncle Sayid Hussein Obama. This is the man who was in attendance with Mama Sarah at Barack Obama's inauguration in 2009.[6]

Musa, Sayid's sidekick and the public promoter of Mama Sarah's non-profit became the family's key advertiser to the social efforts in Kenya. He selects specific Arab media asking wealthy audiences for help, but mandates as a prerequisite that no questions are asked regarding any details of such communications with president Obama or the delving into any political views. Yet, he tells just enough to connect the dots to the wealthy Arab audience of Al-Jazeera. He relays the message to raise all necessary funds since *his mission is to transform Kenya to an Islamic majority by using the Obama household name and his grandmother's non-profit organization.*

The fund has little to do with secular education or the care for widows and orphans. It never once mentions anything in any Arabic media in regards to helping the HIV infected. The bulk of the Sarah's benevolence fund, as Musa explained, goes toward scholarships destined for Saudi Arabia's most virulent Wahhabi Sharia centers—the Islamic University in Medina, Umm Al-Qura University in Makkah and the University of Imam Muhammad bin Saud Islamic University in Riyadh.

The counter-Wahhabist Muslim moderate think tank, the *Gulf Issues Centre For Strategic Studies* describes these institutions as "Salafi schools, which imbibed radical ideas" and are "the spring of Wahhabism":[7]

> "[Wahhabists] grew up in the Wahhabi and Salafi schools which imbibed radical ideas in the *Islamic University in Medina, Umm Al-Qura University in Makkah*, and the *University of Imam Muhammad bin Saud Islamic University* in Riyadh". (see essay, *The Role of Wahhabist Movements*, under a section entitled *The Circle of Violence*)

Musa expresses in classical Arabic how he memorized the entire Quran and how he graduated to become an Islamic scholar on Sharia from the Islamic University in Medina.

"I studied Arabic and Sharia at the Islamic university in Medina in Saudi Arabia," exclaimed Musa while explaining his visit to Umm Al Qura University with his uncle Sayid: "In the month of Muharram we visited the dean of Umm Al Qura University, me and my uncle Sayid," he told Al-Jazeera during the interview.

"The nature of the visit," Musa explains, "was to facilitate scholarship to send students to Umm Al Qura."

Umm Al Qura University has a heritage that includes being one of Saudi Arabia's historical and national monuments. A paragon of Wahhabist education, it takes pride that the university was the first to print the works of Muhammad Abdul Wahhab, the founder of the most virulent brand of Islam—Wahhabism. The history of its Wahhabist connections can be seen.[8]

On a cover-page of one of Wahhab's collections from Umm Al Qura University, one can clearly see in fanciful Arabic calligraphy, the title, *"Writings of Muhammad Abdul Wahhab"* and a stamp that says *"A gift from Umm Al Qura University-Mecca"* is clearly visible.

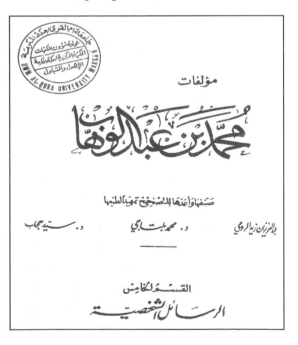

In *The Danger of Wahhabism in The Muslim World,* by moderate Dr. Ahmed Abdul Rahim Al-Sayeh, who abandoned the teachings, he reflects on his studies at Umm Al Qura:[9] "I studied Wahhabism, I studied their curriculum at the University of Umm Al Qura..."

At Umm Al Qura University, Musa and Sayid Obama—president Obama's favorite uncle—are seen in photo-ops and were described by several Arab media sources as diligent workers in advancing scholarships for Kenyans to study Sharia, courtesy of Sarah's fund.

(Sayid Obama on far right standing with Musa Ismail Obama at Umm Al Qura University)

Meetings of President Obama's favorite uncle Sayid can even be seen at the official website of Umm Al Qura University where it proudly states:[10]

> "His Highness the Director of Umm Al-Qura University, Dr. Bakri bin Ma'touk A'sas received at his office in university city at Babidah Mr. Sayid Obama the uncle of His Excellency the President of the United States of America Barack Obama and Mr. Musa Ismail Obama the cousin of U.S. President..."

"When they [the students] submit an application to Sarah Obama Benevolent Fund, they expect to get what they want but we are flooded," explains Musa.

As a result of the flood of students into the Wahhabi Sharia universities in Saudi Arabia, the interviewer then asks regarding the excess: "So you are opening an avenue in other universities?" Musa then explains he had to send the excess to nearby Doha in Qatar, where he visited and arranged everything.

When Al-Jazeera asked, "Do all these scholarships involve studying Arabic and Sharia?" Musa explained, "Some of those do not involve Sharia, like medicine or engineering." Al-Jazeera then asks, "…but the majority involves what?" Musa answers: "Uuuhhh…The majority of course is Sharia schools," adding, "because my connection to the institutions is with Sharia schools."

In what seems like a prepared script, Musa reads what he considers the catastrophe of Kenya, the lack of the process of proselytization, which goes hand-in-hand with Saudi interests seeking help from wealthy Saudis to transform Kenya into a Muslim majority.

مشاهدات «العرب» 2-4

علماء كينيا يناشدون إخوانهم نشر الإسلام وتعليم اللغة العربية

(Photo above of Musa on Al-Arab Newspaper)

This goal is also expressed by Al-Arab Newspaper, which covered the call of the Obamas[11] in an interview with Musa Ismail Obama on the sidelines of the inauguration ceremony of World University Ruff in Nairobi.

Under the title, *"Scholars in Kenya Call Their Brethren to Spread Islam and Teach Arabic"* it states: "Muslims [in Kenya] suffer from the monumental Christianization aided by Zionist expansionism that infiltrates the nation." (Muhammad Lasheeb, *Al-Arab Newspaper*, 8816th edition, published on August 1st, 2012)

Al-Arab Newspaper expounds on the effort to advance "education" by the Obama family in Kenya. Under the title, "Education First" assistant Mufti of the coastal city of Mombasa Ahmad Bimsallam, chimed in explaining that, "the grand destruction that came upon Muslims in Kenya, came from the education and schools that are planted all over the nation by Christian missionary movements."

Al-Arab does not even consider President Obama's conversion to Christianity an issue and included a section entitled, "Obama's Islam" while stating:

"President Obama's Islamic faith was considered a polarizing subject between Muslims and Christians in the Republic of Kenya. It is a center of struggle in the media and continues, as the Anglican Church there attempted to orchestrate a baptismal ordination for his grandmother Sarah in a grand celebration at the Gomokinyata playground in Kizimo, the third largest city in Kenya. It was a trick to trap her, pretending to invite her as a guest, as the church sent out information about her conversion and abandonment of Islam. The young Musa Ismail Obama, the cousin of the American president commented during his interview with Al-Arab that he was with his grandmother during Ramadan in the Holy Land in Mecca to do the Umra festivities after she completed her pilgrimage by invitation from the King of Saudi Arabia. Musa Obama who studied Sharia in Medina spoke to us regarding the situation of Muslims in Kenya calling upon the Arab and Islamic states to put more effort toward aiding the Kenyan Muslim brethren, especially since there is much support coming from Western nations and Western churches, spreading to the rest of Kenyan society from different religions. Musa opined that the situation of Muslims in Kenya is continually getting better, pointing to the village of Barack Obama, Kogelo, which is situated on the shores of Victoria Lake, in Western Kenya, for example, had no Muslims except his family. But now, they are increasing, and that the majority of new Muslims adopted Islam from the kind treatment of their family and that they have now a benevolent institution to raise funds and give important aid to the orphans and the poor, and it also gives scholarships to study Sharia in Medina [Saudi Arabia]. Musa also stated that *despite the fact that Barack Obama hasn't visited his tribe in Kenya since his election in the United States, there is a continual communication between him and several members of his family and his tribe in Kenya, of which the Kenyan prime minister is also a member*. We have also had members of the tribe who came to celebrate the appointment of one of their tribesmen as president of the United States a while ago. Musa also clarified that the election of Barack Obama had an impact for the betterment of the Muslim situation in Kenya to a certain degree, despite the attempts of churches to obstruct Muslim demands and rights, especially what relates to segregation and persecution against them in schools, as well as the issue of hijab and the lack of constitutional rights for Muslims in establishing Sharia courts."

Perhaps most explosive is that president Obama's uncle Sayid Hussein Obama is active in his work with the notorious Muslim World League (MWL) as reported by Saudi media:[12]

"His Excellency Dr. Abdullah bin Abdul Mohsin Al-Turki, Secretary General of the Muslim World League, and a member of the Council of Senior Scholars in Saudi Arabia in Makkah received on Monday Mr. Saeed [Sayid] Hussein Obama, Kenyan businessman, and uncle of President Barack Obama, President of the United States of America, who paid a visit to the Muslim World League, accompanied by a number of Kenyan graduates from Saudi universities."

As we reported, the Muslim World League has extensive ties to terrorism.[13] If Musa's claims are true, that Sayid is Barack's preferred point of contact with his Muslim family and that Sayid is dealing with the MWL, don't the American people deserve to know the extent of their president's connections and loyalties to these individuals and groups?

The MWL has numerous connections with al Qaeda operatives.[14] In fact, several MWL employees have worked with al Qaeda. Osama bin Laden and al Qaeda gained material support and sponsorship—along with a cover—from MWL offices around the world. Dr. Abdullah bin Abdul Mohsin Al-Turki, Secretary General of the Muslim World League, received Sayid, one of the most renowned Wahhabi scholars[15] and a pioneer in spreading Wahhabism through education.

The Kenyan Obamas are too.

FOOTNOTES

1. Wikipedia, *File: Barack Obama's Kenyan relatives.jpg.* http://en.wikipedia.org/wiki/File:Barack_Obama%27s_Kenyan_relatives.jpg

2. Arabic website. http://www.shbab2.com/vb/t74052.html

3. Video in Arabic with English subtitles. http://shariaunveiled.wordpress.com/2012/10/11/obama-family-knee-deep-in-sharia/

4. Sarah Obama Foundation.org. http://sarahobamafoundation.org/index.html

5. Khaleej Times, *Omama!* http://www.khaleejtimes.com/kt-article-display-1.asp?xfile=/data/expressions/2012/June/expressions_June49.xml&section=expressions

6. Political Articles.Net, *Mama Sarah Obama starts historic journey – to witness the swearing-in of her grandson Barack Obama as the 44th American President,* by George Olwenya, Kenya. http://www.politicalarticles.net/blog/2009/01/12/mama-sarah-obama-starts-historic-journey-to-witness-the-swearing-in-of-her-grandson-barack-obama-as-the-44th-american-president/#.UHRes65Ptdh

7. Arabic website: Gulf Issuess Centre For Strategic Studies. http://gulfissues.net/m_p_folder/main_div/derasat/derasat_0012.htm

8. Arabic website. http://alahbash.net/play-651.html

9. Arabic website. http://www.nokhbah.net/vb/showthread.php?t=5745

10. Arabic website. http://uqu.edu.sa/news/ar/6890

11. Arabic website. http://lachyab.wordpress.com/2012/08/01/%D8%A7%D9%84%D8%AD%D9%84%D9%82%D8%A9-%D8%A7%D9%84%D8%AB%D8%A7%D9%86%D9%8A%D8%A9-%D9%85%D9%86-%D9%85%D8%B4%D8%A7%D9%87%D8%AF%D8%A7%D8%AA%D9%8A-%D9%81%D9%8A-%D9%83%D9%8A%D9%86%D9%8A%D8%A7/

12. Arabic website. http://www.sauress.com/aljazirah/1103293283

13. 9/11: 3000 *Americans for Three Saudi Princes, New details about the Troubling Omissions of Saudi Arabia's wealthy from 9/11 Commission Report,* by Walid Shoebat and Ben Barrack. http://www.shoebat.com/wp-content/uploads/2012/09/3000_Americans_for_Three_Saudi_Princes_091012.pdf

14. United States District Court Southern District of New York, http://www.sept11terrorlitigation.com/pdf/Continental_Casualty_Amend_Complaint_.pdf

15. http://www.soufia.org/brahin_sataa.html

new**providence**
MEMORIAL LIBRARY

9/13

377 Elkwood Avenue
New Providence, NJ 07974

297.7
Sho